D1349614

90710 000 477 502

JON YATES is Executive Director of the Youth Endowment Fund, a charitable organisation focused on supporting young people. He has co-founded a series of charities designed to bring people together, and served as a government adviser. He tweets as @jonyates and blogs at jonyates.org.

Further praise for *Fractured*

'This is a lively and interesting account of one of the key challenges facing liberal democracies.'
DAVID WILLETTS, author of *The Pinch: How the Baby Boomers Took Their Children's Future – And Why They Should Give It Back*

'Engaging, punchy, and well-researched. A genuine page-turner – and with inspiring and practical conclusions.'
DAVID HALPERN, author of *Inside the Nudge Unit* and *The Hidden Wealth of Nations*

'*Fractured* addresses an important topic; it is incredibly relevant for each and every one of us – as we head into a new decade of challenges and opportunity, I commend Jon's desire to understand and address fractures together in 2021 and beyond.'
LOUISE CASEY, Baroness Casey of Blackstock

'An enormous contribution … Jon Yates is well-placed to diagnose how ethnic, class and age bubbles have fragmented modern liberal societies – and to work out what to do about it.'
ERIC KAUFMANN, Professor of Politics, Birkbeck, University of London

'A must-read for everyone who is troubled by the growing divisions, hatred and abuse. Accessible and compelling, I cannot recommend it highly enough.'

TED CANTLE CBE, Chair of the Belong Network
for Cohesion and Integration

'If you're passionate about social mobility, buy this highly readable book. It is a challenge to all of us that if we want a more mobile society we have to care about networks as well as knowledge.'

DAMIAN HINDS MP, former Education Secretary

'A compelling review of how and why we're divided that makes a passionate case for the importance of building and protecting a Common Life, including many practical and achievable suggestions.'

BOBBY DUFFY, author of *The Perils of Perception:
Why We're Wrong About Nearly Everything*

'A much-needed framework for understanding the forces that divide and provides a path to healing our fractured societies. This book is an important one: pragmatic, provocative and hopeful.'

JACQUELINE NOVOGRATZ, CEO of Acumen

FRACTURED

FRACTURED

Why our societies are coming
apart and how we put them
back together again

Jon Yates

Harper
North

HarperNorth
111 Piccadilly,
Manchester, M1 2HY

A division of
HarperCollins*Publishers*
1 London Bridge Street
London SE1 9GF

www.harpercollins.co.uk

HarperCollins*Publishers*
1st Floor, Watermarque Building, Ringsend Road
Dublin 4, Ireland

First published by HarperNorth in 2021

1 3 5 7 9 10 8 6 4 2

A catalogue record for this book
is available from the British Library

HB ISBN: 978-0-00-846396-0
TPB ISBN: 978-0-00-847709-7

Printed and bound in Great Britain by
CPI Group (UK) Ltd, Croydon

MIX
Paper from
responsible sources
FSC™ C007454

This book is produced from independently certified FSC™ paper
to ensure responsible forest management.

For more information visit: www.harpercollins.co.uk/green

For Lisa, Chloe, Millie, Bethany, Margaret and Rachel —
my family who make everything possible, everything
worthwhile and put everything in perspective.

Thank you especially to Lisa, who is my rock.

'Our ability to reach unity in diversity will be the beauty and the test of our civilisation.'

Mahatma Gandhi

CONTENTS

PROLOGUE

I can remember it vividly: jumping up and down, beer spilling out of my glass, celebrating with strangers. If I close my eyes, I can see the pub unfolding as we walk in. We came early to get a good spot. We chatted, nestling the beer I thought we wouldn't get served, watching the highlights of the previous match over our shoulders. I can feel the nervousness in my stomach before kick-off. Would we score? Could we stop them scoring? Would I get served another beer? I was sixteen: old enough to sneak into a pub and young enough to believe England could win the European Championship. It was all we talked about that summer. When we weren't revising for our exams, we dreamt of England winning the trophy.

We weren't the only ones. Media interest was intense. England had not hosted a major football tournament for thirty years. The tabloids were making up for lost time. Even the pop charts had surrendered, with the official England song camped at No. 1. Keen to escape the pressure, the England team departed on a pre-tournament tour of the Far East. Away from the media, the players would have a chance to get to know each other on the pitch with a couple of friendly games, and off the pitch with a couple of drinks. Except that it wasn't just a couple of drinks.

Six days before the first game, the front page of the UK's best-read newspaper told the world that the England team had drunk so much before flying home that they'd wrecked the plane. A bill had been sent to the team for damage caused to seats and TV screens. A day later, photos followed. Here were the players: drunk, swaying in a Hong Kong nightclub, their clothes covered in rips. The headline printed above a picture of the team's most famous player, Paul Gascoigne, simply read: 'DisgraceFOOL'. The rest of the media piled in. One paper printed photos of drunken England players next to convicted hooligans and asked its readers to spot which was which.

England's opponents took a different approach. The Dutch had a superb team and were favourites to win. They'd reached the semi-finals at the last European Championships, and won the tournament before. That spring, the majority of their players had represented perennial Dutch Champions Ajax in the final of the biggest club competition in Europe. Unlike England, they had world-class play-ers in nearly every position. Unlike England, their team preparations exuded confident professionalism – as the photo below suggests. As the match kicked off, my heart hoped for a draw, but my head feared a drubbing.

At this point, I'm tempted to encourage you to put down this book, go online now and watch the highlights of the game. I still can't listen to the commentary or watch England's four goals without the hair standing up on the back of my neck. And what goals! It *was* a drubbing – but England were the ones handing it out. As we cheered every goal, the commentator caught the mood of a nation. 'It gets better and better,' he said. My friends and I left the pub that evening on top of the world.

How had it happened? It would be neat to say that it was down to English talent, ingenuity and guts. But the real story of that night was the Dutch. The explanation starts with that photo. Amid the sophistication, class and good food, is another story altogether – one that becomes clear when we spot the difference between the table at the back, on the left, and the other two.

The Dutch national football team with coach Guus Hiddink at
Euro 96, © Guus Dubbelman/De Beeldunie

The Dutch team was mostly White, with a small group of highly
talented Black, Surinamese players. That group – Michael Reiziger,
Edgar Davids, Patrick Kluivert and Clarence Seedorf – felt like
members of a different team. Reiziger told the press: 'The four of us
form a separate group. We talk easily with each other, because we
think the same way, come from the same culture, and make the same
jokes.' Before long, the Dutch press had a name for them – 'the
Cabal' – and were reporting that the Cabal were not happy. They felt
under-appreciated by a manager who thought they should talk less
and listen more; undervalued by an Ajax team that had accidentally
revealed that their White teammates were being paid up to six times
more than them; and underused by tactics that left them watching
more games than they played. Edgar Davids was a superb player,
who dominated Ajax's midfield. Unselected for the first game against
Switzerland, he fumed from the bench and watched in amazement

as another of 'the Cabal' was substituted off just a third of the way into the match. When the game ended in a draw, Davids exploded. Accosting a delighted Swiss journalist, he declared that the problem was the manager, Gus Hiddink, who was clearly in thrall to the older White players. The only solution was for him to 'get his head out of players' asses so he can see better'. That outburst sealed his fate. Hiddink immediately sent Davids home. The Dutch team fell apart. They had fractured well before the game against England.

Why wasn't the English team similarly divided? It was no less diverse, being composed of Black and White players from different clubs on very different wages who just weeks before had been competing passionately against one another. For days since the aeroplane débâcle, they'd faced relentless attacks from the English tabloid press, high on moral indignation; the disapproval of a public readying themselves for disappointment; and even the censure of Parliament, with some MPs demanding players' resignations. But their booze-fuelled antics and the constant criticism that followed did not divide the England team. It brought it together. The players refused to identify who had caused the damage on the plane – despite it being down almost entirely to mercurial midfielder Paul Gascoigne. Instead, they all paid the bill and asked their spokesman to tell the press that they accepted 'collective responsibility'. Years later, Teddy Sheringham, the scorer of the fourth England goal that night, told a reporter: 'We had so much stick going into the Euros in 1996. All we did was make it work for us. There were no real divisions among the squad … the feeling was that we were one unit.'

What weakened the Dutch team wasn't a lack of talent – they were more skilled than the English. It wasn't their differences – the English were just as diverse. What the Dutch lacked was a moment that could overcome those differences; a shared experience that created a sense of being 'us'. What started as a national scandal became a period of intense adversity that unified the team. In the words of England's manager Terry Venables, it 'made all the difference'.

INTRODUCTION

It's a warm Thursday evening. I'm standing just inside the front door of my house in south-west London. My three primary-age children are bunched up behind me, buzzing and bickering about who's going outside first. My wife is checking her watch. It's almost time. We step just a few feet outside. The man from the ground-floor flat on the corner is already there. Every week, he patrols the small patch of pavement in front of his garden wall as if preparing for a roll-call. He stops, and looks up and down the street. It's a good turnout tonight. Faces lean out of upstairs windows; couples stand at open doors.

At 8 p.m. we all start clapping.

It's meant to be a thank-you, this weekly ritual that marks our time. We clap to thank the key workers who are ready to look after us. But I'm not thinking about them today. I'm thinking about the aliens that Karen made up.

Karen Stenner is an Australian political scientist who teaches at Princeton. I met her three years ago at a conference that I organised on the shores of Lake Como. With such a beautiful venue, it would have been cruel and unusual to spend the whole day inside. So, each afternoon after lunch, I allocated everyone a partner and encouraged them to go for a walk. On the first afternoon, I fixed the pairs so that I could talk to Karen. Why? Because I wanted to hear about the aliens.

5

Karen Stenner is fascinated by how you would answer this question: 'Which is more important: that a child obeys their parents well or that they are interested in how and why things happen?' Using this, and two other questions like it, she has identified a group of Americans whom she calls 'Authoritarians'. This sizeable group – one-third of Americans in total, both left- and right-wing – believe that it's more important that children are obedient rather than curious, neat rather than wise, and well-behaved rather than responsible. What is striking about this group is that their preference for order, neatness and consistency applies to much more than the behaviour of children. It describes their view of society, particularly when it comes to diversity and difference. In short, they find high levels of diversity threatening and prefer it when everyone seems the same. When they are questioned, 'Authoritarians' are more likely to hold negative views about other ethnic groups, less likely to unreservedly condemn the Ku Klux Klan and more likely to see Nazis as better than communists. That is, until the aliens arrive.

Karen invented her aliens for an experiment to test our sense of 'us' and 'them'. Her 'Authoritarians' were given a pile of newspaper articles to read. In half of those piles lay a story whose origin was not a newsroom but Karen's imagination. Produced to look as authentic as possible, it told of an official NASA report that had recently been released. The report had reviewed 'billions of radio signals received from outer space over the last 20 years'. Its conclusion was that we are not alone. There are aliens out there who are 'eager to communicate with us'. Not only that, but they are likely to 'make actual contact with us here on Earth within the next few years'. As to the nature of these aliens, the only certainty that the report could muster was that they are 'very different from us in ways we are not yet even able to imagine'. After reading the articles, participants completed a short survey. The survey was about their attitudes – not to aliens, but to other humans somewhat unlike them. Here's the striking thing. Karen's 'Authoritarians' who had considered the arrival of extraterrestrial life had become positively relaxed about human diversity. Faced with a 'them' profoundly different to anything on earth, humans who merely had a different skin colour or religion seemed suddenly very much like 'us'.

Karen's aliens were made up. But ours is real.

We're outside clapping because of an alien that we cannot see, that arrived unannounced and has spread unseen. We didn't invite it in and yet it has entered our homes and taken control of our lives. As we watch for its shadow everywhere, we follow its decrees: when we can come and go, who we can see and what we can do. It is everywhere and nowhere. We only see it when it strikes. It preys on the weak and the righteous. It is an alien 'very different from us in ways we are not yet able to imagine'. It is the ultimate 'them' to our collective 'us'.

The novel coronavirus is Karen's test made real. As I write these words, in the initial phase of this alien's reign, the sense of 'us' is palpable. You can see it in our actions. My neighbours bring us food when we fall ill. Windows have filled up with thank-you notes to refuse collectors, health workers and postmen. The UK government asked for volunteers to support the NHS and 700,000 people signed up. You can hear it in our language too. In the week that the UK lockdown was announced, online searches for the term 'blitz spirit' rose nine-fold. In the US, eight out of ten Americans told pollsters that they now have 'more in common than that which divided them'. Above all, though, you can feel it, especially on a Thursday evening. As we clap for strangers who we do not know and will not know – strangers of all ethnicities, ages and incomes – my neighbours and I are expressing something more than a thank-you. We're articulating a longing to believe that we're all in the same boat. That we're united.

But deep down, most of us know this isn't true. For as I stand and clap, the people I'm applauding are not the only strangers. Looking up and down my street – at windows and at doorways – I recognise just one, maybe two, faces. I'm locked down in a neighbourhood of mostly strangers. I think of another man trapped in his neighbour-hood. Truman Burbank, the hero of Peter Weir's film *The Truman Show* (1998), is an insurance salesman played by Jim Carrey who lives a picture-perfect life in a seaside town called Seahaven Island. What Burbank doesn't know is that his life is a fiction, a reality-TV show. The stars in the sky are studio lights, every step he takes is discussed by studio staff, and his neighbours are actors parachuted into the scene only when he's on the street. As I look around, I realise that I know so few of my neighbours that I wouldn't have noticed if they'd been parachuted in before lockdown began. Unnerved, I look at them again, hunting for familiarity. Something is wrong. The casting director who selected these actors was heavily biased. No one of colour was selected. No one above the age of forty-five. And the costume department has suffered a failure of imagination; everyone is dressed in the style of 'city worker on day off'. The cast of charac-ters that live in my street seems to be the mirror image of me.

Truman did not discover the truth about his neighbourhood until things started going wrong. A star that fell out of the sky crashed onto the street and was revealed as a studio light. His car radio stum-bled upon a strange frequency on which people were talking about him, describing his every move. Normally, Truman never spotted the things that were off in his world. But the accidents revealed reality. The coronavirus is the same. By tilting the world on its axis, it has revealed things hiding in plain sight.

The greatest revelation comes from being forced indoors. Removed from normal daily life, most of us have only two windows into the external world. The first arrives for me every day at 10 p.m. It's the world of the TV news, in all its grisly variety. Care homes struggling to keep residents safe. Minority groups more at risk from the virus. Vulnerable children missing the support of teachers and social work-ers. The second arrives when I open my door on Thursdays at 8 p.m. to clap. It reveals the world of my street – White, affluent young professionals clapping for strangers. Once you spot the disconnect, it's hard to ignore. When the virus first arrived, it created – as with Karen Stenner's aliens – a sense of *us*: it was everyone vs the virus. But as time passes, it has done something else. It has revealed our divisions. We're not all in this together. We're not even living on the same streets.

Over the last few years, elections, referenda, protests and riots have had the same effect. Unexpected results and moments of crisis have fallen like studio lights out of the sky, revealing the world outside of our neighbourhoods, friendships and families, where at least half the people think very differently from us. It has taken accidents and extraordinary events to reveal it, but – like Truman Burbank – most of us appear to be living in a bubble.

My bubble was not imposed upon me like Truman's. It was chosen freely. It's formed from the neighbours in the street I choose to live on; the colleagues at the place where I choose to work; the friends I choose to keep up with; and the parents at the school to which I choose to send my children. These people are not actors. But their back stories, challenges and even appearances seem to mirror my own. Looked at more closely still, most of them vote like me, earn like me, have the same level of education as me and are mostly the same skin colour too. The virus may have forced us to keep our distance, but the truth is that we've been socially distant from those who differ from us for a long time now.

I'm writing this book because that distance matters a great deal. It matters most because it robs us of our greatest human ability: to have concern for each other. For those who need our help, for those who rely on us, for those we stand and applaud.

People are not machines. Our concerns do not arrive by algorithmic deduction. They are not established purely by the weighing of need. Instead, we are social animals whose concerns spring from feelings that, hunter-like, track the changing interests of those we know, care for and love. Unemployment may rise, but it's when our friend loses her job that we really care. A virus may kill tens of thousands, but it will take the death of a loved one to make us truly mourn. The 10 p.m. news can tell me that care-home residents are dying, that children in violent homes are unsafe, that ethnic minorities are more at risk, that manual workers are struggling to balance income with safety, and that small-business owners are seeing their livelihoods crushed. Our deepest concerns, though, remain bounded by our friendships, our connections, our bubbles. If our bubble includes no one in a care home, no one in a violent home, no one from an ethnic minority, no one working with their hands, and no one running a small business, few persistent passions are roused. It is personal experience, not abstract knowledge, that makes us care.

This matters. For as we stand and clap, locked up at home in a socially distanced world, huge decisions are looming. As we consider the routes towards normal, each of them appears to pit different groups against others. Should everyone be allowed out of their homes – enabling those without a garden to get out and breathe fresh air – or should they remain where they are, better protecting the lives of the elderly and vulnerable? Do we open pubs to save their staff from redundancy or keep them closed to save others from disease? Do we keep schools open – helping children from poorer backgrounds to catch up in their learning – or prioritise workplaces so that people who cannot work from home can start earning again? Each decision requires the wisdom of Solomon.

Today, King Solomon of Israel is remembered by most of us for just one story. Two women come before him carrying a baby boy. They argue furiously, each claiming to be the mother. Solomon interrupts. He calls for a sword and orders that the child be cut in two so that each woman can have half the baby. Faced with this horror, the real mother immediately renounces her claim – and is given her child to take home. The Old Testament declares that 'everyone in Israel was amazed'. But it's easy to overlook the fact that Solomon's wisdom was not knowledge; it was empathy. The child returned to his true parent not because Solomon knew who the birth-mother was, but because he understood how she would feel.

Solomon's wisdom is also humanity's greatest advantage. We sit at the top of the food chain not only because we know more than the other animals, but because we empathise better than they do. It is the combination of our empathy and our understanding that has allowed us to form the groups, tribes and nations that dominate the world. What happens, though, if this empathy is restricted? What if our concerns can reach only as far as the edge of our bubbles? What if our priorities are focused solely on those who are 'like us'? Our leaders must then face impossible trade-offs in a society full of people lacking concern for the other side.

This book argues that Solomon's wisdom needs to be recovered by breaking down the barriers that divide us. Right now, the scale of our divisions should trouble us deeply. We should worry about our democracy when so many voters know only members of their own bubble and distrust all others. We should worry about our economy when some bubbles contain the networks and connections required to get ahead while others do not. We should worry about injustice when it is too easy for our bubble to exclude those who are oppressed and those who suffer. We should worry about our security when individuals can be sucked into hard-left, far-right or fundamentalist bubbles that actively hate those on the outside.

This pandemic will pass. When it does, we have a chance to build a society in which we're less distant from each another; in which we venture outside of our tramlines; in which we share many more moments in common. It is a great opportunity to build a better society and we should grab it with both hands. If we can rebuild what I will call a Common Life – a set of shared moments that brings us together with those who seem different from us – our country will be richer, happier and fairer.

I don't want to turn back the clock. These shared moments should be ones we enjoy and gain from, in ways that fit with modern life.

And this book will make some suggestions about the kind of moments these might be. For instance, I will argue that we should consider introducing community service for young people as part of their schooling; funding local groups that bring new parents together; and building a national retirement service that connects us to our local neighbourhood as the time we spend at work reduces.

Get real, you might say. People don't like change, and still less being told what's good for them. Creating new ways to bring us together is unrealistic and impractical, an unaffordable pipe dream. If we're to make changes after this crisis, the priority should be elsewhere. But I would contend that now is a moment of uncommon opportunity, and we should seize it.

As I stand at my door and clap, 150 miles away, in Hereford, a woman stands outside her home and does the same. Born in 1936, my mother turns eighty-five this year. My children, stuck indoors last week, wanted to know about the Second World War, the global crisis that had interrupted her childhood. They were fascinated by her evacuation – how she had been forced to move away from home, from her parents and her friends, and into the home of strangers. I've heard the stories before, but even so my mind filled with images as she spoke. Of my mother, aged six, sheltering in the basement of her school, taught alongside the only other classmate yet to leave London. Aged seven, sent away by her parents to a house she does not know. Forced outside each day by adults who want to help but don't like children, my mother fends for herself between breakfast and tea. She plays alone in the woods and near the village. She longs to leave. Within the year, her parents visit and decide to take her home. Aged eight, so pleased to be home, she watches her mother hide the weekly sugar ration so there will be enough for a Christmas cake.

My mother was just one of 827,000 children to be evacuated. That's 827,000 separate tales of mostly inner-city children sent to country carers. Two worlds collided. Surprised by seeing flowers growing, one wrote home: 'They call this spring, Mum, and they have one down here every year.' Some children refused to drink milk after seeing where it came from, convinced they were being given cow's urine. Surrogate parents in turn were often shocked by the levels of deprivation and poverty they witnessed, with some children arriving in clothes so dirty that they had to be burned. Some smaller children weren't wearing underclothes at all, but brown paper into which they had been stitched for the winter. One woman recorded that the children she received had 'no coats or extra shirts or underclothes. I ... decided to write to the parents for more. The mother wrote back saying she would have to get their suits and shoes out of pawn.' By necessity, the war threw strangers together. Some three million people joined Civil Defence groups at home. Over one and half million women entered industry. Another five million men and women were conscripted into armed service. Many millions, in other words, were forced out of their bubbles and came to understand the lives of the others.

The experience of total war brought us closer together. We saw anew how in need so many of us were. And the result was the National Health Service. That crisis ended – just as this one will. The wisdom we gained from looking beyond our bubbles allowed Britons to build something new: an institution that they saw was necessary, but that for many years had also seemed unrealistic, impractical and unaffordable. It is now never far from the British mind. It has changed lives and lengthened them. It starred in the opening cere-mony of the London 2012 Olympics. It has been described as the closest thing we have to a national religion. As my neighbours and I stand on our street, it is the NHS we are clapping.

The crisis of Covid has distanced us from each other. We see anew how far apart we are. The result must be a new way to bring us together.

Part I

THE HUMPTY DUMPTY EFFECT

Humpty Dumpty sat on a wall,
Humpty Dumpty had a great fall.
All the king's horses and all the king's men
Couldn't put Humpty together again.

English Nursery Rhyme

CHAPTER ONE

THE PROBLEM YOU KNEW
ABOUT ALL ALONG

One of my first jobs when I left school was making sales on behalf of the local milkman. Starting at 10 a.m. after a substantial fried breakfast, I'd pound the streets of my home town of Plymouth, knocking on doors, and trying to persuade anyone unfortunate enough to be at home how much better their life would be if they had milk delivered to their doorstep. If I failed, I earned nothing. But every time I succeeded, I took home £10. Most days I took home about £50, but on one magical day my pocket bulged with five £20 notes. With such clear incentives, I thought a great deal about what would make a sale more likely. How much should I smile when someone opened the door? Too little might seem unfriendly; too much, weird and overfamiliar. How close to the door should I stand? Too near might appear aggressive; but too far, unconfident or aloof. And what was the best opening line? A simple hello or a more formal introduction? The most experienced sales rep in our group was convinced that the best approach was to crack an unfunny joke. If the person smiled, you knew you had someone in the mood to buy; if not, it was time to move on. I copied his approach. 'I'm not as bad as I look,' I would declare with a jaunty smile, standing what I had decided was the optimal distance from the door. That was until one day in May, when the person behind the doorstep looked me up and down, rolled his eyes, declared, 'Yes you are mate,' and slammed it shut.

Francis Evans, an academic at the Chicago School of Business, was more detached from the world of door-to-door sales, but in the early 1960s he became fascinated by the factors that made a sale more likely. In 1963, he analysed every sale of life insurance made by 125 salesmen across the United States. And while he never resolved the issue of how close to stand to the door or whether a joke was better than a 'hello', he did find something fascinating. No matter the competence of the sales rep, the homeowner was more likely to buy if the rep happened to support the same political party that they did. Republicans were more likely to buy if the salesman was a Republican; Democrats were more likely to buy if the salesman was a Democrat. That wasn't all. Sales were also more likely if the rep had the same level of education as the homeowner or if they both earned the same amount of money each week. Incredibly, it even helped if they were the same height.

The preference for 'people like us' that Francis Evans discovered on the doorsteps of America in 1963 has come back to haunt us. Some sixty years later, our societies have become fractured, split into social bubbles comprised of people 'just like us'. These social divisions – by education, age, race, income and politics – have become too large to ignore. Four out of five Americans describe their country as 'mainly or totally divided'. Half of Britons believe that the people of the UK are 'the most divided that we have ever been'. And yet our fractures took us by surprise. As referenda and elections lit up our divisions like an X-ray illuminating broken bones, many of us found ourselves waking and wondering: 'How could it be that close? I don't know anyone who voted the other way.' We were surprised by something we should have known, for the truth was hiding in plain sight. The evidence was there in our own friendships, where we could see groups that were full of people 'just like me'. We have been like children learning the reality about Father Christmas, dismayed by a truth that was obvious all along. For years, we ignored it. As long as the economy grew, we closed our eyes to the parallel lives of the rich and poor while the wealthy worked, socialised and increasingly married solely within their own kind. We looked past our workplaces, divided into firms where either everyone had a university degree, or no one did. Wanting to put issues of race into the past, we ignored the fact that most of us had next to no close friends of a different ethnicity. Not any more. Divisions seem to be all around us. Race, in particular, is back on the agenda.

It has now become too easy to assume that all our divisions are about race. White, Black, Asian, Latino, Somali, Pakistani – these have become the words of the moment to describe our most pressing fractures. Here is a different set of words that are just as relevant: publishers, consultants, bankers, lawyers, doctors, senior civil servants. For, today, no groups in the UK are more fractured than professionals are from lower earners. But – if the word 'professional' describes you as much as it does me – I'm pretty confident that deep down you already knew this. If you are in this group, I'd like to place a small bet. How many people do you know by name for whom life, on a day-to-day basis, is truly financially difficult? My bet is that the answer is none or, at most, one. If so, you are not alone. Outside of a pandemic, the average professional would have to throw a party for a hundred people before inviting anyone who was collecting unemployment benefit. In truth, few of those invitations would even manage to reach someone working class.[1]

Rather than host a party, let's attend a wedding and play a game. You tell me the education level of the first person getting married, and I will tell you the level of the second. It's an easy game for me to win, as most Britons and Americans now marry people with the same education level as themselves. Those with degrees marry those with degrees. Those with MBAs marry those with MBAs. This tendency, known as 'assortative mating', is most pronounced at the highest levels of wealth and education, where the rich and the highly educated marry the rich and the highly educated. It's tempting to console ourselves with the thought that 'it was ever thus'. Tempting, but wrong. During the first half of the last century, the opposite trend was true – more and more people married outside their social class.[2] The rise of assortative mating doesn't just affect the couple getting married. As the American political scientist Robert Putnam puts it, it means that '[f]ewer and fewer working-class kids will have rich uncles or well-educated aunts to help them ascend the ladder'.[3]

Today, about half of Brits and Americans with degrees have almost no close friends without one. Fractures between the young and old have become just as pronounced. Part of the reason older Americans find millennials so puzzling is that they don't talk to them. Just 6 per cent of Americans older than sixty say that they discuss 'important matters' with anyone under thirty-five they are not related to.[4] Europe is equally as divided; a study in the Netherlands found that, in the average week, roughly nine out of ten over-eighties had no contact at all with anyone under sixty, apart from members of their family.[5] These divisions are a key cause of the loneliness affecting older citizens. If, as you head into later life, your friends are mostly your age, they're likely to become less mobile – and less able to visit – at around the same point that you do. It should therefore horrify but not surprise us when half of Britons over seventy tell us that their closest companion is the television, rather than another human being. Millennials are equally cut off. At a point when they need contacts and networks to get ahead, under-thirty-fives have, roughly, just a quarter of the interactions with older generations than would be the case if their friendships mirrored the mix in the local community.

What about politics? On the day after the Brexit referendum, the *Financial Times* sent a journalist on a commuter train into London. One, somewhat stunned, voter described her reaction to the news: 'I woke up and said, "You've got to be kidding me." I don't know anyone who voted Leave – but maybe that says something in itself.' Many Remainers and Brexiteers, Trump-lovers and Trump-haters, live in completely different social worlds. A quarter of Remain voters have no friends who voted Leave, while a fifth of Leave voters have no Remain-voting friends. Two-thirds of committed conservatives in the US have no close friends with a different political view. The same is true of half of the committed liberals. We're now more concerned about our child marrying someone with the 'wrong' political view than with a different skin colour. One in ten Americans would be unhappy if their child married someone of a different race. Two in ten Remainers would be unhappy if their child married a Brexiteer. Three in ten Republicans would be unhappy if their child married a Democrat. Five in ten Democrats would be unhappy if their child married a Republican. Our fractures along political lines may be new, but they're deep.

What about race? American comedian Chris Rock's sarcasm has it roughly right: 'we're living in a time where Dr King and Nelson Mandela's dreams are coming alive … All my Black friends have a bunch of White friends, and all my White friends have *one* Black friend.' In the US, almost half of Whites have no Black friends (as well as no Asian friends and no Latino friends). When asked to list their seven closest friends, most name only White people. When asked to think more broadly – about acquaintances and colleagues – more than a quarter still can't think of anyone who is not White. Chris Rock is too optimistic, though, when it comes to his Black friends. The majority of Black Americans listing their seven closest friends name only fellow Black people. Just under half of Hispanics name only Hispanics. More than a quarter of African Americans and Hispanics can't think of a single friend who is White. The UK is similar. Around half of Brits have friends only from their own ethnic group. Religious divides are also strong. About half of non-Muslim Brits have never had any close contact with a Muslim in their life. The vast majority cannot think of a single close friend who is Muslim. The British writer David Goodhart wrote this about a visit he made to a school in the British city of Huddersfield: 'the mutual ignorance among white and Pakistani children about each other was summed up by one primary school head teacher who heard a Pakistani child expressing surprise to have discovered that white children "liked pizza as much as we do"'.[6] It is time to understand properly why we are so divided, why it matters and how we fix it.

We should start by recognising that our problem is not that we are different from each other. People have always lived with difference. There has never been a country on earth where everyone thought the same, believed the same, looked the same and sounded the same. No, the problem is not that we are different from each other; it is that we are distant from 'the other'. The problem is our lack of inter-action with those who are different; that we live in social bubbles filled with people 'just like me'. It is these bubbles that mean you can live in a diverse country and wake up the day after a knife-edge election and find that none of your friends voted the other way. These divisions between us matter. We will see how they reduce social mobility by robbing poorer children of the networks and contacts they need to get ahead; how they increase terrorism by creating segregated spaces where radicalisation occurs; how they reduce life expectancy by boosting anxiety and exacerbating loneli-ness; and how they slow economic growth by preventing the spread of knowledge and innovation. Worst of all, they poison our demo-cratic debate, making it harder to solve all of these – and other – problems. How, though, will we mend these fractures? Well, first we must understand what causes them. To paraphrase Jean-Jacques Rousseau, we must explain why societies are born together but everywhere have come apart.

Some people will suggest that no explanation is needed, for surely these fractures are 'natural'. Haven't birds of a feather always 'flocked together'? Yes, they have. In fact, ever since Francis Evans's door-to-door salesmen study, researchers have long known that all of us have a small bias towards people 'like us'. This bias, though weak, is so constant that academics believe evolution has hardwired it into us. It has been such a focus of so much research that they have given the bias a name: they call it homophily, meaning 'the tendency to seek out or be attracted to those who are like me'. We will call it the People Like Me syndrome (PLM). It is this syndrome, this natural, persistent bias, that sits at the heart of our divisions into bubbles of 'us' and 'them'. As we will see, People Like Me syndrome is at the core of our story.

But it cannot be the whole story. Why? Because it's a constant bias. It doesn't get stronger or weaker. It can no better explain why we are fracturing more now than the existence of the sun can explain why it is warm today but not last week. You can't explain why it's hot without starting with the sun. But the sun alone can't explain why it's hotter today than it was yesterday. In the same way, you can't understand our divisions without starting with People Like Me syndrome. But PLM can't explain why we are more divided now than before. It becomes hotter because something other than the sun changes – the clouds move, the earth moves, the wind blows. What then has changed to make us more divided? The answer is that although human nature has not changed, our societies have.

To understand this, we need to talk about sugar. Humans love sugar. We have a natural, and pretty constant, bias towards eating it. Doughnuts, cakes, sweets, ice creams – if it has sugar in it, we usually like it. Just like PLM, this tendency is 'natural' and 'constant'. It's baked into our make-up, apparent in our instincts and has evolved over tens of thousands of years. Why? Probably because it was useful for our nomadic ancestors to seek high-energy foods while they travelled great distances, uncertain when they might eat again. However, for today's more sedentary humans an uncontrolled attraction to sugar would be pretty damaging. Rates of obesity and diabetes would go through the roof. And so, in the face of this dangerous bias, societies have stepped in. How? By evolving norms and habits that discourage us from eating too much sweet and sugary food. It has become normal to frown upon those who consume more sugar than they should, who become grossly overweight, whose teeth rot, or who eat sweet food as the main course rather that at the end of the meal. The result is that while it may be 'natural' for an individual to desire too much sugar, it's also now 'normal' for our societies to discourage this desire.

The point is this: when our natural instincts are detrimental to ourselves and society at large, our societies evolve ways to restrain our natural instinct. As individuals, we desire too much sugar, and so our societies have created habits and norms to constrain us. In the same way, as we go through adolescence, we tend to gravitate towards risk-taking, conflict and even violence. Successful societies keep the peace by building norms and habits to channel these impulses. These norms and habits are what many of us call 'civilisation'.

In exactly the same way, successful societies have always found ways to dampen our instinct to divide and sub-divide. How? By creating institutions that bring people together with those who are *not* like them. At different times and places, these social institutions have taken very different forms. The industrial society of our grand-parents connected city dwellers through the school, the workplace and the club. The agrarian societies of our ancestors connected villag-ers through feast days, religious services and rites of passage. The nomadic societies of prehistory connected different families through animalistic rituals. Every successful society in history has evolved different institutions to constrain People Like Me syndrome – but in every case they have the same effect. They bring together those who are different. They build trust. They prevent division. These institu-tions are the hidden glue that is central to our human story. And yet we have no name for them. I will call them our Common Life.

Today, the common life that connected our grandparents – of club and society, local school and local workplace – has fallen away. We have become half as likely to join a club or society. If we do, they tend to be full of people like us. Our schools have become more divided by race and income than our neighbourhoods. Our work-places have become fractured by educational background – increasingly they either have no staff without a university degree or no one with one. The lack of a common life, that can connect us with those unlike us, is the reason we are divided today. It is not because of Fox News or MSNBC, Donald Trump or Brexit. Media-fired culture wars and political conflicts do not help us to unite, but they are not the main reason that we are divided. We are not fractured because our politics are fractious. It's the other way around: our politics are fractious because we are fractured, they are divisive because we, the people, are socially divided from one another. We have an appetite for stories that tell us that 'another group of people' are terrible, untrustworthy and up to something only because we never spend any time with these type of people. There is no market for media or electoral candidates who spread hate and criticism about people who you really like and hang out with all the time. Our divisions create the space for demagogues, not the other way around. The fundamental reason for our fractures is that we lack a common life to connect us, a set of institutions that bring us together with people unlike us. In their absence, we spend our time with the people we choose to see, when we choose to see them. PLM ensures that we choose people who are just like us. And so, long before we were made to socially distance, we became socially distant from those unlike us.

Am I claiming that there was once a period of perfect unity? No. Do I believe that society has been on the 'road to hell' from some earlier golden age? No. Do I believe we simply need to turn the clock back? Again, no. The story is not that things have got endlessly worse. Nor is it that things have got endlessly better. The truth is we've been going around in circles. Things have got worse, and then better, and then worse and then better. How do we know? Because we've definitely been here before. At the start of the Industrial Revolution, our ancestors migrated from their villages to towns and cities in huge numbers. Young men and women left behind their rural communities. Their new neighbours had strange dialects and different habits.

The glue – the common life – that had held them together with their fellow villagers was left behind: the local church that they knew was a day's journey away and there was little prospect of celebrating feast days with your neighbours or inviting everyone to your wedding or child's baptism. On arrival in their new surroundings, people found themselves adrift in a sea of strangers with no social institutions to connect them with those who seemed so unlike them. They therefore clung to people 'like them' – distant family, friends from the old village, those with the same dialect, and, increasingly, those from the same 'class' – living cheek by jowl, but fractured from one another. The historical records describe the consequence: people's trust in each other plummeted. In 1843, the *Illustrated London News* warned that distrust will 'destroy the very fabric of society by shaking every confidence between man and man'.

These divisions into bubbles of similarity proved to be a tinder-box. As the beginning of the coronavirus pandemic revealed, crises can create a short-term burst of solidarity. But without a common life to bring people together, when crises hit the fast-growing cities of the nineteenth century, they combusted. The three challenges of disease, crime and poverty did nothing to create a sense of 'being in it together'. Instead, they created a demand for immediate change, and if this was not forthcoming, violence typically ensued. By 1850, half of Europe was aflame. This was no golden age of unity. The past does not offer us a vision for post-pandemic life. It is a past we should fear, not try to emulate.

Our ancestors would see half a century pass before some semblance of trust and solidarity came to the cities. It didn't happen by turning back the clock. The old ways of connecting villagers – the feast day, the rite of passage, the religious ceremonies – were largely gone. No, they had to wait for a new common life to arrive. In time, clubs and societies sprung up and grew until they had huge memberships; workplaces built solidarity between colleagues; mandatory schools educated children but also connected families with their neighbours.

This new common life, though, did not emerge overnight. It took fifty years to arrive.

We cannot afford to wait that long today. The pandemic has revealed anew our divisions. It has also created an opportunity to act. For the health of our democracy, our society and our economy, we need to take it. Our countries need a new common life – a new set of institutions, different from those of the past, that can pull us out of bubbles and connect us together. With our world turned upside down by the virus, it is time to rebuild it.

CHAPTER TWO

THE VILLAIN OF
OUR STORY

There is a story – in all likelihood apocryphal – that at the turn of
the twentieth century *The Times* of London ran a competition. The
newspaper – troubled by events it was reporting – asked a number
of leading British authors to write articles in response to a single
question: 'What is wrong with the world today?' Most authors
submitted responses that were long, detailed and scholarly. All apart
from one, which reputedly came from the writer and theologian G.
K. Chesterton. It consisted of four words: 'Dear Sirs, *I* am.' If we're
to understand the fractures in our countries, we must begin as
Chesterton did. *We* are the main reason our countries are
fracturing.

Oldham is a small town near Manchester that is home to about
two hundred thousand people. On the morning of 27 May 2001, it
found itself on the front page of every newspaper in England. A
racist attack had led to a street fight, which by the evening had
erupted into a full-blown riot between local White and Asian young
men. It was three days before peace returned.

Despite its small size, Oldham has a proud industrial history. In
the nineteenth century, it produced more cotton textile than
anywhere in the world. Migrants from India came to live and work
there. In the 1980s, the industry on which the town had been built
went into steep decline, and within twenty years Oldham had

become one of the most deprived municipalities in England – and also one of the most divided. On the eve of the riots, Asians and Whites lived in different parts of the town, socialising separately and sending their children to different schools.

In the shadow of the riots, on the west side of Oldham were two such schools, just two miles apart. On the face of it, Breeze Hill and Counthill had much in common. Both had around seven hundred pupils, served mostly lower-income families and achieved mixed results. And yet anyone visiting the schools would spot an obvious difference. It was hard to find a White student at Breeze Hill and equally rare to see an Asian student at Counthill.

Neither Breeze Hill nor Counthill exists today. In the same year, they were both closed. Their students – White and Asian – were transferred to a new, larger school – called Waterhead Academy – where they would be educated together. The most interesting part of Waterhead Academy is the cafeteria. It's here – unlike in many of their lessons – that students express a completely free choice about whom they sit next to. This means that social scientists can see the extent to which the children – Asian and White – choose to sit together or apart. The good news is that White and Asian students sit next to each other more than they used to. The bad news is that they don't do it very much.

But this isn't the most significant thing about Waterhead. It shouldn't surprise us that two groups of students previously educated separately are taking some time to get to know each other. No, the really significant thing about Waterhead is what else the social scientists have found. For they didn't just record the ethnicity of the children having lunch together. They also recorded their hair colour and whether they wore glasses. And what did they find? It turned out that children with ginger hair – like me – were more likely to sit next to others with ginger hair. Children with glasses – again like me – were more likely to sit next to other children with glasses. In short, they found out that you're more likely to sit, eat and be friends with someone who looks a bit like you, whether you've previously been educated in different schools or not.

Christina Bloom needed to rest. The Manhattanite philanthropist had been diagnosed with stage-four breast cancer and was exhausted. But, sitting in her five-million-dollar apartment overlooking Central Park, she couldn't shake an idea that had obsessed her ever since her marriage had failed. Bloom had become fixated on the idea that she had missed out on the man she should have married. A man who – she noticed – looked a lot like her. Despite her friends' protestations, she became convinced that looking alike was the basis for love, and she was prepared to commit some of her not insignificant wealth to the cause. She was so convinced that she hired a team of consultants and coders, and set them to work building a dating website that would scan your face and match you with someone who had the same facial features as you. She appeared on daytime television to promote the business, and before long 50,000 Americans had become members of the marvellously named FindYourFaceMate. com. Although the company closed in 2014 – overtaken by Tinder, Bumble and pretty much everyone else – Christina Bloom was onto something. For we are indeed attracted to people who look like us.

Just a year before the website was launched, two psychology professors, Chris Fraley and Michael Marks, enlisted twenty-two male and eighteen female volunteers to take part in a two-day experiment. On the first day, participants had their photos taken and completed a simple test. They looked at pictures of people's faces and rated their attractiveness out of ten. Then they headed home. What they didn't know was that what really mattered on that day wasn't the test, but the photos that were taken of them. That night, Chris and Michael went to work. For each volunteer they produced fifty new pictures to rate. While ten of these pictures showed entirely normal faces, forty showed faces created on a computer by merging a stranger's face with the photo of the volunteer's own face. The volunteers returned on the next day to the university, where they were given the fifty faces and asked to rate them for sexual attractiveness on a 1 (not at all attractive) to 7 (extremely attractive) scale. Sure enough, the majority of the forty volunteers preferred the faces that most resembled their own. Christina Bloom may not have had the best business idea, but she was right about one thing. Humans appear to like the look of themselves.

Christina Bloom and the researchers at Waterhead Academy had discovered the same thing that Francis Evans had identified on the doorstep: a bias that affects all of us. It's a bias at the heart of why our countries are fractured; a bias in favour of people who remind us of ourselves. This bias can be about looks – recall how Evans found that customers preferred salesmen who matched their height – or about something invisible – Evans also found that customers preferred salesmen with the same level of education or political opinions. Since 1954, social scientists have called this bias homophily. Put simply, it means: 'birds of a feather flock together'. In this book, I am using the simpler, somewhat blunter term: People Like Me syndrome. PLM has been a source of constant interest to social scientists, with around 37,000 articles having been written on the topic.

Readers might reasonably ask: what is the difference between People Like Me Syndrome and racism? Is PLM just a 'nice' term for racism? It is worth spending a moment on what they have in common and how they differ. They are clearly linked concepts. PLM is about a bias (towards people like me) and racism describes a bias against people of a different race. However, they are also each broader than the other. To make an obvious point, PLM is broader than matters of race. As we saw at Waterhead Academy, children were biased towards other children who similarly wore glasses or didn't wear glasses. As Francis Evans discovered with his salesmen, buyers and sellers were biased towards each other by similarity of height, political opinion and wealth. But critically, racism is substantially broader than personal biases. It also describes systems and habits that repeatedly act against people on account of their race. Let me provide an example. In my day job, I am focused on reducing levels of violence in society. This requires addressing the underlying causes of violence – which leads us to education, poverty, the criminal justice system, the employment market and much more. In almost every case, we see repeated disproportionality in the system to the advantage of the ethnic majority group and to the disadvantage of the ethnic minority group. Individual bias is part of the story, but it doesn't fully explain what is going on. The systems, habits or algorithms can bias against a minority group without any individual necessarily being biased. This means that you could reduce PLM and the problem could remain. But reducing PLM helps. Why is this? Because PLM makes it harder to change these systems. If a majority group has the power to change things but are insulated from those who are negatively affected, they are less likely to understand the urgent need for change and are less likely to share power with those from the other group. Throughout this book, I will seek to underline the continuing power of the bias against ethnic minority groups coded into our institutions, habits and algorithms. This is what we call 'systemic racism'. PLM explains much of what we see in the world, but it does not seek to explain it all.

This distinction made, you might wonder what the problem is with PLM. If it propels us to spend time with people like us and we enjoy doing so, why should we be worried about it? Let's reconsider our love of sugar. If we eat too much of it, we tend, nonetheless, to enjoy doing so; it tastes good and gives us energy. The problem is that various negative consequences follow: from diabetes to tooth decay, obesity to heart disease. In the same way, a society in which we surround ourselves with people 'like us' brings some serious consequences. As we will see in Part III, these include reduced social mobility, more fragile democracy, higher risks of terrorism and lower economic growth. For this reason, great societies find ways to clamp down on People Like Me syndrome.

This is difficult, as PLM has very broad effects on human behaviour. It can make us biased towards those with almost any perceived similarity: ethnicity, class, religion, gender, age, job title, attitudes, beliefs, even aspirations. It can also have a very wide impact. As the Evans, Bloom and Waterhead stories begin to show, PLM can affect what you buy, who you love and where you live. Further research reveals that it can affect who you collaborate with at work, which school you send your children to, which ante-natal class you attend and, most of all, who your closest friends are. It can affect the most serious of decisions. Business has known this for some time. It's not hard to find companies that use PLM to sell their goods and services. This doesn't mean they're familiar with the 37,000 articles written on the topic. What they do know is that their customers are biased towards people who remind them of themselves. Advertisers use models who are most likely to resemble an attractive version of their customers; sales companies try to select salespeople who in some way resemble those they will be meeting; and developers have even built housing estates that aim to cluster together people of similar values and ages.

Some people recoil from the idea that we are born with People Like Me syndrome. They argue that such a bias is so terrible that it must be imposed by society and surely only affects some of us: the extremists in our midst. Scientific research resoundingly disagrees. PLM has been identified so consistently in tests across the world (from Kuala Lumpur to Kingston), on so many different axes (from height to eye colour, education to class, name to income) and in so many different contexts (from shopping online to conducting research, attending school to working in an office) that the only credible conclusion is that we're all born this way. We appear to have evolved to be biased towards people who remind us of ourselves. The question is not 'Does PLM exist?' It's 'What is the evolutionary advantage of such a bias?'

To imagine how this bias might have evolved, we need to revisit our ancestors on the savannah. Living in small tribes, we could only fully trust members of our own tight community. Those outside of the group might not be on our side. Living in this world, someone born with an instinctive bias against those who don't look like kinsfolk might well have an advantage. It would give them a few extra seconds to start fleeing or fighting, making them slightly more likely to survive longer, and pass on their genes. Small margins can make a large difference over generations of evolution. These individuals would be marginally more likely to have children, meaning that the next generation would be more likely to have the bias. With each generation, PLM would become increasingly common.

People Like Me syndrome isn't, though, a conscious opposition to those who are 'other'. It's more a sense of comfort gained from the familiar and of nervousness about what feels different. When interviewed by researchers from University College London, these were the exact feelings that parents of children at a socially diverse London school described having about other parents at the school gate. They spoke warmly of the school and of their neighbourhood, but disliked the 'social awkwardness' they felt about approaching people of different ethnicities and classes. They worried about running out of things to say, or finding they couldn't speak the same language, or feeling 'awkward' about earning more than others. The exact same awkwardness was found when King's College London interviewed teenagers about mixing with people from social circumstances other than their own, with almost nine out of ten saying that they felt nervous when they met someone from a 'different background'.

PLM is best understood not as a type of hatred or judgement, but as a feeling of awkwardness and discomfort. It's best recognised in ourselves when we think of a time we felt out of place. Perhaps at a party where we didn't know many people, or at the school gate if you've ever dropped off a child. Try to remember how you felt as you looked around for people to talk to. Did you approach those dressed like you or dressed very differently, roughly your age or much older, about your height or taller? For most of us, a small bias kicks in and we approach the group that we feel most 'comfortable' with. This gentle nudge is PLM at work, and the very gentleness of the nudge raises an important question. How can such a small bias be the villain in our story? The answer is that PLM is a bit like humming.

It's fair to say that my chemistry teacher did not deserve our poor behaviour. Compared to the maths teacher who broke down in class and told us, 'I never wanted to be a maths teacher, I haven't got a maths degree, I wish I wasn't here,' she at least knew her subject. But for some reason – known only to schoolchildren – the chemistry teacher had lost control of the class. We'd done most of the naughty things you could do in a normal classroom, from asking the same question again and again, to swapping seats when her back was turned, to hiding under the desk and shouting out rude words. We'd also done most of the things you could do only in a chemistry lab – many of them fairly dangerous. We had just one weapon left: the Hum. The thing about humming, as every schoolchild knows, is that a single person humming is no big deal. It's easy to ignore and quite easy to identify. But it becomes a real problem when nearly everyone is doing it. At that point, it's an incredibly loud noise that's hard to pinpoint and even harder to stop. Faced by a whole class humming, our teacher took the only obvious course of action. She left the class-room to get help.

The way People Like Me syndrome impacts on our societies is a bit like the effect of humming: one person hardly matters, but when everyone is involved it's a real problem. To see why, we need the help of the American Nobel Prize-winning economist, Thomas Schelling. He was stuck on a long-haul flight and puzzled by something. Why was the place in which he lived so divided by race so many years after legal segregation had ended? Ongoing active discrimination by developers, housing authorities and realtors had continued for many years after legal segregation had ended, but was this all there was to it? With only a pencil and a piece of paper to hand, Schelling started to doodle a model. First, he drew a little grid to represent the houses in his local neighbourhood. He then scribbled either a plus or a zero in each square to represent Black and White neighbours. Finally, he started moving the plusses and zeros around the neighbourhood to reflect people's preferences for where they might like to live. Before long things started to become clear.

It's easy to repeat his experiment. Rather than a piece of paper, we'll use a chessboard. And rather than plusses and zeros we will use grey and white counters. The grey and white counters represent two different types of people living in the same neighbourhood – it could be that they are rich or poor, Black or white, with degrees or without. Whatever difference the colours represent, the first thing we need to do is to fill every square alternately with a white or a grey piece, while leaving the four corner squares empty. As you can see, each person now has several neighbours – some white, some grey.[1]

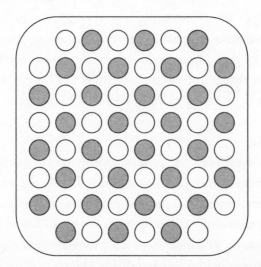

Now let's assume that each person living in the neighbourhood displays a tiny amount of PLM. Greys are not opposed to whites, but they prefer to live in a neighbourhood where they are not outnumbered by whites two to one. We shall assume that whites feel the same way: they are not opposed to greys, but they would prefer to live in a neighbourhood where they are not outnumbered by greys two to one. At present, everything is perfect. Everyone has an exact balance of grey and white neighbours and so nobody wants to move. This position, however, is surprisingly unstable.

Let us imagine that, after a year or so, a few people leave town and some new ones move in. To reflect this, we will remove fifteen pieces at random from the board and then randomly fill five of the vacated spaces. The situation on the board now looks more random.

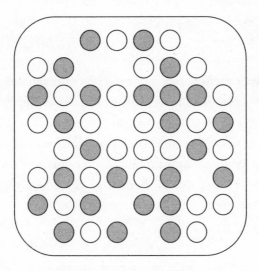

Importantly, there are now a small number of greys and whites who are outnumbered two to one. As a result, they want to move. So, we pick up these counters and move them to the nearest location where they're no longer outnumbered two to one. This is where trouble starts. As soon as we move these people to a new neighbourhood, more of those left behind are outnumbered two to one. More people therefore want to move. As they do so, more of the people left behind are outnumbered two to one. Before long, almost half the board has moved, leaving it increasingly fractured into distinctly grey and white areas.

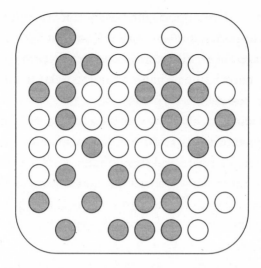

Schelling's experiment shows us how PLM's gentle nudge can snowball into a very powerful force. It may be easy to ignore one person humming, but it is impossible to ignore a whole class. Similarly, one person's People Like Me syndrome may make little difference, but at scale it can divide a neighbourhood, a city or a nation. Unfortunately, this isn't all of the bad news. There's one more factor about human psychology that makes PLM even more powerful.

Even though they didn't know each other in advance, the twenty-two eleven-year-old boys had a great deal in common. They were all White Protestant Americans, from middle-class two-parent families, born in the same year with no history of trouble with the police. Muzafer Sherif, the highly driven Turkish-American social psychologist who had selected them, was determined that no one should be able to point to a reason why these boys might take against each other. He even made sure that they had similar IQs. This was his second attempt at the experiment, and this time it had to work.

Last time around, Sherif had let the boys he had selected become friends. Some had already known each other. Not this time. These boys had never met before and Sherif allocated them at random to one of two teams. Then, one day in the summer of 1954, each team of boys was transported entirely separately to two different locations in Robbers Cave State Park, a remote summer camp in Oklahoma that had once been home to bank robbers and train thieves on the run from the law. Once there, the boys got to know the other members of their team. Unaware of the other team's existence, the boys started to bond with their own team members through a series of activities organised for them by the camp staff – roles played by Sherif's fellow researchers. They swam, hiked, put up tents and ate together. After a few days, each group had chosen a team name, designed a flag and agreed a set of rules for how they would live. Two identities were born: the Rattlers and the Eagles. The two sets of boys, however, remained unaware of the other's existence.

Having formed the boys into these two groups, Sherif and his researchers set out to create tension between them. In their previous experiment – in which some of the boys had existing friendships – that was to prove surprisingly difficult. On this occasion, it was to prove surprisingly easy. Slowly the Rattlers and Eagles became aware that they were not the only team of boys in the park. The Eagles – who were more friendly and supportive – were initially keen to meet the Rattlers, but the Rattlers were immediately much more aggressive. When they spotted the Eagles playing on a baseball pitch in the park, they asked for a chance to compete against them. Sherif and his researchers decided to organise a multi-day competition, with points awarded for winning baseball matches, tugs of war, touch football games, tent pitching, cabin inspections and a treasure hunt. The competition lit the fuse that, with a little encouragement, exploded into a conflict. The first signs of trouble came after the Rattlers won the opening two games. The frustrated Eagles chanced upon the Rattlers' flag, which they had left behind on the baseball pitch. Offered matches, they took the opportunity to set the flag alight. Things now started to escalate. The Rattlers stole the Eagles' flag and beat up the boy who had been holding it. After the Eagles won the next two games, the Rattlers responded by raiding the Eagles' camp in the dead of night. After the competition was won by the Eagles, things got even worse. The Rattlers broke into the Eagles' cabins again and stole the prizes. A few hours later, the camp staff had to physically intervene to prevent violence.

Sherif had wanted to create conflict, but even he was surprised at how divided the two teams had become. After the second raid, the researchers had to keep the boys apart for a day and a night to avoid losing control. When the boys met the next time – for a meal – they shouted abuse at each other and threw food. The behaviour became so bad that the two women doing the cooking threatened to walk out on Sherif. One of the boys – interviewed many years later – described how he had started putting rocks in a sock at night to be ready to defend himself. With a little help, two sets of boys – with vast amounts in common – had fractured into two tribes. The exact experiment was never repeated with girls – and any proposal to do so would today be rejected by universities' ethical committees. However, just two years after Sherif's experiment, a graduate student at New York University, Rozet Avigdor, conducted a somewhat related experiment. Avigdor randomly allocated ten-year-old girls into teams and challenged them to write and perform a play. All went well until – at a dress rehearsal – one of the team's plays appeared to be much better than that of the others. Watching on, the other teams started doing all they could to disrupt the performance. The experiment ended with Avigdor having to forcibly remove them from the room.

What then have we learnt? Schelling's board shows us how People Like Me syndrome can cause division. Sherif's experiment shows us that, once people are divided, active encouragement can lead us from a feeling of discomfort and awkwardness into conflict and aggression. The Rattlers and Eagles had so much in common – age, ethnicity, intelligence, religion, family background. They'd never harmed each other before Robbers Cave and had no reason to dislike one another. Yet, once divided, they became not only biased towards the boys on their own team, but easily turned against the boys on the other team.

It's worth considering how the anger that Sherif brought out among the Eagles and Rattlers impacts on Schelling's experiment. Schelling assumed that the grey and white pieces would happily stay put up to and including the point when they were outnumbered by more than two to one. Is this really credible? After the competition was over, there was no way that an Eagle would have sat and eaten at a dinner table where Rattlers outnumbered him by two to one; members of one team were unhappy just being in the same location as those of another.[2] It is by combining Schelling's and Sherif's experiments that we can see why PLM is the villain of our story. Evolved over thousands of years, it sits – largely harmless – within our psyches. Yet when applied to groups of people, it can snowball, creating divisions that then increase our bias. What is the reason for our divisions? 'Dear sirs, *I* am.' Fortunately, this is not the whole story.

CHAPTER THREE

THE HERO HIDDEN
IN OUR HISTORY

As planned, Muzafer Sherif's experiment had taken two groups of almost identical young boys and made them enemies. After twelve days with them at Robbers Cave, Sherif was elated. But things were also starting to get out of hand. The boys were now unable to interact without name-calling, food-throwing or theft. The coaches to take them home were not coming for six more days, and the mood was getting steadily worse. Sherif and his team were starting to worry that they had uncorked a genie that they couldn't put back. And yet six days later, the boys boarded together happily. Eagles shared seats with Rattlers. Rattlers sat next to Eagles. Everyone sang songs together. Many of the boys exchanged addresses. Halfway home, the Rattlers used their own money to buy every boy – Eagles included – a drink. What on earth had happened in those last six days? How had Sherif united a group of boys who had become such hardened enemies? It all started when the water ran out.

The drinking water at Robbers Cave came from a single reservoir that sat at the top of a large mountain to the north of the campsite. Each day, water travelled from the reservoir down a long pipe into a metallic storage tank. Water then flowed from the tank through another pipe into the latrines, the kitchen and the drinking fountains. There was also a tap on the side of the tank, which the boys used to fill up their water bottles. On the afternoon of day twelve of the experiment, Sherif and his researchers did something drastic. They stopped the water supply. They stuffed sacks into the tank's two exits and blocked both the pipe and the tap. Within hours, the campsite was out of water. Sherif gathered the Eagles and Rattlers together. He announced that vandals had damaged the water supply and volunteers were urgently needed to fix it.

Under the hot sun, everyone volunteered. Rattlers working with Rattlers, Eagles with Eagles, the boys searched for blockages in the pipe. After a few hours a Rattler spotted the sack that was blocking the tap. It was jammed in too tightly. He could not move it. Another boy tried and failed. And then another. The sack was too firmly lodged for a single child to pull it out. Desperate for water, the two teams started working together, pulling and pulling at the sack and asking a member of staff to help. At last, the sack came free. Celebrations erupted. Rattlers high-fived Eagles. Eagles applauded Rattlers. When the tap was turned on, Sherif watched on in delight and amazement as the Rattler boys let the Eagles, who had been working without their water bottles, take the first drink.

Buoyed by his success, Sherif threw challenge after challenge at the boys. A truck broke down and had to be restarted. After a long hike, the tents they were to sleep in had to be erected, but the parts were mixed up between the two teams. Food hadn't been prepared and it would take all of them mucking in to get it ready. The boys were forced into common cause again and again. It worked. By the last day in camp, the Eagles and Rattlers were sitting together, chatting together, performing sketches together and singing together. Two of the boys – an Eagle and a Rattler – suggested that the teams should travel home on one bus rather than two. The boys voted and it was agreed. In less than a week, Sherif had turned the Eagles and Rattlers into a united group. How had he done it? By creating a series of common moments, common events and common challenges that had brought the boys – whether Eagles or Rattlers – together.

In Robbers Cave we saw People Like Me syndrome at work. But in its final act, we see something else – a set of common experiences overcoming PLM and bringing the boys back together again. The truth is that PLM has only ever been one side of the human story. For most of our history, there has been another side – a yin to its yang – that holds it in check. Since pre-history, our societies have relied – just as Sherif did – on rituals, habits and institutions that counteract PLM. How? By bringing us together with those unlike us. These institutions have varied through time – from the animalistic rituals of the hunter-gatherer to the religious feast day of the farmer or the clubs and societies of the factory worker – but in each era, we can find common experiences that connect our societies. If PLM is the villain of this story, these common moments are our hero. And yet we have no name for such moments – for these rituals, habits or institutions that join us with people whom we might see as different. Despite their centrality to the story of humanity, we have never bothered to name them. We will call them the Common Life.

It is not hard to spot the common life that connects the Hadza tribe together. Undiscovered by Europeans until the nineteenth century, the Hadza live as nomads. Based around Lake Eyasi in northern Tanzania, they hunt and gather food in an area roughly the size of Rhode Island. Carrying bows, small axes and slings, their lives deviate little from those of the first Hadza who resided here 60,000 years ago. Members of the tribe live largely unaffected by the information revolution, the Industrial Revolution or even the agrarian revolution. A few earn money once a year protecting crops, and a handful farm small maize fields, but the vast majority of the tribe's nutrition comes from foraging in the wild. Hadza spend most of their time walking, looking for food. Everyone takes part. Women search in a group with a young man standing guard. Men head out alone or sometimes in pairs. Couples search together with their children joining in, as if they were playing a game. At midday, they stop and sleep before starting again. As evening draws near, they settle down together and prepare food. After eating, they talk or tell stories before falling asleep. This is what they do every day of their lives, apart from the day that comes once a month when there is no moon in the sky.

In the evenings when the moon is hidden, and all is dark, the Hadza do not talk. They do not tell stories. They perform a ritual passed down to them by their parents and grandparents, who had received it from their parents and grandparents before. They call it the *epeme* dance. The *epeme* is a dance unique to the Hadza. It takes place in near-complete darkness. All fires from the nearby camp are extinguished. To begin the ritual, the women separate from the men and sit where they cannot be seen. The men gather behind a tree or hut and prepare for the dance. In the pitch dark, as the women begin to sing, the first man starts to dance. He wears a headdress of dark ostrich feathers, on one of his ankles are bells, a rattle is in his hand and a long, black cape on his back. In time with the women's singing, he stamps his right foot hard on the ground, causing the bells to ring, while marking the beat of the music with his rattle. He sings out to the women, who answer in a call and response. As the singing grows in strength, the women rise to join the man, who continues to dance – committing his efforts to a family member, one of the women, a friend or one of his children. At this point, his child may join the dance as well. After each man has danced the *epeme* two or three times, the ritual is finished, by which time it is close to midnight and the Hadza bed down and wait for the new day to begin.

The *epeme* has no religious purpose, for the Hadza have no clear religion. They do not believe in an afterlife. They have no God who needs to be satisfied. The dance serves no administrative function for them either, for they have no chiefs or hierarchy. And yet every month – when the moon vanishes from the sky – they perform it. Which raises a question: why do they do it?

To answer that, we must ask another question. For there is something else that is puzzling about the Hadza. Hunter-gatherers are often thought to have operated in small family groups of ten to twelve people, but the Hadza don't. They live as a larger tribe. They camp in groups of thirty or more, and the four hundred or so nomadic Hadza who are alive today are all likely to interact which each other at some point. Without a chief imposing order or any sense of hierarchy, they have managed to get different families to gather food, hunt and camp together. To use our modern language, they have made diversity work. The question is: 'How?'

A group of researchers decided to find out the answer. For a decade they followed the tribe, tracking individual members. They recorded where each man, woman and child went, who they met with, who they spoke to, who they trusted enough to hunt with and who they cared sufficiently about to share food with. They then crunched the data – looking for any patterns – anything that could explain how they were so 'together'. The first thing the researchers found wasn't very enlightening. After a decade of study, they concluded that Hadza – like us – were more likely to trust closer relatives. They put faith in their parents, their children and their siblings. In other words, people very much 'like them'. Fortunately for us, this wasn't all the researchers found. No, there was something else that made the Hadza trust one another. Something else that seemed to act as a sign that certain people could be trusted. That something else was the *epeme*. A decade of research showed that the Hadza were not only more likely to trust each other if they had danced the *epeme* together, but also more likely to share food, look after one another when unwell, hunt for food together and reveal secrets to each other. Dancing the *epeme* together was, in fact, more important than being related. Hadza were more likely to support, trust or help someone they had shared the dance with than someone with whom they shared a bloodline. What was it that made it possible for the Hadza to work in larger groups than just their families? It was the *epeme*. The *epeme* was the Hadza's common life.

The *epeme* is unique to the Hadza, but nearly all nomadic groups of any significant size have had similar rituals that bonded them together; whether they were performed to celebrate the seasons, a marriage, death, birth or puberty, they had the same key qualities.[1] The qualities of the common life. They brought different groups together face to face, provided equality of status, and were either intense or involved elements of routine. Let's be clear. I don't believe that any of these rituals were organised with the conscious aim of uniting a group. Each has its own purpose. Some celebrate a birth, others welcome someone as an adult to the tribe, and others, such as the *epeme*, remember the dead. But in all cases the real value of these rituals was the way they united the tribe. They were the common life for humanity before we became farmers. They were a set of shared activities that prevented fractures from springing up. Without conscious intent, these common life rituals evolved to best fit the needs and habits of the tribe. A great example of this is the fact that bigger tribes had more intense rituals. Why? Because a bigger tribe faced more risk of division, so a stronger bond was needed to hold it together. Those tribes with a weaker ritual and weaker bond just wouldn't be able to operate at that size.[2] For thousands of years, these common life rituals brought humanity together.

Before we move on from the nomadic hunter-gatherers, we should recognise how much of human history we have just described. The geographer and historian, Jared Diamond, observes that if humanity's existence was represented by a single day, 'we lived as hunter-gatherers for nearly the whole of that day, from midnight through dawn, noon, and sunset. Finally, at 11:54 p.m. we adopted agriculture.'[3] To continue the analogy, the Industrial Revolution, which made us city dwellers, did not begin until well into 11:59 p.m. This means that, without even exploring our time as farmers or factory workers, we have already shown that for 95.6 per cent of humanity's existence we relied on a common life to pull us together. As we will see, not much has changed since.

Starting around 9000 BC in the hill country of what is now south-eastern Turkey and western Iran, humans learnt a new trick. Slowly, step by step, we began to domesticate plants and animals – probably starting with wheat and goats. Why walk and hunt for food when we could grow or breed it? And so we settled down, building homes near our crops and animals. We left behind our nomadic existence and became devoted carers of a selected group of animal and plant species. From daybreak to sundown we tended the soil, planted the seeds, watered the plants and watched over the sheep. Progress. Or was it? When he looked carefully at this pivotal moment in human history, Jared Diamond described it as 'the worst mistake in the history of the human race'.[4] He suggests that – like fools – we swapped a life of nomadic leisure, gathering food from an abundant supply, for a life of slog and hard labour, tilling the ground and managing the crop. Diamond estimates that as hunter-gatherers we worked for twenty hours a week, a number that more than doubled once crops needed our attention. We doubtless felt so clever to have mastered the secret of growing crops and tending animals, but – looking more closely – was it us who domesticated the wheat or was it the energy-intensive cultivation of wheat that domesticated us? Either way, we replaced a wide and varied diet with a narrow one often focused on just a single type of crop. Our food supply became less tasty and less good for us; our average height actually decreased as we adopted agriculture.[5] We became more vulnerable to bad weather, floods and famine. Our newly domesticated animals made us prey to rapidly spreading viruses and bugs. Attacks from neighbouring tribes were more likely to kill us as, with all our crops and animals, we became much less fond of our age-old fallback plan of simply running away. The result? After our great leap forward, our life expectancy fell and didn't recover for thousands of years.[6]

Why on earth didn't we switch back to hunter-gathering? The truth is we were trapped. At first, settling down seemed like a great idea. We found increasing numbers of plants to domesticate. A small number of farmers could use lots of the very best land. But, once we were settled, women, freed from needing to carry their non-walking child between locations, became pregnant more often – with ever-shorter gaps between births. Our population grew – spreading out into smaller parcels of harder-to-farm land. A few generations later, farming had become much tougher work than foraging, but it was too late. There were now too many of us to survive as hunter-gatherers and, besides, we had forgotten how to do it. But what about those who had not yet made the switch? Surely they would spot the error and hold their ground? Unfortunately, the law of the jungle worked against them. Needing more land to feed our growing families, we farmers began to chase off and fight the nomads. The latter learnt a simple lesson: if you can't beat them, join them. Within a few millennia, we were almost all farmers.

Wait a moment, though. This doesn't make sense. How did the farmers defeat the nomads exactly? The nomads were surely the better fighters. Each day, while the farmers tended their land, it was the nomads who honed their skills in hunting, killing and evading. They were more dangerous. They were better trained. Why didn't the nomads just fight off the encroaching farmers?

The answer is the common life. The reason the farmers won was that they attacked in greater numbers. They defeated the nomads not by skill but by scale. Fine, but why didn't the nomads just combine into an equally large group? The answer is that they couldn't. The nomadic common life, brought to life for us in the *epeme*, had evolved to enable nomads to work together. It was great at connect-ing a number of families, but not a number of tribes. The *epeme* is a dance for a few hundred, not a few thousand. The farmers, in comparison, had slowly and fitfully evolved a new common life: one

49

suitable for the agrarian age and that enabled their larger population to work together. What exactly was this common life?

Unsurprisingly, the agrarian common life has varied in shape and form across the eleven millennia that make up the agrarian age.[7] However, three pillars were frequently at the centre of it: the religious meeting, the seasonal celebration and the rite of passage. These three pillars linked farming societies together – and helped them to overcome the nomads. The common life of an English villager in the Middle Ages is even easier to spot than that of the Hadza. It was all around them. In a normal week, the average villager could expect to attend the Sunday church service, celebrate a key religious figure or season through a feast day, and more than likely take part in another villager's rite of passage – whether a baptism, a marriage or a death. It is hard to overstate how significant the common life was. It demanded people's time, their money and their attention.

One estimation suggests that one in four days in the year were reserved as feast days or church celebrations.[8] This is extraordinary – especially when you consider the ever-present challenge villagers faced just feeding their families. The cost to them is best illustrated by the fact that laws had to be passed to prevent villagers skipping the events to work on their land. While these laws – to attend church and collective feasts – were not always complied with, especially by merchants looking to optimise profits, the expectation was clear and most people followed it.[9] The cost was not just in time. In fact, the expenditure on rites of passage became so eye-watering in medieval Europe that administrators started imposing regulations to control it. Limits were put on the number of guests at a wedding, the number of musicians who could perform, even the location of the feast. In German-speaking areas of Europe between the thirteenth and fifteenth centuries, over five hundred such regulations were passed.[10] The rites of passage were often incredibly intricate. Preparation for baptismal feasts sometimes took so long that a sick child died before it began, a serious business in a society that believed unbaptised children went to hell. The common life was so significant to people's lives that – in England at least – it became the basis of how people referred to the date. Today, if you want to tell your friend when your birthday is, you would say how many days into a month it is – for example, my birthday is the twenty-first day of June. In medieval England, you would identify it by telling your friend how many days before or after a feast day it was – for example, my birthday is three days before the Feast Day of Saint John the Baptist.

For almost eleven millennia, the religious meeting, the seasonal celebration and the rite of passage provided a common life for our farming ancestors. They were able to connect a far larger group of people than the nomadic common life ever could, and they would do so successfully until Jared Diamond's day of human history reached one minute to midnight.

A European peasant taken 250 years forward in time from 1400 to 1650 would have discovered a world that felt pretty familiar.[11] Life still largely involved working the land. The common life still revolved around collective worship, feasts and rites of passage. Another 250 years of time-travel would have blown their mind. Between 1650 and 1900, advances in machine technology, water power, steam power, iron manufacturing and chemical production reduced the cost of producing goods radically and transformed economies and societies beyond recognition. The changes were so vast that we describe them today as a revolution: the Industrial Revolution. Thousands of new factory jobs were created in what became fast-growing towns and cities. The urbanised and industrialised society of the late nineteenth century would have contained little that was familiar to a late medieval peasant. The common life they knew so well was hugely diminished. Yes, religion remained a critical element of life, but attendance at Sunday services had fallen dramatically. Feast day celebrations were largely gone, along with the days of enforced holiday required to celebrate them.[12] Rites of passage had become smaller and more private affairs.

The common life of the agrarian age had passed. But does that mean there was no common life? Far from it. A new one had instead sprung up – one that fitted this new industrial age. The new common life was radically different from the old – but once again it had three pillars. We can spot all three of them by visiting the first city that industrialisation created – the city of Manchester. By the third decade of the nineteenth century, Manchester was home to almost a hundred steam-powered spinning factories employing tens of thousands of workers who had left their villages to earn a living. These factories became the main workplace of the early industrialised society. They are seen today, quite rightly, as places of horror – as exhibit A in the case against capitalism. They were places of exhaustion. Before legislation prevented it, men, women and children would work twelve to fourteen hours days, six days a week. They were also dangerous places. Michael Ward, a doctor working in Manchester in the early nineteenth century, was called to give evidence on factory life to a parliamentary committee in 1819. He told the shocked parliamentarians that when he visited a school in Lever Street in Manchester he had found that almost half of the children who spent time working in a factory had received injuries: 'in many instances the muscles and the skin is stripped down to the bone, and in some instances a finger or two might be lost'.[13] The harsh brutality of the Mancunian factories is familiar to us through literature and song, from Coketown in Dickens' *Hard Times* – 'a town of red brick … that would have been red if the smoke and ashes had allowed it' – to Blake's 'Jerusalem' with its 'dark satanic mills'. The grimness of the Manchester workers' lives is made clear by the laws that had to be passed to protect their children, from the 1833 Factory Act that banned nine-year-olds from working more than nine hours a day, to the 1842 Mines Act that prevented under-tens from working down a mine.

Taken alone, however, this dark picture obscures something important about the workplace in Manchester compared to the village. In the villages that Manchester's factory workers had left behind, work was a private endeavour. Whether you owned the land or not, you farmed your own plot and your neighbour farmed theirs. It was a largely independent activity; if your neighbour took a day off or slowed their pace, it wouldn't affect your own work. Factory life was different. Each worker had a role to play. The work – grim or not – was a joint endeavour. Everyone relied on everyone else. As legislation slowly improved the lives of workers, an underlying truth about the industrialised workplace revealed itself – like a statue hiding in marble waiting to be chiselled out. Despite its indignities and dangers, the factory and the production line provided the people of Manchester with an element of common life. For the factories created a space that brought strangers from different villages with different accents together. Factory owners didn't care which villages their workers came from or identified with. Everyone was thrown together.

The factories and mills were not the only source of common life for the people of Manchester. The Acts of Parliament that were slowly improving working conditions in the Manchester factories were also creating a new institution: the school. Back in the village, schools were the preserve of the lucky, the exceptionally gifted and the wealthy. In the fast-growing cities, a combination of religiously inspired charity, legislation and industry self-interest led to the rapid birth of thousands of infant schools. By 1816, half of all the children in Britain attended school for at least one year of their life.[14] Fifty years later, nine out of ten children were receiving two years of instruction.[15] By 1880, when attendance between the age of five and ten became compulsory, 95 per cent of such children were in school. The situation was similar across the West. In 1840, just over half of American under-fifteens attended school.[16] By 1910, this had risen to almost three-quarters, with most states making education mandatory for everyone under fifteen.[17] The rise of secondary school education in the United States at this point was so rapid that the first few decades of the twentieth century are sometimes referred to by historians as the 'high school movement'. Enrolment numbers rose from just 9 per cent in 1910 to 40 per cent by 1935.[18] The fast-growing schools provided a second place in industrial society where people – this time children – from different backgrounds met together face to face. Outside of the Southern states of America, where slavery and segregation ensured that the schools replicated the racial divides in the community, schools brought together children whose families had come from different villages and – in the US case – different countries. Lower and middle classes were increasingly taught together. They were taught the same lessons, at the same pace, under the same threat of correction or punishment, and – in England at least – often wearing the same uniform.

Alongside the school and workplace, industrial societies like Manchester were being knitted together by a wholly new type of organisation: the voluntary association. Back in the village, the idea of starting up a club or society would have been as foreign and strange as the new machines that were whirring in the factories. If you wanted to gather a group of people together, you would simply see your neighbours on the street, find them in the pub or the square, or visit them at home.[19] But in industrialised Manchester, the streets were full of strangers. Searching for support, opportunities and a sense of belonging, the people of nineteenth-century England began to establish and join all sorts of associations, clubs and societies. Once they had started, they did so at a remarkable pace. Consider the groups that just one citizen of Greater Manchester belonged to; British academic James Sunderland records how Reverend James Slade was the:

president of Bolton's savings bank, a Great Bolton trustee, a member of the Pitt Club, Chairman of the Bolton Infirmary, and President of the First Temperance Society and the Bolton Association for the Deaf and Dumb, and sat on various turnpike trusts and on the committee of the Bolton Floral and Horticultural Society and the Exchange newsroom. Along with his fellow clergymen, he also performed chaplainry duties to the freemasons, the Ancient Order of Druids, the Church and King Club, the Pitt club, the Protestant Association and the Orangeman's Club.[20]

This boom in associations included the birth of many that are familiar to us today, such as the Trades Union Congress (est. 1868), the Mothers' Union (1876), the Boys' Brigade (1883), the Scouts (1908), the Guides (1909) and the Women's Institute (1917). Alongside these were countless societies that have not lasted, from the mutual improvement societies providing city dwellers with a basic education to the friendly societies through which groups of people provided each other with employment opportunities and health insurance. Most of these organisations weren't consciously aiming to bring diverse groups of people together, but that is exactly what they did.[21]

The same boom was taking place across the Atlantic. Between 1840 and 1910, the number of associations based in the cities doubled from two per thousand people to over five per thousand. If anything, this understates the rate of growth, as the urban population itself was growing incredibly fast. Every type of association sprang up and expanded. Christian groups expanded rapidly; in the space of four years after its establishment in 1850, the YMCA had created twenty-five local chapters; the Salvation Army followed in 1880. Children joined the Boy Scouts, Girl Scouts or Camp Fire Girls (all founded in the 1910s), while students formed fraternities and sororities. Both women's and men's groups multiplied, with the largest reporting hundreds of thousands of members.[22] Work by American sociologist, Theda Skocpol, has shown that half of the largest associations in American history were born between 1870 and 1920.[23]

What was true of almost all these associations – on both sides of the Atlantic – is that they did not operate by post alone – they relied on physical meetings and pretty much anyone was welcome. Skocpol's research showed that while some American associations sought to serve richer or poorer city dwellers, 'historical directories tell us that hundreds of smaller cross-class federations were born ... [and] churches, religious associations, fraternal and women's groups ... attracted members across class lines'.[24] And so, alongside the workplace and the school, these new associations formed the third pillar of a new common life. Was this common life without fault? No – its reach was incomplete. It failed, in most Western countries, to include people of colour – by norm and by law. We are right to condemn this and right to believe we can and must do much better. It also allowed the very richest citizens, the top 1 per cent perhaps – with their private schools and elite clubs – to stay apart from the rest. And yet, even with their flaws, these three pillars had a significant positive effect. In cities filled with different dialects, backgrounds and flavours of Christian belief, they started to knit our societies together. They created a common life for the industrial society – one that lasted for around a hundred years. For many of us, it was the common life of our grandparents.

Finally, we reach midnight. Our ancestors have gone from foragers to farmers to factory workers; from meeting no more than a few hundred people in their entire life to having that many people living down their street; from relying on a small tribe of extended kin to being part of an interdependent system of many millions. And yet, at each stage, we have found a common life: a way of bringing people from all walks of life together. As our societies changed, so did our common life – from monthly ritual dancing to village-wide feasting, from the baptism of our children to their collective education, from church services to clubs and societies. Whether mandated or voluntarily, we have always found ways of coming together. This, though, still leaves a puzzle. How exactly does bringing people together in this way overcome People Like Me syndrome? Even if we join with those who are different, what makes us trust people who, instinctively, we feel are not like us? The truth is that PLM has a weakness that the common life has learnt how to exploit. If we are to bring our societies back together again, we need to understand this weakness and take advantage of it.

CHAPTER FOUR

A SECRET WEAKNESS

The volunteers had one thing in common. They were all Manchester United fans. The two professors working with them had a lot more in common. While one – Mark Levine – was American and the other – Stephen Reicher – was British, they were both fascinated by human behaviour. Both were experts on human psychology – Reicher would go on to advise the British government on how the public would respond to the coronavirus pandemic. Both were less interested in football and more in how being a football fan makes people act. Finally, both had a theory about a weakness in People Like Me syndrome, and they set out to test it with their Manchester United fan volunteers.

They conducted a short survey in which they repeatedly addressed each volunteer as a 'Manchester United fan'. Survey completed, Levine and Reicher told the volunteer to head over to a different building to watch a video. As the volunteer walked across, a third researcher would jog across their path, head down a grassy bank, lose their footing and fall to the ground, where they would lie holding their ankle and shouting out in pain. Here's where it gets interesting. A third of the time, the researcher would be wearing a Manchester United shirt; for another third, a Liverpool shirt (Liverpool being one of United's greatest rivals); and for the final third, a plain red shirt (the same colour as both Manchester United and Liverpool shirts). Levine and Reicher wanted to know who the Manchester United fans would stop to help. Sure enough – as PLM would suggest – the volunteers were keenest to help fellow Manchester United fans. They were in fact three times more likely to stop and help the researcher if he was wearing a Manchester United shirt than if he wore a Liverpool or a plain red shirt. The fans were – as expected – strongly biased towards those who reminded them of themselves.

But that wasn't the end of the story. Levine and Reicher repeated the test. They did everything exactly the same, except that this time they addressed the volunteers not as 'Manchester United fans' but as 'football fans'. As before, the volunteer walked over to the other building. Once again, the researcher jogged past, ran down the grassy slope, lost their footing and fell over. What was different was the result. This time, as well as helping their fellow Manchester United fans, the volunteers were keen to help Liverpool fans. For the Liverpool fan was, like them, a fellow football fan. When the researcher was wearing a plain red T-shirt, however, they were mostly left to help themselves. PLM was again at work; the fans were still biased towards those who reminded them of themselves. But Levine and Reicher had changed something. They had changed who the volunteers saw as being 'like me'. The scope of people 'like me' expanded and so the volunteers helped an increasing number of them. The secret that Levine and Reicher had discovered was this: it is possible to change who you think is 'like you'.

You have probably experienced this for yourself. Many of us experience it when we travel. For example, when I am at home in London, I feel like a Londoner – other Londoners are 'like me'. When I visit my mother in Hereford, I think of myself as English – other English people are 'like me'. And when I am with my in-laws in Edinburgh, I am British – other Brits are 'like me'. You may have experienced similar variations in the roles you play. When I am with my children, I'm a father, like other fathers; at work, I'm a colleague, like other workers; with my sister, I'm a younger brother, like my other siblings;

at church, I'm a fellow believer. Faced with the threat of coronavirus, many of us found that the person delivering our post seemed more like us than before, as did those collecting our rubbish, let alone those caring for our sick. This malleability of who is 'like me' is the secret weakness of PLM. If we can be convinced that someone who seemed unlike us (such as a fan of a rival football team) is actually very much like us (given that we are both football fans), then PLM's power to divide us is a paper tiger. This is exactly what the common life does. It connects us with those who seemed different and shows us how we are more alike than we imagined. How on earth does it do it?[1]

Few products have been as iconic – or as profitable. In its first six years, Apple sold 100 million iPods. The company built up a $15bn bank balance without a cent of debt. In the next five years, they sold 250 million more.

Most people assume that the iPod was the brainchild of Apple's charismatic founder, Steve Jobs. Except that's not the whole story. The full story of the iPod must include the company that failed to invent the iPod. They were so close. In fact, they invented three different near-iPods, each with a different name. They even conspired to launch two of them on exactly the same day. The story of the iPod is not just about Apple's triumphant success. It's also about Sony's abject failure.

It's hard to overstate the advantages that Sony had over Apple. Steve Jobs wasn't the first to spot that the future of music lay in small portable devices that played digital music. There were plenty on the market by the time the iPod was launched, and lots more on the way. The key to inventing the iPod was being able to nail three very different technologies and get them to work together. First, you had to design a beautiful music player. The best-placed company to do that would surely have a rich history of building music systems and a track record of selling attractive portable music players. Apple had never done this before. Sony was not only one of the largest producers of home stereos; it had also designed what was then the most iconic portable music product of all time: the Sony Walkman. Second, anyone inventing the iPod needed to be able to make the connection between a computer and the music player as smooth as possible. The original digital music players, including the iPod, couldn't connect to the internet to access music. The only way to do so was via a computer. A company with a large laptop computer business would have a tremendous advantage. Apple did, but so did Sony. The final piece of the puzzle was the music. This was Steve Jobs' greatest challenge. Apple owned *zero* music rights and had no history of working with the major record labels. Without music, the iPod was just a nicely designed, colourful piece of plastic and metal. In comparison, Sony owned the second biggest music company in the world. Its back catalogue included Michael Jackson *and* the Beatles. Without these rights, Apple's product was dead in the water.

To grasp how Apple succeeded, we need to understand why, once a year, Apple staff crossed their fingers. Annually, a select few would receive an invitation to the 'Top 100'. This three-day retreat – held in a secret location swept for listening devices – was the occasion when Jobs would bring together his one hundred most favoured staff. Those lucky enough to be invited were chosen using one simple criterion: they were the hundred people who Jobs would take with him if he had to start a new company. Those left behind lamented that they must be in 'the bottom 100'. The chosen few were given a unique and private insight into the future of the organisation. They were the first to see the new iPad; the first to see the iPod; and the first to see the plans for Apple retail stores. The event was designed to be an intense experience that staff would remember for the rest of their lives. One executive described it thus: 'The Top 100 was a horrifying experience for ten or so people [who had to present in front on Jobs] … For the other ninety, it's the best few days of their life.' The pinnacle of the event was always the final session. Jobs would stand in front of a whiteboard and ask one question: 'What are the ten things we should be doing next?' From ten, the list was whittled down to just three: three things for the whole organisation to focus on together – with the 'Top 100' taking the lead. But the ultimate purpose was not about setting priorities. The journalist Adam Lashinsky, who has written widely about Apple, described the Top 100 in this way: 'The meetings were intended to allow … people who in such a siloed and segregated company wouldn't ordinarily interact with one another – to bond.' The aim – above all – was connection.

At Sony, there was no 'Top 100', no list of ten and no whittling down to three. Instead, there were hundreds of different ideas fighting for attention. At the top sat one man, Nobuyuki Idei, who had become CEO in 1999 and brought with him a brilliant idea. The problem with Sony, Idei believed, was that everything was too complicated. The company needed to be much more like his previous employer, Nestlé, which had been split into a number of smaller groups, each focused on different products, from baby milk to chocolate. What Sony needed was to be broken up into separate companies. Then everyone could stop having so many meetings, stop talking to each other all the time, and just get on and be a great success. Idei wanted to set the computer people free to make brilliant computers; the music people free to make brilliant music; and the Walkman team free to make brilliant portable music players. At first Idei's 'brilliant idea' looked like a winner. Profits rose sixteen-fold and, by February 2000, the share price hit an all-time peak of $140. The problem with the 'brilliant idea' was that it wasn't actually brilliant. On 23 October 2001, Steve Jobs walked onto a California stage and launched the iPod. Just eighteen months after its peak, Sony's share price had fallen by 70 per cent.

Working apart may have looked more efficient than working together. It certainly made organisational charts neater. But if the opportunity of the decade requires your portable music team, your computer team and your music rights team to work together, you have a problem. Each separate team saw the opportunity and several launched competitors to the iPod. What they lacked was the design simplicity that can only come from computer experts, portable music experts and music rights experts collaborating. By the time Sony realised its calamitous mistake, it was too late. When the teams working on the portable player approached the music team to get the music rights, they were told they couldn't get them. Why? Because they'd been sold to Steve Jobs. Sony lost to Apple not because its people weren't talented, but because they were never brought together.

The story of the iPod has much in common with a story you read earlier: one that started on the very first page – the story of England vs Holland. Both are stories where the underdog defeats the favourite. Apple and England emerge victorious not through greater talent or more resources but by bringing people directly together. Staff at Apple from different business units and functions are brought together face to face at the Top 100, while the English football players were brought together similarly to practise and party. In the same way, Eagles and Rattlers were working physically together on a series of shared challenges. The first thing every common life does is bring people together face to face. Look again at Robbers Cave. The Eagles and Rattlers weren't separately lectured about the importance of unity. They weren't taught how to be polite and kind. They weren't punished for their rudeness to each other. They were made to do things that got them together. Consider the Hadza's *epeme*. This is not a story that the children of the Hadza hear about in their separate family groups. It is not a set of beliefs that they all agree to. It is a dance performed together.[2] It is not a niche activity that some select group take part in, nor just for the families who have gathered the most food, or those who always set up camp to the east. It is for everyone.

We see the same face-to-face interaction in the common life of the farmer. Villagers from different families and different parts of the village are brought together face to face. The feasts, services and rites of passage were not events attended simply by small family groups. They are open to all comers and were well-attended.[3] Even rites of passage frequently involved nearly the whole village.[4]

The same is true of the common life of the factory worker. The 'factory line' required everyone to be there physically together. Schooling was also a face-to-face endeavour. Despite large class sizes, many nineteenth-century schools operated a 'monitorial' system, whereby the brightest pupils were instructed first and then required to educate a smaller group of students. Clubs and societies likewise provided small groups that physically connected people.

Bringing people together is critical to mending our fractures. Why is this? It is because when brought together we can be incredibly good at building connections. At root, we are deeply social animals. We may be biased towards people like us, but we also have a great ability to form connections with anyone. If a common life can force us to come together with people unlike us – overcoming PLM's desire to keep us apart – then three quirks of our nature make us uniquely good at connecting with others. The first of these is laughter.

Laughing is – at first glance – odd. It appears to be an instinct, much like shivering or flinching. We are cold and we shiver. We feel pain and we flinch. We hear something funny and we laugh. But that's not right. Laughter is not just an instinctive, unavoidable reaction to humour. If it were, you would be just as likely to laugh if you heard a joke at home alone as if you were surrounded by others in a theatre. As any stand-up comedian can tell you, this is not the case. It is much easier to provoke a laugh from a large crowd than a small one. You are thirty times more likely to laugh in company than alone.[5] Whether you do so correlates much more with whether you are in company than whether something is funny. Laughter is so social that you could legitimately describe it as contagious; we catch it from each other. The American psychologist, Robert Provine, illustrates this contagion effect with an extraordinary story of a fit of giggles that broke out at a girls' boarding school in Tanzania:

> The first symptoms appeared on January 30, when three girls got the giggles and couldn't stop laughing. The symptoms quickly spread to 95 students, forcing the school to close on March 18. The girls sent home from the school were vectors for the further spread of the epidemic. Related outbreaks occurred in other schools in Central Africa and spread like wildfire, ceasing two-and-a-half years later and afflicting nearly 1,000 people.[6]

This case is extreme, yet most of us have experience of catching laughter from someone else. We are always more likely to laugh if someone else is already laughing. This is true even if the laughter is fake. Why were so many shows much less funny when the pandemic robbed them of a studio audience? Why do TV comedy shows add fake laughter? Because those of us watching at home are more likely to laugh if we hear someone else laughing. No, laughter is not an instinctive response to humour. It is a social activity, something we do to bond with people that we meet.

The second quirk of our nature is our ability to empathise, to put ourselves in someone else's shoes. How exactly do we do this? Early theories of empathy suggested a process of trial and error was at work. We would consciously imagine how the person might feel, consider how they might act if they did feel this way, and then check if this tallied with their real-life actions. If they did what we expected, we assumed that we had understood how they felt. If not, we would try again. Many researchers now think that empathy is more instinctive than this. We do not need to imagine what the other person is feeling and then test it. No, they argue, we feel it ourselves. As the social commentator David Brooks puts it, when it comes to empathy, we are not line learners but method actors. In other words, we understand others not by reasoning through logic how they might feel but by personally experiencing a lesser dose of what they are going through.[7] When someone tells us of the recent loss of a family member, we do not rationally imagine how that must feel; instead, we actually feel a small dose of their sadness. When we see that someone is in pain, our brain fires some of the very same neurons as when we ourselves are in pain. When we watch someone cry, our brain fires the neurons it uses for when we ourselves are sad. Why do we empathise? Because we are feeling it too.[8] Researchers call this – still hotly contested – quirk 'mirror neurons'. This mirroring is how we enjoy an action film or a thriller; as we watch our heroine driving through rush-hour traffic with the mafia in hot pursuit, our neurons act as though we are doing the same. That's why a truly great action sequence makes our heart rate rise. Outside of a slickly put-together movie, the key to unlocking empathy is to spend time face to face with someone else.

The last quirk is – to my mind – the most significant. To grasp it we need to understand why Gillian Matthews was being paid by the state to feed cocaine to mice. Every day, as a graduate student at Imperial College London, Matthews would open a large cage that was home to a group of mice. She would remove two from the rest of the group, then place 'Mouse 1' in a small cage and give it a dose of cocaine. She placed 'Mouse 2' in another small cage and gave it a dose of salt water. Having given the doses, Matthews would leave the mice for the day. On the next she would return to see if there had been any change to the mice's neurons. Each day she would check a different set of neurons.[9]

The reason for this odd experiment was to see which neurons were affected by cocaine. With this information, scientists might be able to identify what made such a dangerous substance so addictive and help addicts to give up. Matthews was hoping to see a change in the neurons of the mouse who had had the cocaine but not in the other mouse. Returning to the experiment one morning, she was ecstatic to find that the selected neurons in Mouse 1's head had altered. Had she finally found the key neurons that cocaine affected? Before getting carried away, she checked Mouse 2, which had received no cocaine. Something was up. This set of neurons had also changed. Whatever was causing the changes couldn't be the cocaine. What was going on? It wasn't something in the air or the environment, either, as the neurons of the mice who had been left in the large cage had not changed at all.

'We first thought there was something wrong, that we had mixed up our procedure,' said Matthews. How could the two mice who had been separated from the group be affected, but not the rest of the group when they were in the same room, eating the same food, drinking the same water and breathing the same air? Then she realised what it was. 'These neurons are relaying the experience of loneliness.' Matthews had not found a set of neurons impacted on by cocaine; she had found one affected by being alone. To test her new hypothesis, she tried artificially stimulating these particular neurons among the mice that were in the large cage together. Sure enough, whenever she did, the affected mice moved to spend time with other mice. Matthews' experiment suggests that mice have evolved a response to loneliness – a response that makes them seek company.

A similar response seems to affect us humans. Experiments have shown that loneliness doesn't just make us feel sad; it 'hurts'. Brain scans reveal that when we feel lonely our brain fires up in the exact same places as when we stub our toe or cut our finger. This is why painkillers don't just reduce physical pain. They can also make us feel less lonely.[10] Why would our body do this to us? The most credible explanation is the simplest. If physical pain is an evolutionary adaptation to prevent us from injuring ourselves, the pain of loneliness is likely to be an evolutionary adaptation to make us more sociable.[11] We appear to be programmed to seek company.

Understanding these three quirks of our nature – laughter, mirror neurons and the pain of loneliness – gives us a glimpse into why the first condition of the common life is that it physically brings together those who seem different. People Like Me syndrome will cause us to connect with individuals like us – Eagles with Eagles, Rattlers with Rattlers. The common life brings us together with those less like us – Rattlers with Eagles, Eagles with Rattlers. But – to work – it needs to be face to face. We are animals with advanced skills at connecting with others, but empathy and laughter are much less powerful from a distance, and we can't respond to the pain of loneliness unless there is someone to connect with. Once face to face, we have a chance to connect and to realise that we have more in common than we thought, and ultimately to appreciate that these people are in fact surprisingly 'like me'. Perhaps unsurprisingly, just bringing people together face to face isn't enough to achieve this. As Sherif was to prove the hard way, just bringing the Eagles and Rattlers together face to face was never sufficient to create a shared sense of 'us'. Before he took the drastic step of blocking up the only water supply, Sherif had brought the Rattlers and Eagles together to try and start bridging their divides. He had provided parties to attend and short films to watch. Surely at some point the boys would come together and their natural human quirks for connecting would do the rest. Right? Wrong. Once Sherif and his team had divided the teams and introduced some aggravation, any chance for them to connect face to face simply led to more division. The boys would come, fall out with each other and leave. Just bringing people together will not create a sense of 'us'. The common life that we have seen at work down the ages must be doing more than merely bringing people together. What then was the secret sauce that turned the Eagles and Rattlers from enemies to allies, united the English football team, gelled the Top 100 and connected our ancestors? To start to understand this better, we need to go back in time.

Six months after D-Day – the largest seaborne invasion in history – the Allies, led by American general and future president Ike Eisenhower, had advanced through most of France. Rapid success had come at a cost. The troops were exhausted by weeks of continuous conflict, and supplies were running low. The German situation, though, was even worse. Stretched by the Soviets to the East, the Germans had just fifty-five undermanned divisions to the Allies' ninety-six. Hitler, as so often, responded by raising the stakes. He revealed to his astonished generals plans for a surprise counter-offensive that – if successful – would punch through the Allied lines in Belgium, split the Allied Forces apart, encircle and destroy them. It was the ultimate gamble. On 16 December 1944, at 5:30 a.m., the dice were thrown: 406,000 men, 1,214 tanks and 4,224 artillery pieces attacked the Allied Forces. The 'Battle of the Bulge' was underway.

The Allies were taken entirely by surprise. With their air supremacy lost to heavy storms, the US Army began suffering losses greater than in any battle of the war. As the casualties topped a hundred thousand, Eisenhower was desperate for reinforcements, but none were available. Well, almost none. He had a number of battalions of ready and able servicemen who had never been called up to the front. Despite being trained to fight, these men were being deployed only in maintenance roles. They cleared mines, built bases, transported troops and registered graves, but never fought with the other soldiers. The reason was that they were Black. Rules were in place to ensure that the US Army was as segregated overseas as the Southern states were back home. In the space of one day in December 1944, as the Battle of the Bulge raged, Eisenhower decided to ignore these rules. Over two thousand Black servicemen volunteered for the front line and were allocated to White infantry companies. Thus reinforced, and with the weather improving, the Allied line held firm. Three months later, as the Allies advanced into Germany, they did so with growing numbers of Black soldiers fighting side by side with White.

Eisenhower's controversial decision to integrate Black soldiers into White units did not just help to halt Hitler's audacious advance. It permanently changed attitudes among the soldiers fighting in those integrated units. J. Cameron Wade, a Black soldier from the first platoon to integrate, reflected later: 'We ate together, slept together, fought together. There were no incidents. The army couldn't believe it.'[12] The impact on the White servicemen involved was equally striking. When asked if they would like to serve in an integrated unit again, only 7 per cent said no, ten times fewer than in the average White battalion.[13]

What do we learn from the Battle of the Bulge? Does it mean that we simply need to get people who seem too different to mix with each other and, hey presto, division reduces? This would be a terrible misreading of what actually happened in 1944. We need to look much more closely. When we do, we will spot two essential characteristics of the common life that both Black and White soldiers experienced. These two characteristics have been central to the common life our ancestors experienced whether they were foraging, farming or factory working. They are central to creating a sense of 'us' among people who might initially seem unlike. The first characteristic is equality of status.

The Black and White servicemen fighting together came from a country where they were treated radically differently. Daily life was filled with signs, experience, norms and habits that communicated again and again the supposed superiority of one over the other. In the Southern states, Black Americans faced unequal and separate treatment in almost every element of life, with different places to eat, different places to sit, different schools to attend and different neighbourhoods to live in. Five thousand miles from home, under heavy attack in the middle of Belgium, the world was transformed for the Black and White soldiers who found themselves fighting side by side. Men of both colours fought together, slept together, marched together and lived together. They had the same roles, the same clothes, the same equipment, the same rules and the same rank. Even in the South, it was not hard to find the communities interacting. What was missing was any sense of equality. The Battle of the Bulge did more than just bring White and Black Americans together. It gave them an equality of status that allowed them to truly connect.

Equality of status is critical for a common life to be able to unite us. Far away from any war zone, a simple experiment by psychologists Ursula Beermann, Paul Piff and Dacher Keltner shows us why.[14] The three academics selected volunteers with a wide mix of education and wealth and split them into pairs. Some pairs brought together two people who were very similar. Others paired individuals with different levels of education and wealth. With no set uniform, clothes choice, accessories, tattoos and fashion preferences provided participants with subtle signals of their different classes and wealth. The volunteers were instructed to discuss the meaning of life with their partner. It was a topic designed to allow those with more education to demonstrate their wider vocabulary and reading. The psychologists then watched incredibly carefully as the pairs talked to each other, noting every facial expression, every word and every sound. They noted the number of smiles, whether they were real or faked. They recorded how much laughter they heard. The result was striking. The pairs that saw each other as being of equal status got on well; they smiled more genuinely and laughed more often. However, the pairs that mixed rich with poor or highly educated with less educated struggled to connect. Aware of their difference in status, these pairs rarely laughed and frequently pretended to smile.

If we want to build trust between people, we need to do more than just throw them together. We need to do it in a way that avoids them feeling inferior or superior. Look at the activities that bonded the Eagles and the Rattlers. No boy had particular expertise or advantage in finding how to get the water flowing again. No boy was an expert at restarting a lorry. No boy outranked the others at putting up a tent. Look again at the common life throughout history. There is no permanent hierarchy in the *epeme*. All the men dance the same type of dance, all the women take part together. It is not a competitive performance, where the worst dancers are eliminated or where certain families have to wear a different headdress to show their lower position. Even in the hierarchy-infused life of the village, you can see how the villagers' common life tries to reduce a sense of inequality of status. Historians describe rural feasts where there was little indication of attendees' social status, with dances that involved everybody no matter their age, position or background.[15] Town feasts from the fifteenth century onwards often included running contests that were open to participants from all social classes and often involved competitors from lower classes being cheered on by wealthier near-neighbours. This temporary equality is most visible in the European tradition of Fastnacht, or 'carnival'. Taking place in the weeks before Lent, Fastnacht celebrated everything being upside down. Bad behaviour was good, the man dressed as a clown was wise, the rich and powerful were to be mocked, while the common man was lauded. With many participants wearing masks, anonymity further confused the issue of who didn't 'matter' and who did. The common life of the factory worker had a similar degree of equality of status. Once inside the factory – for most of the workers – there was no pecking order. Unless they were one of the lucky few in management, everyone had the same working conditions, doing the same work for the same hours for the same wage. In the schools, students received broadly equal treatment. They mostly sat in ordered rows doing the same work in the same lessons with no one seen as above anyone else. The growing clubs and societies made significant efforts to make everyone feel equal to one another. This often included the swearing of oaths or wearing of uniforms – as practised by fraternity groups like the Freemasons or Elks, membership groups like the Scouts or Guides, and religious groups like the Mothers' Union. Whatever the group, the message was clear: once in the group, everyone was an equally valid member. As one ex-Scout wrote of his troop years later, 'we had boys from the wealthiest families in town, and boys from the poorest parts of town. But when you entered that door, we were all Scouts. If your family couldn't afford a uniform, Roscoe [the Scout Leader] made sure you got one.'[16]

The second characteristic that stands out from the Battle of the Bulge is the intensity of the shared experience that the Black and White servicemen went through. Miles from home, they fought together side by side, risking their lives for each other. Intense experiences like these are critical for a common life to create a sense that people are 'like me'. In fact, the greater the intensity of the experience, the more successful this will be. If this is right, we should expect our veterans to have a greater sense than others of kinship with people from contrasting backgrounds. Sure enough, when American veterans move house – having fought alongside a diverse group of comrades – they are more likely than the average American to choose a neighbourhood with a mixture of ethnic backgrounds.[17] This impact on soldiers is greater the more intense the battlefield experience.[18] A survey of fighters in the 2011 Libyan revolution showed that those who had suffered the greatest losses were the most tightly bonded.[19] American Vietnam veterans who had witnessed comrades being killed or injured felt the most loyalty to other veterans.[20] In the same way, the Black and White servicemen fighting at the 'Battle of the Bulge' were connected not just through equality of status but through the intensity of their shared experience. These experiences are not unique to soldiers. Asking civilians to think and reflect on tough times they have gone through with fellow countrymen makes them more committed to their compatriots.[21] Intense moments when we experience fear, elation or peril alongside others are uniquely effective at bonding people together. This is why so many of us have had to endure team-building days at work that require us to abseil down cliffs or climb mountains. The terror before the task, the extreme focus required to complete it and the joy of having done so creates a bond between colleagues that does not occur simply by sitting in a meeting together.

Why is this? Why do intense experiences bond us? The reason is down to a quirk of how our memory works.[22] Try to remember what your phone number is. Now try to remember your first day at school. You will find that remembering a fact feels very different from remembering an event. These two types of memory are so dissimilar that they are given different names. Remembering a fact – like your phone number – involves 'semantic memory'. Remembering your first day at school is an 'episodic memory'. It is about remembering an episode in your life. What is special about episodic memories is that, unlike semantic ones, they help us define who we are. Think of it this way: if I ask you what sort of person you are, you do not respond by referring to what you do or don't know. You do not say, 'I am the person who knows where Paris is.' But you might say, 'I am the sort of person who hitchhiked to Paris.' When we think about who we are, most of us turn to the most memorable episodes in our lives.[23] We recall the pain of the final, twenty-sixth mile, and think: 'I am the sort of person who runs the London Marathon.' We recall being picked last for the school sports team and think: 'I am the sort of person who's bad at sport.' We remember losing a friend in battle and think: 'I am the person who survived the war.' The more intense the experience, the stronger the episodic memory is and the more likely it is to become part of our identity. If we are mugged on the way home, we may for a while see ourselves as 'a person who got mugged'. If we lose the TV control – even though it may be temporarily annoying – we are highly unlikely to see ourselves as 'a person who lost the TV remote'.

Intense moments in our life – like starting school or joining the army – can come to define how we see ourselves, as they form strong episodic memories. When we think of what sort of person we truly are, we reflect on episodes in our lives and recall the most intense ones. We therefore come to think of ourselves as 'a fighter' or as someone who is 'shy or brave'. That's all well and good, but why would an intense episodic memory bond me with other people? The key is this: most of our intense episodic memories don't just involve us. Think back to an intense moment of your life – maybe quitting a job, getting married or going bungee jumping. Form a picture in your mind. For most of us, we will be in the middle of that picture. But is anyone else also in it? If the activity took place with someone else – a colleague who quit at the same time, a spouse, a person tied to the bungee rope with you – they will probably be in the picture too. When that picture, that episodic memory, forms part of your identity, the other person becomes linked to that identity and therefore feels linked, in your mind, to who you are. You are the person who quit your job alongside them. You are the person who got married to them. You are the person who jumped tied to them.

When we consider who we are, we find we cannot exclude these people, because they are there in our episodic memory. They are people like me. This process – of forming our identity with other people in it – has a name. it is called 'identity fusion'.[24] Identity fusion is why intense experiences play such a key role in building a sense of 'us'. When we share an intense experience with others, it defines them as somehow part of 'us'.[25] This matters hugely. If someone of a different ethnic background is in an episodic memory with you, they form some part of your self-identity. That won't just affect your relationship with them. It means that other people of the same ethnic background will also seem more 'like you'. Remember, those White American soldiers didn't just favour serving with the same Black soldiers again; they favoured serving with any Black soldiers.

This is why intense activity is so important to the common life. If we have a set of institutions that bring us together but no intensity of experience, we are much less likely to connect with each other, and much less likely to see those who are different in some way as 'like us'. The intensity of war was critical to the bond that was formed between Black and White servicemen at the Battle of the Bulge. Not only were they servicemen living together with equality of status; they were also taking part in countless intense shared experiences that were destined to form episodic memories. The same effect was at work among British soldiers serving with men from other classes. This shared intense experience of war made British servicemen see men of other classes as people more 'like them'. We shouldn't be surprised that it also provided the political context for a massive post-war investment in housing and healthcare for Brits of all classes.

Although not a matter of life and death, you can see intensity of experience at work in the activities that finally bonded the Rattlers and the Eagles. From unblocking the water supply to putting up tents before it got dark or restarting a broken-down truck, the challenges that Sherif created were high energy with a clear risk of failure. In comparison, Sherif made sure that the earlier meetings between the boys either pitted them against each other or were remarkably low in intensity – from attending mealtimes to watching films. There was nothing sufficiently intense in these activities to form a shared, episodic memory. The same memory-forming intensity is visible in the England team's drunken night out and the terror of presenting at Apple's Top 100, but it is invisible in the Dutch team's civilised lunches or Sony's separate business units.

About a decade ago, I had my first chance to put this theory into practice. I was responsible for designing the UK's National Citizen Service – a four-week rite of passage for tens of thousands of teenagers that aimed to bond children of different ethnicities and income levels together. On the third day of the programme, we agreed that every small group of twelve young people would have to complete a long hike and then camp together overnight. Few of the young people taking part liked the idea. Many of them worried about it in advance, found it hard work on the day and struggled to sleep at night – mostly because they were scared of being outdoors in the dark. The day after the camp, we found the teams tired and irritable.

But something else had changed too. They were much more united. After the overnight camp, trying to convince a participant to move from one team to another had become incredibly difficult. The hike and the camping had created an episodic memory for those young people, one that included the rest of the group. It had turned a group of strangers into a group called 'us'. Does this mean that the only reliable way to connect people is to engage them in intense activities? Fortunately not; there is another route to bonding groups that relies much less on peril and adventure.

Some primary-age children love playing with beads. My own children – in the right mood – will sit happily for hours making necklaces, wristbands or just pretty patterns. Typically, their output will be as gaudy as possible and then I will be expected to wear the result at work. Nicole Wen, of the University of Texas, had a more serious intent than embarrassing me in front of my colleagues when she designed a game for children to play with beads.[26]

Wen created an after-school club for children aged four to eleven. When they arrived, she separated them into two teams. Each team was further divided into a 'Green' group and a 'Yellow' group. The four groups were initially treated in exactly the same way. They were seated on the floor and given a wristband that corresponded with their group's colour. All the greens had green bands; all the yellows had yellow. Each group had an adult helper. This helper handed every child a bag of beads and some string. The helper then began leading the group by saying, 'Okay green [or yellow] group, we are going to play with these beads in a special way, the way the green [or yellow] group does it!'

This is where things started to differ. The two groups in Team 1 were allowed to make anything they wanted in any way they fancied. Their helpers chatted away with them but didn't give any instructions. Things in Team 2 were very different. Here the children, whether in the green or the yellow group, had to follow a very precise routine. Their adult helpers told the children not to touch any beads until they said so. Then, only when they were told to, the team members were each to find a star bead and string it. After this, they were to string a circle bead, then a square one and finally a heart before starting back at the beginning again with a star. Adding to the routine, before stringing the star or the square, the group members had to lift up the bead and touch it to their forehead. Before stringing a circle or a heart, they had to clap their hands three times.

After ten minutes, the helpers asked all four groups to stop. That was the end of the club for the day. The club met six times over two weeks, with the children always in the same groups following exactly the same instructions as they had in the previous meeting. At the end of the very last session, before the children left, the helpers asked them some questions to see how attached they felt to their groups. They were asked whether they would like a hat that was green or yellow, whether they would like a wristband that was green or yellow, whether they thought it was better for new children to join the yellow group or the green group and whether the next set of helpers should come from the green or yellow group. The results were striking. The children in Team 2, who had followed the very precise routines, were much more attached to their group's colour. They were more likely to choose a gift in their team's colour, more likely to want a new person to join their group and more likely to want any future helpers to come from their group. The children in Team 1, who had just played randomly, cared much less about their team. Across the two weeks, this exercise had lasted just sixty minutes in total. The children had had hardly any time to really get to know each other. They had done nothing dangerous, nothing risky and nothing that was likely to raise their heart rate. And yet – just by following the same routine – a group of children of varied genders, ages and ethnicities had become much more loyal to one another. This is the connecting power of routine in action.

At my secondary school, we didn't string beads, but half of us had our own repetitive activity that the rest were completely puzzled by. Every Wednesday afternoon each pupil had to choose between two 'character-building' activities. You could either volunteer in the local community or join the Combined Cadet Force. I chose the former and, along with half the school, spent the next two years wondering why the others seemed to enjoy marching back and forth so much. It turns out we weren't the only people wondering. In 2009, curious as to why armies invested so much time marching – an activity that is pretty much useless in modern warfare – two American business academics, Scott Wiltermuth and Chip Heath, ran an experiment. They split a selection of volunteers into two groups. Both groups were told that they would be playing a selection of games that would take place at another site a short walk away. Wiltermuth and Heath asked the first group to walk, at their own pace, over to the other site. The other group were instructed to march to the other site in time with one another. On arrival, each group played a series of games. Each one tested their willingness to cooperate and work together. Sure enough, the group that had marched together, stepping closely in time with one another, was able to cooperate much more effectively. Heath and Wiltermuth repeated the experiment twice more – with one group being asked to sing together before playing the games, and another to both march and sing. Once again, whether marching, singing or both, whenever a team performed a synchronised, routine-based process together, they were more able to cooperate.[27]

This process – of creating a sense of 'us' through routine – also has a name. It is called social identification. By completing the same routine together – ideally in synchronisation – humans form a level of connection, of loyalty and of trust. This could be seen in practice again at the 'Battle of the Bulge'. Not only were the soldiers there being bonded through intense experiences; they were also performing a series of everyday routines and rituals together. Whether

marching, making camp, cleaning rifles or saluting, they were following a clear, and often synchronised, process. It is no coincidence that
so many rituals and synchronised activities are built into military life,
where a failure to build loyalty and trust can be a matter of life or
death.

All this shows that routines matter. But it leaves an important
question. Why do they matter? Why does completing a routine
together bond us?[28] It surely operates through a different mechanism
than episodic memory. A soldier is not going to define himself by the
memory of shining and putting on his shoes. To answer this question, a trip to Israel is in order.

One in every sixty Israelis live in a community group called a kibbutz.
These communities, of which there are 270, were founded on principles of strict equality. All income was meant to be put into a pool,
with everyone receiving an equal share. It's fair to say, this didn't
work well everywhere. In many cases, too many members took too
much out of the pot and debts began to build up. As a result, around
a hundred years after their founding, most kibbutzim no longer
share money in this way. However, sixty of them have managed to
continue to operate with a pool without going bust. All members
still put their earnings in the pot, and many happily put in more
money than they take out. What then is special about these sixty
kibbutzim? Why have their members continued to trust and sacrifice
for each other when the other 210 kibbutzim couldn't? What has
created such a strong sense of shared identity that has kept members
working hard and leaving money in the pool for those in need? The
American anthropologist Richard Sosis, and the Canadian economist Bradley Ruffle, designed a simple experiment to find out.[29]

Sosis and Ruffle visited a number of kibbutzim and provided each
of them with an extra pool of money. They told members that they
could take as much money as they wanted out of this pool with no
personal penalty or cost. However, if the group as a whole left money

in the pool at the end, Sosis and Ruffle would double it. This meant that the best thing for the whole group would be if every individual avoided spending any money from the pool. That way, at the end of the experiment the whole pool would be doubled. Everyone would gain. The group's success therefore depended not just on the ability of each member to restrain themselves, but also on their ability to trust each other to do the same. If trust levels were high, it made sense to leave the pool alone. If they were low, it made sense to get your share before all the money was gone. As the experiment unfolded, Sosis and Ruffle took careful note of every member who took money out of the pool. At the end, they put all the records together and started to spot any patterns. This is when it got interesting.

The first thing Sosis and Ruffle noticed was that religious members of the kibbutzim withdrew much less money than secular members. Were these members' religious beliefs encouraging them not to take the money? A closer look at the data suggested that this was only half the story. It turned out that it was only the religious men who were taking less. Religious women took just as much as secular women. What was going on? If a belief in God somehow made the religious men less likely to take the money out, why didn't it do the same for the women? Were the women less committed believers? Were they all secretly atheists? Sosis and Ruffle were puzzled. That is until they remembered the Amidah.

The Amidah is a prayer that religious Jews pray three times a day: morning, afternoon and evening. For Orthodox Jews, the Amidah prayer follows a clear routine. First, you take three steps back – to symbolise withdrawing from the world. Then you take three steps forward – to symbolise approaching God. After that you turn to face Jerusalem and place your feet firmly together. You bow and begin the prayer. The prayer is made silently and has nineteen distinct elements – each of which is to be recited verbatim. The prayer, which must include three further bows, follows a set order: praises to God for your ancestors, then for His power, His holiness, His wisdom, His acceptance of repentance, His forgiveness, His rescuing power, His healing for the sick, His blessings of food, the return to Israel, His righteousness, His justice, His plan to rebuild Jerusalem, His plan to send the Messiah, His mercy, His plan to restore the Temple, the gift of your life and finally His peace.

The key fact about the Amidah was this. In an Orthodox kibbutz, the Amidah was performed only by the men. What Sosis and Ruffle had discovered in their research wasn't the power of belief. It was the power of routine. By praying together – in a very set pattern – three times a day, the Orthodox men had been following a routine more complex and precise than that of the children playing with their beads or the soldiers preparing for battle. The routine had created a bond strong enough to prevent the men from taking from the pool. To prove the point, Sosis and Ruffle examined one last thing. They considered the religious men who never prayed the Amidah. Sure enough, they took just as much from the pool as everyone else.[30] Why were some people taking less from the pool? Because the shared routines of the Amidah were connecting them together.

All of the examples – from marching to singing to stringing beads – show social identification in action. People taking part in a routine together become more loyal, more connected and more collaborative. Why would this be? The clearest hint of how routines have this effect can be seen on the kibbutzim. Each kibbutz tended to have a variety of additional routines alongside the Amidah. These varied in the time they took and their complexity. What is striking is that the kibbutzim that have stayed afloat the longest were those with the most time-consuming and costly routines. It would appear that the more members saw each other committing to routines, the more they trusted each other and the longer the kibbutz survived. The more costly the routine, the more committed a member appeared to be and the more other members trusted them. This is how a routine leads to trust. The routine – whether the Amidah or the act of marching or the task of stringing beads in a set way – serves as a sign of commitment. I see you commit to this ritual three times a day, every day, therefore I can trust that you are really committed to this group. I see that you are prepared to clap three times every time you string a circle or heart, therefore, once again, I can trust you are committed to the group. I can see that you are prepared to march in time, sing in time, clean your rifle in the official way. If I know you are prepared to do this for the group – whether you seemed initially like me or not – I know I can trust you.[31]

Let us turn our attention back to the common lives of our ancestors. Sure enough, we will see that they are full of either intensity or routine. As foragers, our rituals were not forgettable moments of process. Consider the *epeme* dance. It is not some idle swaying to music; no slow dance. It is a ritual performance in the pitch black by men wearing ostrich feathers on their head, bells around their legs and swinging a rattle. This is not a passive, momentary, forgettable interaction. It is intense – something that those who dance will remember for ever. As farmers, our common life provided moments of intensity and routine. Alcohol played an important role. Consider the rites of passage in a fourteenth-century English village. Routine-filled, formal religious services would generally be followed by village-wide drunken celebrations full of gossip and mixing. Someone attending a rural feast could expect to dance in large groups, often with routine, prearranged steps; join a procession, marching in time with others; and then drink and compete against others, whether in archery, wrestling, cockfighting or, perhaps, an early version of football.[32] Even more formal and religious celebrations, such as on a woman's return to church after childbirth ('churching'), were likely to have been followed by a celebratory visit to the pub for the woman and her female neighbours. The common life that grew up in the industrialised cities was also full of routine and intensity. In the factory, routine was everywhere. The working day was built around following a set process in unison with each other and the machines.

Everyone had their role in the routine and relied on everyone else playing their part. And at unfortunate moments – alongside this routine – sat unwelcome moments of intensity, whether caused by an injury to a fellow worker or a strike for better conditions. The school day was also full of routine as the children repeated facts together in unison, learning mostly by rote. To be a member of a club or society was to sign up for more moments of routine and intensity. Quasi-religious routines, such as vows, ceremonies and initiations, were commonplace, while many of the new youth associations expected members to get out of their comfort zone – whether hiking and camping for the first time or undertaking acts of service.

Division does not have to be our destiny. People Like Me syndrome may pull us apart, but we have a weapon for fighting back. It is a weapon that has been so taken for granted that it did not even have a name. As we have seen, throughout history our societies have relied on a common life – a set of rituals, habits and institutions – that can connect us together and build a sense of 'us' across our differences. In this way we have exploited the one weakness of PLM: that who is 'like me' is actually very malleable. Through fostering a perception of equal status and moments of intensity or routinised activity, these rituals, habits and institutions created a sense that those who seemed 'unlike us' were actually just 'like us'. This is what was able to unite Black and White servicemen on the front line in Belgium, Eagles and Rattlers in Robbers Cave, England's footballers, Apple's Top 100, and our ancestors, whether foragers, farmers or factory workers. The reason we are dividing today is that the common life that brought our grandparents' generation together has been withering away.

CHAPTER FIVE

COMING APART

New York attorney Benjamin Brafman was having a difficult day. When your client has been dubbed 'the most hated man in America', it is hard to find a jury that is not biased against him. That client, Martin Shkreli, a thirty-four-year-old businessman, was on trial for fraud. He stood accused of purposely misleading his investors. These were serious charges, but they were not the ones that the court of public opinion had already convicted him of. To the average American, Shkreli was the man who had stolen from the sick.

Daraprim was a drug that around two thousand Americans living with AIDS relied upon. Fortunately, it was relatively cheap at around $14 a pill. In 2015, Shkreli bought the rights to Daraprim. Overnight, he raised the price by 5,000 per cent to $750 per pill. The change made him millions of dollars. People detested him – not just for how he had made this money but also because of what he spent it on. He used $2 million of his new wealth to buy the sole copy of the Wu-Tang Clan's new album. Why? Just so that no one else could listen to it. He appeared to be auditioning for the role of America's pantomime villain. By 2016, Shkreli was so detested that he had achieved the impossible; he managed to unite Hillary Clinton and Donald Trump. The fact that Shkreli was an awful human being was one thing the two candidates could agree on.

85

The task of jury selection is a key part of any American trial. Shkreli's attorney was used to probing potential jurors with searching questions, digging for little hints that suggested who might be biased against his client. On 16 August 2017, sitting in a court in Brooklyn, Brafman didn't have to dig very deep. All he had to do was ask each potential juror what they thought of his client. As the answers came back, he began to realise that the real challenge would be finding twelve people – anywhere in America – who did not hate him.

Juror no. 1 advised that: 'I wouldn't want me on this jury' because 'I am aware of the defendant and I hate him.' Juror no. 144 was asked whether he could decide the case with an open mind. 'I don't think I can because he kind of looks like a dick,' he replied. Juror 59 had sentenced him already: 'Your Honor, totally he is guilty and in no way can I let him slide out of anything.' His main concern wasn't the fraud charge or even the price gouging – juror 59 hated Shkreli because 'he disrespected the Wu-Tang Clan'. Juror 10 was also convinced of Shkreli's guilt. 'The only thing I'd be impartial about is what prison this guy goes to.' Brafman had some hope in juror 52. The latter had never heard of his client, which was a positive, but he had looked at him in court. 'When I walked in here today, I looked at him, and in my head, that's a snake – not knowing who he was. I just walked in and looked right at him and that's a snake.'

Jury service is a remarkable institution. First guaranteed in the UK in 1215 under Magna Carta, in the US it is the only right that appears in both the Constitution and the Bill of Rights. Twelve complete strangers from all walks of life come together for a period of hours, days, weeks, months and sometimes years. They must work together as a team to make a set of decisions that will radically transform the lives of the accused as well as those affected by the alleged crimes. Just over a quarter of the US population will sit on a jury during their lifetime.[1] When they do, they will see what a true cross-section of their society looks like, for jury service is unusual in its ability to bring together people from all ages, ethnicities, income and education levels. If you want to know what your country really looks like, serve on a jury. What makes jury service particularly unusual is how long it has been part of human society. For hundreds of years, when we were still farmers, it was a part of the common life that brought us together. It was also part of the common life that connected us after we migrated en masse to the cities. What is most striking is that it is still connecting people today. This makes it very much unlike the rest of the common life that united our grandparents. Over the last half-century, the three core elements of the industrial common life have all lost their ability to connect us. This loss is most striking in the decline and fall of the voluntary association, which has been as rapid as its initial arrival.

At the start of the 1950s, voluntary associations had been booming for a century. They had accelerated in number and in scale to the point where the majority of adults were members of at least one club or society. A few years later, it was as though someone had found a reverse gear, selected it and hit the accelerator. Every generation of Britons and Americans born after 1950 proved less likely than the one before it to join a club or a society. Across the US, all types of associations declined. Religious groups lost at least 10 per cent of their congregation. Trade unions lost 50 per cent.[2] The Parents–Teachers Asssociation lost 60 per cent.[3] The largest male fraternity – the Freemasons – lost 70 per cent, while other major fraternities were losing at least 50 per cent.[4] The impact on how the average American spent their time was striking. In 1970, two-thirds of Americans regularly attended some form of voluntary meeting; by the end of the century that had fallen to a third.[5] In the UK, groups that had dominated the nineteenth century declined the fastest. Consider churchgoing: in 1900, a third of the UK population went to church so frequently that they considered themselves a 'member'. By 2010, this had fallen to just one-tenth.[6] The number of those who never attended church rose rapidly, increasing by 7 per cent within just the first ten years of the twenty-first century.[7] Men's and women's groups that the Victorians had flocked to declined fast. The number of working men's clubs halved between 1972 and 2015, as did membership of the Women's Institute.[8] Sixty per cent of Brits born at the end of the Second World War were a member of at least one group when they celebrated their fortieth birthday. Just twenty years later, Brits celebrating the same birthday had become half as likely to be involved.[9] By the end of the twentieth century, membership of an association had switched from being an almost universal experience to being a selective one. And yet this dramatic decline in membership is only half the story.

Two blocks from Pennsylvania Avenue and a twenty-minute walk from the White House, you will find a twenty-five-year-old brick building that explains much about what has happened to our clubs and societies over the last seventy years. In this building – so large that it has its own zip code (20049) – sits the headquarters of one of the largest associations in America. Launched in 1958 and with a membership that includes one in every two Americans over fifty, this is the American Association of Retired Persons or AARP. Inside the fortress-like development, behind its gated arches, at the heart of the organisation sits a team of around 165 policy staff including 28 registered lobbyists. It is this team that delivers the core goals of the AARP. It does not do so by bringing people together, but by monitoring and influencing legislation. The vast majority of its members – 33 million of them in all – have never attended any meetings or taken part in any events.

The AARP represents the new type of membership organisation in the West – focused on lobbying, influence and online advice. Members join for individual benefit, not for face-to-face interaction.[10] These large organisations, which range from the AARP to Greenpeace, from the American Automobile Association to Mothers Against Drunk Driving, were all established in the twentieth century.

They play a critical role in our societies, but that role does not include providing us with a common life. Our grandparents joined clubs as a way to meet new people. We increasingly join ones where the members never meet.

What, though, about the clubs that do continue to meet? How well do these continue to provide a common life? Not well, I'm afraid. Not only do these clubs meet less often than they used to; they also increasingly bring people together with others who are just like them.[11] When the American sociologist, Theda Skocpol, looked under the bonnet of the clubs and societies that were still meeting, she found that those that mixed diverse groups of people together had declined the fastest. Associations that mixed rich and poor citizens lost members twice as rapidly as those that involved only the rich.[12] Making this problem worse, across both the US and the UK, blue-collar workers gave up on clubs and societies more rapidly than anyone else. While in the middle of the twentieth century working-class Brits were only a third less likely to join an association than middle-class, by the 1990 they were more than half as likely.[13] This evacuation from associations is fastest among the most disadvantaged. The unemployed in particular became increasingly unlikely to join groups or take part in group volunteering.[14]

In the industrial society, the flowering and growth of clubs and societies created a new type of common life. It is hard to see that common life today. The number of clubs and societies that actually meet has fallen dramatically. Those that do meet have fewer members. Those members attend meetings less often. When they do attend, they tend to find a club increasingly full of people just like them. These shifts sound the retreat of the association from its role in our common life, placing all the weight on the school and the workplace to mix us together.

In early May 1955, West Germany signed papers to join NATO, committing America and its allies to fight back if the Soviet Union crossed the German border. Just five days later, the Soviets corralled the countries of Eastern Europe to sign the Warsaw Pact. The Cold War was heating up and the American people needed a comforting distraction. Corporate America stepped up to the plate. Within this one year, Ray Kroc would unveil his first ever McDonald's, Walt Disney would open the doors to Disneyland, and CBS would launch the first ever big-money gameshow, *The $64,000 Question*. And 1955 was also the year in which, to track the growing number of emerging multi-million-pound businesses, the editor of *Fortune* first published a list of the largest 500 companies in America. It was called – then, as now – the Fortune 500. Little did Smith know that his list would come to outlive Ray Kroc, Walt Disney, *The $64,000 Question* and even the Soviet Union.

The longevity of the Fortune 500 stands in contrast to the companies on that first list. By 2015, nine out of ten of them had either lost their place, gone bankrupt or merged.[15] Yet, throughout this turbulence, the very top slot on the list has shown a remarkable consistency. Since the first publication sixty-five years ago, only three companies have ever sat in the highest position: Walmart, ExxonMobil and General Motors. Over the last few years, however, a new set of barbarians – the West Coast's five big technology companies: Alphabet, Amazon, Microsoft, Facebook and Apple – are clambering at the gate, with every sign that they will one day unseat the present kings.[16] Anticipating booming sales and profits, investors have already made these companies five of the six most valuable public companies in the world. The pace of their rise in value is almost unparalleled. Eight years ago, only one of them sat in the top 10 most valuable. Two were not even in the top 100. As we will see, extraordinary technological advances have always played a critical role in the cycles of division and unity that make up our history. The digital advances these companies are making will come to transform our societies. They are already transforming our workplaces.

Over the last two centuries, our machines have become exponentially more efficient and our computers exponentially more powerful. As a result, we have become much more productive. How so? Here is a simple way to think of it. Picture the number of people needed to run a factory in 1850. Today, with the same number of people, you can run a hundred factories. Two consequences follow. The first is that we can make an awful lot more 'stuff' than they used to. This, in short, is the story of how our societies became so much richer over the last 200 years. The second consequence is initially harder to spot. It is the fact that how well we organise these machines, computers and the people working with them makes a huge difference to how much we produce. Making the wrong decisions about how we are organised massively affects profits much more than it ever used to. We have responded to this by getting more people involved in these decisions and by rewarding them with higher incomes and greater status. Who are these people? They largely fall into five types: those overseeing the work (in other words, senior managers), those making the machines work better (in other words, tech workers), those deciding which machines and workers deserve to receive investment and funding (in other words, bankers), those ensuring that the right agreements are in place so that partners with different machines and workers can work together well (in other words, corporate lawyers), and those providing advice and analysis on how to improve the work (in other words, management consultants). It won't be lost on you that these are all pretty high-paid jobs that have vastly grown in number over the last half-century. There is a name for the people who do these jobs. Because they are meant to bring 'knowledge' to inform decisions, they are known as 'knowledge workers'. The work they do is sometimes grouped together and called the 'knowledge economy'. The growth in this economy over the last fifty years has been one of the biggest changes in our economies. One estimate suggests that up to 50 per cent of the rich world's GDP is now based in this sector. The fast-growing tech world is very firmly in this space.

Unfortunately, the growth of the knowledge economy is making it harder for the workplace to bring people from different backgrounds together in the way it used to. The industrialised workplace had very few knowledge workers in it. Most staff required just basic manual, reading and writing skills to perform their tasks. There would have been a small group of managers who would normally work on site with the manual workers. This way they could quickly resolve any problems on the factory line and ensure the work and work-rate were up to scratch. This changed little over the years, even as companies and the layers of management grew. Senior staff would still be based on site because the connection between worker and manager was critical for the work to succeed. This meant higher-paid and lower-paid workers worked together, lived in the same areas, where the factory was based, and – more than likely – sent their children to the same schools.

The boom in the number of knowledge workers – whether managers, tech workers, bankers, lawyers or consultants – has ended this togetherness. For the knowledge worker, the most important interaction is no longer with the manual worker or the machine operator. It is with other knowledge workers. Designers at Apple need to discuss their plans with software engineers and patent attorneys, not with the workers making the phones. Today, the greater the gap in skill between workers, the less they interact.[17] It's not just that knowledge workers and manual workers don't attend the same meetings. Over the last twenty years, knowledge workers haven't simply moved into different offices from the manual workers producing the product; they have found themselves in different firms and often in different countries. As early as 1937, the British economist, Ronald Coase, arguably foresaw what was coming when he wrote his classic article, 'The Nature of the Firm'. In it, he explained to readers why firms existed at all by posing a deceptively tricky question: 'Why isn't everyone a freelancer?' The reason they weren't, he explained, is that all of their time would be wasted negotiating rates and ways of working. A firm exists – according to Coase – because it saves time. Rather than constantly negotiating ways of working, hours of employment, and prices, better to agree it once, become part of the same firm and get on with the task in hand. Coase concluded that the boundaries of a firm will tend to include the bits that are most complicated to facilitate working together – so that you only have to sort them out once – and the people with the most complex information that needs to be shared. What this means in practice is that firms operating in the knowledge economy tend to put all of their knowledge workers together in one firm and outsource the rest of the work to another firm. Consider Uber.

Uber's marketeers, coders and senior managers need to sit in the same firm. Their complicated, interconnected work requires them to share complex information often and, frequently, to make decisions together. However, the manual workers delivering passengers or food don't need to be in that firm at all. Modern technology means that the information they need can be easily provided automatically and their output can be monitored with very little interaction. Uber is by no means unique. You will find very few non-knowledge workers in Alphabet, Microsoft, McKinsey or the Gates Foundation. When people with lower skills are needed, you can bet they will work for a different firm – that's why those doing the cleaning are not at the office Christmas party. The result is a set of workplaces that are either full of degree-educated, very well-paid knowledge workers or full of non-degree-educated, less well-paid ordinary workers. The French and American economists, Philippe Aghion and Jeffrey Williamson, describe the consequences as being a 'shifting from firms like General Motors, which use both high- and low-skill workers, to firms like Microsoft and McDonald's', whose workforces are full of people just like me.[18] Even in companies that do have both high-skilled and low-skilled workers, they rarely locate them together. Highly educated staff tend to be clustered in headquarters. Amazon may have 341,400 mostly low-skilled workers, but it is the highly educated knowledge workers who cluster together in the HQ. These changes are now visible across the developed world. Researchers looking at firms in France, Britain and America have found evidence that workers are less likely than before to have colleagues from different income brackets or varied levels of seniority or experience.[19]

If the workplace is becoming less able to knit us together by income and education, might there be better news on age and ethnicity? There is surprisingly little data on how much people of different ages work together, but what we can see should concern us. While manufacturing tended to bring young and old together, the new tech firms tend to be silos filled with the young. Line up every member of staff at Google in age order and you'll find that the staff member in the middle is just twenty-nine years old. You will find the exact same at Facebook. Considering that neither firm tends to employ people younger than twenty-one, this means that half of their staff are between twenty-one and twenty-nine years old. This grouping of the young may be at its most extreme in Silicon Valley, but it is visible across the West. While only one in ten workers in the UK are under twenty-one, they make up a quarter of the whole team in 15 per cent of companies.[20]

The picture initially seems more positive on the workplace's ability to connect us with people of different races and ethnicities. Generally, the workplace is more ethnically mixed than the rest of our lives, whether we are British or American.[21] However, as we have seen, this is a low bar and it would be a struggle to describe the workplace as a truly effective common life for citizens of different ethnicities. Professor of Law, and expert on the workplace, Cynthia Estlund, sums up the situation thus: 'the picture of workplace integration … is one of a glass half-full'.[22] The key question is whether the glass has been filling up or emptying. The news here is dispiriting. In the US at least, compared to the 1970s, despite the efforts of larger firms to become more ethnically diverse, the workplace has actually become more divided – largely due to the lack of diversity in newer, smaller firms.[23] There are reasons to doubt whether this situation will improve. Part of the problem is that people tend to recruit those that they already know. A divided society tends therefore to create a workforce divided in its image. Two biases make matters worse. White recruiters continue to be biased towards candidates with European or Anglo-American names, even if they have CVs no better than other candidates. Applicants from all ethnicities, meanwhile, continue to be biased towards certain jobs and sectors. Alongside this, there are cases of managers allocating workers onto different shifts depending on their ethnicity, justifying this on the grounds that it improves communication and reduces tension.[24] There are, though, some reasons for guarded optimism. Larger firms continue to be vocal about their seriousness in diversifying recruitment. However, at present at least, the overall picture is undeniably some-what bleak. The workplace, which did so much to bring many of the people of the industrial society together, has lost much of its ability to connect us. What then about the final element of our grandparents' common life: the school?

Over the last century, in the West, the school has become our domi-nant social institution. It is the sole place – beyond jury service – where we can be compelled, without doing anything wrong, to spend time with people not of our choice. With few exceptions, it is now illegal across the West for children to be denied primary and secondary school education, the vast majority of which is delivered in state-funded schools that are, in theory at least, open to everyone.[25] The school clearly continues to bring people together. Unfortunately, though, those people are now increasingly similar to each other.

Let us start in the United States where the school system unavoid-ably operates in the shadow of centuries of state-sanctioned slavery and segregation. Any description of modern racial division in the

United States describes individuals buffeted by waves of distrust, inequality and discrimination resulting from two hundred years of kidnapping, murder, rape and ill-treatment. It required a civil war bloody enough to kill one in fifty American men to make slavery illegal. Even after that bloodshed, and within living memory, in many parts of the United States, it was state-enforced law – imposed mostly, but not exclusively, by Southern states – that prevented Black Americans from attending 'White' schools, living in 'White' areas, eating in 'White' restaurants, marrying 'White' partners, drinking from 'White' water fountains and even fighting alongside White soldiers. It's impossible to read these laws without being horrified by the banality of their evil. In 1934, Alabama passed a law banning restaurants from serving White and Black people together, specifying that it applied 'unless such white and colored persons are effectually separated by a solid partition extending from the floor upward to a distance of seven feet or higher'. Tennessee's 1905 Streetcar Statute made clear not only that Black people must never travel in the same car as Whites, but also that 'signs must be posted'. Kentucky's 1873 education law specified the exact distance that Black and White schools must be apart: at least one mile in rural areas, but only 600 feet in towns and cities. In Arizona, a 1928 law banning interracial marriage was so badly worded that the state's Supreme Court ruled that it meant that people of mixed race would be unable to marry anyone unless a clarifying amendment was passed. This is recent history. When England last won the Football World Cup, it was still illegal for a Black and White couple to marry in parts of America.

It would be wrong to claim that this history is a solely American story. Many Europeans initiated, maintained, propagated and profited from the evil, while sowing discrimination into their own societies. Every European government accepted a degree of forced segregation by race, even if it was not imposed by law. In Britain, employers, unions and private citizens conspired to maintain a 'colour bar' that excluded ethnic-minority Britons from employment, restaurants, lodging and pubs. Unions passed resolutions against any non-White employees. Employers refused to interview non-White candidates. A 1956 survey of White British landlords found that less than 2 per cent would let a room to a Black tenant. For years, the state did nothing. It would require two Acts of Parliament to dismantle the colour bar.

It is also undeniable, however, that America's history of slavery and state-imposed segregation is distinct. Any description of racial division within the United States describes the continued reverberation of slavery and forced segregation. Much of our racial division comes from this past – especially in the school system. And yet, it is too generous to those of us alive today to assume that all racial division in the United States and in its school system is no more than a preordained consequence of the sins of our forefathers. This sort of 'it is unavoidably so' thinking ignores, for example, the progress that was made in reducing racial division in America's schools in the first forty years after the Supreme Court struck down state-led school segregation in 1954.[26] During that period, efforts to desegregate American schools worked. By 1988, half of all Black children were attending schools that were majority White. Any backsliding from this high-water mark is not preordained at all. It is as much about the actions that followed that moment as about the enforced division that proceeded it. As we will see, there are also divisions that cannot be explained by America's history of slavery and enforced segregation.

Let us start where perhaps we might see some good news: in the state that is home to the 'great melting pot' of New York City. Surely if any state can bring Black and White students together, it is a northern, liberal, diverse, big-city-containing state such as New York. As we will see increasingly, things are not always as we imagine. New York state is not a shining light of unity when it comes to its schools. In fact, of all fifty states, it is the one where Black and White students are the least likely to be educated together. Two out of three Black students in New York state attend a school where at least 90 per cent of their peers are not White.[27] This is despite the state being 65 per cent White.[28] To be fair to New York, the wider country is not much better. In thirteen other states, at least four in ten Black students attend schools where 90 per cent of pupils are non-White.[29] Across the country, one in six Black students attend a school that is 99 per cent Black.[30] Around four in ten schools meanwhile are either almost entirely White or almost entirely non-White.[31] It is easy to get lost in the numbers here and lose the overall picture. A simple comparison may help. Consider the difference between the school of the average White student and that of the average Black student. In the White student's school, around three in four students are White. In the Black student's school, Whites are a minority.[32] The racial divisions are not just Black and White. There is a significant lack of Latino–White mixing. In two of the states with the largest Latino populations, the majority of Latino students attend a school where nine out of ten peers are non-White. In six other states, 40 per cent of Latino students attend schools like this. One of the main shifts that has taken place over the last thirty years has been increasing decisions by White parents not to send their children to mixed schools. What is causing this division? One of the causes is the many thousands of choices made by White families to avoid sending their children to schools where they would be in the minority. The result has been a plummeting of White student numbers in schools where they are outnumbered. Over the last thirty years, the number of schools where Whites make up 10 per cent or less of the student body has tripled.[33] Today, this describes almost a fifth of all schools in America.

The picture is little better in the United Kingdom. Large numbers of British children are divided by ethnicity from their first day at school. While nineteen out of twenty White children will start their first day of education in a majority-White school, only eight out of twenty non-White students will. The situation scarcely improves at secondary school level. Half of all secondary schools in the UK fail to represent the ethnic mix of the local area.[34] In areas where the population is more diverse, the picture is slightly better, but not by much. Consider London, for example, where the majority of school students are non-White. Even here, nine out of ten non-White students attend majority-non-White schools, while half of Whites attend majority-White schools.[35]

If schools remain divided by race, what about their ability to bring children from different income brackets together? This is where the news is worst. Where once schools bridged class divides in local neighbourhoods, they now amplify them. Schools have become more divided by income than the local neighbourhood. A poor teenager in the United States is more likely to find a rich peer living in the house next door than sitting in the next desk at school.[36] Rather than connecting our neighbourhoods together, our schools are further dividing them as increasing numbers of wealthy families move to richer areas to get their children into the best schools.[37] The result is that a child from a rich family has become less likely to either live in the same school district as a child from a poor family or to attend the same school.[38] What about outside of the state system? The private school system has become increasingly exclusive. In 1970, if you were born into a family with an average US income, you had a 13 per cent chance of attending a private school. Those born into the richest families were only slightly more likely to attend than you were. By 2011, private-school fees had risen so spectacularly that the chances of the average child attending had halved, while those of the richer child had doubled. The result is an increasingly exclusive private school system alongside an increasingly income-divided set of state schools.[39] The situation in the United Kingdom is similar. Schools are increasingly divided by income. The Department of Education's own data shows that half of all children poor enough to receive free school meals are educated in just a fifth of the schools.[40] Comparing each school with those nearby reveals that just under a third fail to include both richer and poorer pupils.[41]

The result of all this is a set of schools that divides students not only by race and income but by both at the same time. Consider, as an example, the number of American children who now attend schools where the student body is at least 90 per cent non-White and 90 per cent low-income. This group doubled in size between 2000 and 2013. It now accounts for one in six American students.[42]

Our grandparents inherited a common life that – while far from perfect – largely knitted their societies together. For at least a hundred years, clubs and societies, the workplace and the local school brought people of different backgrounds together. While their societies remained divided by race, the common life brought together people from different villages, with different nationalities, different levels of wealth, different education levels and different ages. Today – as we have seen – this common life has been withering away. Few of us join clubs and societies and those who do are much less likely to meet those who are different. Our workplaces and our schools – meanwhile – have become increasingly divided by wealth and education levels. Why have we become so divided? The short answer is that we have lost a common life to knit us together. Without it, People Like Me syndrome has had free rein and so we have surrounded ourselves with people like us.

Why, though, have we lost our common life? This is the question we must answer. If we can do that, we have made the first step towards getting it back.

Part II

WHY WE'RE FRACTURING NOW

'The country may be more diverse than ever .... But look around: our own streets are filled with people who live alike, think alike and vote alike.'

Bill Bishop

CHAPTER SIX

THE DISRUPTIVE POWER
OF CHANGE

Let us catch our breath. We have seen that our divisions are mostly, sadly, down to us. They spring from an evolved, fortunately weak, desire to be surrounded by people 'like us'. We have named this little bias that sits within us all People Like Me syndrome (PLM). Over time, this syndrome can become surprisingly powerful and divide our societies into bubbles filled with people like us. However, as we have seen, we humans have normally found a way to keep PLM in check. Whether as foragers, farmers or factory workers, we have built a set of institutions that bring us together with those who are unlike us. In each era, these have been different – from the *epeme* to the feast day, from the rite of passage to the workplace – but in each era they have achieved the same goal. They have brought us face to face with those who seem different to us and, through providing a sense of equality, intensity or routine, have created a sense of 'us' where there was just 'us and them'. The reason we are dividing today is that the common life that united our grandparents and their immediate ancestors is now withering away. We are less likely to join clubs and societies, and our schools and our workplaces have become ever more divided by wealth and education. Why though is the common life withering away? There is not one culprit, but two.

To identify these two guilty parties, we must first understand the victim a little better. Or rather, victims. For there is not just one type of common life. There are two: mandatory and voluntary. Consider the school; it became part of the industrial era's common life because it was mandatory. Children had no choice but to go to school and – in nearly all cases – they went to the local one. This threw them together with people unlike themselves. As we will see in the next chapter, these mandatory elements of our common life have been bumped off by a villain who we rather like. However, most of the common life institutions that we have seen have not been mandatory at all. They have been voluntary. Consider the factory workers' clubs and societies, the nomad's *epeme* or the farmer's rites of passage. No one was forced to attend these institutions. People chose to join them. This optionality makes it incredibly hard for voluntary institutions to become part of the common life. To convince most people to participate, such an institution will have to be incredibly well attuned to the needs and habits of the people of the time. This in turn – as we will see – makes them very vulnerable to this chapter's culprit. But before we go any further, I need to tell you about a French farmer and his tomatoes.

Deep in the South of France, about an hour's drive from Toulouse, my friend Nathan almost committed an unforgivable crime. In a farmhouse outside the small village of Lafage, he was seconds away from crushing a farmer's precious tomato seeds. Nathan would plead mitigating circumstances. First of all, he was close to exhaustion. Having committed to cycling through much of France, he had spent every waking hour of the last ten days on a bike. Second, the farmhouse was a mess and the seeds were incredibly small. Last of all, he was there to volunteer and he had to put his bags down somewhere.

The farmer stopped him just in time. She looked down at the seeds – selected carefully from the best tomatoes of the crop – and then back up at Nathan. She fixed him in the eye and declared, 'These seeds are precious … because they know the soil the best.'

Nathan and I laughed when he retold the story. We enjoyed the idea of seeds 'knowing' the soil. For seeds, of course, 'know' nothing. They remember nothing, understand nothing, think nothing. And yet, the farmer is right, and we are wrong.

The key to growing good tomatoes is having the right seeds. And the right seeds are the ones that best suit the soil. There is no way to buy these seeds; they have to evolve. And so, at the end of the season, a wise farmer selects the tomatoes that have flourished best. She picks the reddest, shiniest, juiciest ones with no cracks and no blemishes. She cuts them open and takes the seeds from the middle section of the fruit – where they are fattest and healthiest. These seeds are the 'children' of the tomatoes that suit the soil the best. They will inherit these genes and will produce the best crops next year. The next season, the farmer will do the same. And again the next season, and the next, and so on. This way she will find the seeds that best suit the soil. Or in the French farmer's words, the ones that 'know the soil the best'.

In the same way, the voluntary common life does not spring up overnight. The *epeme* was not created in one day, nor was the religious feast, nor the church, nor the club or society. It takes time and generations of evolution before an institution fits a society so well that most people choose to join in. Ill-fitting institutions die off. Those that are popular grow and adapt until the most suitable ones start to reach nearly everyone. Just like the tomatoes, over time, the voluntary common life adapts to 'fit the soil'.

It is fair to say that the farmer was not the most generous of hosts. Consider the meals that had been promised in return for Nathan's hard work. Most days, lunch was home-made goat's cheese made in a way to make it particularly healthy. To achieve this, the farmer had kept salt out of the mix. The approach was a great success – it was so disgusting that nobody wanted to eat it at all. Dinner proved more of a trial than a treat. On one occasion, the farmer decided to use up cooked but uneaten plain spaghetti from lunch. This could have been delicious – perhaps with a little sauce or some baked vegetables. The farmer thought otherwise – she had a blender and intended to use it. And so the spaghetti was blended and served plain – providing a meal that had more in common with wallpaper paste than with pasta. The mealtime conversation was a distraction from the food, but not a reassuring one. Over one meal, Nathan asked the farmer why she liked to live so remotely and grow so much food – expecting tales of her love of the countryside and her family's long history of farming in the area. The farmer stopped eating. She looked up at Nathan. 'It was obvious,' she said, she had no choice but to leave the city before 'the coming war between all Christians and all Muslims broke out'. After that, Nathan decided to try eating alone. The farmer encouraged him to help himself from a bag in the fridge. Opening the fridge door, Nathan looked inside and saw the bag with meatballs inside. Two of them. Perfect, he thought. He paused. They did look rather large for meatballs. It took a few more seconds for Nathan to realise that the farmer had left him a pair of bull's testicles. He did without lunch that day. Nathan and I chatted for some time – in jest – about how he might get his revenge on the farmer before he left. We imagined him returning to the farm in the dead of night, digging up the soil the tomatoes were growing in and replacing it with soil from elsewhere. The tomato seeds – evolved to fit the farmer's soil – would be much less red, shiny and juicy if the soil suddenly changed.

Something that has carefully evolved to suit one context becomes very ill-suited when 'the soil' changes. This is exactly the situation for the voluntary common life. From the *epeme* to the club and society, these institutions evolved over time to fit the wants and needs of people in a particular era. The *epeme* suits the life of the forager, it does not suit the life of the farmer. The culprit that killed off the voluntary common life was not the internet or social media, populist politicians or media barons – it was change. In the natural world and the business world, organisms and organisations adapt well to change. The same is not true of the voluntary common life. Why is this? A small moth and a large company will help us to find the answer.

For most of us, the peppered moth is an unremarkable creature. Living no longer than a year, with a wingspan shorter than your little finger and no colours in its wings apart from black and white, it is unlikely to have been high on the list of animals you wanted to see, or pretended to be, as a child. And yet, it has played a remarkable role in our understanding of the world around us. For this we have to thank a certain James William Tutt. Thanking Tutt, who died in 1911, would not have been much fun. An English schoolmaster and obsessive collector of moths, he was a man people tended to take against. His own friends described him as sarcastic, impatient and lacking in grace. Two of his contemporaries resigned from notable societies just to avoid being in his presence. In defence of his own overbearing personality, the best Tutt could offer was, 'I can't help it and you know I am right.'[1] What made Tutt even more irritating was that he was, indeed, often right – especially, as it turned out, about peppered moths.

Tutt – in his avid collecting – had noticed that something odd was happening to the peppered moth. It was changing colour. When he was a boy, growing up in the 1860s, nearly all peppered moths that he saw had been white with small specks of black. Only very rarely did he spot a black moth. Forty years later, everything had changed. The white moths were now rare and the black moths were dominant. The question was why. And Tutt – being right again – knew the answer.

The peppered moth was no great fighter. It was weak and fragile, making it easy prey to any predator that saw it. Its great advantage was that, when resting on the trunk of a tree, it was almost impossible to see. Its white and speckled colour perfectly matched the light-coloured lichens that grew on the bark, making it almost invisible.

The peppered moth had survived by adapting to its environment. Like the tomatoes, it 'knew the soil'. It 'knew' the colour of the lichen and fitted it perfectly. The problem for the peppered moth was that someone was 'changing the soil'. Between 1850 and 1900, the lichen that provided its camouflage slowly died off – poisoned by sulphur dioxide from the new coal-burning factories. The trees, where the white peppered moth hid, changed colour – from speckled white to soot black. The moth was invisible no more and was now an easy meal for predators. The exact opposite was true for the rare, black peppered moth. An environment filled with black trees made them the invisible ones. They multiplied rapidly. By the turn of the century, 95 per cent of peppered moths were black. Fourteen years after Charles Darwin had died, Tutt had found a modern example of natural selection at work.

In 1976, Kodak dominated the world of photography, employing over 120,000 people and selling 85 per cent of American cameras. It was so dominant that people took to describing great opportunities for a photo as 'Kodak Moments'. Its business model was unstoppable. Cameras were sold cheaply – pushing others out of the market – while great profits were made on the film that went into the camera. In 1996, Kodak made $16 billion of sales, close to $2 billion of profits and sat at number 67 in the Fortune 500. Like the peppered moth and the farmer's tomato, it had evolved to fit the world around it – a world of cameras and film. But like the moth, everything changed for Kodak the moment that someone 'changed the soil'. The invention of the digital camera was that moment for Kodak. A business that made its profits from selling film couldn't survive in a world without film. By January 2012, Kodak had filed for bankruptcy.

The greatest irony of Kodak's demise was that the first company to build a digital camera had been Kodak. As early as 1975, scientists working for the company had discovered a way to create pictures without film. Even with this head start, Kodak was unable to adapt.

As the American business writer Clayton Christensen, put it, it was like 'seeing a tsunami coming and there's nothing you can do about it'.[2] When Kodak fell, however, there were plenty of 'black peppered moths' ready to flourish in the new environment. Canon and Sony would make billions selling digital cameras. The company that fitted the 'new soil' the best, though, was one that sold neither cameras nor film. In 2012, the year Kodak went bankrupt, a two-year-old little company called Instagram was bought for $1 billion. What the black peppered moth and Instagram show us is that in the natural world and the corporate world, adaptation to 'new soil' can be strikingly rapid. The black peppered moth swiftly filled the gap left by its white cousin. Instagram quickly expanded in Kodak's wake. Rapid change may undermine an individual species or a specific company, but it poses little threat to the natural world or corporate world as a whole. New species and new companies simply replace the old.

Why is this? What is it about the natural and corporate worlds that makes them so good at handling change? The answer is that they have vital qualities that prime them to respond to change. The first of these is '*fast failure*'. In both the natural and corporate worlds, ill-adapted species fail remarkably fast, making space for competitors. A company with an ill-fitting business model – like Kodak's – quickly loses customers and investors to their competitors. With payments to shareholders expected and sales required to pay bills, the company will shrink or fail unless it adapts. The same is true in the natural world: a species ill-adapted to the environment will not survive long. It will increasingly become prey before it can procreate, reducing the numbers of the creature until it becomes extinct. The second quality is '*frequent mutation*'. In the natural world, each generation produces new mutations. They are generally useless, but they stand ready to take advantage if the environment changes. In the case of the peppered moth, each female produces as many as two thousand eggs a year, making the creation of a few alternative colours of moth highly likely. In the corporate world, the attraction of making great profits, and achieving high status, inspires thousands of entrepreneurs to launch alternative business models. Most will fail, but a few are ready to flourish should the environment change. In both environments, therefore, alternatives stand ready to take advantage should an alteration in the environment cause the dominant companies or species to fail. The final quality is '*rapid scaling*'. In both natural and corporate worlds, successful adaptations quickly scale. In the animal kingdom, an animal with a beneficial mutation will survive longer and have more children, passing on its winning characteristics. Within a few generations, those with the new adaptation will outnumber those without it. A few generations can be a strikingly short period of time; two peppered moths, for example, can create nine billion descendants within just three years. If black moths are living longer and having more children than the white moths, it will not take long for them to dominate. The same is true in the corporate world. Businesses that fit the 'new soil' will attract more investors and customers. They will gain more funds to invest, allowing them to serve even more customers, which will attract even more investors. This virtuous cycle leads to rapid growth, while those with an ill-suited business model start to shrink. These three qualities mean that, while change may threaten an individual species or a company, it is rarely a threat to the natural world or corporate world as a whole.

In comparison, the voluntary common life has none of these qualities. It does not 'fail fast'. Committed members will keep a social institution running long after growth has slowed and some time after it starts to go into decline. A visit to a rural church in certain British villages will show the continuation of traditions and rituals long after they have lost their purchase on society. It does not 'frequently mutate'. With no profit motive, few entrepreneurs focus their efforts on designing and launching new elements of a common life. People are not queuing up to create and grow new institutions that bring people together. Existing institutions, meanwhile, have very little incentive to 'mutate', even as they decline. Voluntary institutions are not 'owned' by shareholders wanting growth at all costs. They 'belong' to committed members – who tend to hate changes to an institution that they love. It is a brave individual who calls for change, even if it might help the institution grow. They incur the wrath of existing members, gain no personal benefit if they succeed and face no immediate consequences if they do nothing. Finally, voluntary institutions rarely 'rapidly scale'. Those that involve face-to-face interactions take time to be copied and adapted to different locations. They do not naturally reproduce like successful species in the natural world. They do not attract investors pushing for growth as successful start-ups do in the corporate world. Their members in fact often oppose growth, worrying it will change the precious organisation they have joined. As a result, when the 'soil changes', the voluntary common life is very slow to adapt. It struggles to change as our needs and wants change. Exhibit A is the case of the abandoned village.

The *Mary Celeste* has puzzled historians and the public for 150 years. Many have sought to explain how a hundred-foot merchant ship, in perfect condition with no sign of a struggle, mutiny or attack, could end up abandoned in the mid-Atlantic. And yet, the puzzle of the *Mary Celeste* is small fry compared with the village of Basta, whose remnants can be seen today in modern Jordan. Basta was remarkable. Founded around 8000 BC, it was extraordinarily large for its day. While most settlements had no more than two hundred inhabitants, Basta was home to around a thousand, covering an area as large as twenty modern soccer pitches. At the time of its founding, it was one of the most developed settlements anywhere in the world. Residents used modern technology that would have amazed their ancestors, from cooking with dairy produce to making fired pottery. What is most remarkable about Basta, though, is not its size or its technology. It is the fact that after two thousand years of existence it was completely abandoned.

What makes the situation odder is that Basta is not alone. As our ancestors became farmers, over ten thousand years ago, they formed a number of similarly large settlements. Between 9000 and 8000 BC, the average size of settlement in the Levant grew by a factor of five.[3] Large mega-villages – like Basta – grew up across the Levant and then later across Europe. Then, just as remarkably, the whole process went into reverse. Between 8000 and 7000 BC, the average size of settlement shrunk back again from ten hectares down to two. Basta – and a whole host of similar large settlements – were simply abandoned.[4] Which leaves a rather *Mary-Celeste*-like question: why?

Climate change is an obvious suspect. The climate did become drier across parts of the Levant around this period. But this doesn't explain the abandoned sites in the parts of Europe where there had been no climatic changes.[5] Disease is a possible explanation; in a larger settlement, diseases spread much faster. Yet there have been plenty of much bigger settlements that have endured plagues and famines over the past several thousand years yet were never abandoned. Instead, the population falls and then slowly rises again. What then was the cause? Why would our ancestors construct such large settlements and then abandon them, never to return again?

There are two clues hidden in Basta's remains. The first is the size of the homes. They are incredibly small and closely crammed together. It would appear that, as the population grew, the villages failed to work together to extend Basta's boundaries. Instead, they continually subdivided their homes to make space for their growing families. The need for space was so severe that they even expanded buildings into the gaps between homes. It soon became impossible to get into or out of your home without climbing over everyone else's dwellings. The second clue concerns something missing. There is not a single building in which any group larger than a single family could meet. Not a building anywhere that the villagers built together for everyone to use. There is no place for celebration, no place of worship, no place for storage of things owned in common.

Both clues point in the same direction. Basta was a place where people failed to work together. It was a village divided. But, why was this?

As we know from Chapter 3, the ancestors of those living in Basta were hunter-gatherers. Rituals like the *epeme* had been their common life, bringing their tribe together to ensure cooperation. In the new mega-villages like Basta, as the nomads became farmers, these important rituals started to die out. Archaeologists can find clear evidence of *epeme*-like rituals in the remains of the mega-villages, but only in the first few years of the settlements' existence. Excavations at Çatalhöyük – a large mega-village formed, like Basta, around 8000 BC in the Levant – show the rapid decline of these rituals.[6] A worldwide study of over six hundred nomadic rituals comes to the same conclusion; rituals like the *epeme* died out once farming became the new way of life.[7] In the 'new soil' of the mega-village, the common life of the hunter-gatherers simply didn't fit.

The people of Basta lost their old common life – of intense, *epeme*-like ritual – and never gained a new one. Unlike what we saw in the natural and corporate world, no replacement common life sprung up. Instead, Basta faced a period when the old common life had gone but a new one had not arrived. Without a common life to connect them, the village fractured. Divided, they became acutely vulnerable to disease, overcrowding, conflict and environmental destruction. Eventually, it was too much and they walked away. If this is right, we should expect later, large villages to look different – to have space for people to come together, to have evidence of shared activity. This is exactly what we see. Later settlements founded from 4000 BC onwards have large buildings where residents can come together and bond. They also have a number of more ornate, large houses that are home to those organising the new common life of the agrarian age – the feasts, the religious festivals, the services and the rites of passage that we read about in Chapter 4. In Basta there are no such buildings.

And so, what emptied Basta? The cause was the change from nomadic life to the life of farming. This change killed off the old common life – based around animalistic rituals. No new common life sprung up rapidly to replace it. Why? Because common lives do not fail fast, frequently mutate or rapidly scale. Instead, a period of time follows where there is no common life. We will call this period – when the old common life has gone and the new has not arrived – an *interregnum*. It is in these moments of interregnum that divisions spread and our societies fracture. The rapid change of settling and farming created an interregnum that ultimately emptied Basta. As we will see, the fundamental reason why we are dividing today is because we are again in an interregnum. But we are jumping ahead of ourselves.

Nine thousand years after the abandonment of Basta, the next interregnum hit us. It came because our ancestors faced a change just as large as the transformation from foragers to farmers. Between AD 1750 and 1900, the Industrial Revolution's technical advances transformed Western societies beyond recognition. Millions of villagers migrated to the towns and cities looking for work in the new factories. These urban places expanded rapidly. The way people lived changed just as radically as when we had first settled in villages like Basta. Once again, in this 'new soil', the old agrarian common life began to wither away. Feast days reduced in number – in law and in practice. The village parish church was a long way away for the new urbanites, whose rites of passage became smaller, more family-focused affairs. As in Basta, as the old common life passed away but no new one sprung up, we again entered an interregnum, with no common life replacement to bring the city dwellers together. It would take half a century for a new common life – based on mandatory schooling, the workplace and clubs and societies – to arrive. The interregnum brought great division yet again. Distrust grew alongside fears of revolution. Individuals across Europe turned to demagogues, who promised safety, and the mob, who promised change. By the end of the decade, violence had erupted across Europe. In just one year, 1848, revolutions would take place across France, Italy, Germany, Hungary, the Hapsburg Empire, Prussia and Switzerland.

It was not until the second half of the nineteenth century that peace and stability would begin to return with the slow arrival of a new common life: that of many of our grandparents based on school, the workplace and clubs and societies. With a new common life to unite us, the interregnum ended, trust levels rose again and European societies become calmer and more cohesive.

The pattern is clear. When truly transformational change occurs – whether the move from foraging to farming (the agrarian revolution) or farming to factory work (the Industrial Revolution), the common life that has so effectively brought us together simply doesn't fit any more. It doesn't adapt and so it falls out of use. No new one springs up for many years. Societies face an interregnum – a period with no common life. With no institutions to bring people together, society fractures. Violence and conflict spreads. We are today in an interregnum. As we saw in Chapter 5, the common life of our grandparents is dying. No replacement has sprung up to connect us. If we are to avoid repeating history, we need to understand this better. What exactly changed when we became farmers and factory workers that killed off the existing common life?

The first and most obvious change was the size of the group that people lived in. As small nomadic tribes grew into thousand-people villages, it became impractical to involve everyone in *epeme*-like rituals. Rituals designed to bond the whole community together would now only be able to involve and connect some of the community. Rather than uniting the group, they would become divisive. Similarly, in the nineteenth century, when our ancestors moved from villages of thousands to large towns and cities of tens of thousands, traditional feast celebrations that had united a village would not stretch to the latter.

The second change that matters is to the economy. Consider the production of food for a moment. Nomads often sourced food through high-risk group hunting. Here, a lack of commitment by one member of the group could put everyone in danger. This made them keen on a common life that included highly demanding bonding rituals, which helped to demonstrate that everyone in the group was fully committed to each other.[8] In comparison, farming required much lower levels of trust. You needed to know that other members of the village wouldn't damage your crop, fail to follow through on a transaction or refuse to help in times of crisis. Painful and costly rituals now felt an unnecessary burden. On the other hand, a feast day where no work is done may be manageable for an agrarian farmer, who can store food up, but it would be a nightmare for a nomad who collects their food each day. In the same way, it wouldn't suit factory workers, who must work each day bar Sunday to buy the food they need. Instead, a common life based around the ever-present workplace and their children's schooling was a far better fit. The way the economy works also changes how people think about time and seasons. The nomad's sense of time is likely to be governed by the moon that she sleeps under each night. It therefore makes sense to the nomad that a celebration should fit around the cycle of the moon. For the villager, life is set much more by the seasons affecting her crops. A common life built around these seasons and the activities required in each, whether planting, clearing or harvesting, feels more natural.

The third change that matters is to people's beliefs. When you look closely, a society's common life tends necessarily to fit with people's view of the world. Many modern hunter-gatherer tribes maintain animalist sets of beliefs that require certain rituals to be performed. The Hadza dance the *epeme* in part because they believe it honours their ancestors. In comparison, agrarian societies, which increasingly sought to control the animal world, rejected animalist beliefs. In their place, new beliefs in the existence of one all-powerful, all-knowing God became common among agrarians, as well as convictions validating inequality of status. These beliefs fitted well with a common life largely organised by high-status priests and based around religious services, religious feasts and largely religious rites of passage. Such a common life would have been rejected out of hand by animalist, egalitarian nomads. The industrial era, in comparison, was more secular. A common life based around religion became harder to maintain. However, a new set of beliefs rose up in the cities underlining the importance of education and personal improvement. It is no coincidence that this new common life was based around the school, the workplace and the network-enhancing club and society.

The fourth change that has an impact is the rise of competition for an individual's time. Eating together each night by the fire, the Hadza faced scant competition for their attention to the monthly *epeme*. For agrarian villagers, however, the attraction of having one's own warm, enclosed settlement would loom large on a cold winter's evening. If a common life was to succeed in the agrarian age, it would have to out-compete alternative attractions. Sure enough, the successful new institutions either rely on strong social pressure – like the religious meeting – or provide opportunities to drink and have fun, which feasts and rites of passage did. In the industrial age, with its increasing work demands and leisure distractions, religious feasts and rites of passage struggled to gain enough attention. Clubs and societies took hold because they offered something of value – employment opportunities, social support and friendship. Outside of this, the common life of the industrial society relied heavily on the near mandatory activities of going to school and going to work.

The final change to consider is the movement of people. New arrivals to a community have been shown to be less likely to become involved in voluntary activities that make up a common life. This is not because they are somehow different. It is simply that in a new place we take time to settle, build a network and gain the confidence to take part.[9] This is also true of those who are about to leave. People who plan to move in the next half-decade are 20 to 25 per cent less likely to get involved in voluntary activities. They are less likely to attend religious meetings, less likely to volunteer and less likely to join a club or society.[10] What is striking is that the coming and going of people changes the behaviour of those who stay put. When large numbers of people are coming and going from a village, town or city, everyone who lives there becomes less likely to get involved in voluntary activities.[11] This is true whether those coming and going are moving nationally or internationally. During both agrarian and industrial revolutions, large numbers of people moved. In the former, people moved to the villages. In the latter, they left the villages for the towns and cities.

We have seen that rapid change can entirely disrupt a society's common life and that it can take many years for a new one to evolve. We have seen that the period without a common life – an interregnum – is a time when divisions rise and fractures occur. There are clear signs that we are in an interregnum today. As we saw in Chapter 5, the old common life based on schools, workplaces, and clubs and societies is in rapid decline and there is little sign yet of a new set of institutions that can connect us back together.

But are things changing sufficiently for this to be true? We have identified five ways that society altered during the agrarian and industrial revolutions. How many of these apply to the West today? The answer is that most of them do. The first and obvious change is the shift in the economy from manufacturing to services.[12] With services jobs increasingly clustered in the centre of cities, most of us – from the 1950s onwards – increasingly lived in a different community from the one we worked in. This meant, at least before the pandemic, far greater amounts of our time were being spent on commuting. This has continued to rise over the years. Between 1980 and 2013, the average time spent commuting in the US rose from twenty-two to twenty-six minutes.[13] Between 2011 and 2016, commute times increased in the UK from twenty-seven to twenty-nine minutes.[14] This meant less time to join clubs and societies – a main part of our grandparents' common life. Researchers have shown that just a ten-minute increase in commuting time reduces involvement in community affairs by 10 per cent.[15] If the coronavirus pandemic leads to a permanent change in our work patterns, this may improve things as well as causing further disruption.

Our societies' core beliefs have also changed. The beliefs and values that underpinned membership of clubs and societies, especially religious ones, have declined. Two trends in particular stand out. First is the decline in religious belief. In Britain, 2016 was the first year that the country had more atheists and agnostics than believers.[16] In the US, the latest generation of adults is the most non-religious in recorded history.[17] This shift has weakened religious clubs and societies that had continued to make up a part of the common life during the industrial age. The second significant change has been the rise in materialism. Since the 1960s, we have placed more and more importance on material well-being and success. In the late 1960s, fewer than half of young Americans entering college told pollsters that being well-off financially was very important to them. By 1990, this had risen to 75 per cent. In the UK, adults born after 1980 are twice as likely to agree that it 'is important to be rich' as those born before 1980.[18] This shift in attitudes away from cooperation, and towards personal success and wealth, is helping to drive the decline of more community-based clubs and societies.

At the same time there has been a huge increase in competition for people's time and attention. Too much of the discussion about division and technology has focused on social media, when we should have been focused far more on the role that television has played. It is hard to overstate the extent to which the invention of TV and now streaming has changed how we use our leisure time. In 1950 only one in ten Americans owned a television. Ten years later, nine in ten did. By 1970, we watched 20 per cent more than in

1960; by 1980 it was 8 per cent more than that; and by 2000 we were watching a further 8 per cent.[19] Today, the average Westerner spends around three and a half hours a day watching TV.

TV was the killer competition for the industrial age's voluntary common life. When it comes to disengaging from the local community, Robert Putnam describes TV-watching as the 'single most consistent predictor that I have discovered.'[20] Those who watch the most TV have become the least likely to get involved. They are less likely to volunteer, less likely to be an active member of a club, less likely to join a religious group. Perhaps a cynic might say that this proves nothing but correlation. Couldn't it be that people not involved in a club end up watching more TV rather than TV stopping them getting involved? The best way to put that theory to bed is to understand the history of Notel. Notel is a fake name given to a real place: an isolated community in Northern Canada. The fake name arose as, in the early 1970s, due to the shape of the valley that it sat in, Notel could not be reached by the local TV transmitter. This meant it had 'No Tel'evision. Researchers became fascinated by Notel when it was announced that it was about to gain access to TV for the first time. What made Notel such a perfect natural experiment was that, in all other ways, it was identical to two nearby towns that had been receiving TV for a number of years. The researchers tracked carefully the level of community activity in Notel and in the two nearby towns. Before TV arrived in town, the people of Notel were more likely to attend clubs and societies than the residents of the two neighbouring towns. The question was what would happen once TV arrived. Were the people in Notel more community spirited than their near-neighbours or was the lack of competition from TV the key factor? The answer became clear pretty quickly. Once TV arrived, attendance at clubs and societies fell. This was true of every age group. During the same time period, there was no similar decline in the other two towns. The difference had been the arrival of competition for people's time – in the shape of TV.[21]

Over the last half-century, we have also seen significant movements of population. The change people immediately tend to think of here is the increase in immigration. This has certainly been significant. In 1960, there were around 10 million people living in America who had been born in a different country. Today, there are 45 million. During the same period, the share of the UK population that was born overseas almost tripled. Alongside this, despite recent declines, there has also been significant internal migration – peaking in the 1950s and 60s. As a result, by 2010, Americans were 50 per cent more likely to have moved in their lifetime compared to those asked in 1940.[22] The most significant move of all has been a change in the location of half of the population during daylight hours. The movement of women to work over the last half-century – such a key achievement of the women's liberation movement – may not have changed where many people live, but it has moved millions of people from one location to another for at least most of the working week. This is a change very few of us would want to undo, but it is worth noting that many of these women would have been pivotal figures in the local daytime common life of their community.

And so, four of the five changes that we found during previous interregnums have taken place again over the last half-century as our Western societies have begun to deindustrialise. Our economy has changed – from manufacturing to services; our core believes have changed – from cooperation and faith to personal success; the competition for our time has changed – with the universal spread of television; and there have been significant movements of people – especially through immigration and women's movement to work. As we saw with the agrarian revolution and the Industrial Revolution, this new set of changes has disrupted the 'soil' that the common life operates in. This is why the voluntary aspects of our grandparents' common life have been declining. They have struggled to adapt to the new environment and no new common life has sprung up. And so today we find ourselves in an interregnum again, with no replacement to connect us and with fractures growing around us.

We have unmasked the first culprit. We are dividing because rapid transformation – of a like only seen twice before in human history – has disrupted the voluntary common life that brought us together. But this is only half of the story. Not all of our grandparents' common life was really fully voluntary. The clubs and societies were, but what about the school and the workplace? If change is the culprit that has killed off the voluntary common life, who is the villain that undid this mandatory common life? It turns out it is something we rather like.

CHAPTER SEVEN

THE TRIUMPH
OF CHOICE

A parent wanted to talk to me. They had just watched their child graduate and receive their certificate for completing the UK's National Citizen Service. First piloted in 2009, NCS, as it branded itself, had grown from a small community programme for 150 young people to the fastest-growing youth programme in Europe with just under a hundred thousand graduates each year.[1] I had written the curriculum and oversaw quite a lot of the delivery. If things went wrong, they were normally, in some way, my fault. Usually, if a parent wanted to talk to me, things were either dire or excellent. Luckily, this time it was the latter. The parent's foster-daughter had just completed the programme and it had made a huge difference to her confidence. We talked for a while about the programme, but it was the story the girl's foster-mother told me at the end that stuck with me and made me laugh out loud.

She had dropped off her foster-daughter for the start of the programme and – as parents of teenagers tend to – made a quick exit. Twenty minutes later, her phone rang; it was her foster-daughter. She wasn't totally surprised. She had seen her face when she first met her new team. Each young person on NCS is allocated to a team of eleven other young people – they are likely to be strangers and ideally quite different from each other: different schools, different parts of town, different incomes, different ethnic backgrounds. If we've done our job right, participants should look around and think: 'I have nothing in common with these people.' This is exactly what this girl thought. And so, at the first available moment, she made a trip to the toilet and phoned her foster-mum. 'You've got to pick me up. I have nothing in common with these people. Come and get me.' The foster-mother's response: 'What's that, dear? I can't quite hear you. Must be bad reception.' At which point she had hung up on her daughter and turned off the phone. And now, four weeks later, she was proudly watching as her foster-daughter chatted, hugged and celebrated with those weird strangers who had become her close friends.

One of the reasons that NCS works is that you can't choose your team. You can't put together the team of your dreams with your friends and the people just like you. And once in a team, you rarely see the other teams. This group of you and eleven strangers are all you've got. Twelve is a good number; it's a small enough group that it becomes hard to break off and form a clique. You are just going to have to get to know each other. NCS is effective because, once you are on the programme, there isn't much space for you to choose who to get to know.

As we saw in the last chapter, transformational change disrupts the voluntary common life. Over the last half-century changes in our economy, our beliefs, our entertainment industry and our movements have started to unpick the voluntary common life that brought our grandparents and their immediate ancestors together. However, our grandparents' common life wasn't entirely voluntary. It also included the school and the workplace. Transformational change is the culprit that undermined the voluntary common life, but it is not guilty for the loss of its more mandatory elements. The villain of this crime is something we tend to see as a friend, not a foe. The villain is choice.

Surely this can't be right. Having choice in our lives brings us such joy. I will always be happier if I can choose where I live, which job I do and whether to spend that left-over bit of money on computer games or gin. By providing a critical feedback loop to businesses, choice rewards quality products, drives innovation of better products, improves productivity and ultimately increases wages. I am loath to admit that it might be causing us a problem. What therefore is the evidence that choice is actually one of the reasons we are coming apart? Let us start with Schelling's board. If you recall, this is what the board looked like after we removed fifteen pieces and randomly inserted five new ones.

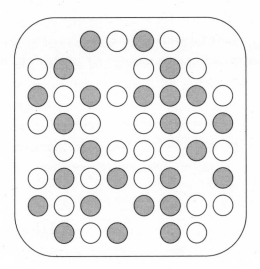

It was at this point that our divisions began. Grey and white pieces found themselves outnumbered two to one and chose to move to a free space. As a result, the board started dividing. But what if there hadn't been any free spaces for the pieces to move to? What if it had looked like this?

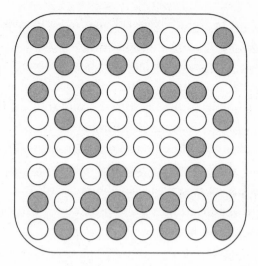

As you can see, I have filled all of the empty squares. As before, there are pieces that would like to move – six of them in total. I have marked them with an x in the picture below.

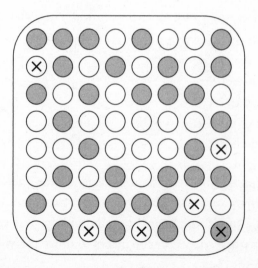

This time, however, they can't move. Not because they don't want to but because there are no options. With no empty squares to move to, they have no choice about what to do. They have to stay put. As a result, there is no knock-on effect on the other pieces and so the board never divides. It turns out that choice is absolutely central to the divisions that appear on Schelling's board. What about in the real world?

How much choice you have about who you hang out with depends on how many people are about. If you are stuck in a National Citizen Service team of twelve for four weeks, you don't have much choice. But if the group becomes larger, your choices expand – about who to talk to, who to be friends with, who to work with. If choice is indeed a key cause of our divisions, we should expect larger groups to be more divided. Is that the case? Surely the opposite is more likely? Won't a larger group provide more diversity and therefore be more likely to bring people who are different together? Let's take a look at some real-life examples, starting with schools.

Daniel McFarland, a professor at Stanford Graduate School of Education, and his team of researchers surveyed students across a variety of schools, asking them to name their closest friends.[2] They then used these answers to produce a map of all friendships. Sure enough, the larger the school, the greater the level of division. When people had more choice concerning who to be friends with, they were more likely to choose friends who were 'just like them'. 'Larger schools that offer more choice and variety are the most likely to form hierarchies and cliques,' said McFarland. 'In smaller schools, and in smaller classrooms, you force people to interact, and they are less hierarchical, less cliquish, and less self-segregated.'[3] Perhaps this result is particular to schoolchildren? We all know that our school years tend to be filled with cliques and groups. What about students at universities? Researchers at Wellesley College and the University of Kansas carefully mapped who was friends with whom within a very large university of more than twenty-five thousand students and four much smaller ones. They then surveyed the student body on issues of lifestyle – how much they drank and exercised, for example

– and values, including where they stood on religion, abortion and politics.[4] They found exactly the same result. In the larger universities, people tended to have friends with the same values and lifestyle as themselves. In the smaller universities, people had friends from across the spectrum. More people meant more choice and more choice meant more division. 'People would expect in bigger and more diverse places you'd come into contact with a bigger and more diverse set of people,' says lead researcher Angela Bahns, a social psychologist at Wellesley. 'But you find the exact opposite.'[5]

But perhaps the link between larger size and greater division is unique to places of education. It is commonly accepted that cities are the great melting pots. They are the places where difference flourishes, where different ideas come together and collide. Surely, therefore, the bigger the city, the more people mix and the less divided we become? I'm afraid not. Study after study shows that the larger the city population, the more divided people become. Let us start in the United States, where we find that the greatest division between income brackets happens in the big cities. The smaller the town, the more richer and poorer families live together. The larger the city, the more they divide. One study selected two hundred smaller cities and found that every single one was more integrated than the largest fifty cities in America. Every one of the ten most united cities had populations smaller than 300,000 people.[6] A further study found that if you wanted to predict how divided the rich and the poor were in a city, the most important fact to know was the city's size.[7] The same is true of our ethnic divisions. These are greatest not in small 'insular' villages, but in the bustling cities. The division is greatest of all in the biggest cities.[8] Just like schools and universities, the bigger the city, the greater the choice and the more divided the people.[9]

This should worry us. As Western populations become more urbanised, more people will have more choice about who to spend time with and therefore we should expect more division. In 1950, two-thirds of the world's population lived outside of cities, with just one-third in the city. By 2050, unless the pandemic causes a reversal, it will be the other way around.[10]

Aside from the size of the group, there is one other thing that changes how much choice we have about who we spend our time with. This is how much control we have over where we go and what we do. Returning to Schelling's board, his game assumes that the grey and white pieces have full control over whether they move or not. Remove this control and the pieces may want to move, but they can't. If they can't move, the grey and white pieces remain mixed up and there is no division. But does this also hold true in the real world? Is it really the case that when we give people more freedom of choice, more division results?

A good place to test this is by looking at those who have the most control over their choices: the wealthy and the highly skilled. If more control means more division, we would expect the rich and skilled to be more divided from those who are different than the rest of us. Is this the case? Yes, it is. It is exactly what we find. As Richard Florida puts it: 'College grads are more segregated than those who did not graduate from high school. The wealthy are more segregated than the poor – indeed they are the most segregated of all, and by a considerable margin.'[11] As people become wealthier and more skilled, they use their power of choice to separate themselves from the rest of us.

What else can we check for? It is easier to choose to change schools than it is to move house. Therefore, if having more control over our choices causes division, we should expect our children's schools to be fuller of people 'like us' than our local neighbourhood is. Again, this is exactly what we find. In both the US and the UK, children are more divided by income and ethnicity in their schools than they are in their neighbourhood.[12] What about if parents get more power to choose schools? If choice is really a key cause of division, we should expect schools to become more divided as parental choice increases.

Again, this is precisely what we see. Since reforms in the late 1980s, parental choice has been central to UK schooling. Parents are encouraged to select the school that most 'suits' them and their children. We see a similar picture in the US with the rise of Charter Schools and voucher programmes. Sure enough, the more choice parents have about where to send their children, the more divided the school system becomes. When there are more schools to choose from, we see more division. When multiple schools are within a short journey, we see more division.[13] When the system makes it easier for parents to choose a school, there is more division.[14] This is true in both the US and the UK.[15]

I propose a final test. There is one place where the cost of choosing who to be 'friends' with, who to 'like' and who to 'follow' is incredibly low. If freedom of choice causes division, we should expect social media to be the most divided place of all. Sure enough, given almost limitless power to connect with absolutely anyone online, we don't choose to connect with absolutely anyone. We don't seek out those who seem different and work to understand them. Instead, we click to follow those who we know, those who are like us and those who agree with us. We use social media to connect with people of the same ethnic background, the same type of schooling, the same place of birth and with the same interests as us.[16] Given the opportunity to understand different opinions, we search out voices that either tell us we are right or remind us of ourselves. This is true in the choice we make about where to get our news, what television programmes we watch, which blogs we read, but also which friends to follow and connect with.[17] Most Facebook users have online friends with the same political views as them. A study of 250,000 tweets by 45,000 American Twitter users identified two almost completely separate universes – one right-wing, one left-wing.[18] Researchers found that a liberal voter in the United States received nine times more tweets from Democrat candidates than from Republican ones.[19] One in five of us have unfollowed or unfriended someone online because we discovered that they had a different political opinion.[20] Those who have managed to maintain more diverse friendships online have been found to actively avoid political discussions on Facetime – including by spending less time on the site.[21]

It is hard to believe it now, but when the internet was in its infancy, many early champions believed it would increase understanding, empathy and connection. They imagined that the ease of connecting people would unite them and transform the world. In 1997, the head of one of the world's most prestigious academic bodies told a conference that the power of the internet would mean that children growing up twenty years later 'are not going to know what nationalism is'.[22] A leading technology journalist wrote of its potential to bring 'true understanding, connection and peace in the world'.[23] One technology writer described a new united 'wonderful human culture' that would evolve.[24] It should be obvious by now that increased choice has not led to the connected, single human community that the internet utopians imagined. Some are today arguing the exact opposite case: that the internet, and social media in particular, is the main cause of our divisions. This is equally over the top. As we have seen, it is the loss of the common life that has led to our divisions, not the birth of social media. However, social media has not helped. It has created a space where People Like Me syndrome is particularly powerful because choices about who we 'follow' and 'like' are unrestrained by social convention, chance and proximity. In this context, more than in any other, we surround ourselves with people 'just like us'. This, in turn, adds to the proof that the more choice we have, the more we divide.

In 1943, John F. Kennedy was twenty-six years old. He had grown up surrounded by privilege. As the son of one of the richest men in America, he had experienced the best education money could buy – spending time at Princeton, Harvard and Stanford. When he fell ill, he recuperated at the family's winter home in Palm Beach, Florida, which they kept as well as the summer home in New York. He seemed to succeed at everything. When he played sport, he flourished, representing Harvard at swimming. When he completed his graduate thesis – on British appeasement of Hitler – it became a bestseller on both sides of the Atlantic.

And yet, despite his uncommon wealth and success, his life was marked by an event that was common to young American men from all walks of life. In October 1941, Kennedy enrolled in the navy and became one of 16 million Americans to fight in the Second World War. By the summer of 1943 he was the captain of *PT-109*, a torpedo-armed patrol boat based in the South Pacific, when it chanced upon the Japanese destroyer *Amagiri*. Kennedy instructed his unit to launch a sudden assault. Turning to start the attack, Kennedy's vessel was rammed by the 2,000-ton destroyer and cut clean in half. Two men died in the collision, but Kennedy's swimming prowess and sheer determinism saved the remaining men's lives as he swam for miles with a damaged back from one small island to another, sourcing his men food, water and rescue. What was almost as remarkable as Kennedy's heroics was the genuine diversity of the men who served within *PT-109*. The American political thinker Mickey Kaus provides these short thumbnail sketches of the sailors who served alongside their privileged captain:

> Andrew Kirksey, 25, a high-school dropout who before the war had been working as a refrigeration engineer in Macon, Georgia.
> Leonard Thom, the left tackle on the Ohio State football team of 1939 and 1940.
> Loan Drawdy, 30, a machinist from Chicago.
> Maurice Kowal, 21, son of Polish immigrants, who had been working in a factory that built engines for Victory ships.
> John E. Maguire, 26, from Dobbs Ferry, New York, who had quit his job at Anaconda Wire & Cable.

George Henry Robertson Ross, 25, another Ivy Leaguer
(Princeton, Class of '41).

Raymond Starkey, 29, a former commercial fisherman who had
been working in the oil fields of California.

Charles 'Buck' Harris, 20, from Watertown, outside of Boston,
who had taken a job at Hood Rubber after high school.

Gerard Zinser, 25, a career Navy man from Illinois; during the
Depression he had joined the Civilian Conservation Corps.

Edmund Drewitch, 30, a jazz pianist who had worked as a steel
inspector at Jones & Laughlin and attended law school at
night.

Harold Marney, 19, who had finished tenth grade at a trade
school and enlisted in the Navy at 17.

William Johnston, 33, who had driven a trailer for Gulf Oil.

Patrick MacMahon, 37, a mechanic for the Detroit Street
Railway Company.[25]

The diversity of these men's backgrounds was far from unique. It was
matched in unit after unit, across army, navy and air force. While
Kennedy may have volunteered for battle, the majority of Americans
who fought had been conscripted. It was this conscription, this
restriction of choice, that brought men from all social backgrounds
together as allies. The UK's conscripted armed forces saw the same
level of mixing between classes and ages as did the continuation of
national service in both countries for a number of years after the war
ended.

Twenty years later, America's Vietnam draft, with its multiple
opt-outs and loopholes, was far from mandatory. While only 20
per cent of American men born in the 1920s didn't serve in the
Second World War, 57 per cent of draft-age men were excused
service in Vietnam or exempted.[26] Among the educated and
wealthy, an even greater number found a way out. As a result, the
Vietnam equivalent of *PT-109* was far from diverse. A diary entry

written by Second Lieutenant William Broyles captures the lack of diversity perfectly:

> I have fifty-eight men … reading through their record books almost made me cry. Over and over they read – address of father: unknown; education: one or two years of high school; occupation: labourer, pecan sheller, gas station attendant, Job Corps. Kids with no place to go. No place but here.[27]

With choice brought back into the equation, diversity vanished.

Over the last half-century, choice has become increasingly central in our lives. We can see this in the stories we tell our children – consider how many of the books they read and films they watch ultimately communicate 'you must be the person you choose to be'. We can also see this in the stories we tell ourselves. A search through every word of every book that Google has ever digitised shows the changing importance of the word 'choice' in our writing and thinking.[28] As the industrial common life began to settle into place from 1820 onwards, the word 'choice' declined in use. Its employment remained quite low up to the end of the Second World War. Then, as television spread, university education rose and the service economy started to replace the manufacturing economy, the use of the word grew and grew, as you can see below.[29]

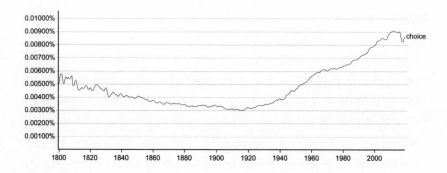

I don't want to turn back the clock. I don't want to go back to the 1950s or any other point in history. I definitely do not want to bring military conscription back. What I want us to notice is that the end of conscription is part of a wider story: the almost total elimination of mandatory elements of the common life in our societies. With the exception of jury service, there is not a single element in UK or US life where one has to spend time with people whom you do not choose to. This is a huge change in a short period of time. Many of our great-grandparents would have served alongside strangers in wars they had to fight in, learnt alongside peers from all social backgrounds in a local school they were required to attend and worked alongside a cross-section of the local adult population for one of a few local employers. We, in turn, have no risk of being conscripted, and have increasing choice over both the workplaces we aim to work in and the schools we send our children to.

Choice has become so central to our societies, its position so unquestioned, and the feeling of exercising it so pleasant, that it is easy to miss how unusual – in the sweep of human history – our present level of freedom of choice is. Ours is arguably the first society in which we can have complete freedom over whom we live alongside, work alongside, befriend, marry and live with. For most of us – in nearly all ways – this has been a great blessing. Choice helps us find the life we wish for, brings a life-affirming sense of agency and – in the case of schools – helps to drive up standards. Unfortunately, it brings with it an unwelcome side-effect. Our love of choice has bumped off the mandatory elements of the common life that previously brought us together. And so, together, two culprits – transformational change and the privileging of choice – have undermined the voluntary and the mandatory elements of the common life that connected our ancestors. Without this common life to link us, People Like Me syndrome has had free rein and it has started to pull us apart. We have found our two culprits. However, they have not been operating alone. Two trends have been aiding and abetting them.

CHAPTER EIGHT

THE DISTANCE
BETWEEN US

At number 40, on Northampton Road in Clerkenwell, East London, sits the London Metropolitan Archives. Amid its seventy-two miles of records, you will find papers from organisations as diverse as the Royal Society of Portrait Painters, the Foundling Hospital and the now-defunct Metropolitan Asylum Board. Among these, you can find a 700-year-old document, written entirely in Latin, called the Assize of Nuisance. The Assize records, in great detail, occasions when the people of London have found their neighbours to be, quite literally, a nuisance. Case 214 concerned Alice Wade and her partial invention of the flushing toilet. In fourteenth-century London, it was common practice to relieve yourself in a chamber pot and, when no one was looking, to empty the pot into the street. Alice had a better idea. She fashioned a long pipe out of wood and used it to connect a hole in her floor, where she had constructed a toilet, to the nearby rainwater gutter. Fairly rapidly, the contents of her pipe blocked the gutter, and her neighbours – who are recorded in the Assize as being 'greatly inconvenienced by the stench' – took her to the authorities. Toilets were a common cause of complaint; a later case was brought by Jean and Andrew de Audrey, who in 1333 asked for action to be taken against their neighbours as they had taken down the wooden boardings from their side of the shared toilets, thus exposing their 'extremities'.

One does not need the Assize of Nuisance or the five series of ITV's true-life *Neighbours from Hell* to know that living next door to one another does not necessarily lead to peace and harmony. As we saw in Chapter 4, living in the same neighbourhood as those who are different from you does not mean you have a common life. Even in the nineteenth century, when neighbours might often share a toilet and even be present at the birth of each other's children (although admittedly that happened to me too), your interactions with your neighbours would not naturally provide routine or intensity in the way the common life requires.[1] Consider the Hadza. They move and camp together, but it is the *epeme* that truly connects them.

However, where people live matters. While change and choice are the culprits for our present divisions, they have been aided and abetted by the growing geographical distance between us. These distances do not destroy the common life, but they make it much harder for it to bring us together. Consider the three pillars of the industrial common life: associations, workplaces and schools. It is far harder for these institutions to mix different groups of people together if everyone living locally is 'just like me'. Most schools draw their pupils from the local area and there is a limit to how far people will travel to join an association or to take a job. As we will see, across both the UK and the US, our neighbourhoods have been becoming more divided by income, education and age. The wealthy increasingly live with the wealthy, the educated with the educated and the young with the young. While there are some signs that our geographical divisions by race and ethnicity are slightly improving, they are not improving fast enough to make most of our neighbourhoods a genuinely mixed environment. If we are to be reunited, we will need a common life that can connect us. The growing distance between us will make that harder.

The fastest-growing divide of all is between rich and poor. In almost every Western country over the last half-century, those with wealth have become much more likely to live in a different neighbourhood than those without. Robert Putnam describes his 1950s hometown as a place where 'affluent kids and poor kids lived near one another'.[2] That is a rare occurrence today. The British geographer Danny Dorling has shown that, in the UK, those with more income and education moved further and further away from those with less of these in every decade between 1970 and 2000. This was true of every advantaged group: those with professional qualifications, those with advanced trade skills, those with degrees and those working more than thirty hours. Every one of these groups became less likely to share a neighbourhood with the less qualified, less skilled, less educated and less employed. No matter who was in government, no matter what the state of the economy, the rich moved away from the poor.[3] The richer the people, the more divided from the rest of society they became. By the end of the last century, the richest fifth of the UK were sufficiently divided from the rest to receive a Segregation Index score of 40. This means that four in ten would have to move home for them to be evenly distributed across the country. Among the richest 6 per cent, the score rose to 60. This is higher than the level of division between Black and White communities seen in the average American neighbourhoods.[4] The result is that rich Brits and poor Brits live in completely different environments. Consider someone moving from the poorest 10 per cent of neighbourhoods to the richest 10 per cent. Their new neighbours are so radically different – behind each door is someone who is fifty times more likely to have attended an elite university, twenty times more likely to be in work, and likely to receive an inheritance forty times larger.[5]

This is not just a British problem. The rich are moving away from the poor across Europe. A study of eleven major European cities found that, in all but one, the rich were distancing themselves from the poor.[6] The same is happening in America. In the thirty years between 1980 and 2010, the rich moved away from the poor in nine out of ten cities, across every region and among people of every race.[7] The change was not insignificant. Take the cities of the south-west of America as an example: the proportion of the rich who would need to move home to achieve an even spread rose from 35 per cent to 57 per cent.[8] The result is that more and more Americans live in either rich or poor neighbourhoods. In 1970, fewer than one in six urban Americans lived in a neighbourhood at either extreme. By 2009, one in three did.[9] In 1970, six out of ten Americans lived in a neighbourhood that pretty much represented America's average wealth. By 2010, just four out of ten did.[10]

Once again, it is the wealthiest and the highest educated who are doing the most to separate themselves from the rest. As the American political scientist Charles Murray has shown, they are increasingly clustering in a small number of zip codes that Murray has called SuperZIPs. These 882 neighbourhoods have become so full of the rich and well-educated that the average SuperZIP family has an income of at least $141,400 and almost two-thirds of the adults have degrees. Not only are the rich and educated clustering together in these SuperZIPs; these SuperZIPs are also clustered with each other. For a start, most of them lie in the north-east or south-west of the country. The bordering zip codes tend to be home to the very wealthy and well-educated. Almost eight out of ten SuperZIPs border a zipcode where education and income levels are in the top fifth. Only 2 per cent border a zip code where the income or education level is below average.[11] To demonstrate the level of clustering among the super-rich, Murray tracks down the 1979 graduates of Harvard Business School.

The 547 graduates ... included 51 CEOs, 107 presidents, 15 board chairs, and 96 others who were directors, partners, or owners of their businesses. In addition, there were 115 who were CFOs, COOs, executive vice presidents, or managing directors. I will consider those 384 to represent people who are extremely likely to fit my operational definition of the broad elite. Sixty-one percent of them lived in SuperZIPs.[12]

To make matters worse, Murray finds that the rich and well-educated are not just divided from everyone else – they are becoming more so. Comparing two sets of graduates from Harvard, Princeton and Yale, he finds that those who graduated in the mid-1960s had a four in ten chance of living in a SuperZIP, while those who graduated thirty years later had a five in ten chance. It is not only the elites who are separating themselves from the less educated. During the last three decades of the twentieth century, the odds of a college graduate living close to non-graduates halved.[13]

Alongside income and education, there is also a significant and growing geographical divide between our oldest and youngest citizens. In the main cities of Britain, the average child and teenager lives in a neighbourhood where just 6 per cent of people are over sixty-five.[14] This is in a country where 18 per cent of the population is over sixty-five. This division is pretty significant – it achieves a Segregation score of 50. In other words, half of all residents over 65 would need to move home to evenly spread pensioners and young people by age. In two of the UK's cities, Nottingham and Cardiff, the score is 60. This divide is deep and becoming deeper. If we split the UK population up into sixteen age groups, we see that eleven of them are becoming more cut off from the rest. This covers 85 per cent of the entire population.[15] The picture is similar in the United States. While divisions have not worsened over the last two decades, different age groups have become increasingly divided from each other since 1950 onwards. As a result, in the average American neighbourhood, adults younger than thirty-five are now as geographically divided from over-sixty-fives as Whites are from Hispanics, with a Segregation score just above 40.[16]

The largest growth in geographical division over the last half-century has been the sorting of Republicans and Democrats into different neighbourhoods. The American journalist and commentator Bill Bishop has described this extraordinary change as 'The Big Sort'. The best way to spot it is through the growing number of Americans living in counties – of which there are over three thousand – where one party won the last election by a landslide margin of at least 20 per cent. In 1976, when Jimmy Carter won the US presidency by a whisper, only 27 per cent of Americans lived in one of these landslide counties. By the time George W. Bush won, with an even tighter margin, in 2000, the share of Americans in landslide counties hit 45 per cent. When Trump won in 2016, 60 per cent of Americans were now in landslide counties. There has also been a huge rise in the number of Americans living in counties where one side won by a margin of 50 per cent or more. In 1992, just 4 per cent of Americans lived in a county that was this one-sided. By 2016, 21 per cent of Americans did. The UK may be less politically divided by geography than the US, but it is moving in the wrong direction. Take the Brexit vote. While the margin may have been very narrow across the nation as a whole, almost half of all voters live in a local authority where one side won by a landslide, leading by twenty percentage points or more. Tory and Labour voters have also become less likely to live near each other. Since 1960, the number of Tory voters that would need to move house so that they were evenly distributed around the country has almost tripled. The distance between us in terms of politics may have grown substantially, but it is still not as great as our distance by race.

To Eric Fischer, the census is a gift from God. Eric, who trained as a linguist, has a rare ability to communicate. His skill lies not in the mastering of foreign languages, but in his talent at transforming data into pictures. If you want to see where tourists and locals used to spend their time in London before Covid, Eric has that information for you – in one picture. If you want to know where people used to go when they took a taxi in New York City, Eric can show you a picture for that. Ever wondered what locations in a city inspire people to write a tweet and prompt them to post a photo online? Probably not – but Eric's got that too. Fortunately for us, Eric is also interested in where different ethnic groups live in a city, which is where the census data comes in. Using different-coloured dots to represent every citizen, Eric's pictures show in an instant the extent to which people from different ethnic backgrounds live in different parts of some of America's cities. I recommend seeing his pictures in full colour online; just search for Eric Fischer and 'Race and Ethnicity'.

Here though, in greyscale, is the most racially divided city in America as you have never seen it before. This is Detroit, with each dot representing a local resident.[17]

Now here is Detroit again. This time without any Black residents.

Downtown Detroit is suddenly empty. You can see the streets, but there are hardly any people – apart from in one or two clusters. The suburbs, meanwhile, remain just as populated as before – full as they are with mostly White residents. This shows just how divided the city is. White residents, and some Hispanics, live in the suburbs, and Black residents live in the centre of the city.

Academics have created a clever way to give this division a score out of 100. The score is created by asking a simple question: 'If the people of this city wanted to end any division and instead be mixed up completely evenly, what percentage of them would need to move to another part of town?' A score of 0 would be a city with no division by geography, a city where zero people have to move for all groups to be evenly spread. A score of 100, in contrast, is complete division – everyone would have to move in order for groups to be evenly spread. This score is called a 'Segregation Index'. Any city or town with a Segregation Index score greater than 60 is highly divided.[18] Detroit scores 79.6.[19]

Eric has produced pictures of the ten most racially divided American cities. More of us may recognise the city that comes in third:[20]

Look closely at the top-centre of the picture. You can see a river running down and to the left. That is the Hudson River. To its right, you can probably make out a thin sliver of land almost in the centre of the picture. This is some of the most expensive real estate in the world. It is Manhattan. Water goes all the way around the bottom edge of it and up the right-hand side. This is the East River. In the middle of Manhattan you can see a big unpopulated rectangle. This is Central Park. Right across the image, the sheer number of dots shows you how densely populated this part of the world is.

Here is the same city again. This time without any White residents.

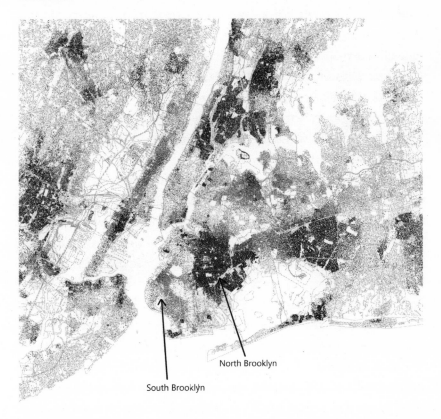

South Brooklyn

North Brooklyn

Let us look first again at Manhattan. Without White residents, the bottom half of the island is almost empty. Meanwhile, the top half – which is Harlem – has lost almost no residents. Turn your attention to North and South Brooklyn, which I have labelled on the map. Once again, you can see the level of division. Without White residents, South Brooklyn is now almost empty. North Brooklyn, meanwhile, has lost almost no residents. Taken as a whole, New York City has a Segregation Index score of 79.1, only slightly lower than Detroit's. The city often seen as the world's greatest melting pot is, in fact, strikingly divided.[21]

In describing this racial division, we need to recognise that more than People Like Me syndrome is at work here. After the Civil War ended in 1865, many Black Americans – freed from slavery – left the South and travelled north. They were met by consistent and persistent efforts to prevent them moving into White neighbourhoods. Partly as a result, between 1880 and 1940, levels of segregation doubled; a Black American became 15 per cent less likely to have a White neighbour. This improved not one jot between then and 1990. While PLM will have played some part in the resulting division, its role was dwarfed by active, racist and abhorrent efforts by some White Americans and the American state to prevent integration. These efforts evolved over time. Terror and murder – ignored or supported by local police forces and politicians – was the initial weapon of choice. Between 1889 and 1922, almost three and a half thousand African Americans were lynched across the United States, while federal efforts to make lynching a crime were rejected again and again by the Senate. By 1934, violence and threat became less necessary, with the newly created Federal Housing Association ensuring America remained racially divided. The new body, born in the heat of Roosevelt's New Deal, was intended to solve a serious problem: a lack of affordable, quality housing. It had two significant tools at its disposal: subsidies to reduce the cost of building, and mortgages to make the resulting homes affordable. The Association was a great blessing – for White Americans. Subsidies to developers were provided with segregationist strings attached – developers' plans were to be frowned upon if they led to greater integration. The Association's official underwriting manual, which all staff had to use, spelt out the intention: 'incompatible racial groups should not be permitted to live in the same communities'. To make matters worse, mortgages were not to be made available to Americans living in predominantly African American neighbourhoods. The intention was again clear – new housing was for Whites only. Excluded from access to credit, the only people who would sell a house to African Americans in the cities were contract-sellers. These unscrupulous individuals would buy a home cheaply, mark up the price four- or five-fold and then 'sell' it to an African American family. Ta-Nehisi Coates describes how the practice unfolded:

> Contract-sellers ... 'sold' homes to Black people desperate for housing at four to five times its value. I say 'sold' because the contract-seller kept the deed, while the 'buyer' remained responsible for any repairs to the home. If the "buyer" missed one payment they could be evicted, and all of their equity would be kept by the contract-seller. This is not merely a matter of 'If.' Contract-sellers turned eviction into a racket and would structure contracts so that sudden expenses guaranteed eviction. Then the seller would fish for another Black family desperate for housing, rinse and repeat.[22]

The discrimination in lending practices that enabled this evil remained legal right up until the 1974 Equal Credit Opportunity Act. Alongside politicians, officials, lenders, contract-sellers and developers, real estate agents were also complicit. African Americans asking to see houses in predominately White neighbourhoods were frequently told that the house had sold when it hadn't or were instructed to look somewhere else. The practice became so commonplace that it also had to be made illegal, which happened in the 1968 Fair Housing Act. While research has shown that the practice is decreasingly common today, Black home-seekers continue to be around 5 per cent less likely to be shown properties than Whites.

With these laws now in place, we might expect the level of racial division to start to reduce. In actuality, the reduction has been remarkably small.[23] Over fifty years after the passing of the Fair Housing Act, more than half of all Americans would need to move for neighbourhoods to fully mix communities. In some places, there has been no progress at all; the average Chicago neighbourhood was in fact more divided in 2010 than it had been in 1950.[24] As a result, White people and Black people continue to live in incredibly different neighbourhoods. While the average Black American lives in a neighbourhood that is 35 per cent White and 45 per cent Black, the average White American lives in a neighbourhood that is 75 per cent White and just 8 per cent Black.

This reality of this division is captured perfectly in a description by journalist Brian Resnick of the place he grew up – Nassau County in New York State:

Two villages, Hempstead and Garden City, lie adjacent to one another in Nassau County. Garden City is 88 percent white; Hempstead is 92 percent black and Hispanic (split about evenly). The transition between the two villages occurs within one block, a visual whiplash … 'Nassau County is becoming more diverse,' says John Logan, a Brown University sociologist who has been studying demographics since the 1970s. 'But within Nassau County … the predominantly minority areas are becoming more minority. And the predominantly white areas are staying mostly white.' … [This] is the story of the nation's suburbs at large. Zoom way out, and it looks like the suburbs are becoming more diverse … But zoom in, block by block, and you see that within those suburbs, stark segregational divides like the one between Hempstead and Garden City still exist.[25]

While the level of geographic division between Black and White Americans improves glacially, a new set of divisions has remained largely constant and increased in importance. Over the last thirty years, Hispanic and Asian populations have grown by over 350 per cent.[26] They now make up one-fifth of the American population. Without the same history, the level of division between these populations and the White population has remained persistently high and has not declined as the population has increased. Between 1980 and 2010, the Segregation Index score for Whites and Hispanics fell by just two from 50 to 48 per cent. During the same period, the score for Whites and Asians stayed constant at 41 per cent.

The UK suffers from a very similar level of geographical division between ethnic groups. Its capital, London, like New York, has often been seen as a melting pot for different ethnic groups, yet in some cases it is more divided that the average American city. Asian communities in London have Segregation Index scores of between 51 and 66 (far above Asian communities in America).[27] Black communities in London may be somewhat less geographically divided from Whites than they are in America, but there is not much here to shout about. In fact, Black and White communities in the UK are more geographically divided than American Latino communities are from White people.[28] Even this may actually be painting too rosy a picture. Many of those who work and spend time in London have tended to commute from some distance away. If one draws a 100 km ring around London to include most commutable towns and villages, a picture of White Britons in one area and minority Britons in another becomes clearer. If you wanted to create an even distribution of Black and White people in this larger area, you would need a higher proportion of these populations to move than in most American cities – at around 58 per cent.[29] The number of Asians that would need to move is even higher still.[30]

Looking at the country as a whole, there is some good news in the UK. Non-White ethnic groups are spreading out around the country and – in this sense – divisions are reducing.[31] The bad news is that, as this happens, White communities are choosing to leave areas that are becoming less White. In other words, Black, Asian and non-British White communities[32] are gradually spreading out and living among each other, while British Whites are tending to leave the newly diverse areas where this is happening. The result is that we increasingly have two types of places in the UK: areas that remain almost entirely White British and areas that bring together a growing number of ethnic-minority Brits with a decreasing number of White Brits. Some of these movements by the British White community are striking. If London were made up of only white Brits, it would have actually declined in size during the 2000s. While the overall size of London grew from 7.3 million in 2001 to 8.2 million in 2011, the number of White Brits fell by half a million. The majority of those who left London settled in areas that were much less mixed.

Of course, people have always come and gone from London and we would expect – as the population overall becomes more diverse – for the share of Whites to fall. However, it is still of note that the number of Whites coming into the city is failing to keep up with the number who are leaving. Also striking is that the decline in the White population is greatest in the London boroughs that have the largest minority populations. In just ten years, the London boroughs of Newham, Redbridge, and Barking and Dagenham have seen around a third of their White population leave. This pattern is repeated across the country, with areas as different as Slough, Birmingham and Leicester all seeing their White population fall by over 20 per cent, in Slough's case by 40 per cent. In comparison, areas that have high White populations have hardly seen any change; both Allerdale and Redcar, which were 98 per cent White British in 2001, saw a decrease of less than 1 per cent.[33] What is the consequence of all this? Ultimately it means that Brits who are not White tend to live in communities where White people are relatively few in number and declining. In 2001, only a quarter of non-Whites lived in areas where Whites were a minority, now almost half do.[34]

Stepping back for a moment, what have we learnt? We have seen that, in both the UK and the US, levels of geographical division by race are very high. Although this is improving in some ways – with ethnic minorities becoming less isolated – in other ways it is hardly moving and even getting worse. Race therefore remains our greatest geographical divide, but it is facing some growing competition.

Schelling's board, that we explored in Chapter 2, showed how easy it was for white and grey pieces – influenced by People Like Me syndrome – to move slowly away from each other until the board was divided. We have seen in this chapter these forces at work, as rich have moved away from poor, educated away from less educated, and old and young away from each other. Alongside this we have seen the continuing consequences of racist housing policies and purposeful racial division alongside continued moves by Whites away from places where they feel in the minority. The result is increasing distance between us and those who seem different to us. Nevertheless, the distance between us is not a primary cause of our divisions. Unlike change and choice, it is not a prime culprit. It is an aid to their work but not a core member of the gang. Why? Because living cheek by jowl with those who are different does not necessarily bring us together. We need a common life for this. A simple experiment conducted by Harvard University's Ryan Enos shows us this truth again.

Enos wanted to know what would happen to the attitudes of White residents in a mostly White part of Boston if they saw more diversity in their neighbourhood. To test this out, he paid pairs of Hispanic Americans to travel around the Boston area and to stop at a series of stations. One of the stations they were to stop at served the community that Enos was carefully watching. The volunteers were instructed to walk around the platform, talk to each other in Spanish, wait on the platform and then catch a later train. They didn't interact at all with local commuters, who simply came and went as normal. Nothing extraordinary or untoward happened. And yet, in just four weeks the attitudes of the commuters changed. In just a month, they became less supportive of Mexican immigration and more in favour of deporting illegal immigrants. Just bringing people together in the local neighbourhood does not reduce division. In fact, it can make it worse. The only way to overcome our divisions is through rebuilding a common life. The distance between us makes that harder but not impossible. It is an aid to our divisions rather than a core culprit. It is not the only aid.

CHAPTER NINE

THE DIFFERENCE THAT DIFFERENCE MAKES

One of the things we learn from history is that we humans tend to think that whatever period we are living through is unique. Our circumstances are ones that 'no one has ever faced before'. Each election is 'the biggest choice we have ever faced'. Each new invention is the one that will 'change the world'. You can see this tendency in the way that we think about diversity today. Many of us tend to assume that our societies are experiencing levels of difference 'unlike anything seen before'. In fairness, we are half right. Our societies do contain more difference than they did half a century ago. The situation is unusual. However, it is far from unique. Earlier, we told the story of the world in three eras: the nomadic age when we were foragers, the agrarian age when we were farmers, and the industrial age when we were factory workers. At the end of each of these ages and the birth of the next, our ancestors lived with a level of difference very similar to today.

Let us start with our move from foraging to farming. It is hard to overstate the level of difference that nomads would have experienced as they first began to settle into villages. People whose ancestors had cooperated with an extended kin of no more than a few hundred people began to live in communities of a thousand people or more. To a nomad, the diversity of habits, traditions and family relationships would have been unlike anything they had seen before. On top of this, as villages grew, diversity of wealth increased. Clerical and religious members of the society gained privileged positions and larger, more ornate houses to recognise their role in either directing the rest of the community or in overseeing the common life. Nomads had moved from a world where everyone came from a small number of families and owned next to nothing to a world where hundreds of people lived together and some had much more than others.

Thousands of years later, the Industrial Revolution would bring an equally dramatic rise in diversity. From around 1750 onwards, millions – in search of work and a better life – moved to growing towns and cities. In Britain, people came from nearby villages where they had lived and worked for generations.[1] In the United States, the change was just as dramatic – with families travelling to towns and cities from both rural areas and overseas. Immigration rose dramatically as new Americans poured in from across Europe. In just ten years between 1850 and 1860, the foreign-born population in America doubled.[2] For those millions starting a new life in the city, the experience of difference would have been overwhelming. In the village, their neighbours were people they had known since birth. Now, they were surrounded by strangers with new accents and different habits – people who had come from across the country and, in American cities, from across the Atlantic. Even within European cities, people would be encountering – mostly for the first time – people who spoke different languages. Consider France; the British writer Kenan Malik notes that at the time of the French Revolution 'only half of the population spoke French and only twelve per cent spoke it "correctly"'.[3]

This was not the only source of difference, for inequality in the new cities was much higher than it had been in the village, with extreme material and cultural differences springing up between the newly rich and the poor. To many of the rich and growing middle classes, the uneducated rural poor who were pouring into the cities seemed like a different type of human. In Britain, the future prime minister, Benjamin Disraeli, described the new rich and the urban poor as being so foreign to each other that they were 'Two nations; between whom there is no intercourse and no sympathy; who are as ignorant of each other's habits, thoughts, and feelings, as if they were dwellers in different zones, or inhabitants of different planets.'[4] One French politician in the middle of the nineteenth century described the rural French as 'not merely one, but several races – so miserable, inferior and bastardised ... their inferiority is sometimes beyond cure'.[5] An 1864 edition of *The Saturday Review*, a well-read middle-class magazine of the era, described the urban poor as 'a caste apart, a race of whom we know nothing, whose lives are of quite different complexion from ours, persons with whom we have no point of contact'.[6] For those remaining in the villages, those who had left for the cities soon became equally foreign. Urban life seemed to be converting their countrymen and women into people they didn't understand and couldn't entirely trust. The new city dwellers were a group who lived and experienced a life radically different from theirs. Family members who moved to the city would return changed and with extraordinary tales.

When foragers became farmers and when farmers became factory workers, they experienced a new world full of difference. Both revolutions – agrarian and industrial – brought with them rapid increases in difference. Our recent move away from the factory is just the same. As we will see, the transformational changes in our society that have happened over the last half-century have created a world full of difference by age, income, education and ethnicity. This may not be unique in human history, but it is rare and it is important. When it comes to understanding division, difference matters.

Why does it matter? Put simply, People Like Me syndrome only matters if there is some difference between people. A bias towards people 'like me' can't have any impact on my choices if everyone I choose between is equally like me. To put it another way, Sherif's boys would never have had any conflict at all if they had all been

Rattlers.[7] Schelling's checkers pieces would never have moved if they were all grey. Without difference (Rattlers *and* Eagles; grey *and* white pieces), PLM is powerless. A world in which we were all alike (same age, same education level, same income level, some ethnicity, same politics) would be pretty awful, but it is worth noting that it would be one where we wouldn't need a common life to unite us. This is a mad and thankfully inconceivable world – there will always be some differences in our societies. For this reason, difference is not one of the two fundamental causes of our divisions – the core culprits remain choice and change's destruction of our common life – but it is an important part of the story. As we will see, as our differences increase, it becomes easier for PLM to divide us. This is why it matters that whether we look at our age, our income, our ethnicity or our education, we are becoming more different from each other. One of the reasons for this change is in fact the most wonderful news – we are living longer than ever before.

Over the last half-century, we have seen dramatic (and very welcome) increases in life expectancy across the West. An average Western baby boy born in 1966 could expect to live to sixty-seven. Fifty-five years later, he can expect a whole extra decade. One in five will reach a hundred.[8] This means we have many more older citizens in our societies. Today in the UK almost one in five of us are over sixty-five. This is not without its challenges for our systems of healthcare, pensions and social care. One challenge that is often unnoticed is an increasing cultural distance between a growing number of older citizens with relatively few shared points of reference, or experiences, with those born in the last twenty years. This distance first came to my attention when I noticed how scared teenagers were of old people.

One of my favourite moments of the UK's National Citizen Service programme has always been when groups of teenagers are told that they are going to visit a residential care home for the elderly.

Organising these trips is not always straightforward. The care homes are sometimes nervous about having a group of teenagers visiting. 'Will they be very loud?' 'How many of them will there be?' 'They will need to be nice and polite.' The greater nerves, however, are always on the side of the teenagers. Most teens spend most of their time with other teens. Interactions with adults are often limited to figures of authority: a teacher, a parent, perhaps a policeman. Even older adults seem like a different tribe. Harold Pinter once wrote that 'the past is a foreign country'. Watching those visits, you could see what he meant. Old and young may be born on the same plot of land, but the countries that they were born into were very different as were their points of reference, culture and values. For many of these teenagers visiting a residential home for the first time and meeting someone seventy years older than them felt like a trip abroad.

This cultural distance affects increasing numbers of us. In fact, within twenty years, almost half of the people living in the UK and the US will be children or pensioners. Half of us will have two generations', and over forty years', distance between us and another quarter of the population. Increasingly, our societies will have three large generations of adults in it – eighteen- to thirty-five-year-olds; those between thirty-five and sixty; and the over-sixties – each with slightly different values, priorities and habits. Differences between old and young are, of course, far from new – but the size of our elder and younger generations is new – and therefore the number of people in our population experiencing this intergenerational distance is far greater than ever before.

Similarly, over the last half-century, the ethnic make-up of our societies has changed. A long and complex history that includes slavery, forced migration, colonialism and periods of relatively open borders has created the basis for increasingly ethnically diverse societies across North America and Europe. Continued immigration, and higher birth rates among new immigrants, have meant that the

White population has become a smaller majority. In the US, within twenty-two years, the White population has reduced from 75 per cent of Americans to a little over 60 per cent. In the UK during the same period, Whites have moved from 93 per cent to 86 per cent. A brief look at the children in these two countries shows why this trend will continue. Put simply, the younger population is much more diverse than the rest. In the US, White children now make up fewer than half of births and have done so since 2011. In the UK, a quarter of all school children are now from an ethnic minority. These numbers grew by a third in just five years between 2008 and 2013.

As these children grow up, their country's ethnic make-up will transform. By 2055, America will catch up with its one-year-olds and become majority-non-White. On the same timeframe, one in three Brits will be non-White, compared to just one in six at present.[9] The change will be most noticeable in parts of the country that have previously seen much less ethnic diversity. In the UK, around half of the country will gain a similar ethnic make-up to the one London has now.[10] A number of cities, including Birmingham, London and Leicester, will become majority-non-White. Religious diversity will also increase, with Muslim Europeans making up one-tenth of the EU population, compared to one-twentieth two decades ago.

Ethnicity and age are not the only places in which we are seeing a rise in difference. Over the last half-century, there has also been a significant increase in the levels of difference between people by income and wealth. In other words, inequality has risen fast. For the thirty years after the Second World War, inequality fell as increasing numbers of people entered the middle class. While the extremes of rich and poor remained, more and more people found themselves in a 'relatively similar middle'. In the early 1980s these trends began to reverse.

In 1979 in the UK, the richest 10 per cent of people took home just over a quarter of all pay. Twenty years later, they were taking home almost four pounds in every ten. Over the same period in the

US, the top 10 per cent went from taking home a third of all pay to also taking home four dollars in every ten. Today that has risen to four dollars fifty. Part of the story here has been the growing wealth of the top 1 per cent.

But more important for us has been a split that is taking place within the 80 per cent of us in the 'relatively similar middle'. A largely homogeneous middle-class group has been splitting into two groups: the higher skilled who are seeing pay increases, and the lower and medium skilled who have been struggling. The trend as a whole can be seen in the growing number of people leaving the middle and finding themselves doing low-skilled, low-wage work. At the end of the 1970s this described only a little more than one in ten British workers; by the end of the century it was one in five. Today it is one in three. This split means a real growth in difference as more and more Westerners, whether they are doing better or worse, find that their experience of life is no longer 'the norm'. This change is so important we need to understand why it happened. There are two reasons. The first brings us back to computers. The second takes us around the world.

In 1965, a computer scientist called Gordon Moore made a bold prediction. Noticing the advances in computing, he published a paper that claimed that the speed of computer chips would double every eighteen months. If true, the impact would be immense. If the power of a computer doubles every eighteen months, then within fifteen years it is not ten times more powerful, it is over a thousand times more powerful. Eighteen months after that, it is two thousand times. More than fifty years later, 'Moore's Law' still just about holds. This revolution in computing power has made radical changes to our lives. Most noticeably, it has transformed much of the world of work. Jobs that previously required a lot of lower-skilled labour – for example, typing or factory work – are now increasingly automated. They are delivered not by humans but by computers or machines.

When Moore first laid down his law, computers lacked the speed and the power to compete with humans at most tasks. With computing speeds doubling every eighteen months, this soon changed as computers became quicker and cheaper at completing certain tasks, especially those that are predictable and repeatable.

To understand why automation is splitting the middle class we need to avoid a simple mistake. It is easy to assume that computers will take over low-skilled jobs first. This is to miss 'Moravec's paradox'. Hans Moravec was a computer researcher, working in the 1980s, who noticed that it was far easier to get a computer to do some things that we find difficult than to get them to do things that we find straightforward. For example, it is far easier to teach a computer to play chess than it is to teach it to put the pieces away after winning. The reason for this is that the human brain has evolved to be remarkably clever when it comes to perceiving distance and judging movement. As a result, a child by the age of two can pick up and move a chess piece with ease. However, our brain is much less capable at analytical thought. The same two-year-old is unlikely to know how to play chess. For a computer the opposite is true. It is far easier to teach a computer the logic required to play chess, and much harder to give it the mobility and perception skills required to pick up the pieces. Moravec's paradox has a very significant impact on the real world. It has meant that middle-income jobs that rely on logic are more vulnerable to automation than lower-income jobs that rely on movement and perception.

This means that automation will affect the highly skilled, medium skilled and unskilled very differently. It is a great blessing to the highly skilled. Those with advanced skills that the computer still cannot perform become more valuable and their salaries rise. For the medium skilled, using logic to make a decent wage, it is the worst news. Valuable and well-paid jobs that they did can now be performed by computers. Skilled workers, such as bookkeepers, will find their work drying up. Unless they are able to retrain to a higher skill level, they will have to take a low-skilled job. These low-skilled jobs – involving movement and perception – will meanwhile start to grow as computers have not learnt yet how to perform them. This process can be seen at work in the taxi industry. Moore's law has enabled Uber, Lyft and others to replace medium-skilled taxi-firm managers and trip organisers with an algorithm. They have then hired a small number of highly skilled programmers to oversee the algorithm, and by bringing down the cost of taxis have created thousands of low-skilled, low-paid taxi-drivers.[11]

The computer chip getting smaller explains part of the rise in inequality; the rest is largely down to the whole world getting smaller. Over the last half-century, the cost and time required to travel around the world has fallen dramatically. Not only has this opened the world to tourists, it has opened the world to trade. Since 1930, the cost of transporting goods by sea has fallen by three-quarters, costs by air have fallen by 90 per cent and the cost of an international phone call has reached zero. The result of these changes is that it is possible, in a way it was not fifty years ago, for both businesses and individuals to move factories and the finished product across borders. Once again, this has impacted on the high, medium and low skilled very differently. For those with high skills, this change presents an opportunity to sell their skills internationally. With a bigger market, their labour becomes more valuable. They also become more mobile, which places pressure on politicians to reduce higher-rate taxes to prevent them leaving. For those with medium skills, globalisation brings competition from abroad, with jobs being relocated to poorer countries where workers are prepared to work for less money. With jobs moved overseas, those who cannot raise their skills, either risk facing static or declining pay or have to move into lower-skilled service jobs that cannot be sent overseas – like shop work, cleaning or delivery driving.

The shrinking of both computer chips and the world is correspondingly shrinking the size of the middle class. In the UK, those earning a middle-class income have fallen from 66 per cent of the population to 50 per cent in just twenty years.[12] In the US – between 1970 and today – the middle-income group has fallen from 62 per cent to 43 per cent. The consequence is a growing divide in income and experience between the winners and the losers. The Serbian-American economist, Branko Milanović, who has spent his career studying inequality, captures the growing risk perfectly.

If the gaps keep on increasing as they've increased in the last 20 years, you would end up with two types of societies within a single country. If there is no sufficient middle class and if the poor really are very far from the rich, then you really cannot speak of a single society.[13]

My father was the first person in his family to get a degree, and my mother was the first woman to do so in hers. When she studied – in the 1950s – fewer than one in twenty young Brits became students. Today this has changed dramatically; in the UK nowadays almost one in two Brits will complete a graduate degree and more than one in two will in the US. For many of these students (most in the UK), university will involve a move to a new city and life away from their family. For many, it will be the first time they have cooked, budgeted and lived independently. Away from family, these students create a new life for themselves far from their existing connections, family and identity. In the UK, where almost half of the population still live within five miles of where they lived as teenagers, it should not surprise us that this time away has a significant, lasting impact on how graduates see the world and the values that they hold most dear.[14] Compared to the least educated, British graduates are 300 per cent less likely to think that 'Britain sometimes feels like a foreign country', to believe that more Muslim immigration would threaten Britain's identity, to believe that women should be housewives, to not accept gay relationships or to believe that things were better 'in the old days'. This difference in attitudes was most clear in the UK's Brexit vote; nothing predicted your vote more than whether you went to university. A population entirely comprising graduates would have voted Remain by two to one.[15] The British commentator, David Goodhart, describes this as the greatest attitude divide in Britain today, writing: 'we have allowed ourselves to drift off into two separate and barely comprehending cultural blocs'.[16]

In some ways nothing here has changed. It is not new for graduates to have different attitudes to the rest of the population. What is new is how many people are graduates – 38 per cent of Brits and 34 per cent of Americans. This is a sharp rise. In the early 1960s, only 8 per cent of Americans had a degree – even fewer Brits did. It is also a recent rise. In the US, it has risen by half in just twenty years.[17] In the UK the number has doubled.[18] With half of all young people now attending university each year, these numbers will only continue to rise. When my mother attended university, she was part of a minority group – if a highly influential one. Today we instead have two large blocks of the population – those who have attended university, with the values that tends to inculcate, and those who have not, with a different set of values. Once again, we are seeing increasing difference within our societies.

So far, though, we have not addressed the main question. Does more difference mean more division? This is a potentially sensitive area, so we will tread slowly and carefully. Let us start with the rather obvious point we made at the start of this chapter; without difference, People Like Me syndrome can have no effect. In a city of clones, where everyone is identical, there can be no division on the basis of difference – as there is no difference. On a simple level, a country cannot divide between different 'types' of people if there is only one 'type'. If the Rattlers had heard rumours that the Eagles existed, but they were just rumours, there would have been no division between the two groups. If the Manchester United fans only encountered fallen

Manchester United fans, there could be no lack of compassion towards Liverpool fans. Let us be clear, though, what a miserable and dull world we are describing. One with a single gender, ethnicity, income level and age; one with no difference in political views or preferences and with no group identities or separate clubs apart from the overarching one of the state. Even North Korea would struggle to meet this hellish description. I definitely wouldn't want to live in this society. However, the underlying point is valuable: difference is required for PLM to kick in. One cannot be biased towards people who remind you of yourself rather than others if everyone is identical.

The second point worth making is that, as smaller groups in a population become bigger and the existing majority group becomes smaller, any existing division will affect more people. This takes a little explaining. Let's use a made-up example to help. Imagine an island of a hundred people where ninety-eight have black hair and I and my brother alone have ginger hair. Imagine that no one talks to me other than my brother and vice versa. The level of division is total – the two of us with ginger hair are just hanging out with each other. While this is unjust and mean, it won't affect many people (though admittedly it will affect the two of us a lot!). Imagine now that the number of ginger-haired people on the island increases so that we make up half the island. Imagine that it is still the case that none of the black-hairs talk to us ginger-hairs. Most measures of division that academics use would say that nothing has changed. The black-hairs still don't talk to the ginger-hairs. But the impact of that division is on a completely different scale. Now that ginger-haired people make up half the island, division defines the whole island. The point is this. As a population shifts from one large majority group to a number of equal-sized smaller groups, the impact of any division is much greater.

To put it another way, if university graduates keep themselves to themselves, the impact is less when there are fewer of them. As they grow to become half of the population, the impact of a lack of mixing and understanding between graduates and non-graduates becomes much more significant. The same is true of a lack of connections between teenagers and pensioners – as more of the populations become under eighteen or over sixty-five, this division becomes harder to ignore. And so, without any further division – the movement away from a population that is majority middle class, majority middle age, majority non-graduate and majority White towards a more diverse population made of low- and high-income groups; young, middle- and old-age groups; graduate and non-graduate groups; and multiple ethnicities will increase the number of people experiencing existing divisions even if the level of division hasn't actually risen. This doesn't mean that difference is a bad thing, just that avoiding division becomes more important.

What then about a more complicated question? Does more difference in a population lead to more coming together or more coming apart? In other words, as we become more diverse by age, income, education and ethnicity, does division become more likely? This is something we can test in the real world. Do we find that cities where citizens are more different from each other are ones that are more united or more divided? The evidence is clear: they are more divided.

Let us consider income first. Two significant studies have examined the income differences in America's main cities and explored how divided the cities are.[19] Sure enough, the greater the differences in income, the more it is that richer and poorer inhabitants inhabit different parts of the city. One study showed that the larger the group was that gained financially from automation (tech workers, graduates and people working in creative industries), the greater the division. The bigger this group becomes, and the more the middle class shrinks, the more the city divides.

What about ethnicity? Are more ethnically diverse cities more likely to be divided? Researchers at Brown University used 2010 census data to answer this question looking at cities across America.[20] They divided everyone in America into one of five fairly broad ethnic groups: Black, White, Asian, Hispanics and 'other'. The researchers then used this to calculate two scores. The first score measured how much ethnic difference there was in the city – the more difference, the higher the score. They called this the 'citywide diversity index'.[21] The maximum score for the most diverse city possible was 80. A number of the larger cities in America score highly here – getting close to complete diversity; New York scores 73, Oakland reaches 75 and Chicago 70. The second score measures to what extent people of the same race are divided. They called this score the 'neighbourhood diversity index'. Once again, the maximum score is 80. The higher the score, the less divided the city. A score of 80 means that every neighbourhood has an equal mix of the different ethnic groups that make up the city. Zero means that the city is completely divided, with each local neighbourhood having residents of only one ethnic group. Every city thus gains a score out of 80 for how diverse it is and another score, also out of 80, for how integrated it is. Let's look at a city and see how it works. I'll try Chicago. Chicago has lots of people from different ethnic groups: in fact, out of a hundred major cities, it has the seventh highest 'citywide diversity index' score in the US with a score of 70 out of 80. However, it is highly divided; its 'neighbourhood diversity index' score is only 36, ranking eighty-second out of the hundred cities. This means that Chicago is very diverse, but not well integrated.

Enough explaining. What do the scores show? Are cities that are more diverse, more or less divided? Fortunately, the statistician Nate Silver has crunched the numbers. The chart below is his and it plots the largest one hundred cities in America with its score for diversity on the x-axis and the score for division on the y-axis. Helpfully, Nate has put a dotted line on the chart. If cities didn't divide at all, this is where you would expect to find them.[22] The further away the cities are from this dotted line, the more divided they are. Unsurprisingly,

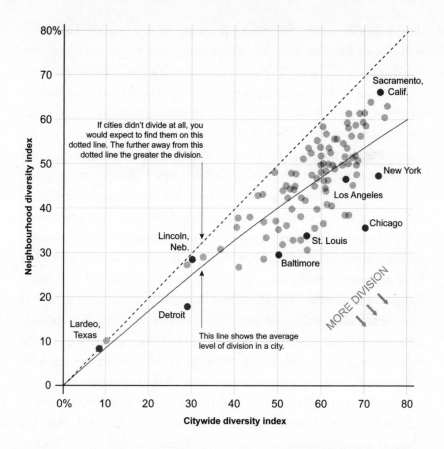

almost no cities are bang on the dotted line as almost no city is perfectly united.

If people within cities didn't divide at all by ethnicity, you would expect the cities to fall on the diagonal black dotted line. This would mean that each neighbourhood perfectly mixes the combination of ethnicities within the city. The further the city is to the right of this dotted line, the greater the level of division within the city.[23]

What is interesting is the differences between cities as to how near or far from the line they are. One can see that Sacramento is quite close to the line (less division) while Chicago is much further (more division). The key question is this: do cities become nearer or further away from the dotted line as they become more ethnically diverse? If they become nearer then more diversity means less division. The non-dotted line that Nate has added shows us where the average city lies. Look closely at it. See how it bends away from the dotted line? As the level of diversity increases from 0 to 80, the non-dotted line becomes further away from the dotted line. The picture is clear and affirms what we have seen about income diversity. As a city becomes more diverse, the level of division between ethnic groups rises. An even larger study by Maryland Professor, Eric Uslaner – this time of 325 rather than 100 locations – found exactly the same: the more ethnically diverse a community was, the more divided it was.[24]

As at previous times of transformational change, our societies have become more full of difference than before. All types of differences have increased – by income, age, ethnicity and education. It is ridiculous to suggest this is purely a bad or a good thing. Most of us feel very differently about our preferred levels of age diversity, income diversity, ethnic diversity and education diversity. Difference is fundamental to our divisions – People Like Me syndrome can't divide us if we all are identical. But none of us want to – or ever will – live in a society where we are all identical. Some difference is unavoidable and therefore all societies – as we have seen through history – need a common life to unite them. For that reason, choice and change are the main culprits for our divisions. Their destruction of the common life is why we are coming apart. But difference is not irrelevant. The more different from each other we become, the more important the common life and the more we feel its absence.

Now we have the full picture. The reason we fracture is because of PLM. It pushes us towards people just like us, creating bubbles and cliques. Over millennia, we have held back this destructive tendency by building a common life that brings people who seem different together. This common life works by using equality of status, intense and routinised experiences to convince us that people who might seem 'unlike us' are actually 'like us'. The reason we are dividing today is that two culprits have taken down the common life.

Transformational change has undermined the voluntary common life by changing the 'soil' so rapidly that it could not adapt. The rising importance of choice in our society has undermined the mandatory common life. Just like the early farmers and factory workers, we face an interregnum with no common life to connect us. Without a common life, there is nothing to hold PLM back and so we divide. This division is aided by two assistants: distance and difference. The growing geographical distance between us makes it harder for the common life to bring us together. The increased difference between us makes it even more important to have a common life. If we want to mend our fractures, we will have to build a new common life to connect us. Without it – as we will see in Part III – our societies will unavoidably continue to become less full of opportunity, less well governed, less healthy, less well-off and less safe.

Part III

WHY FRACTURES MATTER

*'It is hardly possible to overstate the value ...
of placing human beings in contact with other
persons dissimilar to themselves.'*

John Stuart Mill

CHAPTER TEN

SOCIAL MOBILITY

In the shadow of the 1929 Wall Street Crash, as millions lost their jobs, their life savings and their hope for a better life, retired American diplomat James Truslow Adams tried to capture in a few words what he feared his country was losing most. The Pulitzer Prize-winning author, still rich from the investments he had made, believed America was intended to be a place where 'life should be better ... for everyone, with opportunity for each'. He stretched for a simple phrase to capture what was vanishing and settled on two words: the American Dream. That dream is in trouble. Twenty years ago, eight out of ten Americans believed that if you worked hard, you would get ahead. Today, less than half still hold that belief.[1] The UK has become equally cynical. Just one in three Brits believe that the highest-paid jobs are 'open to people of all class backgrounds'.[2]

Our faith is wavering for good reason. In a perfectly mobile society, a child born to a poor family should have the same shot at wealth as anyone else. This would mean that a poor child would have a one in five, or 20 per cent, chance of getting into the richest fifth of the population. In the UK today, their chances are half this. Just 9 per cent of children born to the poorest fifth of parents will reach the top fifth.[3] In the US, the rates are even lower, at 7.5 per cent.[4] And yet there is a city in America where Adams' dream still seems alive. Where, if you are poor, your chances of reaching the top fifth are much, much better. Perhaps you can picture the sort of place? A large city perhaps, bustling with opportunities? Perhaps a diverse, creative location with a reputation for innovation? Lots of manufacturing on the outskirts to provide jobs for all? One of the highest spenders on school education, presumably? Undoubtedly majority-Democrat – with high levels of redistribution from rich to poor? Probably with a population that is left-leaning, secular, even hipster?

If this was your line of thought, you would be wrong. The city in America with Scandinavian levels of social mobility does not lean towards the Democrats. It is very strongly Republican. Seventy-five per cent of its population is White. There is no big manufacturing base. Instead, it is dominated by services. It is not secular. In fact, it is deeply religious. It is not ethnically diverse by American standards. And as for being one of the highest spenders on education, absolutely not. The state in which it sits spends the least – yes, the least – of all states on school education. Our social mobility utopia is Salt Lake City – the home of the Mormon Church and the state capital of Utah. Salt Lake City's success challenges most of what we think we know about social mobility. For a start, how on earth can the poorest children do best in a city that spends the least on education?

The answer brings us back to the common life. What makes Salt Lake City special is that, unlike much of the West, it has retained a common life. While schools across the country have become increasingly divided into rich and poor schools, Salt Lake City's schools have remained largely mixed – with richer and poorer children learning together. While the schools may be low in financial capital, they are high in social capital. While declining church attendance removed a key element of the voluntary common life across much of the West, in Salt Lake City, 40 per cent of people remain members of the Mormon Church. When Bloomberg journalist Megan McArdle travelled to Salt Lake City to understand the social mobility miracle, she found that the networks formed at church were central to it.

When she asked a local economics professor to explain what was happening, rather than expounding on his research he pointed to his church's recent decision to expand its boundaries to include a nearby trailer park.[5] In Salt Lake City, a common life of schools and church is providing something vital to poorer families: networks and connections. Young, low-income students learn and go to Temple alongside their richer peers. They have access to the same friendships, the same contacts and the same expectations. The result is a level of social mobility that countries across the West are investing millions to reach and still falling short.

Is Salt Lake City unique? Or would a stronger common life boost social mobility everywhere? Four economists – led by Harvard-based Raj Chetty – sought to find out. Over a two-year period, they recorded the salaries of almost every American born between 1980 and 1982 and compared them to the salaries of their parents. They split the country into 742 different geographical areas, and produced a map that showed where social mobility was high and where it was low. Then, using every piece of data available, they identified the five attributes that were most important if you wanted to have a high level of social mobility. Sure enough, two of the five are about the common life. The first was the strength of associations and clubs in the area and the second was the avoidance of racial and income division. Chetty and his colleagues found that these two attributes had more impact on social mobility than the level of local investment, the amount of redistribution, the level of university fees, the existence of university grants, the quality of university education, the employment rate, the size of the manufacturing industry, the number of skilled jobs available locally and even the amount of money spent on schools. Not one of these would improve social mobility as much as strengthening clubs and associations or reducing division.[6]

Alex Polikoff was volunteering as an attorney for a charity in the winter of 1966 when he heard the story that changed his life. While he was eating out at a pizzeria to celebrate his birthday, a friend started talking to him about the Chicago Housing Authority. The Authority's job was to provide housing to people in need. To do this they bought land and built homes. What Alex's friend had noticed was that most of the people being housed were Black, and none of the homes were being built near White parts of the town. The result was that the Authority was perpetuating the city's history of racial segregation. The friend saw it was wrong. It was Alex who saw it was illegal.[7] The legal battle that started that day lasted a decade. It ended with the Supreme Court ruling in Alex's favour. It is what happened next, though, that is most interesting.

The Supreme Court instructed the state to offer all Black residents the opportunity to move into wealthier, Whiter neighbourhoods. Between 1976 and 1978, three thousand families took up the offer. These moves had a dramatic effect on social mobility. Parents who moved became more likely to gain work. Children who moved became more likely to graduate from high school, more likely to complete college courses and more likely to end up employed with a high salary. What Alex Polikoff had done was give poor, Black families in Chicago access to the networks and connections that were all around in wealthier neighbourhoods.[8] The lesson was clear: connections between poor and rich families drive social mobility.[9]

Just two months after Alex Polikoff celebrated his birthday with pizza, the esteemed sociologist James Coleman left his academic life at Johns Hopkins University behind, checked into a Washington DC motel and closed the door to the outside world. Armed with one set of clothes and the ability to work with little sleep, Associate Professor Coleman was a man in a hurry. His mission was to change the debate on education in America. The Civil Rights Act of 1964 required a

176

report to be presented to President Lyndon Johnson and the Democratic Congress within two years. It had to detail the extent 'of equal educational opportunities for individuals by reason of race'. The President wanted to know what was going on in his country: were Southern states giving schools that taught White pupils more money than those teaching Black pupils? The job of writing the report had fallen to Coleman. By the time he checked in to the motel, he had just three months left.

Coleman had not wasted the last twenty-one months. With a team of committed students, he had conducted the largest survey of education the US had ever seen. A less ambitious soul would have kept it simple, producing a factual, short report on how money was allocated to different schools. A report like this would have done the job. It would have shown clearly that schools with mostly White pupils were indeed getting more money than schools with mostly Black pupils. But for James Coleman this was not enough. He didn't just want to know about the money going into the schools. He wanted to know about the results coming out. He was determined that his report would tell America whether their White children got a better education than their Black children. If they did, the report was going to say why.

This presented a problem. To understand the why, Coleman needed data on everything: family stability, quality of teaching, size of classes, the ethnic make-up of every school. It is hard to overstate what a huge task this was. Data of this type had never been collected at a national level. There were no records of school expenditure and no standardised tests. Even the task of posting, collecting and storing the questionnaires was a mammoth task; 660,000 questionnaires had to be transported to 4,000 schools nationwide and then collected back in. Analysing the data was no simpler. There was no established way to separate the countless variables that Coleman had insisted on collecting. Whole new statistical methods had to be created. Analysis took so long that it had to be performed on computers in Princeton overnight so that results could reach Coleman's hotel room by morning.

Coleman knew what he expected to find. With the Southern states dragging their feet on desegregation, he believed his report would show that Black children had poorer facilities, larger classes and less adequate teachers, and – critically – that this lack of resources led to worse results.[10] Eventually the analysis was done. At first, it looked like Coleman's instincts were right. Majority-Black schools were getting less money. Black children were doing less well. But – to his immense surprise – the lack of money did not explain the poor results. There were plenty of schools with lots of money that were doing badly and plenty of schools with very little money that were doing well. The careful, precise analysis that Coleman had insisted on revealed the truth. The reason Black children were doing badly wasn't down to money, teaching or facilities. It was down to the other kids in the class.

What Coleman found was that poor children did badly if the other children in their class were also poor. It didn't matter whether they were Black or White. A poor child in a class of other poor children did badly, while a poor child in a class of well-off children did well. As Coleman put it in the report he delivered to the President, whether a child succeeded was a 'function more of the characteristics of his classmates than of those of the teacher'. The priority, his report insisted, must be to ensure that the country had schools 'where children of all different social classes intermingled'. The President was not happy. His administration was ready to deliver increased funding to disadvantaged schools. Coleman's report was meant to provide the justification. Instead, it was telling them that they were solving the wrong problem. They did their best to ignore it.

Half a century later, Coleman's findings have stood the test of time. Study after study have shown the power of educating children of different income backgrounds together.[11] In the 1980s, two

American researchers, Robert Crain and Jack Strauss, showed that inner-city students randomly offered the chance to be bused to a suburban school were more likely to work in a professional job nearly twenty years later.[12] In the 2000s, the labour economist Jonathan Guryan showed that half of the increase in African American students staying on at school was due to schools becoming less divided in the 1960s and 70s.[13] Other studies even showed that a student's achievements at school were more affected by the family background of their classmates than by their own family background. Within a decade of each other, Alex Polikoff and James Coleman had uncovered the same truth: if you want to help poorer kids to get ahead and get great jobs, you need to get them living and learning with richer children. Just as we saw in Salt Lake City, if you want a socially mobile society, you need a common life. The question that remains is 'Why?'

A critical part of the explanation is prejudice. Ethnic-minority children are routinely marked down in teacher assessments and are less likely to be hired when they become adults.[14] Across the West, applicants with a minority-sounding name are half as likely to get an interview – even if everything else in their CV is identical.[15] We know that when people mix and meet with those who might seem different, prejudice is reduced.[16] Having a common life therefore reduces prejudice and provides fairer access to opportunities.

Prejudice is not the whole story, though, as a huge database in Sweden shows us. Sweden has the most amazing data on hiring. Stored on a single database is information on almost every hire made by every Swedish company. The data is so good that it is even possible to identify which hires and which managers were born in Sweden and which were born overseas. This data allowed a team of researchers led by Swedish economics professor Olof Åslund to answer a simple question. By focusing only on small firms where the manager named in the database was likely to be the one doing the hiring, they looked to see whether Swedish-born managers were prejudiced against non-Swedish-born hires? At first look, it appeared so. When given a choice, Swedish-born managers were more likely to hire Swedish-born workers.[17] One thing niggled with Olof Åslund, though. Small companies tend to hire people they know. Had the team discovered prejudice or had they simply underlined that Swedish-born managers tend to hire people they know and that they typically know other Swedish-born people. In other words, was it prejudice that was working against the immigrant workers or a lack of networks? The team found a way to check. They redid the analysis looking only at candidates who had previously worked for the company. This meant that all hires were people known to the hiring manager. Looking at this group, it now made no difference whether the applicant was Swedish-born or not. The issue wasn't fundamentally about prejudice, it was about uneven access to contacts and networks.[18]

Without a common life to even out this access, the rich don't just have more money, they also have far better networks and connections that help them to get ahead and stay there. In comparison, those with less money are less likely to know people who can help them to get on in life. They are less likely to know hiring managers, less likely to hang out with people with professional qualifications, and less likely to be friends with those who have the networks to tell them about job opportunities.[19] This lack of networks really matters because social connections are the main way in which people find out about and get jobs.[20] As many as four out of ten jobs are filled through word of mouth.[21] Lacking a diverse network doesn't just make it harder to find work. It also makes it harder to find the work that suits you and harder to get a decent salary for that work.[22] In comparison, people with wider networks – for example ones that cut across multiple ethnic groups – end up earning more.[23] They receive higher pay offers despite having the exact same skills. Remarkably, your salary can be up to 70 per cent higher if your network includes someone with a higher-status job.[24]

Today, Black African Britons achieve better exam results than White Britons. And yet they remain more likely to be unemployed.[25] Why is this? The cause partly relates to prejudice but it is also due to the lack of networks that ethnic-minority groups have. Both problems are made worse by not having a common life. This lack of networks holds back poor children from all backgrounds, especially those living in poor neighbourhoods. Such children are much less likely to have the mentors or role models they need to advise them on career choices or connect them to opportunities.[26] This has a serious impact on both their chances of finding work and their future income. British children who never meet someone working in business grow up five times more likely to be unemployed. Those who do work earn 16 per cent less.[27] Richer children experience a carousel of alternative career futures just by seeing their aunts and uncles or by meeting their friends' parents. Poorer children in comparison come to believe that 'people like me' simply do not take on professional roles.[28]

The lack of networks doesn't just disadvantage children. The impact is greatest on unemployed adults. The most common way out of an extended period of unemployment is by finding work through a personal connection.[29] In fact, if a long-term unemployed person gains a close friend who is in work, they become 13 per cent more likely to find work that year.[30] Unfortunately, the majority of the long-term unemployed have friends who are mostly either unemployed or in insecure employment.[31] Without networks to help them, they will remain unemployed. This poverty in networks is becoming most common in towns far from the main cities. As the knowledge workers we encountered in Chapter 5 cluster together in the cities, those in the towns are becoming increasingly excluded. With access to highly skilled workers becoming more important to highly profitable – especially digital-based – businesses, corporations are increasingly concentrated in areas that have a pre-existing, high proportion of skilled workers. Like a magnet, this is pulling both opportunities and those with valuable networks further away from those living in low-income areas. You can see this clustering effect at work in the UK in the growing economic, income and academic divide between London and the rest of the country. American academic and author, Charles Murray, describes the same effect in the US context: 'It is difficult to hold a nationally influential job in politics, public policy, finance, business, academia, information technology, or the media and not live in the areas surrounding New York, Washington, Los Angeles, or San Francisco.'[32]

Over the last few decades, Western governments have committed with fervour and funding to building socially mobile societies. And yet nothing has changed. The loss of the common life is the key reason why these efforts have floundered. Without a common life to connect low-income groups to the networks and connections that they need, improvements in social mobility will remain out of reach. Unless we are able to bring people back together, and more evenly spread the access to networks, our societies will feel more like two nations than one. We will have one nation where opportunities seem freely available to anyone who works hard, and one nation where they seem entirely absent no matter what you do.

CHAPTER ELEVEN

DEMOCRACY

Afghanistan, Colombia, Iraq, Sudan and Somalia – the stamps in Keith Mines' passport tell you that he knows a thing or two about civil war. Working for the UN, the US Army Special Forces and the US State Department, he has served in countries and regions plagued by violent division. In March 2017, Mines was asked by *Foreign Affairs* magazine to focus his attention on a country he knows well and estimate the chances of a civil war breaking out in the next decade and a half. With a heavy heart, he put the odds at 60 per cent. The country in question was the United States of America.

There is no greater failure of any system of government than the outbreak of civil war. For a democracy, the failure is greater still. To paraphrase Churchill, the fundamental purpose of democracy is to make jaw-jaw better than civil war-civil war. Through regular, fair elections, open debate and discussion, democracy's great promise is to resolve disputes without violence. If you disagree with the government, you can organise, you can campaign and you can vote. Violence shouldn't be needed.

If democracy is about how many elections you hold, America is more democratic than almost anywhere in the world. There are elections for presidents and vice presidents, for senators, congressmen and governors, for politicians at state, city and county levels, for judges and school boards, for mosquito control boards. In Duxbury,

Vermont, they even elect the dog catcher. One estimate suggests that there are over half a million elected positions across the country.[1] But the act of voting, by itself, doesn't make jaw-jaw better than civil war-civil war, as electorates from Sudan, Syria and the Democratic Republic of Congo can testify. A democracy must do more than just hold a vote. It must make compromise work. An effective democracy must have the backing of us voters to make trade-offs between our competing demands. A democracy must make compromise feel better than conflict. It must be able to decide – in a way we feel is legitimate – where to spend money and on what, whom to tax and how much, what laws to pass and what freedoms to grant. This legitimacy does not ultimately depend on how often the ballot box is used. It doesn't depend primarily on the people whose names are on the ballot. It depends on us – the people filling in the ballot paper and putting it in the box – and how we feel about one another. For democracy to work, we, the people, need to have a sense of shared identity, trust in each other and an understanding of each other's needs. As we will see, democracies struggle to work without these three things, and, as we will also see, maintaining this shared identity, understanding and trust without a common life is incredibly hard.

The word democracy comes from two Greek words. *Kratos* means power and *demos* means 'the people'. It literally means, then, 'power to the people'. The American Constitution begins with these three words: 'We, *the people*'. At the heart of a functioning democracy there needs to be 'a *people*'. Democracies can only make legitimate trade-offs between different preferences and needs if there is an overriding sense of everyone in the society being a group. There must be a belief that we are not just individuals sitting in the same land; we are a group with duties to each other; we are a 'demos'; we are 'the people'.

In my family, my children – after some fussing – will accept us all putting ourselves out so that one of them can take part in a drama performance. Why? Because we are a family; we are a group with duties to each other. At work, my colleagues will accept that when it comes to the annual budget, we might have to all find savings to support a new piece of work. Why? Because we are all 'one firm'; again, this makes us a group with duties to each other. We can make these trade-offs because we are all part of something bigger together – whether a family or a firm. The same needs to be true of us as a society if democracy is going to work. If we have no shared identity with the rest of the country, no 'us' that we all have an ownership of, no 'we' that includes everyone who votes – not just me and people like me – then why should any of us accept losing an election, let alone the trade-offs that follow. Why would you give anything up to benefit people you don't know? The only way we will do such a thing is if we feel we have some sort of shared duty to each other – based on a shared identity. For democracy to work, there must be a sense that we who make up our society are one group, that together we are 'we, the *people*', that we are a group where everyone's needs matter. It is this togetherness that makes us expect our elected leaders to consider the needs of every member of 'the people' equally – rather than just focusing on 'people like me'. It is easy to miss how radical this idea is. It means that we believe it would be wrong for our leaders to prioritise our smaller group – our family, our city, our ethnic group – above another. This idea is as essential as it is radical.

To maintain this sense of shared identity, 'the *people*' need to trust each other. When trust is low, voters start to think about 'them' and 'us'. They worry that someone else in their society ('them') is gaining at their expense, that 'they' are gaming the system. This belief undermines a sense of 'us' – of being in it together. It makes it rational to care more about getting 'my fair share' of the country's wealth than about making the country wealthier as a whole. The result is a society in which people care more about 'us' beating 'them' rather than about what's best for us all.

Without this shared identity and trust in each other, democracy starts to fail. The door is opened to leaders who wish to appeal to just one part of society – 'the good people' rather than 'all the people'. They may gain power through the ballot box, but they will then serve just that one group, feeling entirely legitimate in casting aside institutions that might force them to consider the whole country. I write this on the day after rioters have stormed the Capitol building in Washington. Without a sense of shared identity and trust, democracy shakes.

Shared identity is essential but not enough to make democracy work. We must also have some understanding of each other's needs. While democracy does not require everyone to have a deep understanding of the whole country, it struggles if most of the nation has a collective blind spot. If the majority do not understand the lives and needs of a particular minority – whether an ethnic group, social group or economic class – it is unlikely that an elected government will face any pressure to focus on their needs. Consider the UK's Windrush scandal. For months, thousands of people were threatened with forced deportation and, in many cases, were deported, when they had a legitimate right to be in the country. How did this continue for so long before the scandal broke? The main reason was that the vast majority of the population didn't know anyone affected. The majority of the White population were appalled when they understood what was happening, but hardly any of them had raised the issue because they had no understanding of what was going on.

It is also a problem when the public know about an issue but – due to living in separate bubbles – come to understand it very differently. Without a shared understanding of a problem, it becomes almost impossible for leaders to build the consensus needed to address it. Why do democratically elected governments lack urgency in addressing problems such as climate change, racism or poverty? It is easy to believe that the reason lies with the leaders not caring. In my experience of working with some of these leaders, the problem is just as much with us, 'the people'. If we lack a shared understanding of the scale and nature of a problem, we tend to support the idea that 'something must be done' but are unwilling to accept any of the necessary sacrifices. Issues like poverty and racism struggle to truly animate us unless we know and care for someone who is personally affected. Without the personal connection, we struggle to understand and we struggle to truly care. The result is that we might call on the government to act, but we will likely then punish them at the ballot box for any inconveniences or costs these actions bring, especially significant structural changes. This makes it incredibly hard for governments to act – with higher taxes or tighter laws – without losing the next election. Without a shared understanding among the people of the need for such action, elected governments will rationally choose to ignore chronic problems until they become completely obvious to everyone. At this point, it is of course also clear that the government has acted too late – which in turn leads to growing disillusionment with democratic government and democracy itself.

We have seen that a functional democracy needs its people to have a shared identity, trust in each other and a shared understanding of the country's challenges. What has that got to do with our fractures? The problem is that the latter undermine these things. Consider the Rattlers and the Eagles. Once divided from each other, the two groups of boys had no natural sense of shared identity. After a few days of competition, they felt almost no kinship with the other team. They saw the other group of boys as 'them', not 'us'. They started to become angry and aggressive just because they had to eat together. There was no trust. In fact, trust fell so low that the staff had to physically separate the boys for a day to prevent violence. There was also no shared understanding of the other team's needs. The Eagles suffered from homesickness but the Rattlers never knew. The Rattlers felt pushed around by one of their group, but the Eagles had no idea. In Robbers Cave, division undermined the three qualities that a democracy needs: shared identity, trust in each other and shared understanding. It does the same in the real world.

The best place to spot the damage that division does to any sense of shared identity is by looking at our taxes. These provide a good indication of how willing we are to spend our own money – in taxes – on services that benefit everyone in our society. If we have a strong sense of shared identity with others in the society, we are more likely to support paying for roads, hospitals and state schools. Why? Because the people benefiting – even though we don't know them – are felt to be 'our people'. They are 'people like us'. However, if we lack a shared identity with others in our society, we tend to want to keep our money to ourselves, and our family, rather than see it being spent on roads, hospitals and schools for people who we have no connection with. These types of expenditure – that benefit everyone pretty much equally – are often called 'public goods'. If divisions do reduce our sense of shared identity, we should see it in our taxes. In areas where there is more division, we would expect to see less money being spent on such public goods.

Sure enough, this is exactly what we see. Cities that are more segregated spend less on roads, less on law enforcement, less on parks, less on sewers, less on welfare, less on housing, and less on community development. Cities in the US that are more socially divided spend $100 less a year per resident. This is the equivalent of two-thirds of the average police budget.[2] We see the same picture when we compare countries. Countries that are more diverse – and thus, as we showed in Chapter 9, more susceptible to a lack of mixing – spend noticeably less on welfare payments and public goods. At the extremes, in highly homogeneous Denmark, government spending runs at nearly 60 per cent of GDP, while in more diverse America it is 39 per cent.[3] The same pattern is found within countries. Across America, cities and counties that are more ethnically and religiously diverse, and therefore unfortunately less likely to connect across divides, spend less on public goods and on higher education in particular.[4] Greater difference by age also reduces support for public goods; when the number of elderly citizens increases in a jurisdiction, public spending on education reduces. Strikingly, this reduction is 'particularly large when the elderly residents and the school age population are from different racial groups'.[5] A study in the UK, meanwhile, found that in areas where people were very similar in income and background, more poverty led to greater support for redistribution, but in more ethnically diverse areas the opposite was true. As needs rose, residents living in diverse areas became even less supportive of help being given – presumably because some of those in need were seen as people 'not like me'.[6] Wherever we look, the evidence is consistent; as we become more divided and feel more different from each other, we lose our sense of shared identity. We are also losing faith in each other.

Harvard's Robert Putnam was in Sweden to collect a $50,000 prize, but he had a confession to make first. He hated the conclusion in the research he was about to present. In fact, he hated it so much that he had spent five years reworking it. But the facts were hard to escape. Putnam had found that as diversity in a community increases, trust in one another falls. The analysis – published under the title 'E Pluribus Unum' (out of many, one) – was simple. It looked at the fifty states of America and compared the level of diversity in each one with the level of trust people had in each other. The evidence showed that those living in more diverse communities tended to 'distrust their neighbours ... to expect the worst from their community and its leaders, to volunteer less, give less to charity and work on community projects less often'.[7] The paper caused an immense storm. Before long the work was being repeated elsewhere with similar results.[8] It didn't seem to matter what the nature of the diversity was. Areas and neighbourhoods that were more diverse by income or by ethnicity had lower levels of trust.[9]

Putnam's five-year hunt to disprove his findings had missed one thing: the impact of division. Putnam had shown that areas that were more diverse had lower trust, but he hadn't checked what difference it made whether people in those areas mixed with each other or not. Further research shows that it made all the difference. Communities that were diverse but not divided had just as high levels of trust as areas where diversity was lower.[10] A growing number of experiments conducted by social psychologists has found the same truth: when people from diverse backgrounds, different income brackets or different political tribes take part in activities together, initially low levels of trust rise.[11] The problem for trust in a society is not diversity, it is the level of division. What Robert Putnam had found was the same conclusion as in Sherif's Rattlers and Eagles experiment all over again. Once groups are divided, distrust is likely.

This distrust has a profound effect on our democracies. In particular, it makes it incredibly difficult for our leaders to agree a compromise with 'the other side', even when it is the best deal for everyone. Compromising is easy when a disagreement is between trusted friends. 'I think a small rise is right, you think a big rise is right – let's split the difference.' It is a very different situation if the 'other side' comprises the sort of people who we feel cannot be trusted. Bill Bishop captures this in a story he tells of two legislators – one Republican, Duane Benson, and one Democrat, Tim Penny – trying to get a compromise through Congress.

> Benson recalled how he and a Democratic legislator had put together the rarest of laws, a compromise on abortion. 'The bill would have reduced the number of abortions, but it would have also guaranteed rights,' Benson said. 'We thought naively that we had the formula. It was a wonderful experience and we went through the whole process and we got two votes. His and mine. Because everybody else was pushed to their base.'[12]

This inability to compromise strikes at the core promise of democracy: that disagreements don't need to lead to violence or paralysis. In a divided society, where the people don't trust each other, reaching a compromise becomes elusive. This century, we will face challenges that we cannot ignore, from the aftermath of the pandemic to climate change, from economic shock to automation. Our present inability to make a legitimate decision before the crisis hits is one that we cannot afford. It is the consequence of our divisions undermining good government, and ultimately it reduces trust in democracy itself.

What about shared understanding? Do our divisions make us less able to understand the problems that people face? We should start by being clear that democracy does not require the people to understand everything. Most of us are delighted to leave most decisions with the government as long as we can kick out the politicians if they mess it up. Even referendum-hungry Switzerland, which held thirty referenda between 2016 and 2018, does not take every decision by a mass vote. Should interest rates rise or fall? Is this drug safe enough to prescribe? Which tank should the army buy? We recognise that we don't know and that's quite all right. But some issues are so important that they must go to the people. These tend to be the issues that get discussed at elections. Should we raise or lower taxes on the wealthiest? Should we restrict or ease immigration? Should we allow or ban gay marriage? Should we spend taxpayers' money on greater unemployment benefit or on apprenticeships for young people? Whatever issues dominate the election, democracy relies on 'the *people*' having an informed view on them. In a society where we have friends who are 'unlike us', this can feel like a reasonable expectation, not because we are experts but because we probably know someone who the issue directly affects. In such a society, most of us would have a friend or family member who is a higher-rate taxpayer, unemployed, young or gay. In a divided country, however, we are much less likely to have friends who come from these different walks of life.

How well can 'we, the *people*' be expected to understand an issue we are voting on if we know only people like us?

The answer is 'not well'. In our divided societies, we constantly struggle to understand where our fellow citizens are coming from. We tend to have a poor grasp of their values. During the pandemic we have tended to assume that – unlike us – others are not following the rules. In fact, most people have been. The Dutch believe that one in three of their fellow citizens think homosexuality is immoral. Only one in twenty do. They believe that around four in ten oppose abortion. Only one in ten do. We fail to understand how happy our fellow citizens are with life. We assume many are deeply miserable, whereas in fact they're not. The Canadians – who are actually the most accurate at making this guess – underestimate the number of citizens who are happy by a whopping 50 per cent.

We have a very poor understanding of who is in our country. The British, Americans, Germans and Spanish all believe that around a quarter of their countrymen and women are immigrants. The truth is closer to an eighth. French citizens believe that one-third of people living in France are Muslims. The truth is a thirteenth. The British overestimate the Muslim population by 300 per cent and the Americans by over 1,000 per cent.[13] We have a very poor understanding of what each other earns. We tend to believe that whatever we earn is about normal.[14] We therefore consistently underestimate the amount the richest earn and tend to think our incomes are all much closer together than they actually are.[15] We badly underestimate the level of inequality between racial groups.[16] We equally poorly understand the size of social problems. We overestimate unemployment by 300 to 400 per cent and teenage pregnancy by 1,000 per cent-plus. The average American believes that one in four teenage girls gives birth each year, when the realty is one in thirty-three.[17] These statistics illustrate the general lack of understanding. And yet, the bigger problem for a society without a common life lies not in failing *to know* the number of small-business owners, pregnant teenagers or recent immigrants; it lies in failing to understand what it is like to be a small-business owner, a pregnant teenager or a recent immigrant. The French separate the word 'to know' into *savoir* – which is to know a fact – and *connaître* – which is to know a person. It is the lack of knowledge of each other as people that we should be most concerned about.

At the turn of the twentieth century, two young men moved to the East End of London and became a source of fascination to their neighbours. The workers and their often-hungry children living in the nearby slums had no idea what to make of the two middle-class lawyers, with their private-school education and Oxford degrees. They appeared to have thrown away lives filled with opportunities. They had done so to live in a house they called a 'settlement'. The settlement movement – founded in the UK in the middle of the nineteenth century – bought properties in the poorest parts of the largest cities and used them to provide urgently needed services. They ran nurseries, opened schools and provided doctors' surgeries. None of this was their main aim, however. Their real purpose was to bring rich and poor together in a society that had become deeply divided by wealth. Sure enough, the movement's greatest success was not the nurseries, the schools or the doctors' surgeries. It was not the direct impact it had on the poor factory workers or their children. It was the impression it made on the two wealthy ex-lawyers. Living in the settlement gave these two privileged men a deep understanding of what it was like to live on the breadline in early twentieth-century Britain. It was a lesson they never forgot. Clement Attlee and William Beveridge went on to become, respectively, the prime minister and the lead thinker who established Britain's modern welfare state.

In a society without a common life, there are few opportunities to understand the struggles faced by people from different walks of life. Even if we know the statistics inside out, it takes a step of incredible imagination to understand what life is like for 'the other' if we do not know 'the other'. Without the sort of interaction that the common

life provides – that Beveridge and Attlee experienced at the settlement – it is all too easy to assume that those we don't know are 'up
to something' rather than 'struggling with something'. It becomes
easier to believe that all those on benefits are lazy, that all business
owners are mean and untrustworthy, that all teenagers are feckless,
and that all immigrants are frightening and numerous.[18]

Perhaps you feel I am being overly negative? Surely an effective
demos doesn't need everyone to know someone who's unemployed
to gain an understanding of the challenge they face. Can't we just
learn from our friends and colleagues? Some of us know some facts
and some know others. Surely, we just need to talk and listen to each
other a bit, or watch the news or read the papers. But what if all the
people we talk to and all the news we consume have exactly the same
views as us? This is the problem in our divided societies. One study
in America showed that only 23 per cent of adults have regular
conversations with people who disagree with them politically.[19] This
means that when we talk and listen, we tend to become affirmed in
our instincts rather than widening our understanding. Our existing
views become firmer, completely unaffected by the insights and
experiences of those who are different from ourselves. In a divided
society, the result of more talking about politics is not greater understanding but greater polarisation.[20] Nobody has shown this better
than James Stoner.

In the 1960s, Stoner, an American post-graduate student, became
fascinated by how groups of people dealt with decisions about risk.
He brought together a group of local residents and presented them
with twelve impossible dilemmas. Number 1 presented a dentist in
severe pain. Should he undergo an operation that will remove the
pain if it works but end his career if it doesn't? Number 3 was about
a chess player. Should she make a daring move that will bring victory
if successful but certain defeat if it fails? Number 10 was set in the
aftermath of a plane crash. Should a survivor attempt to rescue his

only child or try to save his wife also and risk losing them both? What surprised Stoner was that while individual members were prepared to take some risk, the group as a whole was incredibly risk-taking. Stoner was puzzled. Perhaps groups were always more comfortable with risk than individuals? When caught up together, perhaps people lose sight of their worries? Stoner decided to try the test again with a different group. In this group, each person was individually more cautious. They were all much less likely to encourage the dentist to have the operation, the chess player to take the shot or the survivor to try to save both family members. Stoner brought the individuals together. Having seen what had happened the first time around, Stoner expected to see this group also become more bullish once they were together. But the opposite happened. When together, this group of mildly cautious individuals become extremely cautious.

What Stoner had discovered was not that groups are riskier than individuals, nor that they are more cautious. He had discovered that – when individuals come from the same point of view – together they become more extreme. Experiment after experiment has found the same thing. Conservative students who join fraternities with other conservative students become more conservative. People who are racially prejudiced become more prejudiced when they discuss their prejudice with others who agree. Democrat-appointed judges vote more liberally when they are sitting and deliberating with other Democrat-appointed judges. In a divided society – where the people we know tend to agree with us – more talking doesn't increase our understanding. It increases our certainty. Where our neighbours and our friends tend to come from the same backgrounds and believe the same things, the more we talk, the more extreme our opinions become – whether about Brexit or Trump, Trans rights or immigration, unemployment or lockdown.

Some of us may feel convinced that we are different. We think we would avoid this trap as we have one or two friends with a different point of view. We would be wise not to overestimate the moderating influence of just one or two diverse views. A set of experiments conducted in the 1950s by American psychologist Stanley Schachter found that like-minded groups quickly ignore anyone with a different opinion. In fact, the more like-minded the group, the faster those with alternative views were excluded. To make matters worse, the experiments found that anyone 'converting' from the minority view to the majority opinion tended to become a minor hero, with the group commending their 'good sense'. The truth is that when just one or two opinions are different, most people either ignore the minority view or successfully convert those in the minority to agree with the majority opinion. As a result, the discussion simply affirms, applauds and makes more extreme your group's original opinions.

In our divided societies, with us talking mostly to people 'just like us', it shouldn't surprise us that we all think 'the other group' is utterly crazy on the major issue of the day – whether Brexit, Covid, the economy or immigration. But this lack of shared understanding makes it near impossible for any leader to carve a path through our present problems that the country as a whole can get behind. American commentator and author Bill Bishop captures the situation perfectly:

> We are living with the consequences of [a] great segregation ... pockets of like-minded citizens that have become so ideologically inbred that we don't know, can't understand and can barely conceive of 'those people' who live just a few miles away ... A segregated society lacks a common political consciousness ... Presidential candidates and op-ed writers often lament the lack of leaders, as if entire generations of Americans were born without the skills of a Johnson, a Franklin D. Roosevelt, or a Dwight D. Eisenhower. There are, of course, just as many leaders as there have always been. What the country is missing is old-fashioned followers.[21]

The problem is not our leaders, it is us, 'the *people*'.

Across the West, people have been losing faith in the democratic system. They have less and less trust not just in their present govern-ments but in democracy itself.[22] Those of us under forty years of age have become particularly cynical. Among this group, shockingly, only one in five Americans believe that a military takeover is not a legitimate response to an incompetent government. In Europe, this is only slightly better at two in five. Just a third of young Americans and two-fifths of young Europeans see civil rights as 'absolutely essential'. Most strikingly, young Americans and Europeans have become much more likely than their parents to see free elections as unimportant.[23]

The problem with our democracies is not our leaders. It is us, 'the *people*'. With us lacking a common life to bring us together, growing divisions have turned us into an electorate that also lacks a shared sense of identity, trust in each other and a common understanding of what needs to be done. Without these, politicians seeking to rule on behalf of us all are often outflanked by the tribalist who talks only to part of the country – magnifying their fears and promising their hopes. Mainstream politicians look increasingly impotent as they struggle with the almost impossible task of uniting a divided electorate that is increasingly unwilling to compromise. The tribal politician avoids the impossible task entirely. Her response to division is to address one section of the population – 'the *real* people' – and ignore everyone else. She accepts wholesale this group's understanding of the country's problems. To them she is a brave and decisive champion: someone who finally 'gets it', someone who isn't afraid to speak the truth, someone who will get things done. Freed from the need to appeal to the whole country, the tribalist can declare that the preferred solutions of their group are obviously right and that leaders of the 'whole country' are elitist incompetents, too corrupt or too cowardly to do what needs to be done. The rise of these tribal, populist leaders should not have surprised us – they are the consequences of a loss of shared identity, trust and understanding – the fruits of our divisions.[24] Their time in power will come and go, but their threat to democracy will not pass until we reunite our societies.

CHAPTER TWELVE

HEALTH

Stewart Wolf was used to giving talks. As a medical doctor, teaching at the University of Oklahoma, he frequently addressed students or local medical societies. There was therefore nothing immediately unusual about a trip he made in the late 1950s to speak to the medical society of the nearby village of Roseto. After the talk, the local doctor invited Wolf to stay for a beer as there was a medical puzzle he'd welcome a second opinion on. The puzzle was the entire village. Despite the doctor's urgings, members of the American-Italian community of Roseto, Pennsylvania, were doing their best to be unhealthy. Their Italian ancestors had cooked with a dash of low-fat natural olive oil; they cooked with lard. Their ancestors made pizza with thin crust and tomatoes; they used bread dough and sausages. Their ancestors waited until Christmas or Easter to eat sugary biscotti; they ate them all year round. They drank wine copiously. They smoked cigars heavily. They hardly exercised. Forty per cent of their daily calories came from fat. Far too many of them were obese or close to it. And yet, the local doctor had noticed something distinctly odd about the Rosetans. Hardly anyone ever had a heart attack.

This sounded extraordinary to Wolf. In 1950s America, heart attacks were the main cause of death for adult men under sixty-five. How could this small community – who ate, drank and smoked with

199

abandon – be immune? Wolf was fascinated. He gathered a group of students and assistants and together they checked the medical records of every person on record who had died in Roseto. They interviewed every person who lived in the community. They conducted blood tests on anyone who would volunteer. The work was laborious. The results were astonishing. Young men living in Roseto had no signs of heart disease. Elderly men had half the rate of the rest of the country. Ulcers were almost non-existent. Mortality rates were a third lower than in the rest of America. Why on earth were the people of Roseto so healthy? It clearly wasn't their diet, or the amount of exercise they took. It couldn't be genetics, as Rosetans who had moved away were no healthier than the average American. There was nothing special about the location; those living in towns nearby had the same mortality rates as the rest of the country.

As Wolf got to know the village, one thing started to stand out. Everyone in Roseto seemed to know each other. Rosetans frequently stopped in the street and chatted. Neighbours cooked for each other in their backyards. When someone had a problem, families and friends were quick to offer help. At the heart of all this kindness sat a set of institutions that bound the people of Roseto together and made sure no one was left out. As the author Malcolm Gladwell describes it:

> [Wolf and his colleagues] saw how many homes had three gener-
> ations living under one roof ... They went to mass at Our Lady of
> Mount Carmel and saw the unifying and calming effect of the
> church. They counted twenty-two separate civic organisations in
> a town of just under two thousand people.[1]

At the heart of Roseto sat a vibrant common life. A set of face-to-face institutions that linked the people of Roseto together. Wolf became convinced that this togetherness was somehow keeping Rosetans healthy. He started tracking the changes in the common life, the growth and decline of the various institutions, and mapped them against the health of the villagers. It took him two further decades to prove the link. He had solved the local doctor's puzzle. Wolf's discovery, however, presents another puzzle. Why is the common life, and the togetherness it builds, so good for our health? It is a puzzle solved in four pieces, and the first piece is about stress.

The North American professors Elizabeth Page-Gould and Rodolfo Mendoza-Denton have conducted a number of fascinating experiments about how we interact with each other. In one of the experiments, they gathered a group of volunteers from a variety of racial backgrounds.[2] Each volunteer took a series of tests that measured whether or not they had negative feelings towards people of different races. The volunteers were then split into pairs and asked to sit, chat and get to know each other. Half of the pairs had volunteers of the same race and half had volunteers of different races. Before the pairs met, and again afterwards, the researchers took a swab of saliva from everyone. They tested it for a hormone called cortisol.

Cortisol is a vital hormone for our body. It helps us regulate our blood pressure and blood sugar levels, supports our immune system, and enables the proper consumption of fat, protein and carbohydrates. Without cortisol, we would become exhausted, dizzy, weak and struggle to digest food. In order to keep the body in balance, we need more of it when we become more active. That's why the body releases extra cortisol when we wake up and when we take exercise.

Page-Gould and Mendoza-Denton found something odd in the swab tests. When a volunteer with negative feelings about other races was paired with someone from a different race, their cortisol levels rose during the conversation. When they were paired with someone of their own race, cortisol levels didn't move. Why would this happen? The volunteers were not exercising together. They weren't waking from a nap. There is, however, one other cause of a rise in cortisol. It rises when we feel stressed. What Page-Gould and

Mendoza-Denton had shown was that spending time with people we feel negatively about causes us stress.

Study after study has found the same result. When confronted by people we see as 'other' or 'not like us' in some way – whether because they are a different class, race, age, education or political persuasion – our stress levels rise. Surrounded by people who seem more educated than us, wealthier, of a different background, a different generation, our mind starts worrying, 'Do I fit in here?' At the same moment, our body activates a 'fight or flight' function, readying ourselves to run away or attack. As we discussed in Chapter 2, this reaction to 'otherness' is the People Like Me syndrome at work, hard-wired into us through years of evolution. One can just about imagine the advantage for our hunter-gatherer ancestors of an instinctive stress reaction to difference. When faced with someone who didn't look like kin, this instinct gave them a split-second advantage, making them first to react. Our modern inheritance, unfortunately, is a boost of cortisol when surrounded by people that we see as 'other'. This is the experience that perhaps you feel when walking past a group of teenagers waiting together for a bus. Unused to inter-acting with teens, your body readies itself. You become super aware of how many of them they are, how loud they seem. The background fades and your heartbeat rises as you walk past. It is not until you are some way past that your breathing slows back down again.

The problem with this reaction to difference, this sense of distrust and worry, is that long-term stress is really bad for your health, partly because you start overdosing on cortisol. The continued supply of it means that your body is constantly readying for an attack that never comes. It releases more and more sugar into the blood. Sugar levels rise, putting the pancreas under pressure and raising the risk of diabe-tes. Obesity becomes more likely as your body demands more energy, instructing you to seek out more high-calorie food. To prioritise the imminent attack, your body draws energy away from less urgent tasks such as fighting inflammation. This suppresses the immune system, increasing your vulnerability to minor ailments like a cold and more serious conditions including cancer. At the same time, it reduces the effort put into digestion. Indigestion becomes more common, as do stomach ulcers. Finally – and most dangerously of all – to ensure oxygen gets to limbs needed for fighting or fleeing – the body narrows its blood vessels, increasing your blood pressure. Perfect for an instant boost. Ruinous when applied chronically. Heart attacks become much more likely.[3] In short, chronic distrust of the 'other' leads to chronic levels of stress, which makes us much more likely to get ill. Our mental health declines. We become less satisfied with life, and – at the extreme – more likely to commit suicide.[4]

Fortunately, Page-Gould and Mendoza-Denton also found some good news. After the first meeting, the pairs of volunteers met two more times – chatting, playing games and getting to know each other. At the start and end of the third meeting, the two researchers once again took swabs of the volunteers' saliva and checked for cortisol. They paid particular attention to those who had had initially negative feelings about other races. Sure enough, during the third interaction, these people's cortisol levels hardly rose at all as they spent time with their partner. Just three meetings had been enough to largely remove the feeling of stress.

And this wasn't all. Page-Gould and Mendoza-Denton asked the volunteers to keep a diary of how they spent their time and who they interacted with on an average day. Most volunteers made no changes to their behaviour. But one group did. Those who had felt negatively towards people from a different race had changed how they spent their time. As Page-Gould and Mendoza-Denton examined their diaries, they found that this group, in their everyday life, were chatting, meeting and interacting with people from different ethnic backgrounds more than ever before. It had taken just three meetings.

The power of the common life is that it turns those who seem 'other' into people who seem 'like me'. For the people of 1950s

Roseto, with such a strong common life, the whole community felt as though it were composed of 'people like them'. When a group of people feels connected in this way, stress levels are lower and health is better. Just the feeling that your community is cohesive can make you less likely to have a stroke.[5] This is exactly how the people of Roseto felt. Living as they did in a cohesive community, united by a strong common life, chronic stress was largely absent, which is the first piece of the puzzle of why their health flourished, despite their diet. The second part is to do with loneliness.

Most division divides the world into 'them' and 'us'. For some people, the situation is worse than this. For those completely on their own, the world can feel like 'them' and 'just me'. Isolation is the most extreme type of social division. Over the last half-century – as the common life that connected us has declined – being isolated has become much more common, especially among the elderly. In both the UK and the US, we have seen a rapid growth in both isolation and loneliness, especially among the retired. Even before the pandemic, one in five British pensioners spoke with family, friends and neighbours less often than once a week. For one in ten it was less than once a month.[6] Just under half of all Britons over seventy told researchers that their main companion was the television. Isolation is not the same as loneliness – some people don't need much company – but for most of us, one leads to the other. That is why a tenth of doctor appointments made by an older person in the UK reveal no other condition than loneliness. In the US, a country where one in four people now live alone, a third of over-forty-fives have been found to be chronically lonely.[7] A former surgeon general, Dr Vivek Murthy, has become sufficiently concerned to describe loneliness in the United States as 'an epidemic'.[8]

The health consequences are significant. As we saw in Chapter 4, loneliness causes genuine pain, probably as an evolved prompt to make us socialise. Chronic loneliness is damaging to our bodies: it hardens our arteries, causing high blood pressure; increases inflammation, damaging your gut, heart and joints; and slows the production of antibodies, reducing the effectiveness of your immune system.[9] All of this makes you more likely to fall ill and, when ill, less likely to recover quickly.[10] You even face a higher risk of death; in some cases up to five times higher.[11] A review of seventy studies on loneliness found you were actually better off smoking ten cigarettes a day than being isolated and lonely.[12] In comparison, isolation was largely foreign to the people of 1950s Loreto. With their flourishing church, three generations living under one roof and vibrant civil society, the chances of getting lost between the cracks were slim. On to the third part of the puzzle.

The more time he spent in Roseto, the more struck Stewart Wolf was by how equal the community was. It was hard to find people with great wealth or in great poverty. Wolf, and his colleague John Bruhn, described Rosetans as morally committed to equality:

> The local priest emphasised [to us] that when preoccupation with earning money exceeded the unmarked boundary it became a basis for social rejection [by the rest of the community], irrespective of the standing of the person outside the community. Similarly, a lack of concern for community needs, especially by those who would spend their money on frivolous pleasures, constituted grounds for social exclusion. Rosetan culture thus provided a set of checks and balances to ensure that neither success nor failure got out of hand.[13]

The result was a society where there was relatively little difference between the way the rich and poor lived. This is the third cause of the Rosetans' good health. Outside of 1950s Roseto, across the West, poorer citizens tend to live separately from the rest. Both their friendship groups and their neighbourhoods tend to be full of people who are also struggling. Each of those factors is bad for their health. Let's start with the friendship group.

My three small children all attend primary school. Even before the coronavirus pandemic, my wife and I had got used to frequent coughs and colds. If one of our children's friends fell ill, it would only be a matter of time before we all had it. After the year we have all been through, we fully expect ill-health caused by a virus to be infectious. What we don't expect is for ill-health caused by lifestyle to be infectious. There is no virus for obesity, none for smoking, nor for taking too little exercise. Sure, we may talk about an obesity 'epidemic', but you can't actually catch obesity from one another, can you?

Twenty miles to the west of Boston sits the small city of Framingham, home to 70,000 Americans and some remarkable medical information. Every two years since 1948, doctors have collected medical information from two-thirds of the adults living in the city. They have also been carefully recording people's social networks, compiling meticulous records of who is friends with whom, who works with whom, who lives next door to whom and who is related to whom. The American sociologists Nicholas Christakis and James Fowler have become experts in the social networks of the people of Framingham. Together, they have systematically mapped over fifty thousand social connections involving more than twelve thousand residents. Having done so, they have sought to answer an extraordinary question: can you 'catch' obesity? The answer would appear to be yes.

Christakis and Fowler found that if a resident of Framingham had a friend who was obese, then they were more likely to become obese too. That was not all; a resident was also more likely to become obese if they just had a 'friend of a friend' who was obese. In fact, they were more likely to become obese even if they just had a 'friend of a friend of a friend' who was obese. The impact was strongest of all if the friendship was reciprocal. If both residents named each other as a friend, and one of them became obese, then the other was three times more likely to also become obese.[14] Studies of three other populations came to the same conclusion: obesity is contagious.[15] What on earth is going on here? Obesity is clearly not a virus. There is no bug that passes obesity through the air. No, what is passing through the air is a set of ideas about what is a 'normal' weight, what constitutes a 'normal' diet and what is a 'normal' amount of exercise to take. We would appear to set these norms based on the people around us. We come to eat what they eat, exercise (or not) like them and weigh roughly the same amount. If our friends are obese, we don't directly 'catch' obesity, but we do 'catch' the norms that lead to it. And our friendship circle doesn't impact merely on our weight. Data from Framingham shows that people are more likely to quit smoking if a close friend stops, or if a 'friend of a friend' stops or even if a 'friend of a friend of a friend' stops. The same pattern is visible for drinking – you are more likely to drink to excess if your friends do, or your friends' friends or your friends' friends' friends do.

Our networks don't just affect bad habits, they also encourage good ones. Researchers found that students are 8 per cent more likely to get a recommended flu shot if an additional 10 per cent of their friends have done so.[16] In fact, we are more likely to visit the doctor when ill and follow their instructions if those around us are doing the same. In short, your friends (and their friends, and even their friends' friends) make a real difference to your health. Citizens struggling to make ends meet face a level of stress that naturally leads to poor mental health, physical health and long-term damaging habits. They also lack the money to pay for healthy food, exercise equipment, gym classes and forms of entertainment that might displace alcohol or smoking. If our societies exclude poorer families so that they cluster together in the same friendship groups, we shouldn't be surprised if their health gets even worse.

The same is true if their neighbourhoods are places where only other people on low incomes live. Part of the reason for this is a lack of investment. Knowing that returns will be lower, businesses tend to avoid investing in neighbourhoods that are predominantly poor. These neighbourhoods therefore lack the private-sector investment that goes into more mixed neighbourhoods. Knowing that poorer citizens are less likely to vote or to have effective routes to complain, governments also tend to underinvest. The result is that, where the need is greatest, less is spent on reducing pollution, designing and constructing housing and maintaining rented homes. There are also fewer places to buy healthy food and fewer places to exercise. Every one of these factors has a negative impact on residents' health. The final factor at work here is violent crime. Violent crime tends to cluster in areas where those lacking access to money live. The sense of hopelessness and a lack of alternatives creates demand for the drugs trade, and the violence, and policing response, that follow it. The result is more anxiety, more stress, more ill-health and even more reason for businesses to avoid investing in the area.

The neighbourhood that you live in and the company that you keep has a huge impact on your health. This is the third part of the puzzle. In 1950s Roseto, those with less were not excluded or clustered. They lived cheek by jowl alongside everyone else. They joined the same clubs. They attended the same church. They had equal status in a society that disapproved just as much of a lack of generosity as of a lack of self-improvement. In the rest of the world, where those with less find themselves increasingly cut off from the rest, we should not be surprised when these citizens' health worsens and their life expectancy falls. This leaves just one final part of the puzzle, which comes down to trust.

Levels of health in the UK and the US don't just vary by wealth. They also vary significantly by ethnic group. In the US, Black people and Native Americans have persistently worse health than White communities.[17] In the UK, Pakistani, Bangladeshi and Black Caribbean citizens have poorer health than the rest.[18] Asian men and women in particular are more likely both to suffer a long-standing illness and to report acute sickness.[19] Mothers born outside the UK are more likely to lose a child in the first year of their life than mothers born in the UK.[20] There are many potential causes of this disparity, from access to healthcare to diet, institutional racism to knowledge of the healthcare system. I would like to focus on one cause in particular: the impact of racial division.

We know, from research in the US, that where doctors and patients have different ethnic backgrounds, the patient–doctor relationship is worse. On average, there is less trust in the relationship, fewer attempts at relationship building, and less joint decision-making.[21] Critically, there is also worse diagnosis and less effective prescribing when patient and doctor are from different ethnic groups. Because doctors tend to be White, this is a problem that mostly affects ethnic-minority patients; Black Americans have three-quarters of their medical interactions with healthcare workers of a different ethnic background.[22] When prejudice is present in these relationships, the results can be very serious. One study found that White doctors, who had a small subconscious bias in favour of Whites over minorities, were less likely to recommend minority patients the appropriate drugs, even when the patient had the symptoms of a heart attack.[23]

As we have seen, these biases are reduced when people from different ethnic groups mix. In a divided society, however, this contact is less frequent. Bias is more likely. The result is worse healthcare for minority groups. As our societies become more ethnically diverse, the number of medical appointments where patient and doctor are from different ethnic groups will increase. Unless there is greater mixing between ethnic groups, the negative impact of biases and distrust is likely to increase.

For 1950s Roseto, healthcare appointments where doctor and patient were from different ethnic groups were very unusual. Not only were most residents Italian-American, but nearly all of them could trace their ancestry back to a single small town in central Italy, called, of course, Roseto. And yet, had they been a more ethnically diverse society, the common life at the heart of the village would have provided the means for Rosetans of all races to mix, meet and build the trust needed to diminish biases. This trust between doctor and patient – even if Roseto patients ignored the dietary advice – is the fourth part of the puzzle.

Before Wolf's team of researchers set to work, the secret of Roseto's good health remained hidden. The secret had been hiding in full view. It was the village's common life. The church, the local societies and the shared houses brought the people of Roseto together. By doing so, they had protected the villagers from stress, loneliness, exclusion and distrust. In some ways, Roseto has not changed much since the 1950s: diets remain just as unhealthy, cigars are still smoked and exercise is rarely taken. But one thing has changed fundamentally: the common life has largely gone. Today, few people attend the local church. Many of the clubs and societies have closed. Those houses that brought three generations together now house just two. And the remarkable health of the people of Roseto? It is also in the past: today, Rosetans die of heart attacks at the same rate as everybody else.[24]

CHAPTER THIRTEEN

THE ECONOMY

By the 1930s, the invention of the car was a problem for the people of Boston. The city had been built for the horse and cart, not the automobile; for an era when a day's adventure was a trip to town, not a trip to the other side of the state. Now people living to the north of the city wanted to drive south to visit Cape Cod and people living to the south of the city wanted to drive north to New Hampshire. The only route was through the city, whose wholly inadequate roads began to grind to a halt. It appeared that nothing could be done. Few of the city roads could be widened and the growth in car ownership was showing no sign of slowing. The only solution was a whole new road – not going through the city but around it. Cynics were everywhere. It was too expensive; at a time when money was tight, surely this was just another Roosevelt boondoggle. There was no one to build it; all the young men were fighting in Europe or the Pacific. Even if it was built, surely nobody would want to use it. Bostonians began calling it the 'Road to Nowhere'. And yet, on 23 August 1951, the first stretch of 'Route 128', which had cost more per mile to build than any road in history, was opened. It was immediately in huge demand. Fifty thousand cars used it on that first day alone.

The greatest gain from Route 128 didn't go to the people of Boston. It was claimed by a young ex-navy officer called Gerald

Blakeley, who had had a eureka moment. Blakeley was just a few months into his new job working for a local real estate developer when he stumbled upon a map of the planned road. What Blakeley spotted before anyone else was that the land on the side of the road was incredibly cheap and would be minutes away from one of the largest universities in the country – the Massachusetts Institute of Technology (MIT). Land was very expensive for companies in Boston and in nearby Cambridge. Wouldn't it make more sense for them to be based together, out of town with easy access to the road and much cheaper rent? Blakeley began buying up land as fast as he could, creating spacious offices, green space and car parks. On the edge of Route 128, he invented the business park. Within fifteen years, over seven hundred companies with sixty-six thousand employees had made their home on Route 128. The park – and the road that fed it – became the most significant tech hub in the United States. By the 1980s, the road had a nickname: America's Technology Highway. It was here that the microwave, the minicomputer and the spreadsheet were invented. Gerald Blakeley, who had had his revelation as a recently hired junior member of staff at Cabot, Cabot & Forbes, made so much money that he bought the whole company.

By 1980, Route 128 had only one serious competitor for technology and innovation. It was a hub of companies based in the Santa Clara Valley just south of San Francisco. You might know it as Silicon Valley. Few took the threat seriously. Route 128 had so many advantages. For a start, there were several great universities nearby. As well as MIT, Harvard, Yale, Tufts and Amherst were all within easy reach. It had a much longer record of success than the Valley. Most significantly of all, the Valley lacked the key asset of Route 128: the transport links. Instead, roads were becoming congested, housing costs were ballooning and salaries were having to rise. The smart money was all on Route 128. And yet by the end of the century, Gerald Blakeley's creation had been overtaken by Silicon Valley. Whether your metric was technological advances, profit creation or the public's imagination, the Valley had reached a different league.

How had this happened? One – perfectly placed – academic had seen it coming. Today, AnnaLee Saxenian is the dean of the School of Information at the University of Berkeley – not far from Silicon Valley – but she grew up just outside Boston near Route 128. Her parents' friends were either engineers at MIT or worked for one of the big tech companies just off the route. In the late 1970s, she moved to California to study how Silicon Valley worked. When she returned to Boston to complete a PhD, she had formed a clear judgement: Silicon Valley was going to win. The reason was simple. Saxenian's time in both places had allowed her to spot the Valley's hidden advantage. People there talked to each other.

At the heart of Route 128 sat a number of large, highly secretive companies. Engineers at Bell, Data General and DEC invested millions in research and development and then did all they could to keep the results to themselves. The much smaller companies of Silicon Valley positively leaked information. Through chance, early fallings-out and bankruptcy, a culture had built up in the Valley of constant job hopping, conspiring together and cooperating outside of your firm. The result was that people met and talked constantly. In 1994, Saxenian published a book laying out her prediction. The connected society of Silicon Valley was going to outpace the divided-by-firm culture of Route 128. The road designed to get things moving was going to be left behind.

Saxenian's book lost her a number of friends in Boston society, but her prediction was spot on. In 2020, when US lawmakers summoned four leading tech CEOs to give evidence to Congress, three of their companies were based in Silicon Valley. Not one was based near Route 128. The power of networks and connections to drive the economy is particularly obvious in Silicon Valley, but it matters everywhere. At every level – the city, the region, the country – the economy grows faster where people who might not normally mix spend time together.[1] Why is this? A successful economy has many parents. Many of them rely on a united and well-connected society.

Let's start with the reason that Silicon Valley trumped Route 128: its ability to spread good ideas fast. The best vantage point for seeing the importance of idea-sharing to the economy is the continued growth of cities over the last twenty years. This growth has been the opposite of what many expected. Why have so many of us been prepared to pay much higher rents to live closer to the office when – since the birth of the internet – many of us could have been working from anywhere? Why have we been paying over the odds to get our commutes down to forty-five minutes when we could have been spending the last decade in the countryside, saving money, and avoiding the commute entirely? Despite predictions of the 'death of distance' and the emptying out of the cities, demand for living in a city has risen steadily over the last two decades and I suspect it will continue to rise even after the pandemic. Ed Glaeser – the Harvard-based economist and specialist on cities – has shown that in a city twice the size, prices are 16 per cent higher, while wages only rise by 10 per cent. Schools are not better, crime is not lower and the air is not fresher. Sure, some large cities offer fantastic cultural opportunities – but far too few of us use them far too rarely to justify a doubling of house prices. Large numbers of us have been choosing to pay more for less space and more noise. What exactly are we paying for?

The answer is 'ideas'. The advantage of a larger city is this: there are more people with more ideas. There is more knowledge and more innovation. And you – just by being there – can pick them up for free (once you've paid your higher rent at least). Why are these ideas worth paying for? Because they make you more productive, better paid and eventually wealthier. As early as 1890, the Cambridge economist, Alfred Marshall, saw what was going on:

> Great are the advantages which people following the same skilled trade get from near neighbourhood to one another. The mysteries of the trade become no mysteries; but are as in the air ... if one man starts a new idea, it is taken up by others and combined with suggestions of their own; and thus it becomes the source of further new ideas.[2]

It is the easy flow of great ideas, whether about better management practices or technological innovation, that makes living in a big city so valuable. Among a large population, ideas are created, built on, tested, improved and shared – all much faster than is ever possible within a small town. The bigger the city, the more ideas, the more they flow and the more they are improved.

But what has this got to do with social division? Here's the key: division interrupts the flow of ideas. If people are not mixing, meeting and talking, ideas find it hard to spread. A lack of connections across divides means that cities are divided into much smaller sub-cities with lines that ideas and knowledge cannot easily cross. Division means that great ideas flow less freely. Less great ideas reach fewer people, are less improved upon and do less good. Everyone is worse off. The greatest loss, though, is felt by the smaller minority groups. The majority group – because it is larger – retains a large network to share ideas with, while the smaller groups have to make do with a smaller network and therefore struggle the most to gain the benefits of the city's large size. The result is that, as cities get larger, we see an ever-widening gap between the wealth of majority and minority ethnic groups.[3] Division is the enemy of great ideas. It slows the economy, damaging the smallest groups, and potentially the most marginalised, the most.

Another critical enabler of economic success is good infrastructure. If we want businesses and government to operate efficiently, we need good roads and effective broadband as well as well-run schools and

world-class hospitals. Without this investment, the economy sput-
ters. Worse roads and slower broadband mean more time is wasted,
whether travelling to meetings, trying to communicate online or
struggling to find the right information. A weak education system
means a less skilled workforce. A lack of effective healthcare means
more days and years lost from productive work. As we saw in Chapter
11, voters living in a divided society are less likely to support investments in infrastructure. They are more likely to think that citizens
who are different in some way belong to another group of people
than they do. They are more likely to question why this other group
should benefit from their taxes. One of the results is that there is less
support for taxes that benefit everyone indiscriminately – in other
words, roads, broadband, education and healthcare: the infrastructure that the economy needs. The result, in turn, is an economy
operating with the brake on.

A lack of investment is one reason for a poorly skilled workforce.
Another is the quality of education. As we saw in Chapter 10, who
you are educated alongside makes a huge difference. To understand
this better, let's turn our eyes away from the West and towards India,
and in particular its capital. Delhi, like much of India, has a highly
divided school system. Children from low-income families, by far
the majority, attend a state-run or very low-fee private school. Sons
and daughters of the rich, however, attend a small cadre of extremely
expensive, elite private schools. Fees for just one child start at the
amount the average Indian family earns in three months and rise far
beyond this. Despite the cost, these elite schools are vastly oversubscribed. Nine children are rejected for every one place.

Aside from the fees charged by these private schools, there is
something odd about them. Despite their wealth, they don't own the
land on which they operate. The government does. The government
lends it to them, charging a very low rent on one condition: that the
schools reserve a number of places for poorer children whose families
could never afford the fees. In reality, no poor children were being

let in and the government was turning a blind eye. That was until 2007, when the High Court ruled that enough was enough, and 395 elite Delhi schools were instructed to reserve one-fifth of their places in the next academic year for children from low-income families who would pay nothing. Any school refusing to do so risked losing its land.

The free places were hugely oversubscribed. Children were selected at random and allocated to classes. The court insisted that the new children must be taught alongside everyone else. And so, with one court judgment, every single entry-level class became a mix of the offspring of the highly wealthy and that of the desperately poor. It is hard to overstate how far apart in wealth and income these families were. The average fee-paying family was richer than 95 per cent of Delhi families. The average free-place family was poorer than 75 per cent of Delhi families. If applied in the West, the same policy would require a private, boarding school where students' parents make an average of £150,000 a year to reserve 20 per cent of places for children whose parents earn £17,500.

The change in policy had a dramatic effect on the poorer children, who made great strides in their Maths, English and Hindi. Just as James Coleman found in his path-breaking report (see Chapter 10), poor children learn better among richer children. A significant part of the reason is that aspirations are infectious. Great sportspeople often talk about the debt they owe to their rivals. Would Muhammad Ali have been 'the greatest' without George Foreman? Would Lionel Messi and Cristiano Ronaldo have been such amazing footballers without each other? Would Venus Williams have won so much without a younger sister snapping at her heels? The same is true of us all. We catch our aspirations from our friends, from those who just assume 'they can do it' or from meeting those who have done it. It therefore shouldn't surprise us that when young people from poorer backgrounds make friends with wealthier, high achievers, their results rise.[4] Unfortunately, in the real world many children often lack the contacts that help them to aspire. Four out of ten state school pupils in the UK leave school saying that they don't know a single person doing a job they would like to do. This rate is even higher among children from the lowest-income families.[5] Robert Putnam summarises the situation like this: 'The influence of peers ... has been shown on teens' academic achievement, educational aspirations, college going, misbehaviour, drug use, truancy, and depression ... High standards and aspirations tend to be contagious – as do low standards and aspirations.'[6]

That is all well and good – but what the rich Delhi parents wanted to know is how this huge change would affect their children. The answer is: they became nicer. Academically, apart from a small decline in English language, they did just as well as before. But their people skills were radically changed – for the better. They became more concerned about equality. They were keener to share their possessions and their time. They were more likely to volunteer to help out at a local charity. They became less prejudiced and were more likely to choose to have poorer children as friends or on their teams in sports competitions. The more the wealthier children interacted with the poorer pupils, the kinder they became.[7]

What happened to these wealthy kids in Delhi has been seen to happen elsewhere. Studies in the West find that children with friends from a different ethnic background develop higher self-esteem, become more socially skilled, and less prejudiced, and are more skilled at relating to and forming rapport with people generally from different ethnic groups.[8] Through mixing children from richer and poorer families together, those from lower-income families learn more and do better, those from more advantaged backgrounds become kinder. When children mix with people from other ethnic groups, they become more socially skilled.

All of these changes matter to the economy. Of course, employers welcome children doing better at school, but they also value having employees who get on well with other people. A whopping 96 per cent of major US employers feel it is 'important' that employees are 'comfortable working with colleagues, customers, and/or clients from diverse cultural backgrounds'.[9] The final piece of good news is that this positive effect is not just limited to children. The same is true of adults; research has shown that staff members who have friends from different ethnic groups outside of work tend to get on better with a wider set of people at work and are more committed workers.[10] Once again, division is a stumbling block for the economy. In a socially divided society, people lack the chance to form those friendships and, with them, the chance to strengthen these skills and raise their aspirations. In our modern, knowledge-based society where low skills are of decreasing value to the economy, children having low aspirations doesn't just damage their futures, it affects us all.

We have seen how being able to share ideas, having a willingness to invest in infrastructure and being able to produce skilled workers makes an economy stronger. However, it is possible to have all of these things and still have a weak economy. All you have to do is focus on the wrong ideas, invest in the wrong infrastructure and get your skilled people working in the wrong jobs. It makes a big difference how good the decisions are on where investments should be made and who does which job. Let's start with getting the right people to do the right work.

In my own family – on a good day – my three primary-school-age children will help to clear the table after we eat. How my wife and I allocate the jobs makes a big difference. We have learnt over time that it is best if the oldest empties the dishwasher, the middle child deals with the plates and the youngest takes care of the cutlery. The same is true in the wider economy. Getting the right people in the right jobs makes a big difference to how much gets done. The economy operates best when the jobs that need doing are done by the most appropriately skilled person. The company I worked for in a previous career had to find the most efficient way to move about two thousand people around the country using a limited number of coaches and minibuses. I was well used to designing a mathematical model to work out the way to do that. Everyone who I have ever given a lift to would tell you that I probably shouldn't be doing the driving.

It is sufficiently important for the right people to be in the right jobs that companies will invest significant time, money and attention to find the right people. A job advert will be written, the exact wording debated, the advert will be paid for, perhaps a recruitment consultant hired, time will be set aside for interviews and follow-ups, references will be sought. The process is not cheap, but we spend the time doing it because finding the right person matters. Social division, however, makes it much harder to find the right person. Why? It comes down to the importance of word of mouth. How do people hear about the job advert? Often through someone they know telling them. How do they know it is a good place to work? Often because someone they know works there. How do they know they have a shot at getting the job? Often due to someone they know being involved in the interview and encouraging them to apply. Research struggles to yield certainty on this, but it is a decent estimate that around half of all jobs are found partly through word of mouth. The problem is that – in a divided society – word of mouth doesn't reach all parts of society. It struggles to cross the lines of difference. For many hiring managers, their own networks and those of their employees are full of people like them. As a result, word of mouth reaches no further than people of the same ethnicity, the same education level and the same background as the hiring manager. Unsurprisingly, this makes it much harder to find the right person and much easier to hire someone who's not right.[11] The result is a less productive firm in a less productive economy.

A divided society is not just bad at allocating people to the right jobs. It is equally bad at allocating money to the right projects. Most of us will have some money set aside that someone else invests for us. For the majority of us, this will be our pension; for some it will include money in the bank or the stock market. Very few of us decide where to invest that money. We simply don't trust ourselves to pick between different companies. And so we often leave that job to the professionals: the investment managers. The decisions that these people make really matter. To understand why, imagine a business – let's call it 'Great Business' – which has invented a new product that people love. The product proves so popular that Great Business can't keep up with the demand. The board therefore decides to rent a new factory and hire new staff to operate it. This will mean that Great Business can create more of the product that people want, create more jobs and put more money in people's pockets. However, Great Business will need to borrow some money to rent the factory and pay the staff. So, the CEO goes to the bank to borrow the money. The bank doesn't understand Great Business, though, and says no. Instead, it lends the money to another business that it knows better. We will call this 'Not-so-Great Business'. Unfortunately, Not-so-Great Business fails to sell much of its product. The result of the bad decision by the bank is less of the product that people like, fewer new jobs and less money in people's pocket. This means that the economy takes a hit. As you can see in this example, the bank's decision mattered. In the same way, the decisions made by investment managers about how to allocate money deeply affect the economy.

Surprise, surprise – these decisions are affected by who knows who. Why did the bank invest in Not-so-Great Business in our story? Because they knew them. Research shows that investors are much more likely to invest if they have met some of the business owners before.[12] In a divided society where most of the investors are White, and most of their friends and acquaintances are White, this means that large numbers of ethnic-minority-led businesses will miss out on funding. Sure enough, a survey of the American venture capital industry in 2020 found that 75 per cent of funding went to all-White leadership teams even though these companies made investors less money.[13] In a divided society, 'who you are' drives 'who you know' – and 'who you know' impacts on whether you receive an investment. The result is not just a lack of justice. It is also a weaker economy.

We have seen that division slows the economy in a number of ways. It slows the spread of good ideas, prevents investment in infrastructure, impedes skills from being developed, and reduces the quality of hiring and investment decisions. There is one other way that it can subdue the economy. To understand this, we need to start by imagining your life turned upside down. Imagine for a moment if, as you finished this sentence, your life changed. From now on you are to be paid a six-figure salary, you own a house with no mortgage and you have in your bank account £1 million that you can spend however you like. How would you feel? Shocked? How about after the shock wore off? Wealthy, perhaps?

If so, you would be unusual. Remarkably, most Westerners with this amount of money don't think they are wealthy.[14] Why on earth not? The reason is that rich people across the world tend to think that everyone else is pretty much as well-off as them. A survey in 2014 found that one in three Australians earning more than double the average income think they earn about the average.[15] Only one Indonesian in three thousand thinks they are in the richest fifth of the population – despite the fact that six hundred of them must be.[16] The poorest members of our societies make the same mistake but in the opposite direction. They tend to think that everyone else is about as poorly off as they are. Six out of ten Australians earning less than half the average wage think that they are earning about the average.

Why are people at the top and bottom of the income spectrum getting it so wrong? Surely, they know just from meeting other people that they're not the average? Here's the problem. The people that they meet are not average. They are people 'just like them'. Because the people you meet are about as hard-up or as well-off as you are, you assume that you are about average. In fact, the more your friends are just like you, the more likely you are to make this mistake.[17] And so, in a divided society, the rich tend to think that everyone is as rich as them, and the poor tend to think everyone is as poor as them. This is not just a curiosity about our societies. It is likely to cause a significant economic problem.

To see the problem, we must first understand a key difference between the rich and the poor. The rich, who have more money than they can spend, tend to save a lot of it. The poor, who have less money than they need, tend to spend all of it. This means that if the rich get richer and the poor get poorer, more money gets saved and less money gets spent. Growing inequality is bad news for the whole economy. Why? Because our economy is hugely reliant on people spending money. If the rich get a greater share of the money and spend less of it, a vicious cycle can start. With less money being spent on things, there is less work needed to provide those things. This means there are fewer jobs, which in turn reduces the amount of money people have. People therefore spend even less and employment falls further, making things worse again. Part of the way out of this problem is to reduce inequality – make the rich poorer and the poor richer. This is a solution we regularly turn to – even if the government might not always want to let the rich know. When things have felt very unequal, the public tend to support, and vote for, a tax system that takes a bit more money from the rich and gives a bit more to the poor. The poor then spend the money rather than save it. More things are bought, creating more work to provide the things. This creates new jobs, which in turn increases spending again. A virtuous cycle arrives.

In theory, this should be a self-correcting system. When things become too unequal, the public notices it, doesn't like it and supports taking more money from the rich and giving it to the poor. But what if the public didn't notice that things were becoming more unequal? In a divided society, they might well not notice it at all. What if instead, as the rich get richer, they increasingly surround themselves with similarly rich people. And as the poor become poorer, they increasingly surround themselves with the poor. Living in our bubbles, we would never spot the growing inequality. In fact, looking around our social circle, we might all think that society is in fact becoming more equal. Everyone we meet is the average – just like me. This is the risk we face today as many of our societies become more unequal and our social circles become more divided by income. We risk failing to spot the need for change. As a result, the income of the poorest might fall unchecked and unnoticed. The danger is that we then end up in a situation that few of us want morally, and none of us want economically. The poor struggle more and more as the economy loses its mojo.

There is one final factor that we must turn our attention to: trust. Studies from across the world have long shown that places where people have more trust in each other are wealthier and have faster-growing economies.[18] In fact, whether people trust each other has as much impact on the economy as whether people are skilled at their work. It has been estimated that a 10 per cent increase in the number of Americans trusting their fellow citizens would grow the US economy by half a percentage point over five years.[19]

Why might trust be such a catalyst for growth? Part of the answer is that if we trust our fellow citizens, we are more likely to hire them, pay up front for something, enter into a business agreement, or lend them some money. Where trust is low, however, the risk can feel too high. The result is that a number of business opportunities get missed.[20] Trust helps the economy by reducing the time and money spent checking whether someone is trustworthy. Where trust is low, contracts are carefully agreed, lawyers get put on retainer and the courts stand ready. In a high-trust society, one's word, one's reputation and the threat of losing that reputation replace much of the need for contracts, lawyers and the courtroom.[21] As a result, the cost of doing business falls, the amount of business worth doing rises and so the economy grows. The final way trust helps the economy is by making corruption less common.[22] If no one trusts anyone, corruption becomes pretty appealing. People start thinking, 'If I can't trust anyone else, then I need to look after number one.' 'I bet everyone else is doing it.' Corruption is poison to the economy. It slows down people's work, prevents the right people from doing the work, and puts money in the wrong place. Trust matters if you want a strong economy. As we saw in Chapter 11, division undermines trust and therefore again weakens the economy.

When I worked in government, once a month I would help the Secretary of State for Education to prepare for sixty minutes of 'Parliamentary Questions'. During the session, any Member of Parliament could ask the Secretary of State any questions they liked about anything at all to do with education. The only rule was that it had to be about education. If it was off topic, the Secretary of State could simply tell the MP to go and ask the correct minister. A new MP with a question might therefore be wise to check with parliamentary officials about which government minister they should be asking. An MP with a question on social division would probably be told that their question should go to the Communities Secretary, or possibly the Home Secretary. I am pretty certain the member would not be encouraged to put their question to the Chancellor of the Exchequer, the minister responsible for the economy. However, as we have seen, our divisions significantly affect the economy.

For too long, we have assumed that the divisions in our society have nothing to do with the economy. This is a mistake. As we have seen, divisions in our societies prevent great ideas from being shared, suppress consumer spending, prevent needed investment in infrastructure, cause us to hire the wrong people and invest in the wrong projects, reduce the academic and social skills of our workforce, and create a low-trust, less efficient environment. All of this reduces the economy's ability to grow. It makes all of us poorer. The Chancellor should be concerned.

CHAPTER FOURTEEN

SECURITY

Strategy consultant Jeff Jones, retired teacher Mark Rudd and retired university professors Bill Ayers and Bernardine Dohrn have some things in common. They are all American baby boomers. They all attended university, becoming involved in student politics and campaigning. They are all married. Three of the four are published authors. All four volunteer time to sit on charitable boards and foundations. They are also all experts in terrorism. In fact, they are all leading experts in one particular now-defunct terrorist group. It was a radical and radicalising group whose aim was to bring onto US soil the violence of America's wars overseas. Their members – most of whom had criminal records for previous acts of violence – lived in communes together studying texts, sharing food and following strict rules. Convinced of the evil of American foreign policy abroad and lifestyles at home, the group sought out military training from countries actively opposed to the US. They used this training to plant bombs, killing American citizens on American soil, including the daughter of a Republican state senator. The group was founded in 1969. It was called the Weathermen. Jeff Jones, Mark Rudd, Bill Ayers and Bernardine Dohrn are experts on this group, the Weathermen, as they were its founders.

Jones, Rudd, Ayers and Dohrn do not fit our stereotypes of terrorists. They are White, highly educated, American citizens who were born and raised in America in stable and well-to-do homes. However, understanding their journey into terrorism will introduce patterns that we will find repeated again and again.

In the late 1960s, the four of them became members of a student society called Students for Democratic Society (SDS). Founded just after the Second World War, SDS had grown at pace to become a national campaigning organisation. Inspired by the Civil Rights Movement and fired up by the war in Vietnam, students set up chapters across the US. By April 1968, SDS was strong enough to organise the largest student strike the country had ever seen, with a million students boycotting classes. However, for an increasingly vocal number of its members – Jones, Rudd, Ayers and Dohrn included – it was not enough. The death toll in Vietnam was rising, not falling. Supposed 'Peace Candidate' Lyndon Johnson had increased, not reduced, the number of troops in Vietnam. Now President Nixon had done the same. The most prominent peaceful demonstrations against the war had failed in the face of police violence. Tear gas and batons had ended the week-long sit-in at Columbia University, leaving 132 students injured, while protestors at the Democratic National Convention in Chicago had been attacked by what the Walker Commission later described as a 'Police Riot'. Jones, Rudd, Ayers and Dohrn had had enough. SDS was losing the battle for America's soul and so it was time to step up the fight. A new breakaway group was formed.

Inspired by the Bob Dylan lyric, 'You don't have to be a Weatherman to see the way the wind is blowing', the group called itself the Weathermen. It immediately began to meet independently of the rest of SDS and adopted goals and tactics that were consciously more radical and extreme. On 9 October 1969, the Weathermen invited all SDS members to a 'national demonstration' in Chicago to show the 'pigs' that they couldn't get away with 'fascist tactics'. Jones, Rudd, Ayers and Dohrn planned a violent attack on the local police force and readied themselves for the arrival of the thousands of SDS members who they expected to rally to their side. It was a bad misjudgement. Scarcely more than a handful of members answered the call and the 'demonstration' became a farce. Abandoned by their peers, they were easily arrested by the police and then further humiliated when their assumed ally, Black Panther leader Fred Hampton, described their actions as 'childish'.

Licking their wounds, Jones, Rudd, Ayers and Dohrn looked for lessons from Chicago. For them, the low turnout demonstrated not their lack of organisational skills but the guilt of their fellow citizens. By not rallying to their side, their previous allies were now complicit in the crimes being committed in Vietnam. As Mark Rudd wrote later: 'at that point in our thinking, there were no innocent Americans. At least not among the White ones. They all played some part in the atrocities of Vietnam … All guilty, all Americans were a legitimate target for attack.'[1] The ease of their arrest, meanwhile, was not a sign of their poor planning but an indication that the only way to succeed was to be more violent. Marching, protesting and rioting were going to achieve nothing. If they were to oppose the military might of America, the only solution was violent attack. In May 1970, Dohrn phoned a local radio station and read out a 'Declaration of War' on America: 'our job is to lead white kids into armed revolution … Tens of thousands have learnt that protest and marches don't do it. Revolutionary violence is the only way.'[2]

In the decade that followed, the Weathermen operated in terrorist cells. Members moved into houses together where they had to submit to extreme collective living. All possessions were to be shared, monogamous relations were banned, every individual decision must be taken collectively, even one as small as a member choosing to go for a walk. Embedded in these intense insular cell groups, members became increasingly supportive of violent action against the outside world. Throughout the 1970s, the Weathermen's cells carried out dozens of bomb attacks on federal buildings, including the United States Capitol, the Pentagon and the Department of State. While phone calls were made in advance to avoid civilian casualties, three deaths were not prevented. In March 1970, three Weathermen – Ted Gold, Terry Robbins and Diana Oughton, the daughter of a Republican state senator – were killed by a nail bomb they were in the process of assembling. The deaths marked the beginning of the end. The Weathermen's leaders went into hiding for close to a decade. Jones was the first to be captured in 1977. By 1981, Rudd, Ayers and Dohrn had all handed themselves in. The four expected significant prison time, but it never came. The police had messed up. Evidence had been gathered illegally. Hardly any charges could be filed against the accused. Rudd and Dohrn paid a small fine and spent less than a year in prison. Jones served a period of community service. Ayers faced no charges at all. The four went on to live remarkably normal and community-focused lives. In 1995, Dohrn and Ayers hosted a gathering to support a candidate for the Illinois State Senate – his name was Barack Obama. In 1997, Ayers received the award for Chicago Citizen of the Year.

I suspect one of your reactions to the Weathermen story is that Jones, Rudd, Ayers and Dohrn are far from 'typical' terrorists. They are too educated, too well-off, too privileged, too secular, too White. What exactly do you imagine a 'typical' terrorist is like? Are they someone who is rich or poor? Are they degree-educated or lacking in education? Are they religious? Do they have mental health difficulties? I would wager that for many of us a 'typical' terrorist is someone who is less educated that the average person – making them more susceptible to radical ideas. They are someone who is vulnerable, perhaps, due to mental health problems. They are probably religious – we may have pictured somebody with a deep Islamic faith. They are relatively poor – and therefore more likely to be radicalised due to the desperation of their poverty. If this is indeed the person you imagined – someone poor, with little education, poor mental health and devoutly religious – you have got it badly wrong. Let us start with the issue of poverty.

After 9/11, both President George W. Bush and his defeated presidential rival Al Gore were in unison on one thing. More aid should be channelled to poor countries to reduce poverty. If poverty could be reduced, they argued, terrorism would be reduced with it. Both men agreed that poverty was a major cause of terrorism. The only problem is that there is scant evidence to back them up. There is no link at all between the wealth of a country and its creation of terrorists. An analysis of almost a thousand terrorist attacks between 1997 and 2003 found that poorer countries were no more likely to produce terrorists than any other.[3] A review of the nationalities of foreign insurgents captured in Iraq between April and October 2005 suggested that in fact poorer countries produced fewer insurgents than wealthier countries.[4]

What about within a country, though? Surely if terrorism does take place, it is more likely to be perpetrated by poorer citizens. Once again, the evidence points in the opposite direction. There is no evidence that poverty makes you more likely to sympathise with terrorism. A study of those of Bengali or Pakistani heritage in the UK found that while 2.5 per cent of the population had some sympathy for terrorist acts, there was zero correlation between individual poverty and sympathy.[5] So much for sympathy. What about those carrying out an attack? Again, there is no correlation between being a terrorist and poverty. In fact, the opposite is often true. Palestinian suicide-bombers recruited by Hamas or Islamic Jihad are half as likely to come from an impoverished family as the average Palestinian.[6] Similarly, Hezbollah fighters are less likely to be from a poor family than the average Lebanese.[7] Looking at higher-profile terrorists, it is all too easy to find examples of well-off individuals from wealthy families. The would-be Times Square bomber, Faisal Shahzad, is the son of a senior Pakistani air-force officer. Umar Farouk Abdulmutallab, who lit a makeshift bomb on a transatlantic flight in the so-called 'underwear plot', is the son of a Nigerian banker who was described by *The Times* as being 'one of the richest men in Africa'.

What then about terrorists lacking education? Again, this is wrong. Shehzad and Abdulmutallab were not just financially well-off. They were also very well-educated. Abdulmutallab had a degree from University College London, while Shahzad had an MBA. This level of education is far from unusual among Western Islamic terrorists or those who sympathise with them. A study of over a hundred UK jihadis found that one in three had a degree, while the previously mentioned study of Brits with Bengali or Pakistani heritage found zero correlation between sympathy for terrorism and a lack of education.[8] If we turn our eye to the Middle East, you are more likely to find sympathy with anti-American terrorist attacks among the more educated.[9] The same is true of the terrorists themselves. In both Palestine and Lebanon, terrorist fighters are more educated than the rest of the population. Sixty per cent of Palestinian suicide-bombers had completed secondary school, compared to just 15 per cent of the general population.[10]

What then about terrorists being devout? It seems intuitive that sympathy for Islamic terrorism will be more likely among more devout Muslims. Intuitive but wrong. A study of Muslims around the globe found that religious Muslims were no more likely than non-religious Muslims to condone attacks on American civilians.[11] In France and the UK, being religious made Muslims less likely to support such attacks. Surveys of Palestinian and Indonesian Muslims found that there was no correlation between the frequency with which they prayed and their sympathy for those committing suicide-attacks. Indonesian Muslims who prayed frequently were actually less supportive than those who didn't pray.[12] Research by the British Secret Service and the International Centre for Counter-Terrorism found that Islamic terrorists and their supporters are often highly ignorant about Islam. They are more likely than average to be religious novices with limited knowledge of the teachings of the Qur'an. Just under half of Islamic terrorists in Europe were brought up outside of a strongly religious home and a third are converts to the faith. Few live a devout Islamic life and many instead dabble with drugs, alcohol and prostitutes. The link between Islamic terrorism and devout faith is weak at best.

Finally, what about terrorists suffering from poor mental health? Surely poor mental health could play a key role in making someone more susceptible to extremist ideas and more open to risking their lives and threatening those of others. This theory is again severely weakened by an examination of the facts. The British Secret Service's research found no greater evidence of mental illness or pathological personality traits among British terrorists than among the general public. The Secret Service report concluded that terrorists 'are a diverse collection of individuals, fitting no single demographic profile'.

If we have ruled out poverty, poor education, extreme religiosity or mental ill-health, what about division? The idea of a link between division and terrorism is not a new one. Neil Basu is the most senior police officer in the UK with responsibility for counter-terrorism. In 2017, he warned a conference of police superintendents that 'segregated, isolated communities ... are a breeding ground for extremist and future terrorists'. But does the evidence back Basu up? This question puzzled the Spanish economist Roberto Ezcurra. And so, in the same year as Basu's warning, he completed a detailed analysis of almost a hundred countries to find out the answer.[13] For each country, he noted down how divided people were by ethnicity and how many domestic terrorist attacks had recently occurred.[14] He then compared the two to see if there was any correlation between division and terrorist attacks. Sure enough, there was. The more divided a country was by ethnicity, the greater the likelihood of a terrorist attack. The correlation was surprisingly strong. Highly divided countries were around nine times more likely to suffer a terrorist attack.[15] In practice, that meant that if India became as divided as the Philippines it would face almost double the number of attacks.

Struck by what he had found, Ezcurra reran his analysis to check that the results were correct. He isolated other factors that might be causing the rise in terrorism and, one by one, removed them from the analysis. He checked levels of diversity, extent of urbanisation, histories of civil unrest, strength of political and individual rights, poverty, size of the country, existence of mountains where terrorists could operate from, openness to international trade, size of government and levels of inequality. None of them explained away the correlation. Ezcurra wondered if this was just a developing world problem. And so he rechecked the data again, looking just at North America and Europe. Again, the results held. On every continent, the same was true. The more divided the country, the more likely it was to suffer a terrorist attack. Two American academics, Bryan Arva and James Piazza, have followed in Ezcurra's footsteps – testing his findings. They found exactly the same correlation.[16]

It is clear that our countries can become safer by reducing division. Is the same true of an individual? Is an individual who is cut off from people who are different more likely to become a terrorist or to sympathise with terrorist activity? It would seem so. Evidence suggests that we are more likely to have sympathy with terrorist activity if our social circles are narrower. Research in the United States consistently shows that white supremacist terrorist attacks are likelier in areas where Whites are less likely to interact with Americans of other races. This lack of connection also makes sympathy for attacks more common as well as increasing the number of anti-Black hate crimes and the membership of racial hate groups.[17]

We noted earlier that there was no link between how often a Muslim prayed and their sympathy for those committing suicide-attacks. However, the same surveys also found that Indonesian and Palestinian Muslims who regularly met with other Muslims were more likely to be sympathetic towards suicide-attackers.[18] Being more religious – if anything – makes you less sympathetic with terrorists claiming to be defending your faith, but spending a lot of

time with people from that same religion makes you more sympathetic. A survey of Israeli Jewish settlers appears to affirm the basic
principle here: religious belief good, bubbles full of the faithful only
bad. Settlers were asked whether they sympathised with the horrific
1994 attack on the Ibrahimi Mosque committed by Israeli terrorist
Baruch Goldstein. The attack left twenty-nine Palestinian Muslims
dead. Before answering, one-third of the participants were prompted
to think about praying to God, one-third were prompted to think
about spending time at the synagogue and one-third were given no
prompt at all. Of those given no prompt at all, 15 per cent described
the attack as 'extremely heroic'. This fell all the way to 6 per cent for
those reminded of praying to God. However, it rose to 23 per cent
among those prompted to think about the synagogue. Deputy
Assistant Commissioner Neil Basu would appear right to be worried
about division. It is clear that division makes our countries more
vulnerable to terrorist attacks and that individuals who don't mix are
more of a risk.[19] Why though would this be?

To answer that question, we need to understand better the journey
from citizen to willing terrorist. Thankfully, it is an incredibly rare
journey. While no two journeys are identical, most follow a pattern
of four steps. As we will see at each step, division pushes the person
further towards terrorism. The first step, at least normally, is to
become a sympathiser.[20] Why do individuals become sympathetic to
terrorist groups? We have seen that it is not simply due to poverty, a
lack of education, religiosity or poor mental health. No, the main
reason that people come to sympathise with terrorists is that doing
so meets one of three deep psychological needs that most of us have:
the need for safety, the need for justice and the need for purity. Most
of us, of course, meet these needs every day without sympathising
with terrorists. However – as we will see – the more divided you are
from the rest of society, the more aligning with a terrorist group can
seem like an attractive solution.

Let us consider first the need for safety. Terrorist groups frequently describe their activities as defensive. They are acting violently only to protect and defend you – and other 'good' people – from another evil group. The Weathermen claimed to want to free America from the sins being committed by a White, militaristic elite. Other twentieth-century far-left terrorist groups like the German Baader-Meinhof Gang or Italy's Red Brigades claimed their atrocities were protecting the working classes from fascism. Baruch Goldstein claimed to be defending Israeli Jews from Muslims. Norwegian White supremacist Anders Behring Breivik claimed to be defending White Europeans from Leftists and Muslims. Osama bin Laden claimed to be defending Muslims from Western crusaders and infidels. Few of us are persuaded by these claims and most see terrorists as a much greater threat than the groups they claim to be defending 'their people' from. Nevertheless, in a divided society, where trust levels are lower and people have less contact with other groups, it becomes that bit easier to believe that you need defending from 'the other'.

The second psychological need that terrorist groups exploit is the need for justice. When interviewed, individuals who express sympathy for terrorist groups often speak powerfully of personal injustices that they have experienced. Those sympathising with Islamist terrorists, for example, often state that the reason for their sympathy is personal experience of anti-Muslim discrimination. This injustice may well create a justifiable anger. It is imaginable that, at its peak, it could create sympathy for those using violence. But this initial, strong anger is normally relatively short-lived. It soon gives way to sadness and frustration. This type of anger – by itself – would struggle to last long enough to maintain much sympathy with terrorist murderers. But what about wider injustices? Those who sympathise with terrorists will also often speak of the anger they feel about the treatment of others 'like them', perhaps in another part of their country or the world. Those sympathising with white supremacist terrorists might speak of fellow Whites facing threat to their voice or power. Those sympathising with Islamic terrorists might speak of the ill-treatment of Muslims overseas. Again, though, it is hard to see how these sympathies with people the individual has never met could make them approve of murder. For most of us, most of the time, the unfair treatment of strangers may trouble our conscience but it rarely spurs us to support violence, let alone murder.

This creates a puzzle. The anger that comes from personal injustices can be fierce, but it is too short-lived to motivate someone to align consistently with terrorists. The injustices that strangers face, meanwhile, may be more long-lasting, but they will probably be too weak to make someone sympathise with terrorists. How then does a need for justice lead to support for terrorism? The path opens up only if our personal injustices and distant injustices become fused together; if, in other words, my personal experience of prejudice feels like part of a wider fight against injustice around the world or across the nation. This would connect the intensity of the short-term, intense anger about my own treatment with the lower-level constant anger about wider injustices. This connection might well create a need to believe that someone out there is acting with purpose to restore justice not just for me but for all 'like me'. This need is one that terrorists can take advantage of. What, though, would cause me to link my personal injustices so closely to a wider struggle? The answer lies in how we think about ourselves.

Most of us have multiple identities. We might see ourselves for example as Black, British, a Londoner, a mother, a Christian and a feminist. One identity does not contradict the other; they all sit together. When one of our identities comes under attack – for example from colleagues mocking our faith – our other identities continue to provide us with self-esteem. Part of us – our faith – has been criticised, but the offending person does not really know us. The criticism was about part of me – not all of me. In a sense, it was not personal. We are angry, but the anger subsides. Similarly, when we read of the ill-treatment of Christians overseas, we care, but we are not completely overcome with anger – this ill-treatment means more to us than it might to a non-Christian, but it again is not totally personal. Our faith is after all just one part of our identity. The story is different, however, if we only have one totally dominant identity. If we see ourselves as exclusively Christian, then the anti-Christian criticism we receive cuts deeper and lasts longer. We cannot rely on other identities to strengthen our self-image. We cannot tell ourselves that the culprit does not really know us – as they have in fact abused the sole identity that defines who we are to ourselves. The criticism is deeply personal. If we have just one dominant identity, we will feel much more profoundly connected with others who are described in the same way, even if we don't know them. If we see our identity as exclusively Christian, then ill-treatment of Christians anywhere in the world is personal. It is an attack on me. For those of us with one dominant identity, our personal ill-treatment and the global ill-treatment of others become very connected. Both are hugely personal injustices. They hurt. They make us feel rightly angry and in urgent and consistent need of justice. The frequency of these global injustices means our anger may not subside into sadness. It may endure. If it does, it is likely to drive sympathy with those who can bring justice. For most of us that won't include terrorists, in fact it may prove a powerful spur for positive action, but – for some – anyone bringing change may be worth sympathising with, even terrorists.

Where does social division fit into this? In an integrated society, where we mix readily with those from multiple backgrounds, we are much less likely to have a single dominant identity. Imagine a woman who has recently moved to London. Despite only recently arriving in the city, she starts getting to know other Londoners at work and travelling with them on the underground. As a result, she begins to see herself as a Londoner. One Sunday she visits a local church with a colleague and enjoys it. She spends time reading the Bible and praying. Over time, she starts to see another key part of her identity as being a Christian. After a friend invites her, she attends a women's march and meets women who call themselves feminists. She likes them very much. As a result, she also begins to see herself as a feminist. You can see how multiple identities start to develop. However, in a more divided society it is easy to miss out on experiences that nurture these multiple identities. The Black and White children playing on different sports pitches from each other miss an opportunity to build a shared identity as members of the same team. The Muslim and Christian pupils attending different schools miss the opportunity to form a shared identity as students of the same school. In a divided society, it becomes far easier to form just a single identity. As we have seen, this reliance on a single identity can make us feel much more personally attacked by our own and others' injustices. This heightened demand for justice can in turn make us far more sympathetic to those who claim to be fighting for us including, in rare cases, terrorists.[21]

After safety and justice, the third need that terrorist organisations can try to meet is our need for purity. In his book *The Righteous Mind*, American psychologist Jonathan Haidt identifies six drivers of our opinions about morality. One of these he calls 'Purity'. He describes it as our desire to avoid doing something that seems in some way evil, unclean or impure. He explains that it is this desire for purity that best explains how we feel when we condemn incest, eating dogs, or people walking outdoors naked. These views are more than simply a desire to avoid harm – they persist even if we are convinced that no harm will occur. It is a desire for purity that partly motivates some environmentalists when they oppose pollution, or people of faith when they oppose blasphemy. Terrorists are able to appeal to our desire for purity by claiming that they are not just fighting against an enemy who *does* evil, but against an enemy who *is* evil. Most terrorist groups paint a picture of an enemy that is dirty, unclean and unhuman, an enemy that should disgust us. This can be seen most clearly in the way that far-right terrorists describe Jews or Muslims as 'dogs' or 'vermin'. It can be seen in the way that Islamist terrorists describe their victims as '*kaffirs*', literally meaning 'unbelievers, infidels, impious wretches'. It is also visible in the language of the Weathermen. They frequently described the police, government officials and anyone they saw as the enemy as dirty 'pigs'. Consider Benedict Dohrn's response to the Manson family's murder of the eight months' pregnant Sharon Tate: 'First they killed those pigs and then they put a fork in pig Tate's belly … Offing those rich pigs with their own forks and knives … Far Out.' This description of the enemy as evil is called 'essentialising'. It suggests that the enemy has an essence that cannot be removed, and that that essence is pure evil. Once a group of people have been essentialised as evil, it becomes easier for normal people to accept their ill-treatment and murder.

For most of us in the West the closest we get to believing that another group is irredeemably evil is when we think of terrorists themselves or perhaps those who harm children. The idea that a whole ethnic or religious group might be evil or unclean seems, to most of us, absurd and abhorrent. However, for some of us it rings true. For a few, that other group does indeed seem in some way impure or unclean. To this minority, the terrorists therefore can hold appeal as deliverers bringing purity – they may be unpleasant but they are opposing evil and purifying the world. Cases of people thinking like this are thankfully rare, but they become more likely in a divided society.

There are two main reasons for this. First, it is very hard to believe that another group is evil if you know and like someone from that group. If you have a diverse group of friends, essentialising myths are hard to accept: 'Hindus can't be evil; my friend is a Hindu and he's not evil.' However, if you know no Hindus, you lack this easy evidence. Second, in a more divided society, as we saw in Chapter 11, you will be much more affected by Group Think. If there is general distrust of another group among your friends, and no one disagrees, you are much more likely to be affected by it. You are not only more likely to hear negative stories about that group; you are also much more likely to feel a pressure to agree with the general negative view. Think again about the Weathermen. After the farce in Chicago, the insular nature of Jones, Rudd, Ayers and Dohrn led their followers to live in exclusive cells, not mixing with the rest of society. This meant they became increasingly surrounded by negative, dehumanising stories about the police, the government and all those working to prevent revolution. In this context it became far easier to believe that those opposing their group were not human, but 'pigs'. Divided from the rest of society, the terrorist claim to be bringing purity can feel much more credible.

Thankfully, the vast majority of those with sympathy for extremist groups and terrorists do not become anywhere near radicalised enough to act on their sympathy. Even if they were minded to do so, their ties to everyday life would make such a step far too costly. Fully accepting the terrorists' radical beliefs would pull them away from their family and their friends. To join a radical group would threaten the career and wealth that they have built. These ties of family, friendship, career and possessions effectively 'freeze' an individual, holding them steady, and preventing them from becoming more radicalised. For the vast majority of people who go on to become terrorists, there needs to be a moment when these ties and bonds are cut – when the person 'unfreezes'. This step of unfreezing is the second step towards terrorist activity.

Why would someone 'unfreeze'? Why would a person's ties of family, friendship, career and possessions become loose? One cause can be a moment of trauma or tragedy – the death of a parent, the end of a romantic relationship or the loss of a job. Another cause is relocating to a place far from old friends – whether a new city, a new country, or potentially a prison. Research by the British Secret Service found that 10 per cent of British terror suspects had indeed lost a loved one, a third had immigrated alone and two-thirds had been arrested and gained a criminal record. For Jones, Rudd, Ayers and Dohrn, it was a traumatic moment of failure that unfroze them. Abandoned by their peers to a police beating in Chicago, they found themselves unmoored. Their plans to lead a series of mass demonstrations were undone. Their identity as leaders of a movement was put in question. Their allies had abandoned them. It was in this unmoored state that the idea of revolutionary violence first took hold.

The causes of unfreezing – whether losing a loved one, a romantic relationship or a job – are sadly very common. However, thankfully for most of us, these losses are insufficient to cut us adrift. Should we lose one spoke of our relationships – our colleagues perhaps or a parent – we retain other links and connections that keep us from unfreezing. However, if we live a life with a less diverse set of connections, then the loss of one important set of relationships could leave us completely isolated. If our workplace is our only connection with others, then losing our job can leave us deeply unmoored.[22] It is for this reason that cults and radical groups will frequently work to purposely undermine new recruits' existing friendships. They know that if the person can be unfrozen from these bonds and connections, they are more likely to accept the cults' beliefs and lifestyle. This is typically achieved either through instructing them to cut off non-believers or through creating a new social world involving only other believers. The Unification Church, for example, requires potential new members to live with existing church members for a weekend, then a week, and then two weeks before deciding to join. These efforts to remove an individual's existing ties often bear fruit, bringing the individual into the church.

For whatever reason it may occur – trauma, tragedy, redundancy, relocation, a break-up or a criminal conviction – when a person is unfrozen from their standard ties, habits and relationships, they find themselves in flux. The majority of individuals unfrozen in this way will simply go on to build new friendships, but in the period before they do they are often lonely, confused and lacking in purpose. A group that can offer friendship, meaning and direction is suddenly much more attractive, even one that brings with it unpalatable beliefs and unreasonable demands. It is this moment of vulnerability that makes unfreezing a gateway to the third step of the journey: radicalisation.

Radicalisation is a key step on the journey to terrorism and it is worth us spending a moment defining it. Some commentators have described as radicalised anyone who holds strongly illiberal positions such as opposing gay rights, women's rights or the rights of other religious groups. Others only use the term for individuals who not only take illiberal positions but also disagree with democracy and the present system of law – for example those who believe that White-only voters or sharia law would be a better system. A third group has reserved the term only for those who also believe that violence is justified in bringing down the present system. I will here side with the latter group and use the words 'radicalisation' and 'radical' to describe only people who approve of violence. This is more than a semantic distinction. It is entirely possible to become convinced of an illiberal position, or favour a non-democratic system, and yet be utterly appalled by any use of violence. Millions of individuals around the world – both Muslim and non-Muslim – hold these positions and detest violence and terrorism.[23]

Becoming unfrozen is not an unusual human experience, especially for those with a smaller, less diverse network of friends. However, the vast majority of unfrozen individuals, including those with sympathies for terrorism, never become radicalised. The majority instead, over time, find a new job, make new friends or reconnect with family members. They 're-freeze' into a new set of relationships that once again encourage and require pro-social behaviour and beliefs. Radicalisation only occurs to those rare individuals who fill the temporary gap in social connections and meaning by joining a radical group.[24] While this is a rare path to take, it is the main route to terrorism.

Before unfreezing, the individual would probably have rejected a radical group's friendship as unwelcome, their beliefs as extraordinary and their lifestyle as unattractive. While unfrozen, however, the extremists' package of friendship, meaning and identity can prove alluring. For those struggling with isolation, the group provides a ready-made group of friends. For those lost without a plan for their lives, it provides direction and activity. For those struggling with self-doubt or insecurity, it provides moral superiority by affirming the individual as one of the enlightened few. Whether unfrozen individuals become radicalised is often simply a matter of timing. We are at our most vulnerable when unfrozen – if extremists step in with an offer of friendship at this exact moment, they may just succeed. The critical role of timing rings out clearly in studies of cult recruitment. Individuals who join cults are disproportionately those who first met cult members soon after a moment of trauma or transition. At this vulnerable moment, the cult formed a welcome friendship group around them and sucked them in. It is not unfreezing that causes cult membership or radicalisation; it is the friendships that are formed while you are unfrozen that do that.

Individuals with narrower, more segregated networks are more likely, once unfrozen, to form these friendships with radicals. This is true for two reasons – one highly practical and one more psychological. First, very practically, a highly segregated individual who loses a parent, a job or a partner is likely to lack the networks and connections to form new friendships easily. If, for example, their sole source of friendships was their workplace, then unemployment is likely to cut off all their main routes to new connections. Denied the opportunity to build their own networks, they will spend longer in this unfrozen state – which means there is more time for radical groups to find them and draw them in with the offer of ready-made friendships. Second, and more psychologically, an individual who lacks connections can easily feel judged, and rejected, by what they see as mainstream society. This can be true of ethnic-majority lower-income groups; in both Britain and the US, Whites with lower levels of education and income often talk of feeling judged and looked down upon by a more educated urban elite, made up of individuals they don't know and have never met. It can also be true of immigrant communities; Muslims living in the West, for example, can feel a sense of disconnection from a mainstream society that sees religion as a largely private affair. This sense of rejection makes individuals who become unfrozen less likely to seek new relationships with those who represent mainstream society.

Imagine a second-generation Muslim immigrant who becomes unfrozen, having fallen out with his parents. For him, the local mosque and mainstream Muslim community bring him back into contact with his parents. If his main friends have always been fellow Muslims then mainstream secular society may seem frightening. In comparison, the Islamist radicals who are inviting him to meetings appear to take his religious beliefs seriously. Why not go along? Imagine the single working-class White man who loses the only job he's ever had and becomes unfrozen. Losing contact with ex-colleagues, returning to the workplace seems intimidating. Local clubs and societies seem dominated by people in work or with more education. In comparison, the far-right extremists that he starts chatting with online seem to respect his patriotism and his way of talking. They affirm him and want him in their group. Why not get more involved?

For the segregated individual, once unfrozen, the extremist world can seem less threatening and demanding than mainstream society. We can, once again, see this dynamic in practice in the journey of the Weathermen. Before they turned to violence, Jones, Rudd, Ayers and Dohrn had publicly cut themselves off from both mainstream society and then from the more moderate left-wing activism of SDS. They had declared them guilty of murder. Unburning these bridges and eating their words would prove a more difficult psychological step than continuing down the path to radical violence.

The final step of the journey is from being a radical, someone committed to violence, to being a terrorist, someone actually committing violence. It is a step that many do not take. Many will leave a radical group or turn away before ever committing an act of violence. Many of those who were beaten up with the Weathermen in Chicago left as the group morphed into terrorist cells. What then marks out those who make this final step? What is it that takes an individual from being a passive member of a radical group to becoming an active terrorist on behalf of the group? The key once again is relationships.

In the final months of radicalisation before an individual becomes an active terrorist, their friendship network becomes even more segregated. Friendships outside of the radical group are dropped entirely as the group spends more and more of its time together away from non-radicals. Cut off from the rest of the world, this small group becomes all-encompassing and the doctrine and rules of the group all consuming. We can see this journey in action in the formation of the Weathermen's cell-like groups. In the final months before the first attack, Jones, Rudd, Ayers and Dohrn moved into small communes where Weathermen lived only with other Weathermen. The cells followed principles of extreme communal living – shared decision-making, shared romantic relationships, shared possessions. Individual members were expected to submit their free time, their beliefs and their personal choices to the group's ideology. The demands became total, with the individual expected to submit their identity and will entirely to that of the group. Social psychologists refer to this way of living as 'totalism'. It is totalism that enables a radical to ignore society's rejection, ethical qualms about murder, and fears concerning personal safety and become an active terrorist. As their group's demands became more 'total', the individuals that remained loyal to the group became more radical in their beliefs, more committed to those beliefs, and more open to using violence to 'defend' them.

Totalism can be seen at work in radicalised groups throughout history. Just one example where we can see its power at work is in the forming of 'The People's Will', a terrorist group active in late nineteenth-century Russia. The group originated in peaceful attempts by students to travel from the city to the countryside to try and convince the ill-treated peasants to demand land reform. The peasants show no interest. Rejected by the peasants, the well-meaning students protect their bruised egos by forming increasingly tight communes, sharing their lives together and reading revolutionary writing. Their thinking becomes more radical and their efforts more extreme. The authorities decide to act. They arrest the leaders, imprisoning them together. Prison provides an even closer, all-encompassing environment for the radicals. By the time of their release, what had begun as a peaceful student movement has become a series of totalistic terrorist cells. The story ends, in 1881, with our utopian students murdering the Russian head of state, Tsar Alexander II.

The role of totalism can also be seen among European far-left radicals in the twentieth century. Half of the Germans who joined the murderous Baader-Meinhof Gang had spent time living in communes. Members of Italy's Red Brigades lived insular, intensely interconnected lives with nearly everything in common. They went on to murder the country's ex-prime minister and five of his body-guards.[25] The same totalistic groups can be detected among the perpetrators of 9/11. While living in Hamburg, the leader of the group, Mohamed Atta, formed a small cell connecting him with other Islamist extremists. The group withdrew entirely from the local culture. They stopped attending the local mosque, prayed together five times a day and avoided all normal student events.[26]

Frequently, it is prison that provides a totalistic environment for terrorists. Partly for reasons of cost, governments, including the

French and the British, have often concentrated terrorists together in one high-security prison. As a result, prison has often made terrorist groups more extreme. Nothing shows this more than the number of terrorist prisoners prepared to make the ultimate sacrifice and starve themselves to death through a long and painful hunger strike while surrounded by fellow comrades in prison. It is noticeable that when the Spanish government began separating out imprisoned members of the Basque terrorist group ETA, an increased number of ETA prisoners – now detached from their cell – started leaving the group.

How, though, does totalism lead a person from radical to terrorist? There are two main causes – the first is loyalty and love. Spending twenty-four hours a day together, sharing an increasingly demanding lifestyle and the risk of arrest, builds an immense bond of loyalty and love between members of the group. This bond makes members more open to violence. Their psychological commitment to each other reinforces the need to turn words into actions. Research in Morocco among communities with known sympathy for Islamic State found that individuals who were tightly bonded to other radicals in that community were much more likely to fight or die for the cause.[27] The support for violence becomes even stronger if one of the group is arrested or killed. The loss of a dearly loved comrade creates the need for revenge and action. The clearest sign of the importance of love and loyalty can be seen in a shift that eventually occurs in most radical groups' communications. Groups start off talking about fighting for 'the people' and end up talking about avenging the death or capture of their comrades.

The People's Will is a great example of this: the group began with peaceful demands for land reform to help peasants and ended up with violent demands for the release of comrades. Growing love and loyalty within the group not only makes violence seem legitimate, it also prevents individuals from leaving. Reflecting on thirty interviews with long-term supporters of Irish Nationalist terrorism, academic Robert White concluded that commitment to other members played a significant part in holding the group together. One Republican tells him, 'There's times I've said to myself, "Why? You're mad in the head, like." But … I just can't turn my back on it … there's too many of my friends in jail, there's too many of my mates given their lives, and I've walked behind … too many funerals to turn my back on it now.'[28]

The second way that totalism pushes someone from radicalism to terrorism is through their desire to fit in. It is easy to underestimate how powerful this desire is. The Polish-American psychologist Solomon Asch conducted an experiment in the 1950s that showed exactly how strong it can be. In the experiment, a volunteer is placed in a room with a number of others. Unknown to the volunteer, the others are not volunteers. They are actors working for the researchers. The volunteer is shown a picture of two lines and is asked to identify which is longer: A or B. It is incredibly obvious that the right answer is A, for it is significantly longer than B. However, before the volunteer can answer, the rest of the group are each asked for their opinion. One by one they all declare – contrary to the undebatable evidence – that the answer is B. The volunteer is asked last of all. Do they give the obviously correct answer of A or do they prefer to go with the group and pick B? Despite the fact that B is obviously wrong, 75 per cent of volunteers at some point choose it rather than face being in the minority.

In a social setting made up solely of other radicals, this natural human desire to fit in pushes the group towards increasingly extreme positions, including the taking of life. When an individual belongs to multiple groups, the impact of one group's view is limited. It is balanced and checked against other opinions and others' judgements. Inside a totalistic cell, the impact of other groups is entirely absent. Contrary views to the extreme are pushed out or excluded. Consider again the Weathermen. Once Jones, Rudd, Ayers and Dohrn were inside their communes, voices that might have advised them to change path were absent. Without any alternative views, a slippery slope towards greater violence develops. Individuals build on each other's increasingly extreme proposals. No one provides a counter-balancing brake until it is too late.

There is no such thing as a typical terrorist. From Bill Ayers to Mohamed Atta, individuals start their journey into terror from all sorts of backgrounds and beliefs. They are no likelier to be poorer, more religious, less mentally well or less educated than the general public. What most have in common, though, is that their journeys to terror follow the same steps: from citizen to sympathiser, through unfreezing to radical, and via totalism to terrorist. At every stage, whether you are a nineteenth-century Russian student or a twentieth-century left-wing activist, you are more likely to take the next step if you live in a divided community separated from those who are different. It should not surprise us then that more divided countries suffer more terrorist attacks. But it should make us wonder why we are not doing more to prevent division.

Part IV

HOW TO PUT OURSELVES BACK TOGETHER AGAIN

'They are our enemies; we marry them.'

African Proverb

CHAPTER FIFTEEN

THE TRILEMMA WE FACE

When I started working on this book, Brexit was a typo and Donald Trump was a brash businessman with a TV show. Since then, Britain has seen its Parliament illegally closed, two prime ministers forced out of their jobs, daily protestors demanding another referendum and eventually its departure from the European Union. The United States has elected and rejected the only president to be impeached twice, seen millions come to believe that democracy is rigged and had its Congress stormed by rioters. After all of that, it is not surprising that four out of five Americans describe their country as 'mainly or totally divided' and half of all Britons believe that the people of the UK are 'the most divided that we have ever been'. And yet, our divisions – as we have seen throughout this book – are much deeper than our politics.

We humans are social animals. We connect, form friendships, fall in love and rely on and enjoy the company of those around us. Our highest highs and our lowest lows are nearly always about our relationships. From our marriages to our divorces, our new introductions to our falling-outs, our acceptances by a new group and our rejections, most of the stories we tell and memories we cherish are about such things. The circle of friends, colleagues and acquaintances around us is who makes us, us. It is in these connections that we have become most fundamentally divided. Our social groups have become full of people 'just like us'. The average British professional knows nobody on unemployment benefits and hardly anyone who is working class. Half of Brits and Americans with degrees have either one close friend who didn't go to university or none at all. Unless they are related, only one in twenty Americans over sixty years old discusses anything important with those under thirty-five, and only three in twenty Dutch over eighty-year-olds have any weekly contact with anyone under sixty.[1] A quarter of Remain voters have no friends who voted Leave. A fifth of Leave voters have no Remain-voting friends. Half of committed liberals in the US have no close friends who are conservatives. Two-thirds of committed conservatives have no close friends who are liberals. Almost half of Whites in America have no Black friends, no Asian friends and no Latino friends. Over a quarter can't think of any acquaintances or colleagues who aren't White. The majority of Black Americans have no close friends who aren't Black, and a quarter can't think of a single White friend. Around half of Britons have friends only from their own ethnic group and half of non-Muslim Britons have never, in their life, had *any* close contact with a Muslim.

The reason for these divisions is as old as human beings. We evolved with a People Like Me syndrome – a bias towards people 'like us'. Left to our own devices, we naturally surround ourselves with people who remind us of ourselves. We have inherited a bias that pulls us apart. Our divisions cannot be pinned on 'populist demagogues', 'media barons' or 'liberal elites'. That is not to say that these forces don't matter; anyone declaring that 'others', whether immigrants or Trump supporters, are *really* different from 'people like us' turbo-charges this PLM. It reinforces the idea that some people are definitely worth avoiding. Our divisions also cannot be pinned on Twitter or Facebook, Snapchat or LinkedIn. Again, these platforms do not help. The power to connect easily with anyone you choose is a gift to PLM. It makes it easier than ever to build a network full of people 'just like me'. But it is a catalyst, not a cause. The underlying problem – I am afraid – is in us. It is *our* People Like Me syndrome.

The good news is that we have learnt how to fight back against PLM. We have found its weakness. The syndrome doesn't decide for us who is 'like you' and who isn't. It relies on us to know that. Fortunately, it is possible to change our mind and convince ourselves that those who we thought were 'unlike us' are actually quite 'like us'. How can this be done? It can be done by creating a common life – a set of institutions that bring people who are different together and bond them. From Israel's kibbutzim to 1950s Roseto, from Robbers Cave to the Battle of the Bulge, from the *epeme* to the feast day, we have seen how the common life pulls off this trick. It brings people from all backgrounds together, providing them with equality of status and involving them in a shared activity that is either intense enough to create a shared memory, or routine enough to show shared commitment. Since our earliest days, PLM has been pulling us apart, but the common life has been keeping us together. In different eras, this common life has taken on very different forms, from the rituals of the nomad or the religious life of the farmer to the schools, work-places and clubs of the factory worker.

The reason we are divided today is that the common life that united our grandparents has been withering away for, at least, the last fifty years. Over that time, we have become half as likely to attend a club or a society. Those that continue to meet are less diverse than before. Our schools and our workplaces have divided by income bracket and education level. The colleague on the Zoom call and the pupil at the next desk are more likely than ever to have the same level of wealth and education as us. As the common life has lost its ability to connect us, People Like Me syndrome has been free to divide us. We can see the result in our friendship groups, our colleagues and our acquaintances. Considering we live in increasingly diverse societies, they are remarkably full of 'people like me'.

Our divisions went unnoticed for a long time. It was the arrival of the consequences that opened our eyes. As I write – a week after the storming of the Capitol – the most visceral consequence is clear. As is the fragility of our democracies. Our systems do not rest on the act of voting alone; they rely on our ability to be one people, one demos, one group who trusts each other and compromises with the other. Our divisions are robbing us of this sense, creating space for the mob and the demagogue to fight on behalf not of 'the people' but of 'our type of people'. As we have seen, this is just one consequence alongside many that ail us. Social mobility is stalling as richer children inherit not just their parents' wealth but also their access to networks, opening up opportunities that others never see. Anxiety about 'the other' and chronic loneliness are making us ill as the anxiety hormone, cortisol, charges through our body, increasing our risk of diabetes, cancer, stomach ulcers and heart attacks. Even after the coronavirus pandemic moves into the rear-view mirror, our economy will continue to operate with the brake on as our divisions slow the spread of good ideas, prevent wise investments and reduce the trust that oils the wheels of business. Amid all of this, our security services are being stretched thin, not by foreign agents, but by potential domestic terrorists, radicalised against us from within our own societies, living – like the rest of us – in groups full of people who think the same way. Our divisions are dangerous. They have arrived because we have no common life to hold PLM in check. To fix our divisions, we must first understand why we have lost the common life that brought our grandparents together.

Like the best murder mysteries, there are two culprits, not one. Each did half the job. The first culprit took down the voluntary part of our common life. Whether we were foragers, farmers or factory workers, most of the common life that connected us was voluntary. No one made us dance the *epeme*, attend the feast day or join a club. Because these institutions were optional, the only way they could get mass take-up was by being incredibly popular. That meant them meeting – almost perfectly – people's needs, wants and habits. To do that, they had to fit with the size of the group, the prevailing beliefs of the time, the way the economy worked, the amount people moved about, as well as being engaging enough to see off any competing distractions. The *epeme* fits the world of the nomad perfectly. It is a ritual sufficiently large to involve everyone who is camping together, it fits with their beliefs about the world and their ancestors, it takes place at a time when everyone had finished gathering food and instead had gathered together, it is more interesting that other distractions, and it could take place wherever the group happened to have settled that night. In comparison, the club and society ideally fitted the world of the factory worker. The associations were so numerous and overlapping that they could involve a whole city, they chimed with the prevailing belief in community and personal improvement, they took place on days that workers were not needed in the factory or in the evening, they easily accepted new people moving into the city, and they provided enough entertainment to attract people in.

The greatest strength of the voluntary common life is this ability to fit the needs and wants of a society. As we have seen, it is also their weakness. For when that society radically changes, it doesn't fit. What makes this so serious is that it also struggles to adapt. Unlike for-profit firms in the corporate world or species in the natural world, the common life does not fail fast, mutate or scale quickly. And so, when transformational change occurs, as it did during the agrarian revolution and the Industrial Revolution, the voluntary common life withers away. That is why deep in the soil, under the deserted village of Basta, you can see the remains of long-forgotten nomadic rituals. They didn't fit the new settled life of the village. And so they died out and were replaced by nothing.

Rapid, transformational change unpicks the voluntary common life. Over the last half-century, it has struck again. It is the culprit that undid the voluntary common life of our grandparents. Our society has transformed from manufacturing to services with more time spent commuting, our values have pivoted from a focus on community to the individual, the television has provided killer competition for other evening activities, and we have become more mobile with higher rates of immigration and larger numbers of women spending their weekdays at work rather than at home. The result is that many of us have lost interest in the clubs and societies that our grandparents joined in large numbers, meeting, in so doing, people 'unlike them'. There is no reason to believe that these institutions will make a comeback.

The second culprit took down the mandatory part of the common life. Our grandparents, and their parents, saw it as normal that they, by and large, went to the local school and worked for the local employer. Many of them accepted the idea of national service – a compulsory responsibility to serve alongside randomly chosen members of society. It was not rapid change that undid these parts of the common life. It was the growing importance to us all of a rather lovely thing called choice. Growing numbers of us simply don't want to send our children to the 'local' school or have to work at the 'local' employer. We want, and expect, to choose the right place for us and the right place for our children. And, of course, when we make that choice, People Like Me syndrome has an effect. It suggests that we might well want to educate our children and earn our living with people who seem quite a lot 'like us'. The culprit that took down the mandatory common life wasn't change; it was choice.

So we have our two culprits: change took down the voluntary common life and choice removed the mandatory common life. They did not do it alone, though. They had two assistants. The first is the growing distance between us. As we saw in Chapter 8, we increasingly live in neighbourhoods full of people that vote like us, earn like us, are educated to the same level as us and have the same age as us. They have become slightly more mixed by race, but from an incredibly low base. This distance matters. For the common life to fight back against PLM, it must be able to bring together people who are different. If those who are different live in completely different parts of town, this becomes very difficult to do. The second assistant is the growing differences among us. As we saw in Chapter 9, our societies have become more diverse. The reasons for this are themselves diverse. Growing life expectancy has increased our diversity by age. Increasing university attendance has made us more diverse by education. Higher rates of immigration and uneven birth rates have increased our diversity by race. Globalisation and automation have made us more diverse by wealth. These changes have created opportunities for longer and freer lives. They are largely to be celebrated. Yet they have also created a world of options for PLM to take advantage of. With more diversity of people to choose from, it becomes, perhaps counterintuitively, easier to find people 'just like me' to spend time with. Greater diversity also means that our divisions are more damaging. When only 5 per cent of us went to university, it mattered much less if those with degrees didn't mix with the rest of us. Now that this group makes up almost 40 per cent of society, this division is much more significant. And so, we have the true causes of our divisions in our sights. Two culprits, choice and change, brought down the common life that was bringing us together, aided and abetted by the increased distance and differences between us.

This part of the book is the most important. In these last three chapters I will lay out exactly how we can put our societies back together again. You may not like everything that follows, but it is an honest, frank description of what we must do. Let us start with something that you will like: the good news. The good news is that we *can* put our societies back together. Our situation is not terminal. Our divisions do not have to last. How do we know this? Because we've been here before and found our way out. During previous times of transformational change, the common life was disrupted and People Like Me syndrome divided us. When we first became farmers and settled into village life, the nomadic common life, made up of animalistic rituals, that had united us for generations withered away. Division and violence spread. We became so unable to solve problems collaboratively that we had to abandon many of the early villages we settled into. And yet, we found a way back. We built a new common life – one based on feast days, religious services and rites of passage. We subdued PLM and overcame our divisions. Millennia later, we lost our way again. As we left the villages for factory work in the cities, we left the villagers' common life behind us. Once again, division and violence spread, with revolutions threatening and breaking out. And yet, once again we found our way out. We built a new common life – this time based on clubs and societies, schools and the workplace. We again subdued PLM and brought our societies back together. If we have done it before, it must be possible to do it again.

In this chapter, we will consider four possible routes out. Each has its attractions. The attraction of the first is obvious; it requires no effort at all. The first route is to do nothing. When the nomadic common life withered away, no one actively sought to build a new one. No one set out to create the monotheistic religions or to plan their festivals, services and rites of passage as a method of bringing diverse people together. Instead, as we saw in Chapter 6, a new common life evolved over time, not through planning but through trial and error. The same is true of the industrial common life. After villagers migrated to the cities and the village-based common life withered away, no one planned the rise of clubs and societies. Schools and workplaces did not spring up in order to bring unity. And yet, over time, these new social institutions evolved. The common life they provided happened by accident, not on purpose. So, why not simply wait it out again?

This is not an impractical plan. I am sure that, in time, a new common life will spring up to replace what we have lost. Our societies are full of change and uncertainty. It is credible that some new way of connecting us, so suitable to our present society that nearly everyone wants to take part in it, will arrive. It may well be something that doesn't exist today, something that we have never heard of, something that we can't even quite imagine. If history is to be our guide, it feels reasonable nonetheless to assume that a new common life will develop. However, if we are to rely on history, we should also assume that this will take some time. After the nomadic common life of animalistic rituals fell away, there was an interregnum of one or two millennia before the new agrarian common life of religious celebration was established. The next interregnum between the agrarian and the industrial common life was around a hundred years long. These interregnum periods were violent and divided. We can wait it out, but we should assume that the problems we identified in Part III won't be going away while we do. I think we should scratch this option off.

The second possible route out of our divisions is to look to reduce the geographical distances between us – one of the two aides that have helped change and choice to divide us. Is it really feasible to do this, though? Surely, it's not credible, let alone desirable, in a Western democracy to force people to move house? Clearly not. However, that doesn't mean there is nothing we can do. For most of us, where we live isn't only a question of where we *want* to live, it is also a question of where we can *afford* to live. At present, choices made by local and national governments make it harder than it should be for those on lower incomes to live in certain neighbourhoods. All too often, in richer neighbourhoods, rules and regulations require that every home is large, every garden is big and no one shares an external wall, let alone a stairway, with a neighbour. The result is a neighbourhood full of wealthy families. Consider the American city of Seattle as an example. Planning rules ensure that almost three-quarters of the land surrounding the best primary schools is reserved for large houses. If we want our wealthier neighbourhoods to be less detached from the real world, the first thing we should do is push back on planning rules that ban flats and small gardens.

The second thing we should do is use government housing subsidies to ensure that less well-off families can afford to live in wealthier neighbourhoods. Some may think this is a 'socialist' step too far. I would merely point out that doing this to some extent has been British and American policy for almost forty years. In America, the main method of providing these subsidies was introduced by that famous socialist, Ronald Reagan. It is called the Low-Income Housing Tax Credit. It gives money to developers to build new homes in rich areas on the condition that they are rented for thirty years to poorer families at below the market rate. Today, two million American families live in homes that have been built in this way. 100,000 more families join them every year. However, over the next decade, that thirty-year period will end for half a million of these homes. The top priority, in the US at least, must be to prevent these rent reductions from lapsing. The second priority should be to build more of these homes.[2] The UK, meanwhile, has a proud history of providing funding, or a home, to those in need of housing. However, during the last decade we placed a relatively low limit on the amount of money that a family can receive to help with this housing. On the one hand, this might seem reasonable; why should a family reliant on government help be able to live in an expensive neighbourhood? But the consequence of such a cap is obvious: more and more neighbourhoods contain only rich people. The limit needs to be removed.

Pushing back on planning rules and providing housing subsidies are the price we must pay to avoid poverty ghettos. We know, from Alex Polikoff's work, that such policies can transform the life chances of children born into poverty.[3] They are the right thing to do for the individual family and for wider society. As these poorer families are more likely to be from an ethnic-minority background, and to have a lower level of education, such planning reform and housing subsidies can also help to make our neighbourhoods more mixed by ethnicity and education level. However, these two policies are about the limit of what we can do. People do not want to be told where to live and they do not want their neighbourhoods suddenly and rapidly transformed. More importantly, as we have seen throughout the book, having a more mixed neighbourhood doesn't necessarily mean less division. As Ryan Enos's experiment with Hispanic commuters showed us in Chapter 8, increasing diversity in the local neighbourhood does not always reduce division. In fact, it can make it worse.

If reducing the distances that divide us is not the silver bullet, what about the other aide to choice and change? For completeness, the third route we should consider is trying to reduce the level of difference in our society. This almost immediately feels like a dead end. Consider the level of age diversity in our societies. It has been caused primarily by us living longer. I've never stood for elected office, but a platform of reducing life expectancy would seem a somewhat unlikely vote-winner. The same is true of any plans to reduce diversity in our levels of education. This has been caused by the increasing number of young people going to university. While most Western countries might benefit from a pivot from academic to technical training, none would be better off if children received less education. And although a good portion of the public support the idea of 'fewer university degrees' in the abstract, they tend to make an exception for their own children and grandchildren.[4] As for reducing ethnic diversity or political diversity, it is simply abhorrent to imagine a free society trying to do either. Some may disagree. They may argue that reductions in immigration provide a legal and morally defensible way to reduce ethnic diversity. I will make a very practical point. This is a mirage. In both the US and the UK, even a total ban on immigration would fail to reduce the ethnic diversity of the population. In fact, it would continue to rise. Even with immigration levels close to zero, by 2060 over half of America's population and a third of the UK's will be non-White. Reducing immigration will slow the rate of change but it will not reduce the level of diversity.

There is one form of diversity that we should work to reduce. It is the level of income and wealth diversity; in other words: inequality. This would be a worthwhile endeavour. As we have seen throughout this book, the rich are the most active in moving away from the rest. Change, here, would make a real difference. However, the tide has not been moving in our favour. In 1979, the top 10 per cent of earners took home just over a quarter of all income in the UK. They now take home over a third. The richest in the US have done even better. In 1979, they took home a third of all income; they now receive almost a half. While the picture has stabilised over the last two decades, probable advances in both globalisation and especially automation will make it very hard to push the tide back out. Nonetheless, a higher minimum wage, stronger labour protections, affordable healthcare and a meaningful safety net are aims worth pursuing. Even with these hard-fought changes, though, we would still need to find ways to bring people together – for even in a perfectly equal society, other differences will remain. Reducing difference by income will help, but it will not hold back People Like Me syndrome. For that, we still need a common life.

There is one more route to consider. Over the last half-decade, many of our discussions around division have drawn us back to two topics. The first is social media – a public space that has become better known for its 'echo chambers' of angry criticism rather than its original promise to connect us. The second is the rise of tribalist leaders – from America's Donald Trump to France's Marine Le Pen, from 'Mr Brexit' Nigel Farage to Hungary's president Viktor Orbán. Often these two topics have become interlinked, with many American commentators suggesting that it is Trump's tweets that are the prime cause of division. Surely, the best route to heal our fractures is to defeat these demagogues at the polls and to remove them from social media. Relying on this approach is instinctively appealing. Divisive rhetoric from such leaders communicated unmediated to their followers is like an 'anti-common life'. While the common life aims to show us that those who 'seem different' are in fact quite 'like us', divisive rhetoric suggests that those who 'seem different' are actively against us. Social media, meanwhile – as we saw in Chapter

7 – makes it so easy to follow and unfollow people that it is the perfect playground for PLM. With each click you can find the perfect online bubble full of people agreeing with you wholeheartedly.

There are two big problems with this approach. The first is that it's not realistic. It is not credible to believe that by defeating demagogues in an election, our divisions will go away. Marine Le Pen has never won a presidential election in France; Nigel Farage has lost seven elections in a row. Defeating these individuals does not remove their voices. What then about silencing them entirely? Again, it is not credible to believe that the tech giants will consistently ban politicians who use divisive language. Trump's online ban arrived only after the Senate recognised his successor; tens of thousands of voices remain online demonising 'the other side'. It is also not desirable to live in a society where unelected technology CEOs can decide who has a voice and who doesn't.

The second problem with this approach is that it does not address the fundamental causes of our divisions. Social media may turbocharge People Like Me syndrome but it did not undermine the common life. Our schools and workplaces have not become divided by income and education level because of Twitter. No one stopped attending clubs and societies because of Facebook. The pull of television has done more to divide us than the roar of social media. As for the demagogues, they are more a consequence of our divisions than a cause of them. Their attacks on foreigners, immigrants, city elites and experts were popular because most of their followers didn't know anybody who was a foreigner, an immigrant, a city dweller or an expert. It is much harder to hate if the person you are being told to hate is someone you know and like. It also should not be lost on us that the election Donald Trump won came after eight years of rule and leadership by a politician more skilled than virtually any other in telling stories of unity and commonality. The divisive Brexit vote came after two prime ministers who had prioritised talking about shared 'British Values'. These votes did not happen because

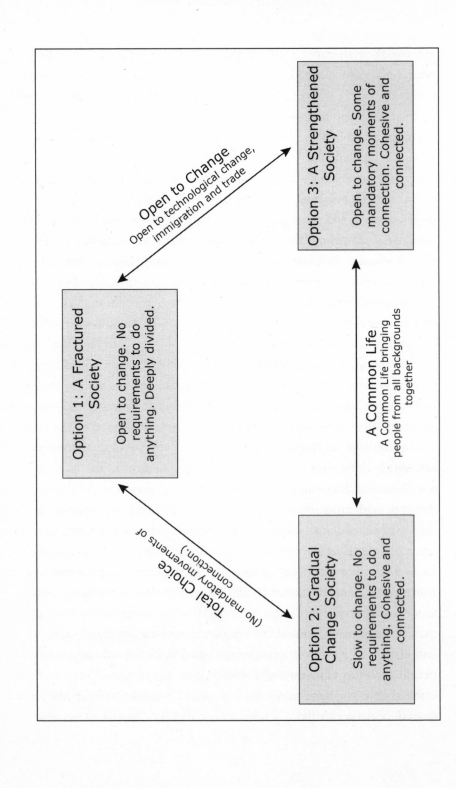

demagogues' rhetoric suddenly divided us. They happened because we were already divided.

We have considered four options: doing nothing, reducing the distance between us, reducing the differences between us, and trying to defeat and silence the demagogues. While we have found some things that are worth doing – supporting housing subsidies, planning reform and seeking to reduce inequality – we have found nothing that will seriously reduce our divisions. This shouldn't surprise us. Throughout this book, one thing has been consistent. Our societies' divisions come not from outside us but from the People Like Me syndrome that affects us all. The only way to bring our societies back together is to put back in place the one thing that can keep PLM in check. The only way to reunite our societies is through a new common life.

We have seen throughout the preceding chapters that the decline of the common life is down to two culprits: change and choice. If we are serious about rebuilding a common life, the only credible options are to take on these culprits directly. We must either slow down the rate of change so that the voluntary common life can adapt and strengthen, or we must reduce the level of choice to allow a mandatory common life to connect us. And so, we face a point of decision. We face a dilemma: if we want to bring our society back together, we must either reduce our openness to change or restrict our freedom of choice. There does remain, of course, the third option. We could put our head in the sand and do nothing. This means we in fact face a trilemma. I call it the common life trilemma. The chart below lays it out most clearly.

Our first option is to do nothing and remain a 'fractured society'. We choose to retain our openness to both choice and change. As a result, we accept the continued decline of the common life. With People Like Me syndrome unconstrained we will see our society become even more divided. This is where most of the West is today.

Our societies are full of change, we have hardly any collective duties (beyond jury service), our common life is withering away and our fractures are growing. The second option is to become a 'gradual-change society'. We refuse to impose any restrictions on people's choices or freedoms but we look to slow down the rate of change. We hope that by doing so we can provide the voluntary common life the breathing space that it needs to adapt, evolve and bring us back together. The third and final option is to become a 'strengthened society'. We remain open to change in our society, from immigration to economic transformation, but we accept some mandatory require-ments to come together. This allows us to build a mandatory common life that starts to reduce our fractures. These are our choices.

CHAPTER SIXTEEN

THE GRADUAL-CHANGE SOCIETY

Was it really possible to avoid the fractures of the last five years? Are there any Western countries that have managed to buck the trend? Yes, there are. In fact, there are four of them. Four societies where, over the last few years, citizens have become more, rather than less, trusting of each other. Levels of trust in these nations are so high today that the average citizen is almost twice as likely to trust their fellow countrymen as the average American. In one of the four societies, the number of people who believe that their fellow citizens can be trusted rose all the way from 47 per cent in 1979 to an extraordinary 79 per cent in 2009.[1] If we ranked the hundred wealthiest countries in the world on the basis of whether people are trusted, respected and included, these four nations would come first, second, third and fifth.[2] The US and the UK, in comparison, would come twenty-third and twenty-fourth.

The four countries are Denmark, Finland, Norway and Sweden – sometimes called the Nordics. How have the Nordics done it? How have they avoided division and distrust while all other countries came apart? The answer is that they have maintained a voluntary common life – the same one that united their grandparents. Just like the rest of the West, the second half of the nineteenth century saw a boom of clubs and societies across the Nordics. The growth was so large that Nordic historians call the period the 'age of associations'.

Just like in the UK and the US, many of the Nordics' biggest charities were founded in this period. Large movements sprang up across the region. Some were class based, like the peasants' movement and the labour movement, while others, such as the sports movement, the religious movement and the teetotal movement, brought people together across these boundaries. These movements spawned hundreds of local chapters. Also, just as in the UK and the US, schools sprang up across the region and gradually became mandatory, while the workplace became a social hub for city dwellers.

Mirroring the rest of the West, change came in the latter half of the twentieth century. The clubs and societies based around the peasant, labour, religious and teetotal movements started to decline. Membership rates fell and chapters closed. But, just as these clubs and societies declined, another group took up the slack. Increasing numbers of Nordics joined sporting, musical and cultural clubs. Between 1981 and 2002, the number of Finns involved in sports clubs grew by a third. One study of a province in Norway found that between 1941 and 1988, at the exact time when clubs and societies were declining across the rest of the West, the number of associations per thousand people rose by a third. A study of Denmark between 1981 and 2008 found a similar increase.

It wasn't just the clubs and societies that were refusing to decline. While Americans and Brits became less likely to visit each other from the 1960s onwards, a study of social habits in Denmark found no such decline. In the early 1990s, the point at which so much of the decline in associations and clubs had taken place in the rest of the West, the average Swede was still a member of three different clubs and associations, with one in three holding some sort of elected position.[3] Over the last half-century, Nordic societies have maintained their voluntary common life. How have they done it?

The answer is that they reduced the speed at which their societies were changing. Rapid transformational change wrongfooted and undermined the voluntary common life in the rest of the West. But in Denmark, Finland, Sweden and Norway, a slower pace of change meant that their voluntary common life could adapt and flourish. This makes the Nordic societies a great example of 'gradual-change societies' – societies without any mandatory common life to bring people together but where change is managed and slowed. Such a slower pace of change protects the voluntary common life, allowing it to continue to flourish at bringing people from all backgrounds together.

How exactly did the Nordic countries reduce the rate of change? They put on the brakes in three important main ways. The first brake was applied to the economy. Compared to the UK and US, Nordic countries remained highly unionised. Unions, employers and government have worked as partners, managing economic change gradually and with consent. Struggling companies were thus less likely to become bankrupt. When disaster was unavoidable and companies needed to lay off workers, generous employment insurance, and significant investments in retraining by the government, meant that the change for the worker and their family was limited. Roughly a third of the workforce was further protected by being employed directly by the state. The level of protection that the Nordics give to their workers and employers is far greater than you would find in the UK, let alone in the US. Data from the Heritage Foundation makes this explicit. In a ranking of countries from around the world, the Nordic countries as a bloc would come twelfth out of 180 for the extent to which they protect workers from unemployment and spend public money on their citizens. The UK and the US, if also treated as a bloc, would be ninety-seventh.

The second brake that the Nordics applied was to immigration. Up until the refugee crisis, with the exception of Sweden, levels of immigration into the Nordics remained lower than the rest of the West. In 2010, 11 per cent of the UK population and 13 per cent of the US population had been born overseas; the same was true of only 9 per cent of those living in Denmark and Norway. This fell to just

5 per cent in Finland. Sweden was the odd one out – as we will return to later – with 15 per cent of its population foreign born. The consequence, outside of Sweden, was a slower rate of change.

The third brake applied was an entirely accidental one. While the rest of the West fell head over heels for television, the Nordics held back – at least slightly. By 2019, the average Briton was watching over three hours of TV a day and the average American over four hours. In comparison, the average Nordic's daily intake was closer to two. In the UK and the US, TV proved to be too fierce a competitor for clubs and societies. In Denmark, Finland, Norway and Sweden, it was more of an even match.

Sure enough, this slower rate of change created the space for the Nordic common life to evolve. The result was that, as the national movements declined, new groups focused on sport, culture and music adapted and grew. Other parts of the common life were also helped by the slower pace of change. Fewer economic winners and losers and a slower shift to services meant that Nordic workplaces were more likely to contain employees with different education and income levels. Employees were also more likely to remain colleagues for longer; while the average American changed jobs every four years in 1997 and the average Briton every eight years, loyal Swedes only moved once every eleven and a half years. The brake on economic change further reduced division by slowing the growth of inequality. As a result, schools are less divided by income. Slower immigration has had a similar effect. A slower rate of ethnic change in the schools has meant fewer White parents sought to move their children to 'Whiter' schools. All of this shows a 'gradual-change society' in practice. There is no mandatory activity that brings citizens together, but the slower pace of change means that the voluntary common life has had the time to evolve and flourish. The result is a less fractured society.

Is this a credible path for the rest of us? Could we protect the clubs and societies that bring people together by slowing down the rate of societal change? What would that even look like? In Chapter 6, we identified four types of change that have been happening at pace for the last half-century. They were economic disruption as our industry moves from manufacturing to services and now increasingly to digital and the increase in commuting that this had brought; a change in society's core beliefs, from an emphasis on community to more of a focus on self-improvement; the movement of people, especially because of immigration; and, finally, new competition for time from the television. Any serious attempt to reduce the pace of change would need to be an unusual mix of left-wing protectionism and right-wing social conservatism. To slow down changes to the economy, the state would have to ban foreign takeovers of larger companies, underwrite failing businesses and protect jobs through strengthening trade unions and giving workers more generous unemployment benefits. To reduce the movement of people, it would have to restrict immigration. To shore up the core beliefs that our grandparents' common life was based on, schools would promote more traditional values of duty over personal opportunity and respect of elders over a critique of authority. Finally, to ward off distractions on our time, the state could put high taxes on forms of digital entertainment, especially streaming services, gaming and social media. We might also seek to reduce time lost to commuting by encouraging people to work more from home and investing significantly in broadband, public transport and roads to speed travel and communication.

Aside from the taxes on entertainment, I think this could be a relatively popular package of reforms for many Westerners. The public tends to be to the left of the average politician on the economy and to the right on social reforms, which is exactly matched by this quixotic package of policies. However, there are two fundamental problems with this approach. The first is that the slowing down of changes to our economy is far from costless. If we use taxpayer money to prop up failing companies, we will have less money to spend on schools and hospitals. We have also removed an incentive for companies to ensure they are making things that we actually want. This incentive enables them to grow and create more jobs and, ultimately, put more money in workers' pockets. Banning foreign takeovers, meanwhile, may be very popular politics, but such buyouts are one of the ways that the UK pays its way in the world. If we can't sell the companies we create, we will need to find something else to sell to fill the gap.

There is, however, a more fundamental problem. For the 'gradual-change society' strategy to work, you have to believe that you can slow down change. You have to be able to slow it down enough to protect the fragile voluntary common life. If change is like a wave crashing against a flood barrier, the barrier has to be bigger than the waves. The problem is that the Nordic barrier isn't actually that big and a huge wave of change is coming.

Sweden is the reason to believe that the Nordic barrier to change isn't enormous. During the last decade and a half, it has experimented with just slightly reducing the size of its barrier to change. It has done this in two ways. First, it has opened its borders and encouraged immigration – not least in a remarkable humanitarian response to the refugee crisis. The result is that, today, 20 per cent of people living in Sweden were born overseas.[4] Second, it has allowed more economic change, with a reduction in unemployment benefits and the removal of regulations and trade barriers. As a result, Swedes move between companies much more than they used to, now spending almost exactly the same amount of time in a job as the average Briton. Inequality has also risen fast; over the last fifteen years, it has risen four times faster than in the US.

The result of these adjustments has been the arrival of the fractures that the Nordics had kept at bay. Swedish cities have started to divide by ethnicity and by income. As in the UK and US, the wealthiest are leading the charge, moving away from poorer members of society. Parents have become keener on choosing where their children go to school and who they go to school with. As a result, schools are now more divided than the neighbourhoods they serve. A study of 356 Swedish schools in 2018 found that over 40 per cent of them were divided either by income or ethnicity. The Danish researcher, Beatrice Rangvid, examined the schools in Copenhagen and concluded that: 'school segregation … for some student groups [reaches] levels comparable to the extreme segregation typical for US cities'. What about Sweden's levels of trust and togetherness? At first glance, it looks like it is holding up okay. The average Swede appears to be just as likely to describe their fellow citizens as trustworthy as they were in the late 1990s. The warning light, though, is flashing among the younger generation – those who are growing up and being educated in this increasingly divided society. In 1998, over half of sixteen- to twenty-eight-year-old Swedes believed that other Swedes could be trusted. Twenty years later, this has fallen to four in ten.[5] A small reduction in the Nordic barrier to change has been enough to let the fractures in.

The Swedish experience is particularly worrying when we consider just how big a wave of change is coming. For the digital revolution has only just begun. An estimate by the McKinsey Global Initiative suggests that automation will require between 75 and 375 million people around the world to change jobs during the 2020s.[6] Up to one in three mechanics, food preparers and repair workers may lose their jobs. Those in office support roles – from IT to payroll, admin to procurement – will fare little better, with 10 to 20 per cent of jobs vanishing. At the same time, we will see a large increase in the number of managers, teachers, builders, designers, care workers, doctors, nurses and children's workers and a huge rise in computer engineers. It is dystopian to expect mass unemployment; it is realistic to expect massive change. The impact of this wave won't be limited to the economy. The agrarian and the industrial revolutions changed where and how we lived, provided new entertainments that vied for our attention, and shook our core beliefs. Now, thanks to the catalyst of the coronavirus pandemic, it seems likely that five-days-a-week-in-the-office is already a lifestyle left in the past.

In the face of this transformational wave, any country trying to be a 'gradual-change society' is going to need to hit the brakes harder than the Nordics have – and definitely stronger than the Swedes have of late. To have a chance of protecting the voluntary common life, it would have to massively slow the changes to the economy and hope that this would slow down wider societal change. As we look at the experience of Sweden and the scale of the change that is coming, I find it hard to believe that the 'gradual-change society' option is viable. The Nordics have managed change to their economy and society successfully over the last half-century. I believe they are going to struggle over the next half-century.

Thankfully, there is another option. In the rankings of trust, respect and inclusion that we saw earlier, the four Nordic countries were first, second, third and fifth. It is time to look at the country that came fourth, which has taken a radically different approach to maintaining its common life. It is a country that never wanted to be a country in the first place.

CHAPTER SEVENTEEN

THE STRENGTHENED
SOCIETY

For most countries, the first day of independence is a cause for celebration. The east Asian island of Singapore is not most countries. Usually, countries fight for their independence. Singapore had strived to avoid it. Ejected against its will from the Malay Federation in 1965, its leader Lee Kuan Yew had no choice. Appearing on television the next day, wiping away tears, he informed a shocked nation that they were on their own. The situation was perilous. Singapore was a densely populated island, half the size of London, without enough land to feed itself. With a population of fewer than 2 million, it also lacked the numbers to defend itself. Graver than both of these threats – in Lee's eyes – was the fact that his new charge was highly vulnerable to ethnic division, unrest and civil war. Why was this his main concern? Because Lee had seen that very threat become all too real in another east Asian island.

The country of Sri Lanka had appeared fully prepared for independence when it came in May 1948. Its future leaders and the soon-to-be departing Britons had worked patiently for many years preparing the ground. They had negotiated a new democratic system of government, agreed a new constitution, and established a government-in-waiting. Yet lying dormant beneath all the planning and negotiating lay a ticking demographic bomb. To understand the explosion that would tear the island apart, we must understand the two main ethnic groups that live in Sri Lanka: the Tamils and the Sinhalese.

The ethnic Sinhalese lived in the south and were largely Buddhist. The ethnic Tamils lived in the north and were largely Hindu. The problem for those planning independence was that the Sinhalese outnumbered the Tamils by five to one. How, in a new democracy, could they prevent the larger group from simply outvoting, out-organising and eventually pushing out the smaller one? The planners were sure that the answer lay in legislation, checks and balances. They agreed laws to ban anti-Tamil discrimination; they set up an independent commission with Tamil members to make government appointments; they made the national language English, not Sinhalese; they created political parties that combined both Tamils and Sinhalese; and they appointed Tamils to important government posts.

None of it worked. Within eight years, a Sinhalese political party had formed and taken power. Sinhalese became the national language; Buddhism became the main religion; and Sinhalese citizens were given priority for jobs and university places. Tamil protests at these changes were met with violence – meted out by a largely Sinhalese police force. By the end of the 1970s, three decades after independence, both the government and the opposition parties were defined by ethnicity. The bomb was ready to go off.

The fuse was lit in the Tamil city of Jaffna, by a group of Sinhalese men. At the heart of the city sat a large, ornate library. Containing over 97,000 books and documents, the library was a source of great pride to the local population, not least because it contained a series of ancient palm-leaf manuscripts recording the history of the Tamil people. On the night of 1 June 1981, under the cover of darkness, Sinhalese men set the library on fire. Everything inside was destroyed. Violence followed immediately. Tamils joined guerrilla groups and attacked Sinhalese soldiers. Within two years, neighbours were attacking neighbours. When one guerrilla group killed thirteen

Sinhalese soldiers in 1983, Sinhalese vigilantes took to the streets of the capital. They slaughtered three thousand Tamils in one day. As the violence spread, Tamils living in the south gathered up their belongings and fled to the north, dividing the country into two ethnic enclaves. Tamil attacks on the state began to grow in number and the Sinhalese government responded with force. Civil war began. By 2009, around a hundred thousand people were dead.

Lee Kuan Yew saw the bomb that was primed to go off under Sri Lanka. He believed it also sat beneath Singapore. The island's ethnic mix mirrored Sri Lanka's. One large group – the Chinese – outnumbered the next largest group – the Malay – roughly five to one. The shadow of Sri Lanka meant that Lee's greatest concern as he sat in the television studio wasn't the lack of land to grow food on, or the possibility of invasion. It was the threat of ethnic division. The day after independence he addressed his citizens thus: 'This is not a Malay nation,' he told them, 'this is not a Chinese nation … We are going to have a multiracial nation.' Action followed.

Where Sri Lanka had built checks and balances, Lee focused on building a common life. He allocated housing so that Chinese and Malay families lived together. He reorganised schools so that Chinese and Malay children learnt together. He introduced national service so that Chinese and Malay adults served together. He did everything he could to prevent People Like Me syndrome from pulling the country apart. The result was spectacular. Singapore didn't just avoid civil war; its stability and togetherness enabled it to reap a harvest of remarkable economic growth. Half a century after their involuntary independence, Singaporeans were the third-richest people in the world. The comparison with Sri Lanka is stark. On its Independence Day, Singapore's GDP was half of Sri Lanka's. Within a decade, it had parity. By 1980, it was four times wealthier. By 1990, six times. This rocket-like progress to riches was based on more than unity.[1] Yet without civil harmony, Singapore's future would have been much less bright. It would have been much more like Sri Lanka's.

Singapore is not a perfect model for the West. It is not a true democracy, the freedoms that its citizens have are less than I want for myself and there are high levels of income inequality. However, we would be foolish not to recognise that we can learn from Singapore.

The approach Lee took to building a common life for Singapore was born of necessity. With threats all around him, and the example of Sri Lanka hanging over him, he knew he could not wait for a common life to evolve. And so, he created one. It had three elements. The most radical was housing. Lee knew full well the power of 'People Like Me' syndrome. Left to the market, he was convinced that the new housing blocks that were springing up across the island would soon be divided up by ethnic group. One would be full of Malay Singaporeans, another full of Chinese Singaporeans and a third full of Indian Singaporeans. He was determined to stop that happening. Here, the Singapore state had an unusual advantage. Unlike in the West, the new housing blocks were being built on land that no individual or company owned. No, the land was owned by the state. Lee was determined to make use of the power this gave him. He instructed his officials to ensure that every housing block had a set of quotas. When the flats were put on the market, no more than a set percentage of flats would be sold to Chinese Singaporeans or Malay Singaporeans or – for that matter – Indian Singaporeans. Citizens were free to sell their flat on, but only if it didn't cause the quota to be broken.

The second element of the common life that Lee built was national service. Singapore desperately needed a defence force. Memories of invasion by the Japanese in the Second World War were recent and, with such a small population, conscription was probably unavoidable. However, it was not lost on Lee that it served a double purpose. It forced Singaporean men from all ethnic groups to live, work and potentially risk their lives together. Still today, all Singaporeans serve for two years in the armed forces or the police. 'All' means 'all'. There is no fitness test to weed people out. In fact, the opposite is true; those who pass a fitness test serve less time. Exemptions are extraordinarily rare. They are reserved for permanent disabilities or severe medical conditions. Punishments for those dodging service are real and significant; anyone caught can expect fines of up to £6,000 and three years in prison.

The third and final element was schooling. Lee was determined to ensure that Chinese, Malay and Indian Singaporeans would be educated together. Much of this was achieved by the country's housing policy, which meant that nearly every school had a catchment area that included all three main ethnic groups. To strengthen this, children were encouraged to take part in volunteering activities. This continues to this day. Singapore has a National Integration Council that issues guidance to schools on how to ensure students mix with those who are different. The latest guidance included encouragements to set up buddy systems, organise volunteering activity and hold celebrations for International Friendship Day, Racial Harmony Day and National Day. In recent years, the government has become concerned about schools becoming divided by income as well as ethnicity. As a result, before the pandemic struck, the state had planned to require all students to take part in a five-day outdoor adventure week to ensure that they spent time with students from across the city.

Singapore's approach to building a common life could not be more different from the Nordics'. The common life that brings diverse Singaporeans together is not voluntary, it is mandatory. Singaporeans are required to live together, serve together and, as much as possible, learn together. With this spine of togetherness in place, the city-state is not just open to change; it encourages it. It seeks to speed up economic changes, not slow them down. We saw in the last chapter that the Nordics came twelfth out of 180 countries for the efforts they took to protect employers and employees from economic change. Singapore comes last. There is no welfare state that Westerners would recognise, and labour protection is very limited. Instead, citizens are expected to save in case of troubles. When it comes to movement of people, Singapore is all for it. It has an incredibly liberal immigration policy. As a result, today, just under 40 per cent of Singaporeans were born overseas. This is three times the level of the United States and more than five times that of Finland. The only area where the pace of change has been slower than it could have been has been in the take-up of television; the Singaporeans consume about the same amount as the Nordics.

Many in the West think of Singapore as some sort of free-market heaven or hell, with the emphasis depending on your politics. The reality is more nuanced. Singapore is very open to the market. It encourages economic change. It also very open to immigration. Yet it can only do this because the state has intervened in housing, national service and schooling to build and protect a mandatory common life. Singapore is a rare example of the third option in our trilemma. It is a 'strengthened society': strengthened by its mandatory common life, it has the freedom to welcome change without fracturing. Lee's choice has worked for Singapore. The accidental country has not fractured, as he feared. It has flourished. But is this really a credible option for the freedom-loving West? The 'strengthened society' overcomes division by requiring people to take part in certain activities. There are moments when citizens have no choice but to mix and meet with people who seem 'unlike them'. That may be fine in the small, Asian, island city-state of Singapore, but surely it is not consistent with a Western view of the world – especially our views on freedom.

For most of us, freedom is the defining quality of the West: freedom to be who we want to be, believe what we want to believe, say what we want to say and do what we want to do. However, we also accept that there are some limits on this freedom. For most of us, the limit is set by an important principle. Philosophers call this the 'harm principle'.

If Western societies have a set of core beliefs, the 'harm principle' is one of them. It says this: 'You are free to do whatever you want, as long as you don't harm someone else.' I once heard it summed it up alternatively as: 'You can put your knife wherever you want, as long as it's not in my back.' The 'harm principle' is over two hundred years old. It is at least as old as the 1789 French Revolution, the victors of which produced a document called the 'Declaration of the Rights of Man and the Citizen' that is now embedded in the French constitution. Clause four of the Declaration begins like this: 'Liberty consists of doing anything that does not harm others.' A century later, the English philosopher, John Stuart Mill, repeated the principle in his essay *On Liberty*. He wrote: 'The only purpose for which power can be rightfully exercised over any member of a civilized community, against his will, is to prevent harm to others.' Centuries later, politics and philosophy students across Europe still study these words and almost everyone in the West accepts the principle. When we complain about an over-officious bureaucrat, we ask: 'But what harm am I doing?' Even small children get the idea. I have lost count of the number of times one of my three daughters has said, 'I didn't even harm her,' before being told off. Westerners will never accept being required to take part in common life activities unless these are needed to prevent harm.

They are. For our divisions are causing us harm. As we saw in Part III, our fractures are making all of us less safe, less healthy, less well governed, poorer and less able to have a fair crack at the whip. Not having a common life causes harm to us all. Hang on, you might say, these are very generalised harms. Westerners might be prepared to accept a law that stops them from putting a knife in someone else's back, but that doesn't mean they will accept further restrictions just to reduce the general risk of stabbings. Are you sure about that? In which case, how do you explain consistent Western support for incredibly controversial stop-and-search or stop-and-frisk policies, which have exactly this justification? People have their freedoms restricted because it may generally reduce crime. Or, more recently, consider our reaction to the pandemic. A narrow view of the 'harm principle' would suggest that all governments should ban us from purposely infecting other people with Covid-19. This isn't what they did. They restricted people's freedoms dramatically (including those who were likely to be immune) in order to generally reduce the number of people dying. We were required to stay at home, wear masks, avoid unnecessary travel, close businesses and restrict the number of people in our homes. I am not arguing here about the rights or wrongs of those decisions. I am pointing out that the people of the West – the children of the French Revolution and John Stuart Mill – were, despite a few outliers, very supportive of these restrictions. Take mask-wearing, for example. Even in the heat of a divisive American election campaign where one candidate attacked mask-wearing, three-quarters of Americans and a majority of Republicans supported the requirement to wear a mask. When asked to explain why, where did they turn? To the 'harm principle'. They supported the rule not because it made *them* safe, nor because they planned to purposely hurt anyone, but because it generally reduced the number of people being harmed.

A pandemic is – hopefully – an unusual event; stabbings should be too. Perhaps, outside of these extreme scenarios, the Western public is in fact opposed to restrictions on freedoms that achieve a generalised reduction in harm. But it doesn't look like it. Consider the public's support for laws to protect our environment. It's hard to think of a more generalised harm than contributing to the loss of the ozone layer or to the increase of plastic in the sea. And yet, Westerners have been hugely supportive both of bans on aerosols that helped to mend the ozone layer and of policies that forced retailers to charge consumers for plastic bags. Maybe, once again, this is a special case? And yet – wherever you look – Western populations support laws that make their societies generally less harmful. Last night I took my daughter to her gym class. I got in the car and set off on the brief ten-minute drive. Despite the shortness of my journey, you would be horrified if I told you that I have never passed a driving test, never insured the car, never wear a seatbelt and always drive at twice the speed limit. We expect the law to do more than ban me from driving into other road users. We expect it to require me to generally reduce the risk of harm. On arrival at the gym club, imagine my own horror if I was told that the building where the class was taking place had not followed any building regulations and the staff who were running the session have not been properly background-checked for any history of hurting children. Again, we expect the law to reduce the risk of these things, not simply to ban buildings from falling down or people from committing abuse. Westerners don't expect the law to merely prevent others from purposely hurting us; we expect it to reduce the risk of harm.

Alongside the harm principle, most Westerners have two other core beliefs about any restrictions on freedom. First, they must be proportionate. Consider our approach to driving tests. Driving tests restrict freedom. Unless you have proven to the state that you can drive safely, you are not allowed to drive, whether you are going to work, to see your friends, to visit your family or to go away on holiday. You are expected to spend your own money on the test and your own time, and probably more money, learning to pass it. We think all of this is proportionate. Now, it is also true that we would be safer drivers if we all took a further, advanced driving test. There would be less harm on the roads. Nevertheless, the public does not think it is proportionate to force people to take this second test. Alongside proportionality, we expect any restrictions to be legitimate. They must be based on an objective set of rules, a rational assessment, some underlying principles. When Covid-19 rules were introduced, many of us wanted to see the evidence and understand the basis for the decisions. In the UK, it was seen to be important that Parliament voted on any changes to the rules.

Any new mandatory common life would have to be both proportionate and legitimate if it is to be accepted by Western societies. To achieve this we should require any such rules to achieve three different types of majority support: from the public as a whole, from those with skin in the game, and from those who have been there and done it. Before any new common life requirement is imposed, the legislative body must have evidence that most of the public are in favour, most of the group required to take part is in favour and most of those who have previously taken part are still in favour.[2] Any legislation should automatically lapse after a small number of years, requiring new evidence of the three majorities and a new vote in Parliament to support it. But could anything actually achieve these three majorities? Definitely. The best proposals would vary by country, and over time, but let me suggest three that I am sure would pass in most Western countries.[3]

The first proposal is a month-long national service programme for secondary school students. Imagine a four-week programme taking place during the school term. Children aged fourteen are formed into teams of twelve. The teams include students from different schools, bringing together teenagers from all backgrounds. The group spends a week camping and hiking together, improving their health and their well-being. They then spend a week learning a skill they care about – drama, sport, music, art or film-making – and use it to serve the local community. One group might make a film about the life stories of elderly residents living in the nearby residential home; another might run sporting activities for younger children after school. In the third week, the teenagers explore their local community, spending time with local businesses, local charity workers and local residents. They conduct a survey to understand the needs of the community and come up with an idea of how they might make a contribution. At the end of the week, they pitch the idea to a panel of experts asking for funding to make their plan happen. In the final week, it is time to put their idea into practice. Throughout the four weeks they will have met, listened to and worked alongside people from all backgrounds. They will have bonded together through moments of shared intensity, whether camping overnight, pitching for funding or organising activities that they are in charge of.

Would such a programme gain the three majorities it needs? Could it achieve the support of the public, the support of those taking part and the support of those who have taken part? It is pretty clear that it would gain the first; there are consistent majorities across the West in favour of some form of return of national service. What about support from the majority of potential participants? Again, I am confident that this could be achieved simply by the activity taking place during term-time, with the alternative being staying in class. I am also confident it would gain majority support from those who have taken part. The programme I have described is very similar to the UK's National Citizen Service, whose graduates were found to be more likely to recommend taking part to others than Apple users are to recommend using Apple products.

The second proposal is aimed at the parents of young children. At the point at which children start at a nursery, parents attend a series of six half-day sessions where they learn what their children will be doing at nursery, how their brains are developing and how they can best help them to learn and be healthy. The sessions are delivered in small groups, with parents spending time with eleven other parents. All come from a different part of town and different walks of life, but all have the same-aged children. Each session ends with lunch, during which parents have the chance to share how things are going for them and gain encouragement and solace from each other's experience. By eating together and sharing stories about the intense and common experience of raising a child, the group starts to connect and build a bond. Members gain friends, who they can WhatsApp with problems, plus a ready supply of babysitters. Because it is a government-backed programme, the government provides a couple of extra sweeteners. No one loses out on money they would have earned because they are not at work; employers are required to release staff to attend and the self-employed are compensated for their time. On top of this, attendance brings with it a reduction in the price of nursery care.

Again, I am confident this would gain the three majorities. The first – majority support from the public – should be relatively easy; the idea of mandatory parenting programmes is consistently popular with the general public, who, rather cynically, always seem to believe that the latest generation of parents are particularly in need of help. The second – majority support from parents – is also likely once the sweetener of cheaper nursery care and time off work is thrown in. The third – majority support from those who have taken part – is also likely. An in-depth review of a parenting programme delivered by the organisation Triple-P found that the average parent gave the course a satisfaction rating of 80 out of 91.[4]

The final proposal is a national retirement service. At the point of retirement, you are enrolled in a three-month course that takes place a short distance from where you live. You join a group with eleven others who have also recently retired and come from a variety of walks of life. At the first meeting, you have a meal together and start to get to know each other. A facilitator helps to get everyone talking and you have a chance to hear about the other participants' careers and what everyone is hoping for from retirement. The group meets three times a week. The Monday sessions help you think through what you might want to do with your retirement, covering a range of topics such as financial planning, holidays, supporting family, taking up hobbies, volunteering in the community or continuing to work. The Wednesday sessions involve volunteering in the local community. You are able to pick from a variety of options, from reading to children at the local school to visiting residents at the local care home or helping with the upkeep of a local park or a community building. The Friday sessions are entirely social. As a quid quo pro for being required to take part, the group is given a small budget to socialise together – enough to cover a meal out each week. Members are also given a small top-up to their state pension.

Again, I am confident that this would gather the three majorities. Majority support is likely to be the easiest. Westerners of all ages are very supportive of expenditure in support of those who are older, even in times of recession. They are keen for 'something to be done' about isolation and loneliness. The second – achieving majority support from those required to take part – is likely to be the toughest, but a top-up to the state pension in return for mandatory participation is likely to swing the vote. Majority support from those who have taken part should be entirely possible. A two-day programme that was piloted in the early 2010s in the UK resulted in very positive feedback. Participants found that they were more confident, better informed and had built a useful network.

These three proposals are just one way that a mandatory common life could be built.[5] There are countless other ways it could be done that might better suit the wants and needs of a specific society. My aim is merely to show that a mandatory common life is not incompatible with our Western values. Providing a service programme for teenagers, a parenting programme for new parents and a national retirement service will not undermine Western society. In fact, it will do the exact opposite. Unless we take some form of action to bring people together, the things we hold most dear in our societies are at risk: our sense of fair play, safety, trust, opportunity, health and even our democracy itself. Many others have made similar points about the danger our fractures pose, but too few have proposed a solution. There is only one solution that will make a genuine difference: it is to rebuild our common life. The only way to do that is to either slow down the rate of change or use the power of the state to bring us together.

Of course, there are things that we as individuals can and should do. I list thirty-two such things in the Epilogue. There are worthwhile things you can do that will make a difference. Doing them will help to mend some of our fractures. It will also draw attention to the fact that more must be done. More will have to done. For the problem of our fractured societies is too big to be solved solely by these individual actions. It requires the state to act as well. If we want to reduce climate change, there are things we can all do. But the state must act as well. The same is true here.

We are left with one final objection. It is not an objection based on logic. It is more of a feeling. A feeling that says – no matter how strong the argument, how compelling the evidence, how reasonable the proposals – the idea that a Western state could ever compel its citizens to do something together is simply inconceivable.

Britain's National Health Service feels like an inevitable invention today. It is the one piece of public policy that no serious British politician will question or criticise. Retired Chancellor, Nigel Lawson, described it as 'the closest thing the English people have to a religion'.[6] Even outside of a pandemic, National Health Service doctors and nurses are revered as heroes. Pollsters regularly find that they are the people that Britons trust the most and the National Health Service itself is the single thing that the country is most proud of. It could never have been any other way.

Except it could have.

In the 1940s, when the National Health Service was first suggested, those heroic doctors did not cheer for its arrival; they opposed it root and branch. Within two years of the Second World War ending, the ex-Chairman of the British Medical Association – the organisation that represents all British doctors – described the proposal to create a National Health Service as the 'first step, and a big one, to National

Socialism'. Note his words. He did not say 'socialism'. He said, 'national socialism'. To the doctors, the National Health Service was not an inevitable, fundamentally British, marvel; it was an inconceivable, potentially Nazi, disaster.

The doctors weren't the only 'heroes' opposed to the National Health Service. The leader of the opposition, Winston Churchill, was also against it. Twenty-one times he led his party to oppose the Bill that eventually created the health service. In a typically Churchillian flourish, he warned the health secretary, Aneurin Bevan, whose job it was to get the Bill passed, that he was at risk of making himself 'as great a curse to his country in time of peace as he was a squalid nuisance in time of war'. Many charities, churches and local authorities across the country were opposed – appalled at the prospect of the government taking control of *their* hospitals. Despite the opposition, the Bill was finally passed and Bevan took a moment to celebrate. His joy proved premature, for the doctors refused to go along with it. Holding a vote in 1948, they lined up ten to one against having anything to do with the new system. The National Health Service was dead on arrival – Bevan had everything he needed but no doctors. He decided to do a deal. He promised the doctors that they could still continue with their lucrative private practices, and they agreed to get the National Health Service up and running. Bevan later told supporters that he had 'stuffed their mouths with gold'.

Right up until the moment when it first opened its doors, the NHS was far from inevitable. In fact, for many of the bravest and the brightest in Britain, it was inconceivable and ill-judged. Before 1939, the public largely agreed. It would take a crisis to change things. The Second World War threw people of all backgrounds together – in war, in evacuation, in work and in bomb shelters. Confronted with each other, wealthier Britons saw just how unhealthy their country was. A mental Rubicon was crossed. The idea of a National Health Service moved, in the public's imagination, from inconceivable to desirable; only after its birth and success did it ever seem inevitable. The truth is that nearly all big political ideas – from the welfare state to privatisation, from the European Union to Brexit – start off as inconceivable. Through argument, clarity, imagination and crisis, they slowly become imaginable, desirable and eventually inevitable.

This aim of this book is to start that journey from inconceivable to inevitable. To encourage you that we do not have to live with our present divisions. To show you that there is another option. And to make of you a small request. The next time you hear one of our politicians tell you that they want to heal our divisions, to mend our fractures, or to bring our country back together again, would you mind asking them what they actually plan to do? Do they intend to copy the Nordics and apply the brakes to change? Do they plan to copy Singapore and build a new common life to bring us together? Or do they plan to just do nothing? With only warm words and appeals to shared values, our leaders are like Aneurin Bevan prematurely celebrating a new National Health Service when he didn't have any doctors.

We have lived in our divided societies for long enough. It is time that someone put down the warm words and did something about it. Now that would be something worth standing outside the front of our homes and clapping for.

THIRTY-TWO THINGS YOU CAN DO RIGHT NOW

We need the government to act if we are going to overcome our divisions. But there are things each of us can do to make our societies more united. Here are thirty-two suggestions.

Think well

Assume the best: It is easy to be nervous of people who seem different from you – whether they are teens waiting for a bus, people talking with a different accent or a different generation. Try assuming the best instead.

Accept other points of view: People have opinions that you won't agree with. If it feels like it's your job in life to convince everyone of something or to police a moral line, relax a little.

Be honest: Pick up your phone and look at the last ten people you sent a message to. How different are they from you?

Make peace with awkward moments: Sometimes in life you might start a conversation with someone and they won't want to talk to you, or you might end up with an awkward silence. Don't let this stop you interacting with people you don't know.

Change your habits

Say hello: Try defaulting towards saying 'Hello' and 'How are you?' when you see a neighbour at the park, or on the commute or in the supermarket.

Watch less TV: Try having a day a week when you watch only thirty minutes of TV or none at all. With the time you save you can do some of the other things in this list.

Change who you follow on social media: Follow some new people on social media who are different from you in some way, especially those with different opinions.

Take a different path: Is there part of your neighbourhood that you think of as being 'not for people like you'? Go there and have a drink, eat a meal out, take a walk.

Help out

Help at your local school: Contact your local school and see if they are looking for someone to help read to the children.

Help with young people: Contact your local Scouts or Guides and see if they are looking for helpers.

Visit the elderly: Contact your local residential care home and see if you could visit and talk to residents. Or contact a befriending charity and sign up.

Help at the food bank: Contact your local food bank and offer to help.

Join something

Join a club: Take up a hobby and join a club where you can share it with others. Try one that doesn't cost much money; that way you'll meet a more mixed group of people.

Join a class: Sign up for a class at your local college. Say hello and be friendly to the other people in the class. Suggest you all go out for a drink or some food.

Visit a place of worship: If you've never been to a church, a mosque or a temple, try and organise a visit. If you're a person of faith, try going more often.

Start a book group: Start a book (or film, board game or card game) group and invite a group of neighbours, colleagues or fellow parents from the local school to join.

Be a great neighbour

Invite your neighbours around: Open your house up once a year and invite all your neighbours to pop by for a drink or a bite to eat.

Cook for any old or new neighbours: Offer to cook for someone in your local neighbourhood who is older or who has a baby.

Ask for and give help to your neighbours: Ask your neighbours when you need some advice with DIY or need to borrow something. Offer to help when they do.

Do seasonal cards: Drop a card through people's letterboxes at Christmas to say hello and wish them the best.

Open up your workplace (especially if you're a manager)

Review your job adverts: Take a look of your job adverts. Remove jargon. Be explicit that you welcome people from all backgrounds and with all opinions. Ask yourself: does this role really require someone to have a degree?

Advertise somewhere new: Try advertising somewhere new and see if you get a different set of applicants. Consider taking on an apprentice if you haven't before.

Mix up your interview panels: Rejig your interview panels so that not everyone on them is from the same walk of life.

Consider a 'Rooney Rule': Is there a type of person missing from your organisation? Consider insisting that all final interview rounds include someone like this.

Support your local state school (especially if you're a pupil, parent, teacher or governor)

Make state schools great: Support the local school so that parents want to send their children there. Encourage teachers, support fundraisers, join the Parents Association.

Support community activity: Ask the head teacher if pupils could get involved in volunteering or perhaps visiting a local residential care home. See if you can help.

Ask about school linking: If your pupils are mostly from one background, ask the head teacher about making a link with another school with a different set of pupils.

Open up the school: Ask your school governors to reserve a certain number of places for children from lower-income families.

Get political

Write to your councillor: Write to your local councillor asking what they are doing to help poorer families to afford local housing and get into the better schools.

Write to your MP: Write to your Member of Parliament and ask them what they plan to do to heal our divisions.

Use your vote: Use your vote to support politicians who will do the most to take on the four causes of division:

> Distance: Will they support subsidised housing and planning reform so that poorer families can live in wealthy areas?
> Difference: Will they seek to reduce inequality?
> Change: Will they protect workers' rights and manage immigration?
> Choice: Will they support national service for schoolchildren and incentivise parenting classes and a national retirement service?

Share these ideas: Tell others about these thirty-two ideas, send them a copy of the book, organise a book group to discuss the ideas.

FURTHER READING

In writing *Fractured*, I benefitted hugely from a wealth of wisdom and facts gleaned from academic articles and books. You can find most of these in the Endnotes. If you are looking for something accessible and enjoyable to read having finished *Fractured*, here is a selection of the books and articles that I would most recommend:

Allport, Gordon, *The Nature of Prejudice*, Addison-Wesley, 1954

Bishop, Bill, *The Big Sort: Why the Clustering of Like-Minded America is Tearing Us Apart*, Houghton Mifflin, 2008

Brooks, David *The Social Animal: A Story of How Success Happens*, Short Books, 2012.

Chetty, Raj et al., 'Where is the Land of Opportunity? Geography of International Mobility in the United States', National Bureau of Economic Research, 2014, https://www.nber.org/papers/w19843

Coates, Ta-Nehisi, 'The Ghetto is Public Policy', *The Atlantic*, 2013, https://www.theatlantic.com/national/archive/2013/03/the-ghetto-is-public-policy/274147/

Diamond, Jared, 'The Worst Mistake in the History of the Human Race', *Discover*, 1987, https://www.discovermagazine.com/planet-earth/the-worst-mistake-in-the-history-of-the-human-race

Fowler, James H. and Nicholas Christakis, *Connected: The Surprising Power of Our Social Networks and How They Shape Our Lives*, Hachette, 2009

Goodhart, David, *The Road to Somewhere: The Populist Revolt and the Future of Politics*, Hurst, 2017

Halpern, David, *Social Capital: The New Golden Goose*, Cambridge University Press, 1999

Halpern, David, *The Hidden Wealth of Nations*, Polity Press, 2010

Harari, Yuval Noah, *Sapiens: A Brief History of Humankind*, Vintage, 2014.

Kaus, Mickey, *The End of Equality*, Basic Books, 1987

Marlowe, Frank, *The Hadza: Hunter-gatherers of Tanzania*, University of California Press, 2010

McArdle, Megan, *How Utah Keeps the American Dream Alive*, Bloomberg, March 2017, https://www.bloomberg.com/opinion/articles/2017-03-28/how-utah-keeps-the-american-dream-alive

McCauley, Clark and Sophia Moskalenko, *Friction: How Radicalization Happens to Them and Us*, Oxford University Press, 2011

Murray, Charles, *Coming Apart: The State of White America, 1960–2010*, Random House, 2012

Perry, Gina, *The Lost Boys: inside Muzafer Sherif's Robbers Cave experiment*, Scribe, 2018

Putnam, Robert, *Bowling Alone: The Collapse and Revival of American Community*, Simon & Schuster, 2000

Putnam, Robert, '*E Pluribus Unum*: Diversity and Community in the Twenty-first Century', *Scandinavian Political Studies*, 2006, https://onlinelibrary.wiley.com/doi/abs/10.1111/j.1467-9477.2007.00176.x

Putnam, Robert, *Our Kids: The American Dream in Crisis*, Simon & Schuster, 2015

Sachs, Jonathan, *The Politics of Hope*, Vintage, 1997

Skocpol, Theda *Diminished Democracy: From Membership to Management in American Civic Life*, University of Oklahoma Press, 2013

Uslaner, Eric, *Segregation and Mistrust: Diversity, Isolation, and Social Cohesion*, Cambridge University Press, 2012

Whitehouse, Harvey, *Arguments and Icons: Divergent Modes of Religiosity*, Oxford University Press, 2000

Willetts, David, *The Pinch: How Baby-Boomers Took Their Children's Future, and Why They Should Give it Back*, Atlantic Books, 2010

ACKNOWLEDGEMENTS

Someone once said that gratitude is to life what salt is to food. It brings out the flavour; spread it liberally. When it comes to *Fractured*, there is a lot of gratitude to spread.

I should start at the beginning with Matthew Taylor who was wise enough to suggest that a book needed to be written and unwise enough to suggest I should do it. I would have had nothing to write, though, without my many co-conspirators who have worked – very patiently – with me on my passion of bringing people from all backgrounds together. There are a lot of you but I particularly want to thank Benny Goodman, Craig Morley, Doug Fraley and Alexis Meech for The Challenge; Emma Jenkins for HeadStart; Afua Kudom, Rosie Evans and Rich Bell for the Social Integration Commission and APPG; Andy Smith, Charlotte Hobson, (Rosie again) and Rick Miles for Step Forward; and Brendan Cox, Gemma Mortensen, Matthieu Lefevre and Tim Dixon for involving me in More in Common.

I benefited hugely from everyone who was prepared to read elements of the book and provide thoughts. Thank you to those who came to the house for a *Fractured*-focused dinner both for being prepared to eat my cooking and for being an impromptu focus group. I know which was the braver step. I am particularly grateful to Brendan Cox, Rich Bell, Rachel Hursey, Margaret Yates, Charlotte

Hobson, Rob Collett and Peter Babudu for reading large sections and sending through thoughts and suggestions. I also owe Nathan Sansom a thank you for gifting me the story of his time in France.

The fantastic team at HarperNorth have been flexible, fast, supportive, kind and talented – all at the same time. Thank you Alice, Jon, Gen, Megan and Oli. The irony was not lost on me that a book about the biases we have towards people like us was snapped up by someone with the same first name as me. Thank you, Jon. None of this would have happened without my peerless agent Toby Mundy. I count myself very privileged to have an agent who gets what I am trying to say, knows the world of publishing inside out, and has an excellent sense of humour (in other words, he laughs at my jokes). Thank you also to Nick Fawcett for his marvellous hunter-gathering of typos and poor writing. His consistent attention to detail was remarkable to me. The most important correction came from my brother-in-law. Thank you Jamie Youth for spotting that the book should be called 'Fractured' not 'Fracture'.

The last phase of book writing coincided with my work at the Youth Endowment Fund. Sir Kevan Collins – my Chair – was a great support in my finishing the book and I owe him my thanks, as I do the rest of the wonderful team I work with.

I have three thanks that go together: to illness, ignorance and love. Illness first. This book would never have happened if I hadn't sneezed so hard that I slipped a disk (genuinely), confining me to my bed every weekend for six months. Having watched everything on Netflix, I ran out of things to do and excuses not to start working on the book. As for ignorance, there is no way I would have started writing this book if I had any idea of how much work would be required. Finally, love. My wife, who had already had to put up with me sitting on my behind for six months with a bad back, was sufficiently smart to know that a book was actually a lot of work. And yet, she has supported me throughout from encouraging me, reading drafts, typing things up, being fantastic with the family in my absence and gently mocking me when I needed a sense of perspec-tive. Thank you, Lisa – this book would still be a bundle of thoughts without you.

And finally, to my mum and dad. They gave me a faith that taught me that we are all children of the same Father and a hair colour that meant I would be a rather solitary soul if I only hung out with people 'like me'. Thank you.

NOTES

Chapter 1: The Problem You Knew About All Along

1. If you're British and a professional, you know half as many working-class people as the average Briton. The picture in the United States is much the same.
2. This went into reverse from 1960 onwards as increasing numbers of women completed degrees and gained senior positions at work. This of course is something to be celebrated. However, once in senior positions, these women met and married men who had done the same. In the 1950s, male, heterosexual doctors married nurses or secretaries; today they marry other doctors.
3. Robert Putnam, *Our Kids*, Simon & Schuster, 2015.
4. The average age difference between any two Americans is two decades but the average age difference between two American friends is half that.
5. The average Briton, meanwhile, has almost half the number of friendships with people of other generations than demographics would suggest.
6. David Goodhart, *The British Dream*, Atlantic Books, 2013.

Chapter 2: The Villain of Our Story

1. The figures that follow and are reproduced later in the text take inspiration from a diagram first published in Tim Harford, *The Logic of Life*, Little Brown, 2008.
2. In the real world, we know that once you become used to being surrounded by people like you, you can become easily discomforted by quite low levels of diversity. This helps to explain why White Americans and White Britons are the most likely groups to leave ethnically diverse

areas and schools: they're simply much more used to being in the majority. While the majority of African Americans are happy to live in neighbourhoods that are split evenly between White and Black, the majority of White people are not. The more we live surrounded by Eagles, the more uncomfortable we feel mixing with Rattlers.

Chapter 3: The Hero Hidden in Our History

1. In the case of the Hadza, the puberty ritual is normally the most intense. Lasting as long as a month, it can include dramatic enactments as well as a series of physical ordeals culminating in a celebrated return to the community.
2. Frank Marlowe, *The Hadza: Hunter-gatherers of Tanzania*, University of California Press, 2010.
3. Jared Diamond, 'The Worst Mistake in the History of the Human Race', *Discover* magazine, 1987.
4. Ibid.
5. Jared Diamond (ibid.) notes that, 'Skeletons from Greece and Turkey show that the average height of hunter-gatherers toward the end of the ice ages was a generous 5' 9" for men, 5' 5" for women. With the adoption of agriculture, height crashed, and by 3000 BC had reached a low of only 5' 3" for men, 5' for women. By classical times heights were very slowly on the rise again, but modern Greeks and Turks have still not regained the average height of their distant ancestors.'
6. Ibid.
7. Just as each hunter-gathering tribe or group had a common life that differed from each other – the *epeme*, for example, was unique to the Hadza – we should expect the way in which the common life operated in each period and location to differ. Even if we focus just on what became the West, that short phrase 'agrarian societies' can cover periods from the ninth millennium BC to the second millennium AD – periods as diverse as Ancient Rome, the Holy Roman Empire, Elizabethan Britain and pre-revolutionary America.
8. Fifty-two of these days would have been Sundays when attendance at the local church was expected. The remainder – around forty to sixty – were commemoration days, which would include collective feasts, or days to rest following significant feasts, such as Christmas and Easter. (Christian Rohr, 'Feast and Daily Life in the Middle Ages', lecture at Novosibirsk State University, 2002.)
9. Ibid.

10. Ibid.
11. Even a farmer travelling from 7000 BC to AD 1600 would recognise many of the elements that made society work, even if they didn't understand the words being used to describe them.
12. Urban life would have included a number of public pageants to mark special occasions, but these declined throughout the eighteenth and nineteenth centuries and were much less universal than the rural feasts. (David Sunderland, *Social Capital, Trust and the Industrial Revolution*, Routledge, 2007.)
13. Michael Ward, 'Minutes of Evidence taken before The Lords Committee appointed to enquire into the state and condition of the children employed in the Cotton Manufactories of the United Kingdom', House of Lords, 1819.
14. Raymond Williams, *The Long Revolution*, Parthian Books, 1961.
15. Ibid.
16. 1840 Census Data as presented here: George Tucker, *Progress of the United States in Population and Wealth in Fifty Years*, Publishers various, 1843.
17. P.A. Graham, *Community and Class in American Education, 1865–1918*, Wiley, 1974.
18. C. Goldin and L. F. Katz, 'Human Capital and Social Capital', in *Patterns of Social Capital*, Cambridge University Press, 2001.
19. While some associations had existed in towns before industrialisation, the rate of establishment in the nineteenth and early twentieth century was unparalleled.
20. David Sunderland, *Social Capital, Trust and the Industrial Revolution*, Routledge, 2007.
21. The Scouts here are an exception. Just a year before the organisation was formally established, Baden-Powell took twenty boys to Brownsea Island, off the coast of Poole, to camp, ensuring that half of them came from the local Boys' Brigades and half from exclusive public schools (https://www.nationaltrust.org.uk/brownsea-island/features/scouting-and-guiding-on-brownsea-island).
22. Gerald Gamm and Robert D. Putnam, 'Voluntary Associations in America', in *Patterns of Social Capital*, Cambridge University Press, 1999.
23. Robert Putnam, *Bowling Alone*, Simon & Schuster, 2000.
24. Theda Skocpol, *Diminished Democracy: From Membership to Management in American Civic Life*, University of Oklahoma Press, 2013.

Chapter 4: A Secret Weakness

1. There are other things to learn from Levine and Reicher's football fans. Their experiment gives us a valuable insight into what People Like Me syndrome feels like when it strikes. It's not a conscious hatred or dislike of 'the other', especially the 'ethnic other'. In fact, first and foremost, it isn't conscious at all. When interviewed at the end of the experiment, hardly any of the football fans mentioned the researcher who had fallen over. The second thing is that it doesn't apply only to ethnic difference. In our test, the researcher was always the same person. Their ethnicity didn't change. Just their shirt. The third thing to note is that PLM syndrome is much more of a bias towards those 'like us' than a strong opposition against those 'unlike us'. In both of Levine and Reicher's tests, the Manchester United fans were equally likely to help someone wearing a Liverpool shirt as to help someone wearing a plain red shirt (despite Liverpool being their arch-rival).

2. Yuval Noah Harari, in his book *Sapiens*, details the role that shared stories or 'myths' – from animism to Islam, from capitalism to communism – can play in enabling human groups to work together for a greater shared purpose. Without a common life, however, this shared story is a weak force to connect groups. This is partly because it is through the common life that these myths and narratives become created and shared; without them, separate groups will form their own myths, leading to division and separation. It is also because, as the research into the Hadza shows, a shared story in itself builds less trust than a shared interaction. Researchers found that trust rose between Hadza only when they performed the *epeme* together. Dancing it apart had no effect.

3. The same inclusiveness is evident when fairs, with a greater variety of entertainments, start to spring up. Emma Griffin writes: 'The fair, then, was both universal and inclusive, attracting both genders, all ages and individuals of all social status' (Emma Griffin, *England's Revelry: A History of Popular Sports and Pastimes, 1660–1830*, The British Academy, 2005).

4. Weddings, for example, would include a celebration at Sunday mass that all would attend, as they would on the return to church of a new mother after childbirth.

5. Robert Provine, *Cracking the Laughter Code*, Penguin, 2000.

6. Ibid.

7. David Brooks, *The Social Animal*, Random House, 2011.

8. Remarkably, our neurons act as mirror neurons when watching relatively inconsequential actions. Just watching someone else brush their teeth

will make your neurons fire as though you were brushing your own teeth.

9. The experiment is fully written up in Matthews et al., 'Dorsal Raphe Dopamine Neurons Represent the Experience of Social Isolation', *Behavioural Neuroscience*, 2016.

10. Robby Berman, 'Your Brain Interprets Prolonged Loneliness as Physical Pain – Why?', http://bigthink.com/robby-berman/the-powerful-medical-impact-of-loneliness, 2017.

11. This helps to explain why our tendency to feel lonely is partly hereditary. For more information on loneliness and evolution, see the work of John Cacioppo, the director of the Center for Cognitive and Social Neuroscience at the University of Chicago.

12. Matt Schudel, 'J. Cameron Wade, World War II veteran and activist for forgotten Black soldiers, dies at 87', *Washington Post*, 2012.

13. Gordon Allport, *The Nature of Prejudice*, Addison-Wesley, 1954.

14. Stéphane Côté et al., 'Social Affiliation in Same-Class and Cross-Class Interactions', *Journal of Experimental Psychology*, Vol. 146, No. 2, 269–85, 2017.

15. Christian Rohr, 'Feast and Daily Life in the Middle Ages', lecture at Novosibirsk State University, 2002.

16. David Alexander, 'Man with the Black Hat' (http://manwithblackhat.blogspot.co.uk/2012/01/my-scoutmaster-died-today.html, 2012).

17. Jacob Rugh and Mary Fischer, 'Military Veterans and Neighborhood Racial Integration: VA Mortgage Lending Across Three Eras', *Population Research and Policy Review*, 2018.

18. H. Whitehouse, 'Dying for the Group: Towards a General Theory of Extreme Self-sacrifice', *Behaviour and Brain Sciences*, Cambridge University Press, 2018.

19. H. Whitehouse et al., 'Brothers in Arms: Libyan Revolutionaries Bond Like Family', *Proceedings of the National Academy of Sciences of the United States of America* (*PNAS*), 2012.

20. Researchers found that respondents who thought of these tough times were more willing to risk their life to defend their fellow countrymen. H. Whitehouse et al., 'The Evolution of Extreme Cooperation Via Shared Dysphoric Experiences', *Scientific Reports*, 2017.

21. J. Jong et al., 'Shared Negative Experiences Lead to Identity Fusion via Personal Reflection', *PLoS ONE*, 2014.

22. H. Whitehouse, *Modes of Religiosity: A Cognitive Theory of Religious Transmission*, Altamira Press, 2004.

23. H. Whitehouse and J. A. Lanman, 'The Ties That Bind Us: Ritual, Fusion, and Identification', *Current Anthropology*, 2014.

24. W. B. Swann et al., 'When Group Membership Gets Personal: A Theory of Identity Fusion', *Psychological Review*, 2012.
25. C. M. Kavanagh et al., 'Exploring the Pathways Between Transformative Group Experiences and Identity Fusion', *Frontiers in Psychology*, 2020.
26. Wen et al., 'Ritual Increases Children's Affiliation with In-group Members', *Evolution and Human Behaviour*, 2016.
27. Scott Wiltermuth and Chip Heath, 'Synchrony and Cooperation', *Psychological Science*, 2009.
28. I am grateful to Professor Harvey Whitehouse for this distinction between high-intensity versus routine activities. He first laid this out in *Arguments and Icons: Divergent Modes of Religiosity*, published in 2000.
29. Richard Sosos and Bradley Ruffle, 'Ideology, Religion and the Evolution of Cooperation: Field Experiments on Israeli Kibbutzim', *Socioeconomic Aspects of Human Behavioural Ecology*, 2004.
30. Ibid.
31. What is striking is that those praying do not appear to be consciously aware that this is an effect that the Amidah is having. In the same way, the marchers, singers and bead stringers are not consciously aware that the task is making them appear more trustworthy. Instead, we have evolved to make this judgement subconsciously. Trusting those who follow the same routine as us must have become a useful rule of thumb for our ancestors. Those who followed the rule instinctively clearly gained an advantage that led to the instinct being passed down the genetic line. The soldiers in the Battle of the Bulge knew consciously that they were Black and White men. But subconsciously the world of routine told them that they could trust each other.
32. This was especially likely if the feast celebrated a saint who was particularly important to the village.

Chapter 5: Coming Apart

1. Mona Chalabi, 'What Are The Chances Of Serving On A Jury?', *FiveThirtyEight*, 2015.
2. One in three non-farm workers were members of trade unions in the 1950s. This had fallen to one in six by the year 2000. (Theda Skocpol, *Diminished Democracy: From Membership to Management in American Civic Life*, University of Oklahoma Press, 2013.)
3. In 1960, almost half of all American parents were members of a Parents–Teachers Association; by the 1990s, less than one in five were.
4. Theda Skocpol, *Diminished Democracy: From Membership to Management in American Civic Life*, University of Oklahoma Press, 2013.

5. Robert Putnam provides these statistics in *Bowling Alone*. He goes on: 'Measured in terms of hours per month, the average American's investment in organizational life (apart from religious groups) fell from 3.7 hours per month in 1965 ... to 2.3 in 1985 and 1995. On an average day in 1965, 7 percent of Americans spent some time in a community organization. By 1995 that figure had fallen to 3 percent of all Americans. Those numbers suggest that nearly half of all Americans in the 1960s invested some time each week in clubs and associations, as compared to one quarter in the 1990s ... active involvement in face-to-face organizations has plummeted, whether we consider organizational records, survey reports, time diaries, or consumer expenditures' (Robert Putnam, *Bowling Alone*, Simon & Schuster, 2000).
6. 'Church Statistics', *Introduction: UK Christianity 2005–2015*, https://faithsurvey.co.uk/download/csintro.pdf.
7. NatCen, 'Losing Faith, NatCen Social Research: British Attitudes Survey', https://www.bsa.natcen.ac.uk/latest-report/british-social-attitudes-28/religion.aspx.
8. See both Cherrington, *Not Just Beer and Bingo: The Story of Working Men's Clubs*, AuthurHouse, 2012, and The Women's Institute, 'About the WI', The Women's Institute website.
9. See John Mohan, 'Shifting the Dials? Stability, Change and Cohort Variations in Voluntary Action', Third Sector Research Working Paper, 2015. The forensic work of Andrew Leigh finds the same pattern in Australia. Summarising the situation in 2011 he writes: 'Organisational membership is down. We are less likely to attend church. Political parties and unions are bleeding members. Sporting participation and cultural attendance are down. We have fewer friends and are less connected with our neighbours.' (Andrew Leigh, *Disconnected*, UNSW Press, 2010.)
10. The rise in these types of organisation meant that initial analysis of membership groups in the UK suggested that the decline Putnam had identified in America was not present in the UK. Further examination has shown that membership is in fact decreasing in organisations where you find face-to-face interaction. (See Helen Cameron, 'Social Capital in Britain: Are Hall's Membership Figures a Reliable Guide?', unpublished paper presented at ARNOVA Annual Conference, November 2001.)
11. Robert Putnam, *Bowling Alone*, Simon & Schuster, 2000.
12. Theda Skocpol, *Diminished Democracy: From Membership to Management in American Civic Life*, University of Oklahoma Press, 2013.

13. Peter Hall, 'Social Capital in Britain', *British Journal of Politics*, 1999.

14. In an analysis of levels of participation in Britain, the National Council for Voluntary Organisations and the Centre for Civil Society commented that 'for the unemployed, levels of participation are fourteen percentage points lower than twenty years ago' (Grenier and Wright, 'Social Capital in Britain: Exploring the Hall Paradox', *Policy Studies*, 2007). Volunteering among people who are unemployed fell from 50 per cent in 1991 to 38 per cent in 1997 (Grenier and Wright, 'Social Capital in Britain: An Update and Critique of Hall's Analysis', CCS International Working Paper Number 14, 2003).

15. Mark Perry, 'Fortune 500 firms in 1955 vs. 2014; 88 percent are gone, and we're all better off because of that dynamic "creative destruction"', AEI website, http://www.aei.org/publication/fortune-500-firms-in-1955-vs-2014-89-are-gone-and-were-all-better-off-because-of-that-dynamic-creative-destruction/.

16. Alphabet is the holding company for Google.

17. Kremer and Maskin have shown that the larger the skills gap becomes, the less interworking there is between the high and low skilled. (Kremer and Maskin, 'Wage Inequality and Segregation by Skill', Working Paper, National Bureau of Economic Research, 1996.)

18. Philippe Aghion and Jeffrey G. Williamson, *Growth, Inequality, and Globalization: Theory, History, and Policy*, Cambridge University Press, 1998.

19. Michael Kremer and Eric Maskin, 'Wage Inequality and Segregation by Skill', National Bureau of Economic Research, 1996.

20. David Willetts, *The Pinch: How Baby-Boomers Took Their Children's Future, and Why They Should Give it Back*, Atlantic Books, 2010.

21. Miles Hewstone, 'Levels of Integration Within the Workplace', Social Integration Commission Research. Xavier de Souza Briggs, *"Some of my best friends are ...": Interracial Friendships, Class, and Segregation in America*, MIT, 2005.

22. Cynthia Estland, *Working Together: How Workplace Bonds Strengthen a Diverse Democracy*, OUP, 2003.

23. Ferguson et al., 'Firm Turnover and the Return of Racial Establishment Segregation', *American Sociological Review*, 2018.

24. Trevor Phillips, *Race and Faith: The Deafening Silence*, Civitas, 2016.

25. The Amish in the United States are one example.

26. This was done in 'Brown vs Board of Education'.

27. Gary Orfield et al., *Brown at 62: School Segregation by Race, Poverty and State*, The Civil Rights Project, 2016.

28. 2010 American Census.

NOTES

29. Ibid.
30. Sean McElwee, 'Beyond Ferguson: 5 Glaring Signs That We're Not Living in a Post-racial Society', *Salon*, 2014.
31. Gary Orfield et al., *Brown at 62: School Segregation by Race, Poverty and State*, 2016.
32. Jason Breslow, *The Return of School Segregation in Eight Charts*, PBS, 2014. C. Kristina, '10 Reasons Segregation in Schools Still Exists', *Care2*, 2012.
33. This has risen from 5.7 per cent (in 1988) to 18.6 per cent (2016) of all public schools (Orfield et al., *Brown at 62: School Segregation by Race, Poverty and State*, 2016). It is interesting to note that the same source suggests that non-White minority groups appear much less concerned about being in the minority. During the same period, non-White pupils increasingly joined schools in which they comprised less than 10 per cent of the school population, with the result that there was a sharp decline in the percentage of schools that have a tenth or fewer non-White students.
34. The Challenge, the Institute of Community Cohesion (iCoCo) and SchoolDash, 'Understanding School Segregation in England: 2011 to 2016', 2017.
35. All statistics from 'Demos Integration Hub – Education', http://www.integrationhub.net/module/education/.
36. Hanley Saparito, 'Declining Significance of Race?', published in *Choosing Homes, Choosing Schools*, Russell Sage Foundation, 2014.
37. Researchers examining the tendency of rich and poor American families to live in different school districts found that the level of separation was growing twice as fast if families had children, suggesting that school considerations were driving rich and poor families to live further apart from each other. (Ann Owens et al., 'Trends in School Economic Segregation, 1970 to 2010', CEPA, 2014.)
38. Ibid.
39. Richard J. Murnane and Sean F. Reardon, 'Long-Term Trends in Private School Enrolments by Family Income', CEPA, 2017.
40. Department for Education Statistics for under-12s, updated August 2011. As referenced in 'Concentrations of poor children', The Poverty Site, http://www.poverty.org.uk/19/index.shtml.
41. The Challenge, the Institute of Community Cohesion (iCoCo) and SchoolDash, 'Understanding School Segregation in England: 2011 to 2016', 2017.
42. Gary Orfield et al., *Brown at 62: School Segregation by Race, Poverty and State*, 2016.

Chapter 6: The Disruptive Power of Change

1. Michael A. Salmon et al., *The Aurelian Legacy: British Butterflies and Their Collectors*, University of California Press, 2000.
2. Clayton Christensen, *The Innovator's Dilemma*, Harvard Business Review Press, 1997.
3. The Levant describes an area of the Middle East that would now include Syria, Jordan, Israel and Lebanon.
4. Ian Kujit, 'People and Space in Early Agricultural Villages', *Journal of Anthropological Archaeology*, 2000.
5. Stephen Shennan et al., 'Regional Population Collapse Followed Initial Agriculture Booms in Mid-Holocene Europe', *Nature Communications*, 2013.
6. Harvey Whitehouse, 'Rituals Define Us: In Fathoming Them, We Might Shape Ourselves', *AEON*, 2012.
7. Q. D. Atkinson and H. Whitehouse, 'The Cultural Morphospace of Ritual Form', *Evolution and Human Behviour*, 2011.
8. A large number of studies have shown that groups facing significant collective risks willingly participate in painful and costly rituals, whether they are modern hunter-gatherers or soldiers being initiated into a unit. Studies include Irons, 1996; Jong et al., 2014; Sosis and Alcorta, 2003; Sosis and Bressler, 2003; Sosis et al., 2007; Whitehouse et al., 2012; Whitehouse, 2018.
9. Ade Kearns and Elise Whitley's study of 1,400 migrants living in deprived areas of Glasgow showed that engagement in the neighbourhood was initially low and rose only after some time in the area. (Kearns and Whitley, 'Getting There? Effects of Functional Factors, Time and Place on the Social Integration of Migrants', *Journal of Ethnic and Migration Studies*, 2015.)
10. Robert Putnam, *Bowling Alone*, Simon & Schuster, 2000.
11. When those arriving come from another part of the country, those who receive them become less likely to get involved in local clubs and societies. When those arriving are immigrating from overseas, those receiving them become less likely to volunteer in the local community. This would appear to happen for two reasons. First, as people come and go, the key relationships that underpin elements of the common life become disrupted. Clubs, societies and faith communities tend to rely on a core set of committed relationships. Bonds of trust build up over time between the most committed members of the group – those who do the work to ensure it continues to run. In a fast-churning population, much like a plough cutting through the roots of a plant,

these relationships are frequently disrupted. All too often, one of the core group leaves, making it harder for the remaining core members to run the group. Second, with soon-to-be leavers and new arrivals less likely to join the club or society, groups are correspondingly less likely to have the critical mass they need to operate. When they close – or never open – this affects the whole population, including those who are neither coming nor going. (Robert Sampson, 'Local Friendship Ties and Community Attachment in Mass Society', *American Sociological Review*, 1988; Florence Neymotin, 'Immigrant Influx and Social Cohesion Erosion', *IZA Journal of Migration*, 2014.)

12. From the 1950s onwards, services become the dominant mode of production. In the UK, between 1961 and 1981, they reach more than 50 per cent of employment. They also did in 1931, but this was largely due to the Depression's impact on manufacturing. (Census data, ONS, http://visual.ons.gov.uk/five-facts-about-the-uk-service-sector/.) In the US, manufacturing begins to decline while services flourished from the start of the 1950s. Between 1931 and 2014 it went from a ratio of two to one to ten to one (Department of Labor's Bureau of Labor Statistics, reported here: http://www.businessinsider.com/growth-of-us-services-economy-2014-9?IR=T).

13. Decennial Census 1980 and American Community Survey 2013, US Census Bureau.

14. ONS Labour Force Surveys.

15. Robert Putnam, *Bowling Alone*, Simon & Schuster, 2000. Sidney Nie and Norman Hie, *Participation in America*, University of Chicago Press, 1987.

16. YouGov poll, *The Times*, https://www.thetimes.co.uk/article/post-christian-britain-arrives-as-majority-say-they-have-no-religion-5bzxzdcl6p3, 2016.

17. Pew, '2014 Religious Landscape Study', 2014.

18. Ipsos Mori, 'Millennial Myths and Realities', 2017.

19. Robert Putnam, *Bowling Alone*, Simon & Schuster, 2000.

20. Ibid.

21. Tannis Williams, *The Impact of Television*, Academic Press, 1986.

22. Raven Molloy et al., 'Internal Migration in the United States', *Journal of Economic Perspectives*, 2011.

Chapter 7: The Triumph of Choice

1. I was always struck that NCS had managed to be a great success despite its full name being made of three words that would struggle to excite most teenagers – National, Citizen and Service. In this it reminded me of one of the UK's favourite museums – at a time when there is little love for Empire, war or (in some quarters) museums, the Imperial War Museum remains one of the UK's most popular visitor attractions.
2. Daniel A. McFarland et al., 'Network Ecology and Adolescent Social Structure', *American Sociological Review*, 2014. Sergio Currarini et al., 'An Economic Model of Friendship', *Econometrica*, 2009.
3. Stanford Report, http://news.stanford.edu/news/2014/november/cliques-high-school-110514.html, 2014.
4. Angela J. Bahns et al., "Social Ecology of Similarity', *Group Processes & Intergroup Relations*, 2012.
5. Quoted in 'How big cities can lead to small thoughts', *Wall Street Journal*, 2012.
6. Richard Florida, *America's Most Economically Segregated Cities*, Bloomberg, 2015.
7. Kendra Bischoff and Sean F. Reardon, 'Residential Segregation by Income, 1970–2009', Stanford University, CEPA, 2013.
8. Research conducted by Xavier de Souza Briggs at MIT concluded, 'Segregation is by far the most serious in the central cities of the largest metropolitan areas' (Xavier de Souza Briggs, *Interracial Friendships, Class, and Segregation in America*, MIT, 2005).
9. It is important to note that this does not mean that a White person is more likely to spend time socially with someone from a different ethnicity in relatively all-White Cornwall than in 40 per cent non-White London. What it does mean is that a White person's friendship group in London is much more unrepresentative of the city, as each ethnic group has more friends of the same ethnic group than would be expected if friendships were allocated at random. Xavier de Sousa Briggs puts this very well: 'People living in ... metropolitan areas ... are generally more likely to have friends of other races but less so than a random choice of friends in the local "pool" would predict.' While less research has been conducted on this topic in the UK, the results that exist paint the same picture. The UK's Social Integration Commission found that the largest city, London, was more divided by income, age and ethnicity than the rest of the UK.
10. *2014 Revision of World Urbanization Prospects*, UN Population Division, 2014.

11. Richard Florida, *America's Most Economically Segregated Cities*, Bloomberg, 2015. The same is found in Ann Owens, 'Inequality in Children's Contexts', *American Sociological Review*, 2016.
12. Simon Burgess et al., 'Parallel Lives? Ethnic Segregation in Schools and Neighbourhoods', *Urban Studies*, 2005.
13. Ibid.
14. Simon Burgess et al., *Sorting and Choice in English Secondary Schools*, University of Bristol, 2004. Hayley Potter, 'Do Private School Vouchers Pose a Threat to Integration?', The Century Foundation, 2017.
15. In their national examination of charter schools, they found that the percentage of Black students in 90 to 100 per cent minority schools was twice as high as that of Black students in traditional public schools. Frankenberg, Sigel-Hawley and Wang found that US Charter Schools, where parents and pupils have more choice about whether to attend, were more ethnically divided than traditional public schools (Erica Frankenberg et al., *Choice without Equity: Charter School Segregation and the Need for Civil Rights Standards*, Los Angeles: Civil Rights Project, 2010.)
16. Lewis Wimmer, 'Beyond and Below Racial Homophily', *American Journal of Sociology*, 2010.
17. A study of blogs in America found that you were four times more likely to read a political blog that agreed with your opinion than one that disagreed (Eric Gilbert et al., 'Blogs are Echo Chambers: Blogs are Echo Chambers', *IEEE Xplore*, 2008.) On television, with the rise of choice in television channels, including channels based in other countries, we have seen a decline in 'water-cooler' moments – moments when a large proportion of the whole country is watching the same thing. These choices vary significantly by age, education, political persuasion and ethnicity. For example, Trevor Phillips notes how in the UK in 2015 the top twenty most popular programmes among all viewers shared just ten titles with the top twenty among minority viewers. (Trevor Phillips, *Race and Faith: The Deafening Silence*, Civitas, 2016.)
18. Michael D. Conover et al., 'Political Polarisation on Twitter', Proceedings of the Fifth International AAAI Conference on Weblogs and Social Media, 2011.
19. Yosh Halberstam and Brian Knight, 'Homophily, Group Size, and the Diffusion of Political Information in Social Networks', National Bureau of Economic Research, 2014.
20. Catherine Grevet et al., 'Managing Political Differences in Social Media', Computer Supported Cooperative Work, 2014.
21. Ibid.

22. Nicholas Negroponte, ex-director of MIT's Media Lab, speaking in Brussels in 1997.
23. Louis Rosetto, co-founder of *Wired*, quoted on the BBC website, 2007.
24. Harley Hahn, technology writer and author, speaking in 1993.
25. Mickey Kaus, 'The End of Equality', *New Republican*, 1951. The original source is Robert J. Donovan, *John F. Kennedy in World War II*, McGraw-Hill, 1961.
26. John Blum, *V was for Victory*, Harvest, 1976.
27. William Broyles, *Brothers in Arms*, Knopf, 1986.
28. J. Michel et al., 'Quantitative Analysis of Culture Using Millions of Digitized Books', *Science*, 2010.
29. https://books.google.com/ngrams/graph?content=choice&year_start=1800&year_end=2019&corpus=26&smoothing=0.

Chapter 8: The Distance Between Us

1. Until the end of the nineteenth century, most neighbours shared water supplies and WCs. Even as late as 1951, 21 per cent of the population shared a toilet with a neighbour. Meanwhile, a baby born before 1950 was more likely to be born at home in the presence of a neighbour than in hospital in the presence of the father. (Emily Cockayne, *Cheek by Jowl: A History of Neighbours*, The Bodley Head, 2012.)
2. Robert Putnam, *Our Kids*, Simon & Schuster, 2015.
3. Danny Dorling and Phil Rees, 'A Nation Still Dividing: The British Census and Social Polarisation 1971–2001', *Environment and Planning*, 2003.
4. Danny Dorling et al., 'Poverty, Wealth and Place in Britain, 1968 to 2005', Joseph Rowntree Foundation, 2007.
5. Danny Dorling and Bethan Thomas, *Identity in Britain: A Cradle-to-grave Atlas*, Bristol: Policy Press, 2007.
6. On average, the share of the rich who would need to relocate for an even spread rose from around 30 per cent to 36 per cent. The eleven cities were Vienna, London, Amsterdam, Stockholm, Madrid, Oslo, Tallinn, Budapest, Vilnius, Athens, Prague and Riga. Income data was not always available outside of Amsterdam, Oslo and Stockholm, therefore for Madrid, Tallinn, London, Budapest, Vilnius, Athens, Prague and Riga the researchers used data on managers and elementary occupations, and for Vienna they used university degree and compulsory education. (Marcińczak et al., 'Inequality and Rising Levels of Socio-economic Segregation: Lessons from a Pan-European Comparative Study', *Socio-Economic Segregation in European Capital Cities*, IZA, 2016.)

7. A 2012 report by the Pew Research Center found segregation between upper- and lower-income households rose in twenty-seven of America's thirty largest metros between 1980 and 2010 (Richard Fry and Paul Taylor, 'The Rise of Residential Segregation by Income', Pew Research Center, 2012). British epidemiologists Kate Pickett and Richard Wilkinson write in *The Spirit Level*: 'Analysis of Census data by Rutgers University Professor Paul Jargowsky has found that in 2011, 7 percent of poor whites lived in high poverty neighbourhoods, where more than 40 percent of the residents are poor, up from 4 percent in 2000; 15 percent of poor Hispanics lived in such high poverty neighbourhoods in 2011, up from 14 percent in 2000; and a breath-taking 23 percent of poor blacks lived in high poverty neighbourhoods in 2011, up from 19 percent in 2000' (Pickett and Wilkinson, *The Spirit Level: Why More Equal Societies Almost Always Do Better*, Penguin, 2009).

8. Similar rises occurred across the country. In the north-east the proportion rose from 40 per cent to 48 per cent, the mid-west rose from 34 per cent to 44 per cent, the west from 31 per cent to 38 per cent and the south-east from 28 per cent to 35 per cent. The regional scores are computed by averaging the scores for the large metros in the region. The averages are the simple unweighted averages. (Source: Pew Research Center tabulations of 2006–2010 American Community Survey five-year file and Geolytics 1980 Census data in 2000 boundaries.)

9. A rich neighbourhood is here defined as one with an average income greater than 150 per cent of the national average. A poor neighbourhood meanwhile has an average income less than 66 per cent of the national average. (Kendra Bischoff and Sean F. Reardon, 'Residential Segregation by Income, 1970–2009', Stanford University, CEPA, 2013.)

10. Ibid.

11. Charles Murray, *Coming Apart: The State of White America, 1960–2010*, Random House, 2012.

12. Ibid.

13. Researchers found that the isolation index of college graduates increased from 0.19 to 0.36. The isolation index measures the likelihood of someone from a group living next to or having contact with another group. (Massey et al., 'The Changing Bases of Segregation in the United States', *Annals of the American Academy of Political and Social Science*, 2013.)

14. David Kingman, 'Generations Apart? The Growth of Age Segregation in England and Wales', Intergenerational Foundation, 2016.)

15. Danny Dorling and Phil Rees, 'A Nation Still Dividing: The British Census and Social Polarisation 1971–2001', *Environment and Planning*, 2003.

16. Richelle Winkler, 'Research Note: Segregated by Age: Are We Becoming More Divided?', *Population Research and Policy Review*, 2013.

17. Maps of racial and ethnic divisions in US cities, inspired by Bill Rankin's map of Chicago, updated for Census 2010. Produced by Eric Fischer using data from Census 2010 and shared under a CC BY-SA 2.0 license. Base map © OpenStreetMap, CC-BY-SA https://www.flickr.com/photos/walkingsf/5560480146/in/album-72157626354149574/.

18. Douglas Massey, 'Residential Segregation and Neighborhood Conditions in U.S. Metropolitan Areas', in *America Becoming: Racial Trends and Their Consequences. Volume I*, National Academy Press, 2001.

19. This score is based on how many people need to move for Black and White to be evenly distributed. The data is based on the 2010 Census.

20. Maps of racial and ethnic divisions in US cities, inspired by Bill Rankin's map of Chicago, updated for Census 2010. Produced by Eric Fischer using data from Census 2010 and shared under a CC BY-SA 2.0 license. Base map © OpenStreetMap, CC-BY-SA https://www.flickr.com/photos/walkingsf/5559914315/in/album-72157626354149574/.

21. The full list of cities is as follows: Detroit (80 per cent), Milwaukee (80 per cent), New York City (79 per cent), Chicago (76 per cent), Philadelphia (74 per cent), Miami (73 per cent), Cleveland (73 per cent), St Louis (69 per cent), Boston (68 per cent), Los Angeles (65 per cent).

22. Ta-Nehisi Coates, 'The Ghetto is Public Policy', *The Atlantic*, 2013.

23. At the last census in 2010, the Segregation Index sat at 59, only 17 points lower than in 1950 (John R. Logan and Brian J. Stults, 'The Persistence of Segregation in the Metropolis: New Findings from the 2010 Census', US2010 Project, 2011). Some analysts of this Census (see *The End of the Segregated Century: Racial Separation in America's Neighborhoods, 1890–2010*) have suggested a more rapid improvement in neighbourhood division. Their method of analysis has effectively left aside the lack of mixing between Black and White communities and focused more on the growing connection between Hispanic and Black people. This highlights a genuine area of improvement, but can be misleading if interpreted to mean that Black–White segregation is improving at a faster rate than it is.

24. The average neighbourhood in 1950 had a Segregation Index of 76, just four points less than Chicago in 2010.

25. Brian Resnick et al., 'The State of Segregation in the Suburbs', *The Atlantic*, 2017.

26. There were 50.7 million Hispanics in the United States in 2010, and 17.3 million Asians. In 1980, there were 14.8 million Hispanics and 3.5 million Asians.

27. The score varies by ethnic group as follows: Indians 51 per cent, Pakistanis 55 per cent, Bangladeshis 66 per cent. This is the Segregation Index calculated for each individual ethnic group and their spread among the rest of the population. (Rich Harris, 'Evidence and Trends: Are We Becoming More Integrated, More Segregated or Both?', in *Mapping Integration*, ed. D. Goodhart, Demos, 2004.)

28. The score varies by ethnic group as follows: Black African 46 per cent, Black Caribbean 46 per cent. In each case and the numbers in subsequent notes, this is the Segregation Index calculated for each individual ethnic group and their spread among the rest of the population (ibid.).

29. The score varies by ethnic group as follows: Black African 57 per cent, Black Caribbean 60 per cent (ibid.).

30. The score varies by ethnic group as follows: Indians 56 per cent, Pakistanis 67 per cent, Bangladeshis 73 per cent (ibid.).

31. Segregation Index scores for all non-White groups fell between 2001 and 2011 by an average of six percentage points (ibid.).

32. Normally EU citizens who have not become British citizens.

33. Academics Ted Cantle and Eric Kaufman sum up the situation thus: 'For most of the districts and counties that had a disproportionately high number of White British population in 2001 (i.e., above the English average of 86.8 percent), this had reduced by 2011 though not in proportion to the reduction of White British in the population as a whole (i.e., 79.8 percent) and therefore became less proportionately mixed than previously, despite being more diverse. In other words, they have moved further away from the national averages' (Ted Cantle and Eric Kaufman, 'Is Segregation Increasing in the UK?', Open Democracy, 2016).

34. Ibid. A similar tendency of Whites to not settle in and to leave areas that are majority non-White is evident in the United States. John Logan writes of his work on the 2010 American Census: 'Unfortunately the same analyses demonstrated that whites rarely enter all-minority neighbourhoods, and they still have a tendency to leave diverse neighbourhoods' (John Logan, 'The Persistence of Segregation in the 21st Century Metropolis', *City & Community*, 2013).

Chapter 9: The Difference That Difference Makes

1. The change was dramatic; in 1750, 85 per cent of the British population lived in the countryside; by 1990, 85 per cent lived in cities. (Eric Evans, *The Forging of the Modern State: Early Industrial Britain, 1783–1870*, Routledge, 1993. Geoffrey Best, *Mid-Victorian Britain 1851–75*, Fontana Press, 1985.)

2. Campbell Gibson and Emily Lennon, 'Historical Census Statistics on the Foreign-born Population of the United States: 1850–1990' (Table 4), Population Division Working Paper No. 29, 1999.

3. Kenan Malik, 'The Failure of Multiculturalism', https://kenanmalik. wordpress.com/2015/02/17/the-failure-of-multiculturalism/, 2015.

4. Benjamin Disraeli, *Sybil, or the Two Nations*, OUP, 1845.

5. Philippe Buchez, address to the Medico-Psychological Society of Paris, 1857. Quoted in Kenan Malik, 'The Failure of Multiculturalism', https://kenanmalik.wordpress.com/2015/02/17/the-failure-of-multiculturalism/, 2015.

6. Kenan Malik, 'The Failure of Multiculturalism', https://kenanmalik. wordpress.com/2015/02/17/the-failure-of-multiculturalism/, 2015.

7. Sherif himself proved this point in an experiment he conducted at a place called Middle Grove, which took place a year before the Robbers Cave experiment. On this occasion, he allowed the boys to spend time together and become friends before splitting them into teams. On the basis of these friendships, despite his attempts to turn the boys against each other, they refused to become enemies.

8. These benefits remain themselves unevenly distributed, with life expectancy varying greatly within Western societies.

9. Estimates vary. David Coleman estimates 38 per cent by 2050 (David Coleman, 'Projections of the Ethnic Minority Populations of the United Kingdom 2006–2056', *Population and Development Review*, 2010). Policy Exchange estimates 20 to 30 per cent by 2051 (Rishi Sunak, *A Portrait of Modern Britain*, Policy Exchange, 2014).

10. Projected by Philip Rees of Leeds University. (Trevor Phillips, *Race and Faith: The Deafening Silence*, Civitas, 2016.)

11. You might think that surely this increase in computing power can't continue for ever. Moore's Law has largely relied so far on miniaturisation. Every eighteen months, we have discovered new ways to make the items on a computer chip even smaller. This has meant we can cram more on each chip, making each more powerful. These gains will have to slow down at some point as we approach the atomical limit to how small we can go. And yet new innovations loom over the

horizon. We are seeing quantum computers that can operate at a small enough scale to use an electron – with its multiple quantum locations – to make many calculations rather than just one. Advances are being made in 'neural networks', which enable a computer to mimic the human brain's faster method of learning by trial and error. At the same time, the growth of 'the cloud' is allowing computers to connect to larger, more powerful computing via the internet. This doesn't just mean you can access a file anywhere; it also means that chip size is less important than before as the chip can always access another more powerful chip to help it. It would be a brave soul who wagered that the pace of development will slow.

12. Daniel Dorling et al., *Poverty, Wealth and Place in Britain, 1968 to 2005*, Joseph Rowntree Foundation, 2007.

13. Branko Milanovic, BBC website, https://www.bbc.co.uk/news/business-34987474, 2016.

14. Ludi Simpson and Nissa Finey, *Understanding Society: How Mobile Are Immigrants After Arriving in the UK?*, University of Essex Institute of Social and Educational Research, 2012.

15. YouGov, *How Britain Voted*.

16. David Goodhart, *The Road to Somewhere*, Hurst & Co., 2017.

17. Camille Ryan and Julie Siebens, 'Educational Attainment in the United States: 2009', US Census Bureau, 2012.

18. ONS Labour Market Survey, 2013.

19. Kendra Bischoff and Sean Reardon, 'Residential Segregation by Income, 1970–2009', Stanford University, CEPA, 2013. Richard Florida, *America's Most Economically Segregated Cities*, Bloomberg, 2015.

20. See the 'American Communities Project'.

21. Simply put, this is a measure of how many people in the city are likely to be in a different ethnic group from the 'average person'. This is scored from 0 to 80. A score of 0 means that there is no diversity as everyone is from the same ethnic group, and 80 means there is a lot of diversity with the population completely evenly split between the five groups.

22. The reason for this is that the method of calculating the scores means that you can't get a higher score on the second than you did on the first.

23 Figure based on the original produced by FiveThirtyEight entitled 'A Two-Dimensional View of Urban Diversity: City and neighbourhood diversity indices for 100 largest U.S. cities.' Based on data from Brown University's American Communities Project. https://fivethirtyeight.com/features/the-most-diverse-cities-are-often-the-most-segregated/.

24. Eric Uslaner, *Segregation and Mistrust*, Cambridge University Press, 2012.

Chapter 10: Social Mobility

1. Gallup and Brookings polling, available at: https://www.economist.com/
news/united-states/21595437-america-no-less-socially-mobile-it-was-
generation-ago-mobility-measured and https://www.
democraticunderground.com/10025582886.
2. YouGov polling, available at: https://yougov.co.uk/news/2013/11/12/
social-mobility-problem-no-solutions/.
3. Jo Blanden and Stephen Manchin, 'Up and Down the Generational
Income Ladder in Britain', *National Institute Economic Review*, 2008.
4. Chetty et al., 'Where is the Land of Opportunity? Geography of
International Mobility in the United States', National Bureau of
Economic Research, 2014.
5. Megan McArdle, *How Utah Keeps the American Dream Alive*,
Bloomberg, 2017. The role of churches and other places of worship in
improving social mobility is picked up by American academic Robert
Putnam in his book *Our Kids*. He writes: 'Churchgoing kids have
better relations with their parents and other adults, have more
friendships with high-performing peers, are more involved in sports
and other extracurricular activities, are less prone to substance abuse
(drugs, alcohol and smoking), risky behaviour (like not wearing seat
belts), and delinquency (shoplifting, misbehaving in school, and being
suspended or expelled). As with mentoring, religious involvement –
when it happens – makes a bigger difference in the lives of poor kids
than rich kids, in part because affluent youth are more exposed to their
positive influences' (Robert Putnam, *Our Kids*, Simon & Schuster,
2015).
6. The other factors that made a significant difference were primary-school
quality (though not expenditure), income inequality, and two-parent
families. (Chetty et al., 'Where is the Land of Opportunity? Geography
of International Mobility in the United States', National Bureau of
Economic Research, 2014.)
7. As a trained lawyer, Alex knew that the authority had a duty, laid down
in the Constitution, to provide all people 'equal protection under the
law'. He also knew that, following the Supreme Court's ruling on
segregated schools, 'separate was not equal'. If the Chicago Housing
Authority was building racially separate housing then it was not treating
people as equal. This meant it was breaking the law.
8. An attempt to replicate what happened in Chicago showed that it was
the mixed nature of the neighbourhood that mattered, not the quality of
the home. A large government programme – Moving to Opportunity –

tried and failed to match the success of Polikoff's intervention. While
the Chicago families moved at least ten miles away to areas where the
children could attend new schools and play in new neighbourhoods,
'Moving to Opportunity' families hardly moved at all. They moved
house but stayed much more local, mostly remaining in the same areas,
maintaining the same social connections and carrying on attending the
same school. Unsurprisingly, outcomes did not improve.

9. Studies in both the UK and US have found the same effect. In the US,
   Raj Chetty studied people moving from Cincinnati to Pittsburgh. The
   two cities are only 300 miles apart, yet poor children born in Cincinnati
   will grow up to earn $5,000 less per year by the time they are twenty-
   six. An analysis of families that moved from Cincinnati to Pittsburgh
   showed that the earlier they moved, the more their children went on to
   earn. A child born in Pittsburgh will earn $5,000 more, a child moving
   to Pittsburgh at the age of nine gains $2,500. Families with two children
   making the move found that the younger child went on to earn more.
   In the UK, researchers found that even when you control for all personal
   factors that contribute to poverty – including income, wealth, health
   and education – researchers found that people living in poorer areas
   were significantly less likely to escape poverty. (Nick Buck, 'Identifying
   Neighbourhood Effects on Social Exclusion', *Urban Studies*, 2001.)

10. In an unguarded moment, before publication Coleman told a reporter
    that, 'the study will show the difference in the equality of schools that
    the average Negro child and the average white child are exposed to …
    [T]he difference is going to be striking.'

11. The research has been summarised well in Reyn van Ewijk and Peter
    Sleegers, 'The Effect of Peer Socioeconomic Status on Student
    Achievement: A Meta-analysis', *Educational Research Review*, 2010. A
    key study is the work by Heather Schwartz, which tracked what
    happened to 858 primary school students whose families were allocated
    new housing by a lottery. Half the students ended up in schools where
    most children were well-off and half attended schools where most
    children were poor. Sure enough, the children at the mixed schools
    gained the better results – even though these schools received less
    funding. In maths they outperformed those in the higher-poverty
    schools by eight whole percentage points. Richard Kahlenberg, from the
    Century Foundation Studies think-tank, summarises the research as
    follows: '95 percent of education reform is about trying to make high-
    poverty schools work. This research suggests there is a much more
    effective way to help close the achievement gap. And that is to give
    low-income students a chance to attend middle-class schools.'

12. Robert Crain and Jack Strauss, *School Desegregation and Black Occupational Attainments*, National Institute of Education, 1985.

13. Jonathan Guryan, 'Desegregation and Black Dropout Rates', *The American Economic Review*, 2004.

14. This is one reason why exams can be fairer than coursework or teacher assessment.

15. US data: Marianne Bertrand and Sendhil Mullainathan, 'Are Emily and Greg More Employable than Lakisha and Jamal?', National Bureau of Economic Research, 2003. UK data: M. Wood et al., 'A Test for Racial Discrimination in Recruitment Practice in British Cities', Department for Work and Pensions, 2009.

16. A meta-review of 515 experimental studies involving 250,000 participants in 38 nations confirms that intergroup contact significantly reduces prejudices and negative emotions. (T. Pettigrew et al., 'A Meta-analytic Test of Intergroup Contact Theory', *Journal of Personal and Social Psychology*, 2006.)

17. Olof Åslund et al., 'Seeking Similarity: How Immigrants and Natives Manage in the Labor Market', *Journal of Labor Economics*, 2009. These results are consistent with similar racial and ethnic hiring biases documented in studies of hiring by Giuliano et al. (2009) and Bandiera et al. (2009).

18. An almost identical study in the US covering the hiring decisions at one large tech firm showed the same picture. Initial analysis showed that White candidates were hired more frequently than their Black competitors. Further analysis showed that White people had much stronger networks than Black people connecting them to the firm and were sixteen times more likely to use them when looking for work at the firm. Once those finding work through personal networks were removed, there was no hiring difference. (T. Petersen et al., 'Offering a Job: Meritocracy and Social Networks', *American Journal of Sociology*, 2000.)

19. Those with less money don't just have less useful connections; they have fewer connections full stop. They have fewer friends. A White American with a socio-economic status in the top fifth, for example, has 50 per cent more close friends than a Black American with a socio-economic status in the bottom fifth. (*Social Capital Community Benchmark Survey*, Roper Center at Cornell, 2000). They also have fewer acquaintances. (N. Smith et al., 'Status Differences in the Cognitive Activation of Social Networks', *Organization Science*, 2012.)

20. Research underlining the importance of personal networks for hearing about jobs includes: M. O. Jackson, 'A Survey of Models of Network Formation', in *Group Formation in Economics*, Cambridge University

Press, 2004; A. Rees, 'Information Networks in Labor Markets', *The American Economic Review*, 1966; M. Granovetter, 'The Strength of Weak Ties', *American Journal of Sociology*, 1973; and M. Granovetter, *Getting a Job: A Study of Contacts and Careers*, University of Chicago Press, 1995.

21. There is no definitive measure of the number of jobs filled through word of mouth. Various researchers, including Granovetter (1974, 1995), Corcoran et al. (1980), Holzer (1988), Gregg and Wadsworth (1996), and Addison and Portugal (2002), coalesce around the figure of four out of ten.

22. For more information on this, see S. Pedulla and K. Newman, 'The Family and Community Impacts of Underemployment', in *Underemployment: Psychological, Economic and Social Challenges*, Springer, 2011.

23. 'How are Poverty, Ethnicity and Social Networks Related?', Joseph Rowntree Foundation, 2015.

24. Emi Ooka and Barry Wellman, 'Does Social Capital Pay Off More Within or Between Ethnic Groups?', in *Inside the Mosaic*, De Gruyter, 2006.

25. CoDE, 'Addressing Ethnic Inequalities in Social Mobility', available at https://hummedia.manchester.ac.uk/institutes/code/briefings/policy/code-social-mobility-briefing-Jun2014.pdf, 2014.

26. Robert Putnam, *Our Kids*, Simon & Schuster, 2015.

27. This remains true when controlling for academic results. (Anthony Mann, 'It's Who You Meet: Why Employer Contacts at School Make a Difference to the Employment Prospects of Young Adults', Education and Employers Taskforce, 2014).

28. For example, see 'Race for Opportunity: Aspiration and Frustration', Business in the Community, 2010.

29. Perri 6, 'Escaping Poverty: From Safety Nets to Networks of Opportunity', Demos, 1997.

30. Lorenzo Cappellari and Konstantinos Tatsiramos, 'Friends' Networks and Job Finding Rates', *IZA*, 2011.

31. N. Buck, *Working Capital: Life and Labour in Contemporary London*, Psychology Press, 2002. This damaging division begins at the point that someone becomes unemployed. On losing their jobs, 40 per cent of people also lose contact with their friends in work. (Taylor et al., 'The Impact of Long-term Unemployment: Lost Income, Lost Friends – and Loss of Self-Respect', Pew Research Center, 2010.)

32. Charles Murray, *Coming Apart: The State of White America, 1960–2010*, Random House, 2012.

Chapter 11: Democracy

1. Jennifer Lawrence, *Becoming a Candidate: Political Ambition and the Decision to Run for Office*, Cambridge University Press, 2012.
2. Jessica Trounstine, 'Segregation and Inequality in Public Goods', *American Journal of Political Science*, 2015.
3. K. Desmet et al., 'The Political Economy of Linguistic Cleavages', *Journal of Development Economics*, 2012.
4. A. Alesina et al., 'Public Goods and Ethnic Divisions', *The Quarterly Journal of Economics*, 1999. Claudia Goldin and Lawrence Katz, 'The Shaping of Higher Education: The Formative Years in the United States, 1890 to 1940', American Economic Association, 1999. The same pattern holds in the developing world; primary-school funding is lower in more ethnically diverse districts in Kenya (Edward Miguel, *Ethnic Diversity and School Funding in Kenya*, UC-Berkeley, 2001).
5. James Poterba, 'Demographic Structure and the Political Economy of Public Education', National Bureau of Economic Research, 1996. The loss of the sense of 'we' is not uniquely about public goods. It can be found almost anywhere that a sacrifice is required – be it taxation or risking one's life. For example, economists Matthew Kahn of UCLA and Dora Costa of MIT found that American Civil War soldiers serving in companies that varied more by age, occupation and birthplace were more likely to desert.
6. Kearns et al., '"All in it Together"? Social Cohesion in a Divided Society', *Journal of Social Policy*, 2014.
7. Robert Putnam, '*E Pluribus Unum*: Diversity and Community in the Twenty-first Century', *Scandinavian Political Studies*, 2006.
8. Peter Dinesen and Kim Sønderskov reviewed surveys of Danish municipalities from 1979 to the present and found that increasing diversity was correlated with diminished social trust. Similar reviews have taken place in the UK, including James Laurence, 'The Effect of Ethnic Diversity and Community Disadvantage on Social Cohesion', *European Sociological Review*, 2011.
9. Eric Gould and Alexander Hijzen, 'Growing Apart, Losing Trust? The Impact of Inequality on Social Capital', IMF, 2016.
10. James Laurence, 'The Effect of Ethnic Diversity and Community Disadvantage on Social Cohesion', *European Sociological Review*, 2011.
11. A meta-review of 515 experimental studies involving 250,000 participants in 38 nations confirmed that contact between people from different groups significantly reduces prejudices and negative emotions,

including distrust. (T Pettigrew et al., 'A Meta-analytic Test of Intergroup Contact Theory', *Journal of Personality and Social Psychology*, 2006.) These findings are confirmed in another meta-review of 123 real-world contact interventions with more than 11,300 participants of different ethnic groups. (Gunnar Lemmer and Ulrich Wagner, 'Can We Really Reduce Ethnic Prejudice Outside the Lab?', *European Journal of Social Psychology*, 2015.)

12. Bill Bishop, *The Big Sort: Why the Clustering of Like-Minded America is Tearing Us Apart*, Houghton Mifflin, 2008.
13. Ipsos Mori, *Perils of Perception*, 2016.
14. Ariely Norton, 'Building a Better America – One Wealth Quintile at a Time', *Perspectives on Psychological Science*, 2011.
15. Peter Taylor-Gooby, 'Why Do People Stigmatise the Poor at a Time of Rapidly Increasing Inequality', *The Political Quarterly*, 2013. Ariely Norton, 'Building a Better America – One Wealth Quintile at a Time', *Perspectives on Psychological Science*, 2011.
16. Michael W. Kraus et al., 'Americans Misperceive Racial Economic Equality', *PNAS*, 2015.
17. Ipsos Mori, *Perils of Perception*, 2016.
18. Robert Putnam captures this tendency well in his honest reflections upon revisiting his home town: 'Because of growing class segregation in America, fewer and fewer successful people (and even fewer of our children) have much idea how the other half lives. So we are less empathetic than we should be to the plight of less privileged kids. Before I began this research, I was like that. I've worked hard, I thought, to rise from a modest background in Port-Clinton – much of the time heedless of how much my good fortune depended on family and community and public institutions in the more communitarian and egalitarian age. If I and my classmates could climb the ladder, I assumed, so could kids from modest backgrounds today. Having finished this research, I know better.' (Robert Putnam, *Our Kids*, Simon & Schuster, 2015.)
19. Diana Mutz, *Hearing the Other Side: Deliberative versus Participatory Democracy*, Cambridge University Press, 2006.
20. In the UK, voters are increasingly polarised on the issues of immigration and the economy, with Labour and Conservatives moving further away from each other on both of these between the 2015 and 2017 elections. Jonathan Wheatley captures this movement expertly here: http://blogs.lse.ac.uk/politicsandpolicy/the-polarisation-of-party-supporters-since-2015/. In the US, Republican and Democrat voters are more far apart ideologically than ever before, while the proportion of voters holding consistently conservative or liberal views has nearly doubled

from 12 per cent to 21 per cent of the population in ten years. ('2014 Political Polarisation in the American Public', Pew Research Center.)

21. Bill Bishop, *The Big Sort: Why the Clustering of Like-Minded America is Tearing Us Apart*, Houghton Mifflin, 2008.

22. We have also seen a rapid decline in trust in our governments. In the late 1950s, three in four Americans trusted the government. Today that is closer to one in four ('Beyond Distrust: How Americans View Their Government', Pew Research Center, 2015). Between 1987 and 2009, the proportion of Britons who trusted their government fell by a third from 37 per cent to 25 per cent ('British Social Attitudes Survey', NatCen).

23. Young here means 'born since 1980'. (Roberto Foa et al., 'The Danger of Deconsolidation', *Journal of Democracy*, 2016.)

24. Support for Trump, for example, was highly correlated with changes in your local ethnic population, concerns about rising diversity and a strong sense of 'being White'. It correlates much more weakly with wealth and income, with poorer Whites being more likely to have voted for Hillary Clinton. For more information see Janet Adamy and Paul Overberg, 'Places Most Unsettled by Rapid Demographic Change Are Drawn to Donald Trump', *Wall Street Journal*, 2016; Ryan Enos, *The Space Between Us: Social Geography and Politics*, Cambridge University Press, 2017; Jonathan Rothwell, 'Explaining Nationalist Political Views: The Case of Donald Trump', *Social Science Research Network*, 2017.

Chapter 12: Health

1. Malcolm Gladwell, *Outliers*, Penguin, 2008.

2. Elizabeth Page-Gould et al., 'With a Little Help from My Cross-group Friend', *Journal of Personality and Social Psychology*, 2009.

3. Theresa Seeman, 'Social Ties and Health: The Benefits of Social Integration', *Annals of Epidemiology*, 1996; C. U. Mitchell and M. LaGory, 'Social Capital and Mental Distress in an Impoverished Community', *City & Community*, 2008.

4. John Helliwell and Shun Wang, 'Trust and Wellbeing', *International Journal of Wellbeing*, 2011; Theresa Seeman, 'Social Ties and Health: The Benefits of Social Integration', *Annals of Epidemiology*, 1996; C. U. Mitchell and M. LaGory, 'Social Capital and Mental Distress in an Impoverished Community', *City & Community*, 2008.

5. E. Kim et al., 'Perceived Neighbourhood Social Cohesion and Stroke', *Social Science & Medicine*, 2013.

6. 'Safeguarding the Convoy: A Call to Action from the Campaign to End Loneliness', Campaign to End Loneliness, 2011.
7. Knowledge Networks, 'Loneliness Among Older Adults: A National Survey of Adults 45+', AARP, 2010.
8. Surgeon General Dr Vivek H. Murthy, quoted in Jena McGregor, 'This former surgeon general says there's a "loneliness epidemic"', *Washington Post*, 2017.
9. V. Cattell, 'Poor People, Poor Places, and Poor Health', *Social Science & Medicine*, 2001.
10. J. Barefoot et al., 'Trust, Health, and Longevity', *Journal of Behavioral Medicine*, 1998; Theresa Seeman, 'Social Ties and Health: The Benefits of Social Integration', *Annals of Epidemiology*, 1996; and Rosenheck et al., 'Service Delivery and Community: Social Capital, Service Systems Integration, and Outcomes among Homeless Persons with Severe Mental Illness', *Health Services Research*, 2001.
11. L. Berkman et al., 'From Social Integration to Health: Durkheim in the New Millennium', *Social Science & Medicine*, 2000.
12. Julianne Holt-Lunstad, 'Loneliness and Social Isolation as Risk Factors for Mortality', *Perspectives on Psychological Science*, 2015. A separate review by many of the same authors of 148 separate studies involving over 300,000 people found that people with weak social connections faced a greater risk of death than those with strong social circles (J. Holt-Lunstad et al., 'Social Relationships and Mortality Risk: A Meta-analytic Review', *PLoS Medicine*, 2010.)
13. John Bruhn and Stewart Wolf, *The Roseto Story: An Anatomy of Health*, University of Oklahoma Press, 1979.
14. Nicholas Christakis and James Fowler, 'The Spread of Obesity in a Large Social Network Over 32 Years', *New England Journal of Medicine*, 2007.
15. James Fowler and Nicholas Christakis, 'Estimating Peer Effects on Health in Social Networks', *Journal of Health Economics*, 2008.
16. N. Rao et al., 'Social Networks and Vaccination Decisions', Federal Reserve Bank of Boston Working Paper, 2007.
17. The Office of Minority Health, 'Data and Statistics: Racial and Ethnic Profiles', US Department of Health and Human Services, 2010.
18. 'Postnote Number 276: Ethnicity and Health', Parliamentary Office of Science and Technology, 2007.
19. Kerry Sproston and Jennifer Mindell (eds), *Health Survey for England – Volume 1: The Health of Minority Ethnic Groups*, The Information Centre, 2006.

20. Seeromanie Harding and Roy Maxwell, 'Differences in Mortality of Migrants', in *Health Inequalities*, The Stationery Office, 1997.
21. L. A. Simonoff et al., 'Cancer Communication Patterns and the Influence of Patient Characteristics', Patient Education and Counseling, 2006. A. Koerber et al., 'An Exploratory Study of Orthodontic Resident Communication by Patient Race and Ethnicity', *Journal of Dental Education*, 2004.
22. L. A. Penner et al., 'Interpersonal Perspectives on Black–White health Disparities', *Social Issues and Policy Review*, 2007.
23. A. R. Green et al., 'The Presence of Implicit Bias in Physicians and its Predictions of Thrombolysis for Black and White Patients', *Journal of General Internal Medicine*, 2008.
24. John Bruhn and Stewart Wolf, *The Power of Clan*, Routledge, 1998.

Chapter 13: The Economy

1. Studies on this topic include A. Rupasingha, 'Social Capital and Economic Growth: A County-level Analysis', *Journal of Agricultural and Applied Economics*, 2000; Jonathan Helliwell and Robert Putnam, 'Economic Growth and Social Capital in Italy', *Eastern Economic Journal*, 1995; Terrence Casey, 'Social Capital and Regional Economies in Britain', *Political Studies*, 2004; and Tom Kemeny and Abigail Cooke, 'Urban Immigrant Diversity and Inclusive Institutions', *Economic Geography*, 2017.
2. Alfred Marshall, *Principles of Economics*, Macmillan, 1890.
3. E. Ananat et al., 'Race-Specific Agglomeration Economies: Social Distance and the Black–White Wage Gap', National Bureau of Economic Research Working Paper, 2013.
4. Simon Burgess and Marcela Umana-Aponte, 'Raising Your Sights: The Impact of Friendship Networks on Educational Aspirations', CMPO Working Paper, 2011.
5. Future First, 'Social Mobility', Careers Advice & Alumni Networks, 2011.
6. Robert Putnam, *Our Kids*, Simon & Schuster, 2015.
7. Gautam Rao, 'Familiarity Does Not Breed Contempt: Diversity, Discrimination and Generosity in Delhi Schools', Working Paper, 2013.
8. Frances Aboud and Sheri Levy, 'Interventions to Reduce Prejudice and Discrimination in Children and Adolescents', *Journal of Personality and Social Psychology*, 2006 (The Claremont Symposium on Applied Social Psychology). A. Fletcher et al., 'The Extension of School-based Inter-

and Intraracial Children's Friendships', *American Journal of Orthopsychiatry*, 2004. Lisa Hunter and Maurice Elias, 'Interracial Friendships, Multicultural Sensitivity, and Social Competence: How Are They Related?', *Journal of Applied Developmental Psychology*, 1999.

9. A. Wells et al., 'How Racially Diverse Schools and Classrooms Can Benefit All Students', The Century Foundation, 2016.

10. Steffanie Wilk and Erin Makarius, 'Choosing the Company You Keep: Racial Relational Demography Outside and Inside of Work', *Organization Science*, 2015.

11. A. Calvo-Armengol et al., 'The Effects of Social Networks on Employment and Inequality', *American Economic Review*, 2004; Elin Bjarnegård, *Gender, Informal Institutions and Political Recruitment*, Palgrave, 2015; M. Bentolila et al., 'Social Contacts and Occupational Choice', CEPR Discussion Paper, 2004; and Susan Hanson and Geraldine Pratt, 'Job Search and the Occupational Segregation of Women', *Annals of the Association of American Geographers*, 1991.

12. D. Liu et al., 'Friendships in Online Peer-to-Peer Lending: Piples, Prisms, and Relational Herding', *MIS Quarterly*, 2014; and Erik Hekman and Roger Brussee, 'Crowdfunding and Online Social Networks', CARPE Conference Papers, 2013.

13. C. West et al., 'Deconstructing the Pipeline Myth and the Case for More Diverse Fund Managers', Kauffman Fellows, 2020.

14. UBS Investor Watch, 'When is Enough ... Enough? Why the Wealthy Can't Get Off the Treadmill', UBS, 2015.

15. David Richardson and Richard Denniss, 'Income and Wealth Inequality in Australia', Australia Institute, 2014.

16. T. Indrakesuma et al., *A Perceived Divide: How Indonesians Perceive Inequality and What They Want Done About It*, World Bank, 2015.

17. Lisa Windsteiger, 'The Redistributive Consequences of Segregation', International Inequalities Institute Annual Conference, 2017.

18. Looking at UK regions over the period 1980 to 2000, Terrence Casey finds that the correlation coefficient between the economic index and social trust is +0.7 (Terrence Casey, 'Social Capital and Regional Economies in Britain', *Political Studies*, 2004). Other relevant studies include Stephen Knack and Philip Keefer, 'Does Social Capital Have an Economic Payoff? A Cross-Country Investigation', *The Quarterly Journal of Economics*, 1997; Paul Whiteley, 'Economic Growth and Social Capital', *Political Studies*, 2000; David Halpern, *Social Capital: The New Golden Goose*, Cambridge University, 1999.

19. Oguzhan Dincer and Eric Uslaner, 'Trust and Growth', *Public Choice*, 2010.

20. One can see the impact of trust on economic activity in the very rapid growth of online platforms such as eBay, Uber or Airbnb. By providing a system in which poor behaviour is punished – mostly through customer ratings – we have started to trust that strangers will look after our homes, drive us safely around and send the goods we have paid for. While this was not achieved by raising overall levels of trust in each other, it shows the power of well-placed trust to enable economic activity.
21. As shown in David Halpern, *Social Capital: The New Golden Goose*, Cambridge University Press, 1999; and Frances Fukuyama, 'Social Capital and Civil Society', IMF Working Paper, 2000.
22. Eric Uslaner, 'Trust and Corruption', in *The New Institutional Economics of Corruption*, Routledge, 2005.

Chapter 14: Security

1. Mark Rudd, unpublished memoir.
2. Bernardine Dohrn, quoted in Harold Jacobs, *Weatherman*, Ramparts Press, 1970.
3. Alan Krueger and Jitka Malečková, 'Education, Poverty and Terrorism: Is There a Causal Connection?', *Journal of Economic Perspectives*, 2003.
4. 'Exploding misconceptions', *The Economist*, 2010.
5. K. Bhui et al., 'Is Violent Radicalisation Associated with Poverty, Migration, Poor Self-Reported Health and Common Mental Disorders?', PLOS, 2014.
6. Claude Berrebi, 'Evidence about the Link Between Education, Poverty and Terrorism among Palestinians', *Peace Economics, Peace Science and Public Policy*, 2007.
7. Alan Krueger and Jitka Malečková, 'Education, Poverty and Terrorism: Is There a Causal Connection?', *Journal of Economic Perspectives*, 2003.
8. Rachel Bryson, 'For Caliph and Country: Exploring How British Jihadis Join a Global Movement', Tony Blair Institute for Global Change, 2017; and K. Bhui et al., 'Is Violent Radicalisation Associated with Poverty, Migration, Poor Self-Reported Health and Common Mental Disorders?', PLOS, 2014.
9. Surveys of adults in Jordan, Morocco, Pakistan and Turkey found that respondents with more education were more likely to believe that suicide-bombing aimed at American or other Western targets in Iraq was justified. (Pew Global Attitudes Project, 2004.)
10. Claude Berrebi, 'Evidence about the Link Between Education, Poverty and Terrorism among Palestinians', *Peace Economics, Peace Science and*

Public Policy, 2007; and Alan Krueger and Jitka Malečková, 'Education, Poverty and Terrorism: Is There a Causal Connection?', *Journal of Economic Perspectives*, 2003.

11. Dalia Mogahed and John Esposito, *Who Speaks for Islam? What a Billion Muslims Really Think*, Gallup, 2008.

12. J. Ginges et al., 'Religion and Support for Suicide Attacks', *Psychological Science*, 2009.

13. Roberto Ezcurra, 'Group Concentration and Violence: Does Ethnic Segregation Affect Domestic Terrorism?', *Defence and Peace Economics*, 2017.

14. A domestic terrorist incident is one in which the venue, target and perpetrators are all from the same country. Ezcurra used data on domestic terrorist attacks between 2001 and 2007. He sourced this data from W. Enders, 'Domestic Versus Transnational Terrorism: Data, Decomposition, and Dynamics', *Journal of Peace Research*, 2011.

15. Ezcurra found that an increase in the measure of ethnic segregation by one standard deviation increased the expected number of domestic terrorist attacks by a factor of 8.75.

16. Bryan Arva and James Piazza, 'Spatial Distribution of Minority Communities and Terrorism: Domestic Concentration versus Transnational Dispersion', *Defence and Peace Economics*, 2016.

17. Mason Youngblood, 'Extremist Ideology as a Complex Contagion', *Humanities and Social Sciences Communications*, 2020; A. Gladfelter et al., 'The Complexity of Hate Crime and Bias Activity', *Justice Quarterly*, 2017; R. Medina et al., 'Geographies of Organized Hate in America', *Annals of the American Association of Geographers*, 2018.

18. J. Ginges, 'Religion and Support for Suicide Attacks', *Psychological Science*, 2009.

19. We should be careful not to overstate what the research shows here. There is a clear correlation between segregation and terrorist attacks and terrorist sympathy. This of course does not mean that everyone who is segregated will become sympathetic to terrorist activity, or that everyone who commits a terrorist offence comes from a segregated background. Nor does it mean that there are no other important causes of terrorism. There is clear evidence that those who commit terrorist attacks have often been affected by individual experiences and traumas. We will explore all of this in more detail in the subsequent pages.

20. I say 'normally' as, rather surprisingly, sympathy with terrorist activities is not always necessary to become a terrorist. Several studies have shown that recruitment into a terrorist movement can sometimes precede any sympathy for the cause. For example, see Joel Busher, 'Understanding

the English Defence League', LSE, 2015, and Katrine Fangen, 'Right-wing Skinheads – Nostalgia and Binary Oppositions', *Young*, 1998. Nevertheless, it is more normal that individuals joining a terrorist group have first become a sympathiser.

21. One example of this process in practice can be seen in the attitudes of young Serbians growing up in East Sarajevo in the aftermath of the civil war. The Serb children who had frequent and friendly contact with children from other ethnic groups had built a sense of identity that included Croats and Bosniaks. They were unlikely to see themselves as victims and were relatively ready to accept that there was guilt on the Serb side. In comparison, the Serb children who had no regular contact with Bosniaks or Croats were unwilling to accept that the Serbs held significant responsibility for the conflict. They saw themselves as the victims of the war and retained a feeling of being treated unjustly. (Sabrina Čehajić-Clancy and Michal Bilewicz, 'Fostering Reconciliation through Historical Moral Exemplars in a Postconflict Society', *Journal of Peace Psychology*, 2017.)

22. Research by Kamaldeep Bhui and others has shown that those with a wider network of contacts and friends are less likely to have sympathy with terrorist actions (K. Bhui et al., 'Is Violent Radicalisation Associated with Poverty, Migration, Poor Self-Reported Health and Common Mental Disorders?', PLOS, 2014).

23. My preferred definition of radicalisation comes from Dina Al Raffie and is as follows: 'A gradual and intentional process that consists of a set of activities that aim at changing the beliefs, feelings and behaviours of individuals with the intent of 1) Aligning them against the core values of societies in which individuals are based; and 2) Readying them for intergroup conflict, whereby society constitutes an out-group that must be fought.' (Dina Al Raffie, 'Social Identity Theory for Investigating Islamic Extremism in the Diaspora', *Journal of Strategic Security*, 2013.)

24. Examples of supposed 'lone actors' are frequently used to suggest that individuals can in effect radicalise themselves without the influence of others. In practice, there are very few lone terrorists and many who are supposed to be so have in fact been heavily influenced by other radicals. For example, Mohammed Merah, an Islamist terrorist who killed seven people in France in 2012, was described by the head of the French domestic intelligence service as a 'lone wolf'. Later research showed that he had been trained by a jihadi group in Pakistan and had connections with other local radicals. A comprehensive review of 119 supposed lone actors found that 85 per cent had in fact engaged with other radicals,

the majority doing so face to face. (P. Gill et al., 'Bombing Alone: Tracing the Motivations and Antecedent Behaviours of Lone-actor Terrorists', *Forensic Science*, 2014.)

25. Donatella della Porta, *Social Movements, Political Violence, and the State: A Comparative Analysis of Italy and Germany*, Cambridge University Press, 1995.
26. Mitchell Silber and Arvin Bhatt, 'Radicalization in the West: The Homegrown Threat', NYPD, 2007.
27. S. Atran et al., 'Devoted Actors Sacrifice for Close Comrades and Sacred Cause', *PNAS*, 2014.
28. Robert White, 'Commitment, Efficacy, and Personal Sacrifice Among Irish Republicans', *Journal of Political and Military Sociology*, 1988.

Chapter 15: The Trilemma We Face

1. The division isn't just between the oldest and youngest. The average age difference between any two Americans is two decades, but the average age difference between two American friends is half that. The average Briton, meanwhile, has almost half the number of friendships with people of other generations than you might expect if their friendships reflected the population.
2. That means even more subsidies for the housing market at a time of serious financial strain. Is this realistic? The US government already spends a whopping $185bn a year (that's almost $400 per American) on housing subsidies. Surely they can't afford even more. But if we look more closely at that $185 billion, we will see something extraordinary. Just one dollar in four goes to the low-income families that we have been talking about. More than twice this goes to families earning $100,000 a year or more, through subsidising their mortgages. If Americans want to live in neighbourhoods that aren't divided by wealth, there is enough money to do something about it. It is just being spent on the wrong people.
3. Making such a move before your thirteenth birthday from a poor to a rich neighbourhood makes you more likely to graduate from college, more likely to get married and more likely to earn an extra third each year.
4. You could also try to reduce the level of diversity around education levels by trying to get everyone to degree level. In practice, this would require sending huge numbers of older citizens to university, which would be deeply impractical, ruinously expensive and very poor value for money for the economy.

Chapter 16: The Gradual-Change Society

1. This is in Denmark.
2. These measures are based on surveys of members of the public. The respect data is based on Gallup surveys across all countries, answering the question: 'Were you treated with respect all day yesterday?' The inclusion data is based on Gallup surveys across all countries, which asked: 'Are you satisfied with opportunities to meet people and make friends?' The trust data is based on the percentage of people responding 'Most people can be trusted' to the question, 'Generally speaking, would you say most people can be trusted, or you can't be too careful?' This final question comes from the Integrated Values Survey, the Afrobarometer, the Arab Barometer, and the Latinobarómetro.
3. 'Society Activities in Sweden: A Statistical Illustration', Statistics Sweden, 1993.
4. This is higher than both the UK and the US – it is roughly three times higher than in Finland.
5. Sören Holmberg and Bo Rothstein, 'Social Trust: The Nordic Gold?', *Social Europe*, 2020.
6. J. Manyika et al., 'Jobs Lost, Jobs Gained', McKinsey Global Institute, 2017.

Chapter 17: The Strengthened Society

1. It also required a world-renowned civil service, an open climate for business and security, the absence of corruption, and investment from American government and companies.
2. The first rule by itself would clearly be insufficient to defend liberty. It cannot be right that the majority of the public could impose new mandatory activity on one part of society that did not themselves support it. For example, most Western populations support the reintroduction of two years' national service for school-leavers, while most future school-leavers do not.
3. As you can see from my examples, I do not believe that Westerners will ever accept the Singaporean approach to allocating housing. This is a constraint on freedom too far for us. It is worth noting that some have tried to impose such rules in a Western context. In Germany, more than fifty thousand residents of Stuttgart live in apartments ultimately owned by the city in the same way that the Singapore state owns the majority of Singaporean housing. To prevent ethnic division, the city imposed a rule requiring that no more than 20 per cent of homes in any one block

go to non-EU citizens. In practice, however, this has had no impact, as more than 50 per cent of the demand for housing comes from non-EU citizens, making the rule impossible to follow.

4. A. Fives et al., 'Parenting Support for Every Parent', UNESCO, 2014.
5. It is worth noticing one thing that all three proposals have in common. They all take place during moments of transition: from childhood towards adulthood, into parenting and then into retirement. This is likely to be a good place to focus for other possible proposals. Moments of transition are times when we most feel the need for new friendships and connections as things change around us and it becomes harder to keep up with existing friends and connections who perhaps have not retired, have not recently had a child or are not approaching adolescence in the same way. Moments of transition are also times when our own identity is in flux. We tend to be less sure who we are and where we stand. This makes others who are in the same state of flux seem very 'like us'. That person from a completely different walk of life is now also someone who has just retired, or had a baby or become a teenager. There are therefore likely to be similar opportunities to design moments of common life around people starting their first job, buying their first home, changing careers and becoming older.
6. Nigel Lawson, *The View from No. 11*, Bantam, 1992.

INDEX

choice, triumph of
conscription and 131–4, 135
freedom of choice and scale of division
129–31
mandatory common life, role in loss of
123–35, 137, 151, 156, 168, 169, 258,
259, 261, 263, 267
National Citizen Service and 123–4, 127
restricting freedom of choice 267–8,
269–98 *see also* gradual change society *and*
strengthened society
Schelling's board and 125–7
size of group and scale of division 127–9
word 'choice', changing importance of 134
Christakis, Nicholas 206
Christensen, Clayton 109
church attendance 26, 50, 56, 57, 60, 83,
87–8, 110, 114, 174–5, 200, 205, 208,
210, 238, 242, 291, 295
Churchill, Winston 183, 291
'churching' (woman's return to church after
childbirth) 83
cities
citywide diversity index, US 165–8
geographical segregation in 136–52,
165–7, 181–2
'ideas', power of and 214–15
income segregation in 128, 137–40,
154–5, 181–2, 274–5
Industrial Revolution and move to 25, 26,
51, 53, 83–4, 87, 114, 115, 117, 118,
154, 155, 260
racial segregation in 96–7, 128–9, 142–52,
158, 165–8, 188
Civil Rights Act, US (1964) 176–7
Civil Rights Movement, US 176–7, 228
civil war 96, 146, 183, 184, 277, 279
'civilisation' 24
climate change 112, 186, 191, 290
Clinton, Hillary 85
Coase, Ronald: 'The Nature of the Firm'
92–3
Coates, Ta-Nehisi 147
Cold War (1946–91) 90
Coleman, James 176–9, 217
'colour bar', UK 96

Common Life (set of rituals, habits and
institutions) 11
agrarian common life *see* agriculture/
farming
collapse of modern 84, 85–100
causes of 101–69 *see also* change; choice;
difference *and* distance between us,
geographical
consequences of 171–250 *see also*
democracy; economy; health; security *and*
social mobility
recovery from/restoration of common life
251–98 *see also* gradual change society;
strengthened society *and* suggestions for
action, thirty-two
connection with those who seem different,
power of 58–84
defined 11, 24–5, 44
empathy and 10–11, 65–6, 68, 131
equality of status and 70–6, 84, 117, 168,
205–8, 255
historical span of 44–57
hunter-gatherers/nomadic societies and 23,
24, 44–8, 49–50, 51, 63, 72, 83, 104,
105, 106, 113, 114, 115–16, 117, 137,
153, 154, 202, 255, 256, 257, 259, 260,
261
Industrial Revolution and 25–7, 44, 47–8,
51–6, 64, 114–15, 118, 121, 154–5, 257
intensity of experience, shared and 73–7,
79, 83, 84, 103, 137, 287
interregnums (when the old common life
has gone and the new has not arrived)
26–7, 114–15, 118, 121, 122, 169, 261
laughter and 64–5
loneliness and 66–8, 204–5, 210, 256, 289
mandatory *see* mandatory common life
People Like Me syndrome (PLM) and *see*
People Like Me syndrome (PLM)
restoration of 251–98 *see also* gradual
change society; strengthened society *and*
suggestions for action, thirty-two
routine, connecting power of and 77–84
school and *see* school
trilemma 266, 267–8, 282
voluntary *see* voluntary common life

INDEX

Segregation Index/Segregation score 138, 140–1, 144, 146, 149
semantic memory 74
settlement movement 193–4
Shahzad, Faisal 231, 232
shared identity 80, 184, 185–9, 198, 239
shared understanding 186, 187, 188, 191–4, 196
Sherif, Muzafer 38–40, 41, 42, 43, 44, 68, 76, 155–6, 190
Sheringham, Teddy 4
Shkreli, Martin 85–6
Silicon Valley, US 94, 212–14
Silver, Nate 166–7, 168
Singapore 277, 279–82, 292 *see also* strengthened society
$64,000 Question, The (gameshow) 90
Skocpol, Theda 55–6, 89
Slade, Reverend James 54–5
slavery 54, 95, 96, 97, 146, 157
Slough, London 150
social animals, humans as 9, 64–8, 253–4
social bubbles 18, 22
social identification 79–84
social institutions 24, 26, 95–6, 110, 260 *see also individual institution name*
social media 106, 119, 273
  changing who you follow on 294
  choice and 130–1, 264–5
  common life and 254, 264–5
social mobility 22, 32, 173–82, 256
  common life and 175–9
  decline in 173–5
  hiring and 179–80
  housing and 176
  networks and 179–81
  prejudice and 179–80
  Salt Lake City 174–5
  schooling and 177–9
Solomon of Israel, King 10–11
Sony 60–1, 62–3, 76, 109
  Sony Walkman 61
Sosis, Richard 80–2
Soviet Union 90
Sri Lanka 277–80
Stanford Graduate School of Education 127

status, equality of 47, 70–6, 84, 117, 168, 205–8, 255 *see also* inequality
Stenner, Karen 5–7, 9
Stoner, James 194–5
Strauss, Jack 179
strengthened society 266, 268, 277–92
  education/schooling and 281
  freedom, restrictions on 282–6
  harm principle and 282–5
  housing and 280–1
  immigration and 282
  mandatory common life and 279–82
  National Health Service and 290–2
  national service and 280–1
  national service programme for secondary school students 286–7
  parenting sessions 287–8
  retirement service, national 288–9
  Singapore as 277, 279–82, 292
  volunteering activities and 281, 288
stress, cohesive communities and 201–4, 207, 208, 210
Students for Democratic Society (SDS) 228–9, 244–5
sugar 23–4, 32
suggestions for action, thirty-two 293–8
Sunderland, James 54–5
SuperZIPs, US 139–40
Supreme Court, US 96, 97, 176
Sweden 179–80, 269–70, 271–2, 274–5, 276

Tanzania 44–5, 65
Tate, Sharon 240
taxes 161, 184, 187, 188–9, 191, 216, 223, 262, 273
team-building days 73–4
television 20, 119–21, 130, 134, 204, 257–8, 265, 272, 273, 277, 279, 292, 294
Tennessee, Streetcar Statute (1905) 96
terrorism *see* security/terrorism 227–50
The People's Will (terrorist group) 247, 248
thinking well 293–4
totalism 246–50
Trades Union Congress 55
trade unions 55, 87, 96, 97, 271, 273

353

Harper
North

BOOK CREDITS

HarperNorth would like to thank the following staff and
contributors for their involvement in making this book a reality:

Hannah Avery
Sebastian Ballard
Fionnuala Barrett
Claire Boal
Charlotte Brown
Sarah Burke
Alan Cracknell
Jonathan de Peyer
Anna Derkacz
Gavin Dunn
Tom Dunstan
Kate Elton
Mick Fawcett
Nick Fawcett
Simon Gerratt
Alice Gomer
Monica Green
Tara Hiatt
Graham Holmes

Megan Jones
Jean-Marie Kelly
Alex Kirby
Oliver Malcolm
Simon Moore
Ben Murphy
Alice Murphy-Pyle
Adam Murray
Melissa Okusanya
Genevieve Pegg
Agnes Rigou
Dean Russell
James Ryan
Florence Shepherd
Zoe Shine
Hannah Stamp
Emma Sullivan
Katrina Troy

For more unmissable reads,
sign up to the HarperNorth newsletter at
www.harpernorth.co.uk

or find us on Twitter at
@HarperNorthUK

**Harper
North**

Rifling Paradise

Jem Poster

Rifling Paradise

THE OVERLOOK PRESS
Woodstock & New York

This edition first published in the United States in 2009 by
The Overlook Press Peter Mayer Publishers, Inc.
Woodstock & New York

NEW YORK:
The Overlook Press
141 Wooster Street
New York, NY 10012

WOODSTOCK:
The Overlook Press
One Overlook Drive
Woodstock, NY 12498
www.overlookpress.com

Cataloging-in-Publication Data is available from the Library of Congress

Manufactured in the United States of America
ISBN 978-1-59020-048-3
10 9 8 7 6 5 4 3 2 1

For Kay, Tom and Tobi

I

1

It occurred to me later that I must have registered their approach a minute or so before the first stone struck the window. Certainly something had disturbed me as I dozed beside the fire – a murmured word perhaps, the click of the gate latch, a shoulder brushing the overgrown laurels beside the path – and I was already out of my armchair and moving towards the window at the moment of impact. Quite a small stone by the sound of it, such as one might imagine tossed against a young girl's casement by an importunate lover. I put my face against the glass, cupping my eyes with my hands, and peered out into the night.

The second stone must have been flung with considerable force. It struck one of the panes at waist height, sending shards of glass skittering across the floorboards. I remember starting backward, my head averted and my right hand held protectively to the side of my face, and then seizing the lamp from the chiffonier and stumbling through the hallway to the front door.

In those days – why not confess it along with the rest? – I was usually half cut by the time I turned in for the night, and possibly the claret was responsible on this occasion for what might have looked to my persecutors like a display of courage. But you have to realise that when I threw open the door and stepped out into the garden I had no particular reason to consider myself in danger. I had in mind, I suppose, a gang of mischievous schoolboys up from the village, a misguided but essentially innocuous prank.

Not schoolboys. The figures hovering at the margin of the oil-lamp's muted glow were all but featureless, but I could see at once from the stance and bulk of the two nearest that I wasn't dealing with children. I hesitated. Away to my right, someone cleared his throat and spat. Nobody spoke.

It was difficult to assess the situation. I was, in the first place, uncertain of the size of the gathering. Besides the half-dozen men dimly discernible at the lamplight's edge, there were indications – a stifled cough, the crack of a snapped twig, feet scuffing the damp leaf-litter where the beeches overhung the lawn – of perhaps as many again in the deeper shadows beyond. And what had brought them to the Hall at such an hour? I could hardly interpret their visit as a conventional courtesy, though I could see, on rapid reflection, a certain wisdom in treating it as such. I forced a smile.

'You were lucky to catch me,' I said. 'Another twenty minutes and I'd have been sound asleep in bed.'

'We'd have been sorry to have had to rouse you, Mr Redbourne.' The voice was quiet and even, but not entirely reassuring. I felt my pulse quicken.

'Might the matter not have waited until morning?' I asked, peering uncertainly towards the speaker.

'Might have. But the sooner the better, we thought.'

'In that case, you'd better come directly to the point.'

'I'll come to it soon enough. We were in the Dog, drinking a drop to poor Daniel's memory – you'll remember Daniel Rosewell – and it came to us that, living such a tidy step from the village, you mightn't have heard of his passing and that you needed to be told.'

'Daniel dead? How?'

'Six foot of rope and a milking stool. Hanged hisself last night in Waller's barn. Janie Waller found him this morning when she went out for kindling – his toes not two inches off the ground, she says, but two inches or twelve, it makes no difference.'

I was silent, thinking, I confess, less of the dead youth than of the trail that must have led this dubious company to my door.

'That'll grieve Mr Redbourne, we said. Or if it doesn't, it ought to.' Just the faintest hint of venom now. It was vital, I knew, to keep the discussion on a civilised footing.

'Thank you,' I said. 'It was good of you to bring the news. Would you convey my condolences to the boy's mother?'

5

'Thanks and convey be damned.' A second voice, less measured than the first and with a harder edge to it, speaking out of the shadows to my left. 'You're to blame for the lad's death, Mr Redbourne, and you know it.'

'But that's absurd. I barely knew him.'

'That's not true. Five years back you fed and lodged him at your own expense for a month and more. The whole village knows it.'

'I gave him such employment as he was capable of and quartered him in one of my cottages while he worked for me. I'm accommodating three labourers in a similar fashion at this very moment.'

'Yes, but you visited him.'

I stared into the murk, wondering how much more my faceless accuser might know.

'At night. He told Nathan Farr. He said you put your arms about him.'

'Daniel was a troubled soul, and I offered him such consolation as I could. I may have embraced him on occasion.'

'Other things too. It wasn't only what you'd call embracing.' I thought I heard the trace of a sneer in the speaker's precise articulation of the word.

'What kind of things?' I asked. There was, I could see, a degree of risk in pressing for greater specificity, but I needed to know exactly how matters stood.

'That's not for us to say. You know better than we do what kind of mischief you visited on the lad.'

Jem Poster

'You touched him, Mr Redbourne.' A third voice cutting in now, reedy, distinctive. I listened intently, trying to place it. 'Wrongfully. Like you touched Nathan Farr.'

'Nathan? Is Nathan here?' I lifted my lamp and leaned forward, scanning the shadows. It was as though I had bent suddenly over a rock pool: the same instantaneous spasm of alarm, the same collective recoil.

'Not with us tonight, Mr Redbourne. But he'd take an oath on it. The touching. And the photographs. He told us about those too.'

I had it now. 'Maddocks,' I said sharply. 'Maddocks, is that you?'

A strained silence suggested that I had hit the mark. When the voice resumed, it was with a shade less aggression.

'It makes no matter who, sir. What I have to say goes for us all. For the whole village.'

'I doubt that,' I said, my spirits rising. Maddocks – a wastrel, a petty schemer, a hen-pecked nonentity. Who was he to set himself up as my inquisitor? 'I very much doubt it, Maddocks. And in any case, you've had your say and I've heard you out. Now I suggest that we all get to our beds.'

'You may have heard us, Mr Redbourne, but you've not heeded us.'

I hadn't had a word from Samuel Blaney, civil or uncivil, since he had left my employ, but I should have recognised his voice anywhere. He must have known as much. He strode forward and stood squarely in front of me, his massive head thrust defiantly forward into the lamplight.

7

'It's a subtle distinction,' I said.

I've heard you out.' Blaney's mimicry of my own clipped tones was at once inaccurate and offensive. 'I've heard you out. That's what you told me when you dismissed me. My children will go hungry, I said – and so they did, believe me, for a good twelvemonth after – but you wouldn't heed my words. Hearing and heeding, Mr Redbourne – they're not the same thing, now, are they?'

'I had others to consider, Blaney. I'll not have my workforce intimidated, by you or by anyone else. And I'll not have you sneaking in now to settle old scores under cover of other business.'

I'm a tall man myself, but Blaney stands a good couple of inches taller. He reared himself to his full height and stepped up to within a yard of me. I edged back, bringing the lamp between his body and my own.

'Sneaking, is it?' he breathed. 'Well, you'd know all about that, wouldn't you? Creeping like a thief around your own grounds after nightfall, dodging in where you'd no call to be. That's sneaking, Mr Redbourne, the way a man acts when he doesn't want to be seen.'

I gestured out to the shadowy figures behind him. 'And this?' I asked. 'What's this?'

'Samuel's right, Mr Redbourne.' I tried to locate the voice, anxious to re-establish connection with the group from which Blaney had so pointedly and menacingly detached himself. 'If you'd heeded what we've told you tonight, you'd be weeping now – weeping for the lad and for what you brought him to.'

This was outrageous. I sidestepped Blaney and thrust myself angrily forward, feeling the blood rise to my face. 'A man doesn't grieve to the orders of a mob,' I said heatedly. 'And I'll not be held responsible for what the lad chose to do to himself.'

'But why did he choose it?' the voice insisted. 'Why would a young man want to do away with himself? And as a child – well, you'd not have found a happier face for ten miles around. Bright as an April morning till he fell in with you.'

'Daniel?' I felt my self-control slipping, heard my own voice as though from someone else's mouth, shrill with incredulity. 'That's nonsense. The child was beaten black and blue from the time he could walk. Go and stand outside his mother's door if you want an answer to your questions.'

'A mother strikes her child to keep him on the straight and narrow. That's natural, and what's natural does no harm to a youngster. But what you've done—'

'Listen,' I said, 'I'll not stand for any more of this. Let me advise you, as a magistrate, that your accusations and innuendo amount to slander, and furthermore' – I glared around me as though my gaze could penetrate the enveloping darkness – 'that I could have the whole pack of you charged with trespass and malicious damage. Now get back to your homes and leave me in peace.'

I swung round and, as I did so, Blaney took a step to his left, positioning himself between me and my doorway.

'The Farr boy,' he said softly. 'He'll take an oath, remember. In the witness box if need be.'

'Let me pass.' I made a move to circumvent him, but he was too quick for me.

'You'll pass when I give you leave,' he said. And he reached forward and laid the flat of his hand against the lapel of my smoking-jacket.

It was a surprisingly unemphatic gesture, casual, almost caressing, but I knew at that moment that Blaney was prepared to steer us all into deeper and more dangerous waters. The men at my back knew it too, I could tell, sensing in their stillness a new expectancy, a sharpened focus. 'When I give you leave,' he repeated, slowly withdrawing his hand but without yielding ground. He was staring into my face with an expression of such malevolent intensity that I was obliged to avert my eyes. And as I did so, I was aware of some faint stir, subtle but unmistakable, in the group behind me. Nothing, I remember thinking – not a word, not a glance, not the smallest gesture – would be lost on this audience. I looked up at Blaney again, forcing myself to answer his gaze.

'With or without your leave,' I said, as firmly as I could, 'I intend to retire to my bed. You must excuse me.'

His silence made me think momentarily that I had retrieved the situation; then he reached forward again and gripped me by the right wrist, pressing his thumb sharply into the flesh just beneath the edge of my cuff and making the glass chimney of the lamp jitter in its housing. I tried to pull away but he held me fast and drew me, with a horrible suggestion of intimacy, to his breast.

'I could put you on the ground,' he whispered, the stink of ale coming off his breath, 'as easy as I could put out that lamp.'

And then, after a tense pause, viciously, gratuitously: 'You've hands like a girl's, Mr Redbourne. I hate that in a man.'

'You can't threaten me like that, Blaney. The law doesn't allow it. And no one, let me remind you, is beyond reach of the law.'

'Just so, Mr Redbourne. No one. That's a lesson you've still to learn. A lesson' – his gaze flickered briefly outward – 'we're here to teach you. Because there are those who learn of their own accord, and there are those who won't learn until they're taught. And you' – he released my wrist and, before I had time to step back or even to register his intention, struck me across the cheek – 'you need teaching.'

Blaney was, I knew, capable of considerable brutality, but this was not in essence a brutal action. It was, rather, a finely calculated insolence, delivered without force and with a knowing eye on his audience.

'How dare you!' I was trembling violently now, caught between rage and fear. 'I could have you charged with assault.'

'Assault? How do you make that out, Mr Redbourne?'

'You just struck me in the face. I don't imagine you're going to deny it.'

'A tap, that's all. A friendly tap.'

'An unprovoked act of aggression, and in the presence of witnesses.'

'Witnesses, sir?' He was playing shamelessly to the gallery now, grinning hugely, sweeping the shadows with exaggerated movements of his heavy head. 'I can't see any witnesses.'

'Don't act the fool, Blaney. There must be a dozen men out there, any one of whose testimony would be enough to convict you.'

The grin faded. He leaned close, his mouth against my ear. 'We'll see who's the fool,' he said quietly. And then, lifting his head and voice: 'Did anyone see me assault this man?'

There was a long, uneasy silence. Blaney bent towards me again. 'Like I said, Mr Redbourne. No witnesses.'

In my father's time, a cry would have brought a dozen servants running from the house and its outbuildings, but those days were long gone. Under my own straitened regime, the groom and the cook, man and wife, lived in a cottage at the far side of the estate, housework was attended to on an irregular basis by a girl who came up from the village as required, and only Latham slept on the premises. Well into his seventies, deaf as an adder and barely able to carry out his routine duties, he was hardly a man to be counted on in a crisis, and I could have nourished no realistic hope of assistance from that quarter. Even so, I found myself, in my agitation, turning helplessly towards the house. Blaney was quick to spot the movement.

'The old man won't hear you,' he said. 'Not even if he was awake, which I doubt. And don't go fancying you might make a break for it neither. I'd have you before your foot was off the ground.'

A sudden gust of wind, raindrops spattering the laurels. I spread my hands in a gesture of appeasement. 'What do you want of me?' I asked.

The question seemed to catch him off guard. He glanced outward as though in need of a prompt.

'After all,' I continued, heartened by his momentary discomfiture, 'we can't stand around talking in the garden all night.'

My attempt at levity was clearly a misjudgement. He turned slowly back to me, his eyes glittering dangerously. 'You're in no position to say what can or can't be done, Mr Redbourne. I'll do what I damn well like, on or off your blasted property.' And, as though to reinforce the point, he lunged clumsily towards me.

I stepped sideways, anticipating another slap, and felt my right heel sink deep in the freshly turned soil of the flowerbed. I might have retained my balance; but Blaney, seeing me stagger, put out his hand, fingers extended, and prodded me in the chest. The barest touch, but it was enough. I fell awkwardly on my side among the lavender bushes with the lamp beneath me. I heard the glass crack against my ribs, felt the heat of the wick and its fitting through my jacket. In the darkness that engulfed us, I imagined Blaney towering above me, poised to deliver whatever kicks or blows would satisfy his appetite for revenge.

In my sometimes confused memory of the events of that night, this stands out with the most extraordinary clarity. You have to think of me huddled there among the crushed foliage, knees drawn up to protect my midriff, the side of my face hard against the damp earth. Whatever faint hope I might have entertained up to that moment – hope of rescue, some vestigial trust in the essential humanity of my tormentors – had been extinguished with the lamplight. And yet out of my very hopelessness, something – grace is the word that comes to mind, though I find myself more comfortable with the notion of some profound form of resignation – rose like the fragrance from the bruised lavender, stilling my agitation; and I lay quietly in that merciful state of suspension, waiting incuriously for events to unfold around me.

I remember the strangest sense of leisure, of time frozen or protracted, but in actuality my trance could hardly have lasted more than a few seconds, broken, I think, by the voice of one of the men.

'Let him be now, Samuel.' There was a nervous urgency in the man's tone, as though he were calling back a vicious and intractable dog. I looked up. Blaney still stood above me, his broad frame silhouetted against the sky, but I thought I detected a certain irresoluteness in his stance.

'We came here to teach him a lesson,' he said.

'You've given him lesson enough, Samuel.'

Blaney seemed to consider this for a moment.

'He'll not tell,' he said at last. 'Not with what we know about him.'

'You lay into him the way you laid into Arthur Cotteridge that time and there'll be no hiding it, whether he wants to tell or no.'

There was another long pause. I saw Blaney shift position but was unprepared for the kick he aimed at my legs as he turned. His boot struck my left shin a little below the knee, glancingly but not without force. I rolled sideways, anxious to avoid worse, but he was already moving away down the slope of the lawn to rejoin his companions.

'You just mind that,' he called over his shoulder, 'next time you're thinking of putting your milksop hands where they've no right to be.'

I lay still until I was sure the men had all left the grounds. Then I limped back to the house and groped my way painfully up the stairs to my bedroom.

2

My leg throbbed and my hands shook so violently that I was scarcely able to light the lamp. I removed my shoes and my muddied jacket and threw myself face down among my pillows, trying to compose myself sufficiently to summon Latham. But as my breathing returned to normal and the trembling subsided, it struck me that it would be unwise to make more of the incident than was absolutely necessary; and having satisfied myself that my injuries were essentially superficial, I eased myself from the bed, drew a chair to the fire, raked up the embers and settled back to consider my situation.

The decision I reached as a result of my deliberations seemed at the time to involve some radical shift of perspective, yet the plan I formulated that night was really nothing new. From childhood on, I had been fascinated by the exploits of those naturalists who, with scant regard for their own personal comfort and safety, had obstinately pursued their quarry – their specimens, their theories – to the most remote corners of the earth. Throughout my youth and early manhood, I had dreamed almost daily of following, more or less literally, in the footsteps of Darwin or Waterton; and though my own travels had been considerably more modest than theirs, I had made forays sufficiently gruelling and fruitful – into the Camargue, across the Pyrenees – to convince myself that my ambition wasn't entirely unrealistic.

What I suppose I lacked was precisely that obstinacy I so much admired in my heroes. At all events, in the years after my parents' early deaths I lapsed first into trivial habits of mind and then into a form of melancholia – a deep-seated ache or long-ing that I learned to dull with occasional doses of laudanum and regular recourse to the good red wines laid down by my father for a future he had no doubt imagined he would live to enjoy. I continued to add new specimens to my collection, I contributed notes and articles to minor periodicals; but the invigorating dreams – those vivid fantasies of exploration and discovery – were put aside like childhood toys.

I might ascribe my loss of vision to the more sombre view of reality that comes with experience or, more specifically, to the responsibilities I rather unwillingly shouldered when I inherited the estate. Neither explanation is misleading in itself, but both skirt the darker truths of my inward life – the passions nursed in secret, the delicate liaisons screened from public view. What had begun as a sentimental camaraderie tinged with philanthropy (I would give the boys this, I thought, I would give them that – a few shillings, an education, eternal friendship) became an obsession, drawing me deep into some shadowy world of troubled pleasure and stifled aspiration.

What was I looking for, stalking my prey across the bright meadows or leaning over the bridge with assumed nonchalance, waiting in breathless ambush while the waters churned and boiled beneath me? The cynic's answer is too simple, too obvious. I was, after all, the gentlest of predators, subsisting for long periods on the most rarefied diet – a glance, a greeting, an inept pleasantry (Nathan Farr, lazing in the March sunlight with his back against the churchyard wall, looking up at me from beneath his unruly fringe: 'We're alike, Mr Redbourne, gentlemen of leisure' – the suggestion of fraternity, of easy complicity, haunting me for days). What was it – I mean, what was it precisely – that I had in mind? And what outcome could I possibly have anticipated but humiliation and disgrace?

Despite the pain from my leg, my thinking seemed unusually lucid, as though the shock of the night's events had purged my mind of its customary clutter. I could see clearly that my situation was all but untenable and that decisive action was required; it followed from that – since staying put could hardly be accounted decisive unless I were prepared to face my accusers in the open – that I should have to distance myself from the village, almost certainly for some appreciable time. And the moment the idea presented itself, I was gripped by a subdued but unmistakable excitement: the old ambition again, but now in more resolute form. I should travel, I should add significantly to my collection and I should contribute my quota to the sum of human knowledge. That was how I formulated my intentions; and as I did so, I was struck by the thought that what had been a bright but insubstantial dream had now transformed itself into a plan of action.

I saw at once that there were practical matters to be addressed. Firstly, and most importantly, I had no available funds; and secondly, I should have to find a competent steward to manage the estate in my absence. However, I had some confidence that the necessary finances could be found reasonably close to home, while the fact that my own management of the estate had in recent years proved considerably less than competent inclined me to view the second matter as an opportunity rather than an impediment.

I was so taken by the apt simplicity of it all that I began, in imagination, to pack for my voyage. That to be left, this to be taken – and this, and this, nets and collecting-boxes, coats and collar-studs, books and papers, my mind running freely over my belongings until, quite unexpectedly, it faltered and stuck.

The photographs. What about the photographs? I rose awkwardly to my feet, limped over to the wardrobe and took the heavy portfolio from its hiding-place. Village Types: a Photographic Record – the title, neatly inscribed in violet ink on the front cover, was intentionally misleading. There had been half a dozen sitters but, in truth, only one type: a young man somewhere between fifteen and eighteen years of age, well muscled and firm-featured, with a certain unreflective openness in his gaze. A representative record had never, in fact, been my aim. I was, as collectors phrase it, a specialist.

I set the portfolio on my bedside table and untied the fastening, feeling again the familiar quickening of the pulse, the flickering thrill of guilty anticipation. Yet the portraits were, I reminded myself as I leafed through them, innocuous enough. Luke Wainwright, perhaps divining something of the nature of my interest but more probably prompted by his own notorious self-regard, had stripped to the waist for his sitting, squaring up to the camera like a prizefighter; but all the others sat or stood in their shirt-sleeves, informally posed against the plain white wall which, I had realised from the beginning, set off to perfection their tanned features and the strong outlines of their lightly clothed bodies.

No, the meaning of the portraits wasn't to be found in the images themselves, but in the memories they enshrined: the sharp reek of sweat as I helped Matty Turner out of his jacket, my face so close to his sunburned neck that I might easily have put my lips to it; my fingers resting lightly on Luke's shoulder as I showed him how to look through the view lens or, more audaciously, brushing the inside of Nathan Farr's thigh as I leaned over him to adjust the angle of his chair.

I'd touched Nathan, yes, and one or two others besides, but neither those fleeting moments of physical contact nor the earnest, oblique and largely one-sided discussions that had led up to them would have been sufficient in themselves to keep me in thrall to Blaney and his mob. Whatever power my persecutors might have exercised under cover of darkness, I should probably have faced them down in public if it hadn't been for Daniel.

Daniel, poor, bewildered Daniel, skulking aimlessly in all weathers through the narrow lanes around the village, afraid to return to a house in which cuffs, punches and worse were meted out more regularly than meals by a mother whose name was a local byword for erratic and unreasonable behaviour; Daniel, whose hooded gaze and pinched, melancholy features had drawn me into territory far darker and more dangerous than any I had negotiated in the company of his handsome confreres. The fact that those boys hadn't needed me had been a perverse part of their charm; Daniel's need, on the other hand, had been urgent, palpable. He had clung to me – sometimes literally – like a frightened child in a storm and I, for my part, had responded with a tenderness of which I had not, up to that point, believed myself capable.

Tenderness? That's the word that comes most readily to mind, though I sense how much it leaves unacknowledged – the relentless cycles of longing and shame, the corrosive despair undermining every look, protestation or act. And yet the word holds good.

I had set him apart from the others, folded in a sheet of cream-coloured paper at the back of the portfolio, and now I searched him out: a single portrait, a little underexposed, emphasising the hollows beneath the sharp cheekbones, the shadows around the deep-set eyes. The photograph had been taken at Daniel's instigation, not my own, and had borne out my intuitive suspicion that his beauty was a thing too delicate and equivocal to be captured by the camera. Sullen, tense and slightly stooped, he looked out at me with the fixed stare that had always seemed to hold some unspoken challenge or reproach, and now frankly unsettled me. Smudged death's-head: Daniel as *memento mori*, Daniel leaning forward, thin lips parted, to remind me of the night I'd let him go.

A foul night, rain sluicing down, the wind thrashing the untended laurels in the shrubbery and buffeting the house. I had been dozing in front of the fire, a book open on my lap, when I heard a soft tapping at the window. Daniel peering in, his white face an inch from the blurred pane. I lurched to my feet and hurried to open the front door.

'What is it, Daniel? What are you doing here?'

No answer. He stood blinking in the muted light of the hallway, his black locks plastered to his cheeks, rainwater pooling at his feet. I could hear Latham moving slowly along the corridor at the back of the house.

'Come through.' I ushered Daniel into the study and helped him out of his sodden greatcoat. His shirt, scarcely less wet than the coat, clung to his thin shoulders. He moved over to the fire and stood on the hearthrug staring into the flames, pale and tremulous, his arms folded across his chest. I draped his coat over the back of the nearest chair.

'Are you ill?' I asked.

'I'm well enough. No thanks to you, though, treating me the way you do.'

I was taken aback, both by the accusation itself and the asperity of his tone.

'What do you mean?'

'You know what I mean. You keep me out there like an old dog in a kennel.'

'Hardly a kennel, Daniel. The cottage is more than large enough for you. You've coals in the grate, food on the table, a warm bed—'

'And not much else. It's no life for a human soul, holed up out there in the woods with no company but owls and flittermice.'

'A better life, I'd have thought, than the alternative. Would you rather be back with your mother?'

A long silence and then, surlily: 'I was waiting for you. You hadn't said you weren't coming.'

'The weather, Daniel. Surely you weren't expecting me to come out on a night like this?'

He spread his hands, holding them wide and a little towards me, a gesture all the more poignant for its clumsy theatricality. 'Why not? After all, I came out to see you.'

I stepped forward, meaning to take him in my arms, but a sudden clattering from the far end of the house reminded me of Latham's presence and I started guiltily, stifled the impulse. Daniel eyed me narrowly. 'You don't want me in here, do you? Not where you live. Only out there, where you can choose to visit me or not, as you see fit.'

The observation was more accurately perceptive than I cared to admit. I hesitated an instant too long, and Daniel pounced. 'It's true, isn't it? Even now, you're wondering how to get me out of the house.'

'Come now, Daniel. You know that's nonsense.'

'Is it?' He fixed me with his challenging stare. 'In that case, I'll stay.'

'It's not as easy as that. I shall have to make arrangements.'

'Arrangements? What arrangements would you have to make? You live alone in a house with more rooms than a family of ten could make use of, and you can't find space for a friend.'

He was working himself into a passion, a hint of colour rising to his cheeks. I could see clearly enough the risks involved in letting him stay, but I could see, too, that outright rejection might well fan his anger to an uncontrollable blaze.

'Some other time,' I said. 'Maybe next week.'

'Tonight,' he said fiercely. 'I want to stay tonight.'

It struck me then that Daniel had determined, perhaps long before setting out for the Hall that night, to put me to a test I could hardly be expected to pass. His dark eyes glittered with a wild exultation and I sensed that nothing would please him more, at that particular moment, than to tear apart the delicate, precarious structure we had created. Youth tends to seek resolution and truth; maturity knows with what compromises and half-truths our irresolute lives must be shored up. I reached out and gently touched his arm.

'Leave it now, Daniel. We can talk tomorrow.'

'You're sending me away, aren't you? Just like I said.' He brushed my hand aside, gestured towards the streaming panes. 'Sending me out in weather you'd not walk abroad in yourself – not for my sake, anyway. And if I catch my death—'

'Keep your voice down. Listen, I'll walk back with you.'

'Damned if I'll let you.' He lunged forward, snatched his wet coat from the chair-back and was out in the hallway before I had time to think of stopping him. I followed, to find him wrestling with the heavy bolt on the front door.

Even now, it cuts me clean to the heart to think of it. As the bolt slammed back in its groove, he half turned and looked up at me over his shoulder. The dangerous glitter was gone from his eyes, replaced by an expression of bewilderment and helpless entreaty. If I had wanted to hold him back, to hold him close, that was the moment to do so.

Anything would have served – a word, a gesture, the merest touch. I did nothing; I said nothing. And Daniel turned away again, wrenched open the door and stepped out into the dark.

I set the portrait to one side and turned my attention to the others. In retrospect my action seems freighted with significance, yet I'm not aware of having given a great deal of thought to it. I simply leaned forward and fed the photographs into the fire, singly at first and then, as the flames took hold, in thin sheaves. I remember the heat on the back of my outstretched hand, the smell of singed hair in the air; yes, and the way the lovely faces warped and darkened in the instant before the flames consumed them.

As the blaze died down, I turned back to Daniel's photograph. I should like to be able to say that what followed was a gesture of love, or at least of loyalty; but in preserving something of the image – a little oval, roughly snipped out with my mother's rusted sewing scissors, head and shoulders, like a ragged cameo – I was actually responding to darker promptings. Treat me as you treated them, the rigid stare seemed to say, and you'll be sorry. I'm not sure that I saw the matter so clearly at the time, but this was an act of propitiation, a sop to Daniel's aggrieved and possibly vengeful spirit. I slipped the scrap between the leaves of my pocket-book before consigning the remainder of the photograph to the flames.

There was more to be done. I returned to the wardrobe and withdrew the negative plates – six small maroon boxes, each representing a different sitting, a new obsession. I opened each box in turn, tipping its contents into the hearth; then I set to with the handle of the poker, methodically at first but with increasing wildness, the shards of dark glass flying about my hands as I worked. Only when every plate had been shattered beyond hope of recognition or repair did I pause for breath.

It was then that I began to cry, the tears coursing down my face as I squatted there in the hot afterglow of the blaze. Crying for Daniel, of course, for the poor soul lost in the drenching dark, but not for him alone. My tears were for myself too, for the chastened dreamer hunkered among the splinters of his own unsustainable illusions; and for those other lost ones, the beautiful boys already slipping away into unremarkable manhood in worlds utterly remote from my own.

The throbbing in my leg had become almost intolerable. I took the hearth-brush and shovel from the stand and tidied up as best I could. Then I poured myself a generous measure of brandy, knocked it quickly back and retired to bed.

3

I remember hearing the clock in the hallway strike four as I slipped between the sheets, and then nothing more until Latham came up with my shaving-water at eight. I rose on my elbow as he entered, and a flash of pain shot through my leg from shin to hip. I groaned softly and sank back against the pillows.

'If you'd prefer to sleep a little longer, sir . . .'

'Thank you, Latham, but I have matters to attend to. Is there any post?'

'No, sir, but an odd thing . . .' He set down the ewer, fumbled in his pocket and produced, with as much of a flourish as his stiff joints allowed, my silver cigarette case. 'From the garden. The girl found it by the flowerbed when she arrived for her duties this morning. And one of the lamps out there too, smashed to smithereens. I thought the house must have been burgled – there's a pane broken in the study – but we've gone over the downstairs rooms from end to end, and there's no sign anything's been so much as breathed on.'

'No, it was a matter of far less consequence – just a few lads up from the village looking for mischief. One of them shied a stone through the window and when I gave chase I stumbled and fell. No great harm done, though I imagine the flowerbed may be looking a little the worse for wear.'

'Your smoking-jacket too, sir – caked with mud. I'll have it seen to.' He placed the cigarette case gently on the bedside table and reached the jacket down from the back of the door. 'Look at this,' he said, lifting the sleeve between finger and thumb and holding up the filthy underside for my inspection. There was a hint of reproach in his voice, as though I were still the troublesome child he had once had to swab down in the stableyard after a wet afternoon's fossil-hunting in the local quarry.

'Get Mrs Garrett to attend to it after breakfast.' I eased myself gingerly up the bed and leaned back against the headboard. 'And I'd be grateful if you'd ask the girl to make arrangements for the reglazing when she returns to the village. I have business in London and I don't expect to be back before Friday.'

Latham stepped over to the window and drew back the curtains. I leaned forward, swivelling towards the light, and the pain flared again, making me grimace and catch my breath. He returned to my bedside and stared down at me, his thin face creased with concern. 'With respect, sir, I think you should postpone your journey. You don't look fit to travel.'

'I'm well enough. Perhaps a little more shaken by my fall than I'd thought.'

'If you'd like me to send for Dr Griffiths—'

'There's no need. I shall leave immediately after breakfast.'

'You'll miss the early train, sir.'

'Then I shall take the next.'

'If you insist, sir.' He draped my jacket carefully over his forearm and withdrew without another word.

My uncle's house was barely fifteen minutes' walk from my hotel, but my leg was aching and the sky threatened rain, and it seemed sensible to take a cab. The city, I thought, as we bowled down Tottenham Court Road, was even more crowded and more frenetically busy than I remembered, and I was glad when the cab swung off down Bedford Avenue and into the quieter reaches of Bloomsbury.

The exterior of the house gave little indication of my uncle's wealth and status. Less recently painted than either of its immediate neighbours, it seemed to give off a faint air of gloom although, looking up as I stepped down from the cab, I could see the soft flicker of firelight reflected from the ceiling of a first-floor room. I paid the driver, limped up the front steps and rang the bell, hearing its muffled clang reverberating upward from some basement room or passage.

My uncle Joshua – my father's younger brother – was a banker by profession, but had accumulated most of his considerable fortune through shrewd investment in land and housing on the northern fringe of the expanding city. More successful than my father, he was also generally reckoned to be appreciably less scrupulous. A vicious scoundrel, my mother once called him in the course of an ill-tempered conversation with my father as we awaited his arrival one summer afternoon, and I remember very clearly the shock of her uncharacteristically scathing judgement, as well as the subsequent loosening of a family connection I had imagined, in my childish innocence, to be unshakeable. My uncle was never, I think, barred from the house, but he must have recognised at some point that he was unwelcome there. At all events, some time around my sixteenth year his visits ceased altogether.

Yet this sketch, I realise, misses the essential point. For, whatever else he may have been, my uncle was also the man who fanned to a flame my childhood interest in the natural world, taking me with him on his long, meandering excursions, answering my incessant questions with genuine erudition and exemplary patience, revealing what lay hidden behind the dazzling surfaces of things. I can see him now, twisting back a spray of privet to show me the hawk-moth larva clasping the stem, or withdrawing from the dark interior of a hawthorn hedge the pale, translucent egg of a linnet.

For two or three years after he had ceased to visit, we maintained a regular correspondence. I remember the impatience, faintly tinged with guilt, with which I used to wait for his long, detailed letters – meticulous descriptions of specimens newly received from collectors in remote regions, affectionate recollections of our own excursions and general advice more accessible and more pertinent than any I can recall hearing from my father. And my replies were equally warm and full, quite different in tone from the dutiful letters I dispatched to my parents during the school term or the flippant chronicles of home life sent, during the vacations, to my schoolfellows. Only in writing to myuncle did I feel that the words on the page were in harmony with my deepest and most serious thoughts.

And perhaps it was some subtle embarrassment at my own openness with him which, as I grew to manhood, insinuated itself between us. At all events our correspondence shrank, during the course of my nineteenth or twentieth year, from a flow to a bare trickle, and the fault undoubtedly lay with me. I would put aside his letters to be answered later and then forget them for weeks on end, eventually responding with a hasty note and the promise of a fuller reply when time allowed. But time, for reasons my uncle may have understood more clearly than I, never did allow.

The door was opened by a manservant so coldly formal in his bearing and so supercilious in his manner that I wondered for a moment whether the telegram I had sent to announce my visit might have gone astray. 'I'm Charles Redbourne,' I said. 'I believe – I hope – that my uncle is expecting me.'

'Indeed.' He led me up the stairway, stopped outside one of the front rooms and knocked gently. There was a brief pause, and then the door swung open.

I hadn't seen my uncle since the day of my father's funeral, and though I should have recognised him anywhere, it was apparent that the intervening years had not dealt kindly with him. His tall frame was stooped, and he seemed to hold up his head with difficulty. The skin of his face was slack, and pale as tallow; his eyes were dark in their hollow sockets. As he took my hand I could feel the distortion of his arthritic fingers and the weakness of their grip. He drew me forward and pushed the door shut behind me.

The room was large and well lit, furnished richly but with the restraint characteristic of an earlier and less assertive age. No clutter: just two fireside chairs, a low mahogany tea-table, an inlaid bureau and a wooden chest carved in high relief with scenes from the Greek myths. The carpet, I noticed, as my uncle propelled me gently towards the hearth, was unusually soft and thick.

'You're limping, Charles. Not your father's trouble, I hope.'

'I've been spared the gout. The limp is the result of a recent gardening accident. Nothing serious.'

'Apt punishment for undermining the order of things. If you want my advice, I suggest you leave the gardening to those who are employed to do it. Half of society's ills might be averted if men knew their appointed places, and it's our duty – the duty of our class – to lead by example. When I ring this bell' – he leaned over and tugged at the tasselled bell-pull beside the chimney-breast – 'Mrs Fraser will put three spoonfuls of Darjeeling into the pot and fill it with scalding water. There's nothing difficult about the task, and I'm perfectly capable of doing it myself. I've no doubt that, if I were obliged to do so, I could eventually lay my hands on the milk-jug, the sugar-bowl and the best china. But my point is that nobody's interests would be served by such an intervention, neither Mrs Fraser's nor mine. Gardening is for gardeners, Charles; our part is to enjoy the fruits of their labours.'

He motioned me to one of the chairs and seated himself in the other, holding his crooked hands to the blaze. 'And what brings you,' he asked abruptly, with a hint of asperity, 'knocking on my door?'

'It struck me that we had become strangers to one another. And because I regard you as pre-eminent among those who influenced my early intellectual development—'

'Thank you, but perhaps a little plain speaking would be in order. As you can imagine, your visit comes as something of a surprise.'

'Not too much of a surprise, I hope. My telegram—'

'Come now, Charles, your visit can hardly be accounted less surprising for having been announced five hours in advance. You don't write to me – not a word in the past three years and no more than half a dozen carelessly scrawled pages in the past fifteen – and then you turn up on my doorstep with the air of a man who wants something. I'll tell you now, my will has already been drawn up.'

The barb, delivered with only the faintest suggestion of humour, struck sufficiently close to the mark to disturb my composure. I sank back into my chair and cleared my throat.

'It's true,' I began carefully, 'that I'm here to request a favour, but I'm also offering something in return.'

'Forgive me, Charles, but when you've spent as many years in the world of business as I have, you develop a peculiarly sensitive nose for what's in the wind. I can tell without hearing another word that, whatever you're offering, your proposal is likely to serve your own interests far better than it will serve mine. That said, I'm willing to listen. Tell me what you have in mind.'

This was not at all the conversation I had imagined as I travelled up. I had convinced myself that my uncle, delighted to see me after so many years, would be doubly delighted when he heard my proposal. The idea that the man who had set me on the path of scientific enquiry should subsequently provide me with the funds for an important collecting trip had seemed so apposite that I had scarcely troubled to examine it. Now I was mumbling, stammering, losing my thread, like a schoolboy called upon to explain himself to an unsympathetic master.

'And of course,' I heard myself saying, 'the specimens – such as you needed for your own collection . . . I mean, it's understood that I should be collecting on your behalf as well as my own, and any significant discovery—'

'Have you no funds of your own? Your father left you tolerably well provided for.'

'He left me the estate.'

'And, if I remember correctly, a substantial proportion of his savings.'

I shifted uncomfortably beneath his gaze. 'The fact is,' I said, 'that I've handled my financial affairs rather badly. The sum in question has been seriously depleted.'

'Depleted?'

I felt my face grow hot. 'There's nothing left,' I said. 'Nothing at all. And the income from my tenants barely pays my bills.'

'Then your proposed journey would seem singularly ill-timed.' He leaned suddenly towards me, his eyes searching mine. 'You're not in any kind of trouble, are you, Charles?'

The particular predicament in which I found myself would not, perhaps, have diminished my standing in my uncle's eyes and it might have been preferable in some respects to have made a clean breast of it, but I could see that anything less than a firm denial risked leading our discussion off at a tangent to my central concern. 'No,' I said. 'I've decided that this is the moment to go. That's all there is to it.'

A soft tapping at the door heralded the arrival of the tea, borne on a silver tray by a diminutive maidservant. The girl placed her burden on the table and stood at my uncle's elbow, her eyes downcast. He looked up sharply and waved her away. 'That will be all, thank you, Alice. We'll attend to it.'

She gave a little bob and withdrew, her footfall almost silent on the thick carpet. As the door clicked shut behind her, my uncle turned back to me and resumed his questioning. 'Has it occurred to you that you might sell part of the estate?'

'I'd rather not.'

'Of course you'd rather not. But when the alternative is to come cap in hand to relatives who have managed their affairs more wisely than you appear to have done, selling would seem perhaps the sounder option and certainly the more gentlemanly one. I'm sorry, Charles, but I'm at a loss to understand your thinking on this matter. And besides . . .' He lifted the lid of the teapot and stirred the brew. 'Will you take milk with your tea?'

I nodded. 'You were about to say something.'

He was silent, apparently preoccupied with the matter in hand. I sat back and waited.

'There was a time,' he said at last, handing me my cup, 'when I dreamed of being able to help you in some way – of being in a position to offer you the support a father might offer his son. But in those days you were not fatherless, and by the time you were, you had turned your back on me.'

His phrasing was a little melodramatic for my taste, but it was impossible to dispute the essential fact. I sat staring into my teacup, listening to the rain driving against the window-panes. After a moment, my uncle rose to his feet and crossed to the bureau. He opened the top drawer and drew out a bulging file.

'Do you know what these are?' he asked, bending back the cover to reveal a thick sheaf of papers. He returned to his seat and flicked through them, eventually extracting two sheets, held together at the corner by a rusted dressmaker's pin. He leaned forward with an odd, tightlipped smile and handed them to me.

There is something strangely disconcerting about being confronted with one's own letters, particularly when those letters belong to the period of childhood or youth. The careful schoolroom script seemed simultaneously alien and familiar, and though I knew at once that I was holding a fragment of my own past, I was slow to acknowledge the fact.

'Do you remember writing that?' He was staring intently at my face. 'Look at the second page.'

I folded back the top sheet and scanned it quickly.

. . . deserving of my gratitude, since you have been a second father to me, a second father and more. More, because you have also been friend and tutor, and I dare say that what you have taught me on our walks together will prove more important to my future life than anything I have learned in school. If I ever make a name for myself as a natural scientist – and I am more than ever convinced that is my true vocation – my success will be due in large measure to you.

There was another paragraph in similar vein. The whole passage, I noticed, had been marked with two parallel pencil-lines in the right-hand margin of the page. 'Yes,' I said uneasily. 'Yes, I remember.'

He tapped the file. 'They're all here,' he said. 'All of your letters to me, from the first to the last. An object lesson in the callous ways of the world.'

'That seems a little harsh,' I said, struggling to suppress my anger.

He shrugged. 'Life is harsh,' he answered, and with the words he sagged suddenly in his chair, his sallow face creased with grief. Tears gathered and fell, the slow, unimpassioned tears of the old.

'I meant what I wrote,' I said. And then, with regret, sympathy and cunning so finely blended as to confuse even myself: 'I'm sorry to have disappointed you, Uncle, but the arrangement

I'm proposing may go some way towards making amends. I should be glad to think that in adding to your collection I was also doing something to restore the connection between us.'

He drew a large linen handkerchief from his pocket and dabbed at his eyes. 'The collection,' he said quietly, 'is neither here nor there. Think about it, Charles. I'm seventy-one years old. There's not a single organ in my body that works as it should, and the various passions that serve to keep a man alive are all gone. Sometimes at night, when the house is quiet, I drift upstairs like the ghost of my younger self and take a few choice specimens from my cabinets. I stare at them, I finger them, I put them back again. Whatever glamour they once seemed to possess is lost. Dead matter, Charles – rows of stiffened skins in an old man's attic. Why should I add to their number?'

'Then you won't help me?'

In the stillness I could hear the cluck and gurgle of rainwater from the gutters below. My uncle placed his gnarled hands on his knees and gazed down at them for a long time as though lost in contemplation of his own decrepitude.

'I'm prepared to pay your passage to Australia,' he said at last.

It was not a destination I had considered. Although I had not thought very carefully about the matter, it was South America I had in mind. I was about to say as much when it struck me that I would do better to hold my tongue.

'I know a fellow,' he continued, 'who can help you. Edward Vane – owns a substantial property just outside Sydney. A very substantial property indeed. Large house, extensive grounds, acres of grazing. He's made more in twenty years – mainly from coal and shale-oil – than I've made in a lifetime. But the point is' – he lowered his voice, though it was inconceivable that any of the servants could have overheard him – 'that he owes his fortune to me.'

He leaned back in his chair and ran his hand wearily across his eyes. 'I'll leave if you're tired,' I said. 'I can return tomorrow.'

He gave no indication of having heard me. 'We were close in those days,' he said, 'Vane and I. I mean, during his early months in London. He had come to the city with the express intention of making his fortune here, and I've no doubt his life would have unfolded exactly as he'd planned it if he hadn't been knocked off course by a woman. The usual story – passion, pregnancy, a hasty marriage on an inadequate income. She was a Cornish girl, a sweet enough thing but very dreamy and delicate, and not the slightest use to him. And, of course, she brought no money with her, none at all.'

'But you provided for them?'

'Eventually, yes. I don't mind telling you, Charles, I felt betrayed. I'd given Vane my friendship and assistance, introducing him into circles that would otherwise have remained closed to him, and it seemed to me he'd proved himself unworthy of my attentions. For a while I refused to have anything to do with him. But as time went on, I began to realise that I might have been unduly hard on him. And one morning I met him in the street, very pale and down-cast, with his wife on his arm, and for the first and perhaps the only time in my life I was moved to an act of charity.

There and then I told him that I would put a sum of money at his disposal so that he might make a fresh start elsewhere. That sum of money was the cornerstone of his fortune, and though he repaid it long ago, I know for a fact that he still considers himself in debt to me. When do you propose to leave?'

The question, characteristically incisive and practical, caught me completely off my guard. 'As soon as I've made the necessary arrangements,' I answered evasively.

'Two months? Three?'

I was suddenly and acutely aware of my own unpreparedness for the venture. Twenty-four hours earlier I had no notion of going anywhere; now I was poised to embark on a voyage to the far side of the world. I felt my innards tighten, tasted the tea's bitterness at the back of my tongue.

'Longer,' I said. 'I shall need longer.'

'Well, let me know when matters become clearer and I'll write to Vane, informing him of your plans. I've no doubt that you'll benefit both from his hospitality and his connections.' He leaned back in his chair as though to suggest that our business was at an end.

'Thank you, Uncle.' I glanced through the window at the darkening sky. 'It's time I left,' I said, rising to my feet. He rose with me, moving beside me through the gloom, but stopped at the door as though loath to let me go.

'I'm sorry we've become such strangers to one another,' he said.

'That can be remedied in time.'

'Perhaps, though time isn't a commodity I'd care to speculate on these days. You're no longer so very young yourself, Charles, if I may say so. I take it you're still a bachelor.'

'Yes. I've thought now and then that a wife and family would give direction to my life, but I've never met a woman I felt I might be able to love. Over the years, I've come to regard myself as temperamentally unsuited to marriage.'

'Love,' he said with a dismissive little gesture, 'is neither here nor there. A man is not obliged to love his wife. He provides for her, and she for him. And those of us who resist marriage – because they can't love, because they value their liberty, because they consider themselves unsuited – would do well to think carefully about the alternative while they're still in a position to make choices. Companionless old age, Charles – I don't recommend it. Naturally, I try to convince myself that I chose wisely, but if I could turn back the clock, knowing what I know now, I believe I should choose differently.'

'It may be that in matters of that kind the choice isn't ours to make.'

He seemed to consider this for a moment, his head drooping on his thin neck. I felt the grief and loneliness coming off him like the stink from a street-beggar, and I shifted uncomfortably to and fro until he raised his eyes again.

'You may stay here if you wish,' he said. 'The guestroom's not much used nowadays but I could have it made ready in no time.'

'Thank you, Uncle, but I've left my belongings at the hotel. I shall call again on Friday, if I may, before I leave town.'

It struck me, as we walked down to the hallway, that my refusal might have offended him; but as we reached the door his face broke into a weary smile, and he ushered me out with a gesture as delicately solicitous as if the linnet's egg still nestled there in the hollow of his upturned palm.

II

4

A little over an hour's ride from the harbour and set in spacious, well-managed grounds, Tresillian Villa amply confirmed my uncle's claim that Edward Vane was a man of substance. Meeting me on the quayside, he had seemed awkward and unimpressive, and our conversation as we journeyed out of Sydney had been strained, but as the carriage entered the drive and approached the house he seemed to puff up like a courting pigeon, suddenly amiable and expansive, his broad features animated by a boyish eagerness. He barely gave the horses time to come to a standstill before flinging back the door and leaping out, appreciably nimbler on his feet than, considering his bulk, one might have expected.

Standing on the quayside earlier, in the shadow of the rust-coloured warehouses, I had hardly been aware of the heat and we had travelled, rather to my disappointment, with the blinds half down; now, stepping from the carriage on to the shimmering drive, I felt the full force of the December sun. I stood blinking, a little unsteady, the perspiration breaking out on my face and body.

Vane turned to give instructions to a pair of servants and then took me by the elbow and walked me down the sloping lawn. 'This is the finest view of the villa,' he said, turning me so that we looked back up the slope towards the front entrance, 'and for my money the finest view in the colony.' The remark was accompanied by a sidelong smile in my direction, but I sensed that it would be unwise to treat it simply as a joke.

Certainly the villa was imposing, though not entirely to my taste. It was an odd hybrid, the house itself brickbuilt along essentially modern lines, but fronted by an incongruous stucco portico in the Palladian style. The effect of structural incoherence was heightened by the stable-block, which had been tacked on to the side of the house in such a way as to unbalance the whole of the front elevation. Even so, the building had its attractions: I was particularly taken by the generous proportions of the windows and by the railed verandah, raised a couple of feet above the level of the terrace and festooned with swags of mauve wisteria flowers.

I sensed that my host was waiting for my response.

'What a house,' I said, 'and what a prospect. You're a fortunate man, Vane.'

He turned to face me, beaming broadly. 'Well, Redbourne,' he said, 'we're a long way from England but I think we can offer you something of what you're accustomed to.'

There was, in fact, all the difference in the world between this luminous panorama – the wide lawns washed in sunlight, the little grove of citrus trees, the elegant eucalypts shimmering beyond – and my own shadowy wilderness of an estate, but I saw no reason to say so.

'I'm sure I shall be very comfortable here. If your men have finished attending to my luggage, I wonder if you'd be good enough to show me to my room? I'm in need of a wash and a change of clothing.'

'I've asked Mrs Denman to prepare a bath. If you'll follow me . . .' He led the way towards the house and was about to usher me up the front steps when the door was flung back and a girl stepped out and stood in front of us, staring down, her eyes narrowed against the sunlight.

If it hadn't been for the assurance of her stance and her unabashed gaze, I might have taken her for one of the servants. Her face was tanned, and her thick brown hair had been pinned back with a carelessness that, if not exactly slatternly, hardly suggested good breeding. Her clothing, though clean and reasonably neat, had evidently been chosen for comfort rather than elegance, and as she came down the steps towards us, I was struck by the natural fluency of her movements. Although she seemed, to judge from her face and figure, to stand on the threshold of womanhood, she moved with the ease of a child, swaying a little from the waist, her feet light and quick on the hot steps.

'My daughter, Eleanor,' said Vane.

Eleanor came to a halt on the bottom step and placed her hand fleetingly in mine. 'I'm pleased to meet you, Mr Redbourne,' she said. 'I hope you've had a good journey.' And then, barely waiting for my answer and with the air of having discharged a slightly tiresome duty, she made off across the lawn towards the citrus grove.

'You'll find Eleanor somewhat lacking in the social graces,' said Vane apologetically as he ushered me into the house, 'but I hope you'll make allowances.' He guided me up the staircase and along a dim corridor, stopping outside the last of four identical doors and pushing it open. 'This is your room,' he said. 'Mrs Denham will let you know when your bath is ready. I need hardly say that I should like you to be as easy here as if you were in your own home. If there's anything you need, you've only to ask. I shall look forward to continuing our conversation in due course.'

I could see at once that my new quarters were remarkably spacious, and not merely by comparison with the cramped and dingy cabin I had grown accustomed to over the preceding weeks. The room was, in fact, considerably larger than my bedroom at home, and far more pleasingly appointed. The bed was high and wide, the coverlet printed with a bold, modern design. Between the two large windows stood a writingdesk, equipped with ink, blotter and an array of pens; against the opposite wall, a heavy washstand, topped with a thick slab of pale, veined marble. The lower sashes of the windows had been raised, and the scent of flowers, sweet and faintly peppery, wafted in on the warm air, mingling with the smell of the polished furniture and floorboards. I sat on the edge of the bed, breathing deeply and waiting, without impatience, for Mrs Denham to call me.

I took my time over my bath, and then shaved with particular care, leaning close to the wall-mirror and persisting with the task until I was satisfied that my skin was as smooth as the razor could make it. And as I stepped away, wiping the blade on my towel, I was struck by something unexpected in my own reflected image, something that drew me back to examine it more carefully.

It had been a long time since I had looked at my face with any pleasure. As a schoolboy I had considered myself tolerably handsome, but my appearance had not, by and large, improved with age. True, I had been blessed with the Redbourne brow – an ample forehead which, still clear and unfurrowed in middle life, had continued to give my face some semblance of nobility; but my jawline, never a strong feature, had grown increasingly fleshy and indeterminate with the passing years, while my eyes had lost the gleam of youth without acquiring any of the compensatory qualities usually associated with maturity. Now, however, no doubt as a result of the abstemious regimen I had adopted during the voyage – a sparer diet, enforced at first by seasickness and continued by choice, the daily bottle or two of claret reduced to a single glass – my features had become leaner and more resolute, my gaze clear and steady. My hair, untrimmed since my departure, had thickened into a leonine mane, the streaks of grey at the temples barely discernible among the mass of darker curls; and looking into the mirror in the sharp white light of that uncluttered bathroom I felt a surge of elation as though I were re-encountering, after long separation, a well-loved but half-forgotten companion.

There was more to it than this, of course. Although I had come to realise, during the months of planning and preparation following my visit to my uncle, that I was in no further danger from Blaney and his mob, there were signs that my standing in the village had been seriously undermined. Sitting in my pew on a Sunday morning or strolling through the lanes around the Hall, I had noticed how reluctantly the villagers' eyes met mine, how hollowly their greetings rang in my ears. Imagination? In part, perhaps; but little by little I had become obsessed by the notion that I should need to refashion myself, heart and soul, if I were ever to regain any degree of authority in the one corner of the world I could call my own. Australia was to be the crucible in which I should be made new. My arrival there was an event of extraordinary personal significance and my elation a natural response to the beguiling suggestion that, after years of inertia, I was once more in command of my own destiny.

I dressed with what I imagined was appropriate informality but, emerging on to the veranda, I discovered that Vane had divested himself of his jacket and necktie and was sitting at ease with his waistcoat unbuttoned.

He raised his eyes from his newspaper as I approached and looked me up and down as though appraising the cut of my suit.

'I'm not a man who stands on ceremony,' he said simply, giving me leave, as I took it, to remove my own jacket. I did so, and sat down beside him.

He was, I guessed, a little above my own age, though his face was scarcely lined and his lightly oiled hair almost untouched with grey. He might have been described as distinguished but there was a certain brutality in the set of his mouth and chin, noticeably at odds with the lively intelligence of his eyes. Almost a gentleman, as my father used to say of certain acquaintances: the double-edged phrase came back to me as my host wiped his shirt-sleeve across his brow and drew a monogrammed cigarette case from his waistcoat pocket.

'Will you have one?' he asked, flipping open the case and holding it out to me.

I shook my head. 'I haven't touched tobacco since leaving England,' I said, 'and I feel much the better for it.'

'My daughter would approve.' He glanced down the garden to where the girl reclined in the shade of a lemon tree, propped on one elbow, her book open on the grass before her. 'A filthy habit, she says, and one I should have had the strength of will to abandon years ago.' He lit up and drew deeply on his cigarette before resuming.

'Eleanor is an outspoken young lady, Redbourne, and I must warn you now not to expect genteel conversation from her. She's quick and clever – some might say too clever for her own good – but she presumes on the privileges of an indulged child-hood. In the aftermath of her mother's death she seemed to need those privileges, but I've had cause in recent years to regret what

I now see to have been a damaging lack of firmness in her upbringing. To put it bluntly, she appears to have no idea how to conduct herself in polite society, and no intention of learning.'

'There's plenty of time, Vane. She's still very young.'

'She's twenty years old.'

'Twenty? I must say, that surprises me. I'd have taken her to be three or four years younger.'

'You're not the first to be misled. And if she'd learn to bear herself more like a lady—'

'No, it's not that. Or not that alone. There's something about her features – some brightness or clarity of a kind that rarely persists far beyond childhood.'

'She has her mother's looks. I mean she's the very image. Sometimes, when I glance up suddenly from my work and she's there, reading perhaps, or just gazing into the air the way she does, it's my wife I see. That's really how it feels – as though I'd slipped back into the past and found her there waiting for me, just as she used to be.' He stubbed his cigarette savagely against the leg of his chair and flicked it away over the veranda rail. 'Believe me, Redbourne, it's no easy matter sharing the house with a girl who might be the walking spirit of her dead mother.'

'Even so,' I said, sensing his agitation and anxious to steer our conversation into calmer waters, 'you must be thankful that she has inherited those looks. Beauty isn't everything, but it's not a negligible gift.'

He shot me a swift glance. 'Joshua gave me to understand,' he said sharply, 'that you're not a ladies' man.'

It had not occurred to me either that my well-intentioned remark could have been construed as indicative of an unseemly interest in the girl, or that my uncle might have discussed my character in his correspondence with Vane. Caught off balance, I mumbled and stammered until my host, doubtless regretting both his rudeness and his indiscretion, came to my rescue. 'He also told me,' he said, tacking neatly about, 'that I should benefit greatly from your company and conversation, and I can see already that we shall hit it off together. Let me tell you, Redbourne, I consider myself extremely fortunate to have you here as my guest.' And at that moment, as if on cue, one of the maidservants stepped up behind us and announced that luncheon was served.

5

Luncheon was a protracted affair. Eleanor stayed only long enough to satisfy her hunger before returning to her reading in the shade of the citrus trees, but Vane clearly wanted to make an occasion of the meal, toasting my arrival in good wine and maintaining a constant and eventually exhausting flow of conversation. I sensed something of the emigrant's homesickness in his insistent questions about the country he had last seen more than twenty years earlier, and though I was naturally disposed to respond fully to his enquiries, I was relieved when he pushed away his coffee-cup and rose to his feet.

'I have business to attend to,' he said. 'It might wait until tomorrow but procrastination, as your uncle was fond of telling me, is the thief of time. It's a maxim I've lived by for many years, and I've found no reason' – he spread his hands in a gesture I understood to embrace the villa, the gardens and a good deal more besides – 'to doubt its essential wisdom.'

'Of course. Please don't disturb your routines on my account. I'm used to fending for myself, and I have business of my own. Assuming that my rifle is in reasonable order, I may as well begin this afternoon.'

'I wish you luck, but I'm afraid you'll find nothing remarkable hereabouts. Tomorrow I shall introduce you to Bullen. He'll take you further afield and show you what's what.' He chuckled softly, as if at some private joke. 'Quite a character, our Mr Bullen.'

'A local naturalist?'

'I don't know whether you'd call him a naturalist. He's not a particularly well educated man – not, by any stretch of the imagination, a scientist – but he has an eye for a rarity, and I know for a fact that several of the big collectors in Sydney regularly buy from him. He has made something of a name for himself in the region, though the Grail, as he calls it, has so far eluded him.'

'The Grail?'

'He wants to discover a new species of bird or mammal – thinks they'll name it after him. I can't understand it myself, but for him it's an obsession.'

I might have tried to explain, on Bullen's behalf, the nature and power of an obsession I understood only too well, but

I sensed that my efforts would be wasted on Vane. 'I'm sure,' I said, 'that we shall find we have a good deal in common, Mr Bullen and I. I look forward to meeting him.'

How easy it is, I thought, reflecting on Vane's words as I strolled later among the eucalypts, to dismiss as unremarkable the marvels that lie most immediately about us. To me, everything was new, and everything a source of wonder, from the vivid green mantis rocking slowly back and forth on its twig to the cockatoos that rose at my approach, lifting into the bright air like a host of raucous angels, their wings suffused with sunlight. There was brilliance there but also, I realised as I began to examine my surroundings more carefully, a remarkable subtlety: I was particularly struck by the delicate coloration of the woodland foliage – the greens more muted than ours but no less various, interfused with soft shades of grey and touched with pale metallic lustres. I was so entranced by my discoveries that for some considerable time I was content simply to observe, and it was with something like regret that, coming upon a small group of parrots feeding in the undergrowth, I eventually unslung my rifle.

My shot was not, I confess, a particularly good one, but one of the birds sat tight as the others scattered, and I knew at once that it had been hit. As I approached, it tried to launch itself into the air but fell flapping to the ground, beating the dust until it died. I lifted it up and wiped the blood from its beak with a leaf.

I had always felt a degree of confusion at such moments, but on this occasion the combination of sorrow and excitement was peculiarly unsettling. I remember pacing up and down, gazing through a film of tears at the curve of the slack neck, the brilliance of the ruffled plumage. Breast upward, the bird glowed rich crimson, its throat patched with blue of an almost equal intensity; as I turned it on to its front, letting its head hang forward over the edge of my palm, I saw how the crimson seemed to bleed between the darker wing-feathers, accentuating their contours with a boldness that reminded me of an Egyptian wall-painting I had once coveted.

'We call them lories,' said Vane when I showed him the bird on my return. He had evidently completed his business and was sitting on the veranda steps cleaning his nails with a small pocket-knife. 'Crimson lories. Ten a penny round these parts – though they're handsome enough creatures, I grant you.'

I replaced the body carefully in my satchel. 'I shall have to presume further on your hospitality,' I said. 'Do you have an outhouse where I might prepare my specimens?'

'There's the barn. Ideal for your purposes, though I shall have to conduct some rather delicate negotiations on your behalf.' He folded his knife, slipped it into his waistcoat pocket and hauled himself to his feet. 'Leave the matter in my hands.'

'When you say negotiations . . .?'

'With Eleanor. The barn is her studio.'

'She's an artist?'

'She likes to think so and, to tell the truth, she has a certain talent – though, as with so many things, she makes too much of it. Young women need something to keep their hands and minds busy – patchwork, sketching, embroidery, it doesn't matter what – and I've always encouraged her. But in recent years her art, as she insists on calling it, has become an unhealthy preoccupation. When the mood takes her she'll spend the entire day in the barn, refusing to let anyone in, hardly bothering to come out. She misses meals, or she comes to the table but won't speak, bolts her food and scampers away again, like a half-tamed animal.'

'It doesn't sound as though she'll welcome my company.'

'I can guarantee that she'll accept it. And it's just possible' – he gave a wry smile – 'that your presence will exert a civilising influence. Heaven knows, she's in need of it.'

'You flatter me,' I said lightly, 'but civilising influences certainly exist. Indeed, I shouldn't be at all surprised if she were to be taken off your hands within a year or two and exposed to the civilising influence of matrimony.'

I had intended the remark to be simultaneously humorous and reassuring, but Vane's expression darkened suddenly and I realised at once that I had struck entirely the wrong note. 'What I suggest,' he said abruptly, 'is that you leave me to settle matters with Eleanor. You might like to continue your exploration of the estate and return in twenty minutes or so.' He gestured vaguely up the drive, turned on his heel and marched into the house.

Twenty minutes would have seemed time enough, but as I turned the corner of the house and stepped up to the veranda, I heard Eleanor's voice ring out, shrill and raw, through the open windows of the day-room. 'If you won't listen to what

I say, then why trouble to ask me? I'm telling you, I shan't be able to work with him sitting there.'

And then Vane's voice, half angry, half cajoling: 'He has work of his own, Eleanor. He'll not trouble you. And besides—'

'It's my studio. I'll not have it turned into a poulterer's shop.'

'Don't be absurd. And let me remind you that the barn was handed over to you with certain conditions attached. I've told you before, either you respect those conditions or—'

'Just try it,' she cut in viciously, lowering her voice so that I had to strain to catch the words. 'Just you try keeping me out.'

One hears of families in which the children are perpetually at loggerheads with their parents, but my own upbringing had impressed upon me the importance of filial obedience. 'You may disagree with me,' my father had told me on one occasion, 'but while you're under my roof you do as I say.' As I grew to manhood, I found myself dissenting more and more frequently from his opinions, but it would never have occurred to me to express my opposition in any but the mildest terms. Eleanor's words shocked me into embarrassed retreat, but as I walked back up the drive I found myself reexamining them with what I can only describe as a kind of excitement. I imagined the unseen tableau with vivid precision – the girl backed, quite literally, into a corner, but staring directly into her father's face as she spat defiance at him – and I was almost sorry when, a good ten minutes later, Vane strode out to where I was loitering in the shade at the edge of the garden and told me that Eleanor would be delighted to share her studio with me for the duration of my stay.

Predictably enough, our conversation at dinner that evening was not leavened by any expression of delight on the girl's part. Vane talked loudly and a little wildly, as though he were desperate to distract my attention from Eleanor's sullen silence, while I did my best to follow, through a haze of fatigue, the twists and turns of his rambling discourse. Only at the end of the meal, as the maidservant cleared away the dessert plates, did he change his tactics, leaning over to address his daughter directly. 'I'm sure Mr Redbourne will be interested to see your work, Eleanor. Tell him what your instructor said about it.'

'My instructor was a fool,' said Eleanor curtly.

Vane turned apologetically to me. 'There was a falling out,' he explained. 'But Mr Rourke is an artist of some local reputation and he told Eleanor in my presence' – he glanced sideways as though for corroboration – 'that she had a rare talent as a watercolourist.'

'What he admired in my work,' said Eleanor, scratching irritably with her fingernail at a small stain on the tablecloth, 'were the very qualities I despised in his. My father doesn't agree with me, Mr Redbourne, but I'm certain that I paint a good deal better without Mr Rourke's guidance than I ever did with it.'

'You owe him a considerable debt,' said Vane sharply, 'and it's neither kind nor honest to pretend otherwise.'

Both glanced my way at precisely the same moment, and I saw with sudden clarity that their argument was an old one, now being rehearsed for my benefit. I wanted no part in it. I lowered my gaze and sat staring stupidly at my empty wine-glass until Vane, rising abruptly from his chair, drew the uncomfortable proceedings to a close.

6

The barn had been built in the English style, plain and sturdy, with thick walls of rough-hewn stone and a tiled roof. It would scarcely have looked out of place in a Cotswold village, I thought, setting down my satchel and instruments beside the pathway and shading my eyes against the early morning sunlight. The front wall was pierced by four small unglazed windows, two on either side of the double doors; the aperture in the gable – originally, I supposed, the loft doorway – had been incongruously fitted with a large, rectangular sash, while two square skylights, evidently of recent construction, had been inserted in the roof.

Eleanor was there before me. Seated at a trestle table just inside the building, she was clearly asserting ownership both of the space she occupied and the light that fell on her through the open doorway. She raised her head as I entered, lifting her paintbrush and fixing me momentarily with a vague, unseeing gaze; then, without a word, she returned to her work.

As promised by Vane, I had been supplied with a trestle of my own but, whether accidentally or through Eleanor's machinations, it had been placed against the wall beneath one of the small windows. The light that fell on its surface was adequate for my purposes, but I could see at once that its positioning was significant: I should be working under Eleanor's eye, but without the opportunity of observing her activities. It crossed my mind that I might simply move the trestle to a more favourable position but, on reflection, I decided against it. There would be time later, I told myself, for such adjustments.

I unbuckled my satchel, took out the lory and laid it belly upward on the rough surface. 'Is there a chair?' I asked.

For some time she said nothing, her gaze flickering between the paper pinned to her drawing-board and the bright orange nasturtium flower on the table in front of her. She continued to paint, but I sensed something faintly suspect in her concentration, a subtle hint of the theatrical. 'Under the hayloft,' she said at last, jerking her head sideways without looking up at me. 'In the corner.'

The battered chair I discovered there among the debris was hardly ideal – a little low for the table and with curving arm-rests that impeded my movements – but by placing a thick plank beneath its back legs, I was able to adapt it to my needs.

I untied my canvas roll and laid it flat on the table, with the handles of the instruments towards me; then I drew out a scalpel and set to work, parting the crimson breast-feathers with my fingers before running the narrow blade down the body from throat to vent.

There is nothing particularly difficult about skinning a bird, but the job requires immense patience. The thickness of the plumage is deceptive: the skin itself is thin and delicate, and separating it from the flesh is a necessarily slow process. I've learned by experience not to apply undue pressure but simply to use the end of the blade to tease the skin free of the tissue that binds it to the body. It's not an entirely agreeable task, but I've always found it an absorbing one, and I'm apt, when engaged in it, to lose all sense of my surroundings.

I don't know how long Eleanor had been standing there when I became aware of her, close behind me, paintbrush in hand, looking over my shoulder at my handiwork. I started violently, sending the scalpel clattering across the table-top, and twisted round in my seat. 'Don't do that,' I snapped.

She backed away, but without taking her eyes off mine. 'I've a right to do as I please in my own studio,' she said. 'Haven't I?'

I was at a disadvantage, embarrassed by my own outburst. 'You frightened me,' I said lamely. 'I mean, I'd forgotten where I was.'

'It happens to me too. I hate it when anyone comes in while I'm drawing or painting.'

'How am I to take that, Eleanor?'

She shrugged. 'Take it as you please. You told me how you felt. I'm telling you how I feel.'

'Would you rather I found somewhere else to work?'

'My father says you're to work here. I've no choice in the matter.'

'I'm sorry. I'd never intended—'

'It's not your fault. But it isn't easy for me, having you here. I don't like being disturbed in my own work, and I don't like the look of yours.' She glanced down at the exposed flesh of the bird's breast. 'What's it all for, anyway, this killing and skinning?'

'All science,' I said, easing my chair round so that I faced her directly, 'is grounded in facts. A collector's cabinet is a repository of facts from which important scientific truths may be deduced, and new theories constructed. We need these collections, Eleanor, if we're to understand the world we live in – it's as simple as that.'

'You're talking to me as though I were a schoolgirl. I know what science is, and I know what collectors think they're doing. But what kind of a fact is it, your dead lory? You'll take the skin back to England with you and you'll lay it in your cabinet with a label round its neck. Now and again you might bring it out, perhaps for your own private satisfaction or to take a few notes on it, or perhaps to show it to another collector. This is a crimson lory, you'll say. But it won't be true. You know that as well as I do, Mr Redbourne. Whatever it is you imagine you're laying hold of – for yourself, for your precious science – it's gone the moment you pull the trigger.'

I knew what she was driving at, and might have acknowledged as much, but she was working herself into a state of high excitement, the words tumbling out in a breathless torrent, and there seemed no opportunity to respond.

'What you're left with is a handful of skin and feathers – the sort of thing a milliner might use to dress a hat. It's dead stuff, dry as dust, and nothing's going to bring back the bird you had in your sights when you took aim. You'd do better,' she added, turning nimbly and darting back to her table, 'to try to catch something of its life. This' – I saw her dip her brush twice and lunge at the paper on her drawing-board – 'is a lory. And' – another quick flourish – 'so is this.' She tilted the board to show me two running streaks of red slashed diagonally across the paper.

'You've spoiled your painting.'

She let the board fall to the table and put down her brush. 'I don't care,' she said, but her jaw was set hard and tight as though she were biting back some unallowable grief. 'Anyway, it was already spoiled.'

'Let me see.' I rose from my chair and stepped over to examine the painting more closely. I saw her move protectively towards it, one hand outstretched; then, with a little shrug, she stepped back and let me by.

It was not, I saw at once, the kind of study that might have graced the pages of a botanical handbook. Bounded by the two bright slashes of red pigment, it glowed with a similar brilliance, rich and vibrant, but it notably lacked the precision we conventionally associate with scientific illustration. Yet the longer I gazed at the work, the more clearly I recognised in it something of the vital essence of the flower – the extravagance of the flared petals, bright as flame but stained and streaked with darkness, the honeyed light far down in the throat, the cool translucence of the stem.

'It's lovely,' I said encouragingly. 'Truly lovely.'

'Oh, lovely,' she said scornfully, reaching over and tugging the paper roughly from the board. 'I've had enough of lovely.' And then, with a quick, angry movement, she ripped the sheet across and flung the two halves to the earthen floor.

If it had been an act of pure spitefulness, I should no doubt have been well advised to ignore it and return to my work. But something in the girl's face – distress, I thought, and a kind of bewilderment, as though she had been caught unawares by her own action – held me there. I stooped and picked up the pieces.

'There was no call for that,' I said gently. 'If you didn't want the painting, you might have offered it to me. I should have been glad of it.'

'You said it was spoiled.'

'I didn't mean—'

'Then it's yours. Have it.' It was gracelessly done and I, for my part, had no time to thank her before she turned away and stalked out into the sunlight.

I was sitting in my room early that evening, aligning the two halves of the painting on my writing-desk, when I heard Vane call my name softly outside the door. With an obscure feeling of guilt, I gathered up the pieces and slipped them into the left-hand drawer.

'Are you there, Redbourne?'

I opened the door just as he was readying himself to rap on the panel. 'Bullen has arrived,' he said. 'He'll be at dinner tonight, but I thought it advisable to have the two of you meet in advance. That way you'll be able to address matters of business before our other guests arrive.'

'Business?'

'Bullen is more than willing to act as your guide, but he has made it clear to me that he'll be obliged to treat any excursion as a professional engagement.' He glanced uneasily down the corridor. 'The fact is,' he went on, lowering his voice to a murmur, 'that the man has fallen on hard times. A few years ago he owned seventy-five acres of good grazing, but he's been brought to the brink of ruin by unwise speculation. Sugar plantations, the hotel business – knows nothing about either, of course. If it weren't for his collecting he'd have gone under. I tell you, Redbourne, your arrival is a godsend for him.'

Vane's account fell some way short, it seemed to me, of a reassuring character reference. 'I assume,' I said, 'that the arrangement will be equally beneficial to me?'

'No doubt of it,' he said hastily, 'no doubt at all. He's already planning an itinerary for you – local excursions first, and then a trip out to the mountains. Come down and let him tell you about it.' He turned, evidently expecting me to follow at once. I hesitated for a moment, then fell into step behind him.

Bullen was sprawled at ease on the sofa in the dayroom, his hat beside him on the padded arm-rest. He sprang up as I entered and advanced to meet me, a tall man, big-boned without any hint of fleshiness, his features hard and angular above a full brown beard. His handshake was firm and his voice, as he greeted me, deep and resonant, but there was something in his demeanour – the hunched shoulders, the evasive eyes – that disconcertingly offset the initial impression of physical strength. Vane had no sooner introduced us than he withdrew, pleading business of his own.

'And what,' asked Bullen, reseating himself on the sofa, 'made you fix on Australia?'

'I'm not sure that the decision was entirely mine.'

I could see him weighing up my reply. 'I mean,' I explained, 'that matters seemed to fall into place without a great deal of effort on my part.'

'You're a believer in the workings of a divine providence, Mr Redbourne?'

I laughed. 'That's a very serious interpretation of a casual observation.'

'Speaking for myself,' he said, for all the world as though I had pressed him to give me an account of his personal philosophy, 'I believe that our destiny lies in our own hands. And once we recognise that fact, our power is virtually unlimited.'

I thought of the man's failed business ventures and wondered what his philosophy made of those. 'I understand,' I said, shifting ground with more firmness than tact, 'that you've offered to act as my guide to the region. Perhaps we might discuss practicalities.'

Reflecting later on the moment, I realised that I had decisively undermined Bullen's attempts to engage with me on terms of equality – to present himself as civilised conversationalist and fellow gentleman – but if he resented my less than dextrous manipulation of our discussion, he gave no sign of it, turning his attention immediately to matters of business. We easily agreed terms for the local excursions, but it quickly became apparent that his real interest lay in the possibility of accompanying me on longer expeditions, at my expense.

'But no fee,' he added quickly, 'apart from this: of the specimens killed on any of those expeditions, five go to me. My choice.'

It might have seemed a small enough matter, but I could see at once that his proposal had serious implications. By creaming off the best of our bag – and I had a fleeting vision of him out there in some shadowy wilderness, gloating over his cache of rarities – Bullen would seriously diminish the quality of my own collection. I resisted, diplomatically at first but then more vigorously, and we were still debating the point when I heard Vane returning, his footsteps ringing out on the bare boards of the hallway. 'Three specimens,' said Bullen quickly as the door opened and our host entered.

I have often noticed that an angry conversation seems to leave some residual stain on the air and, even if he had not overheard our altercation, Vane must have realised as he stepped into the room that my first meeting with Bullen was not proving a success. I saw his eyes flicker between the two of us as though he were assessing the situation.

'Well,' he said lightly, gesturing towards the deepening shadows outside, 'at least we shall all be a little cooler now. We'll be dining in half an hour.'

'You mentioned other company,' I said.

'The Merivales. The family has farmed the opposite slope of the valley for three generations. Walter Merivale died last year, but his widow and son have kept things running smoothly enough. An admirable family, Redbourne – I can guarantee that you'll enjoy their society.'

I took leave to doubt it, though I naturally kept my opinion to myself. Vane had presumably imagined that Bullen – a man prepared to haggle like a fairground huckster in pursuit of his own dubious ends – was fit company for me, and I saw no reason to suppose that his other guests would impress me any more favourably. I excused myself, perhaps a shade abruptly, and went up to dress for dinner.

7

I could hardly have been further from the mark. From the moment Mrs Merivale stepped over the threshold, sweeping into the house a few paces ahead of her son and daughter, I realised that Vane's neighbours were people of considerable distinction and refinement. Mrs Merivale herself was thin and strikingly tall, but with none of the awkwardness that so often afflicts women of unusual height. On the contrary, she held herself imposingly erect, her shoulders back and her head high so that, as we were introduced, she looked me directly in the eye. She was dressed in widow's black and this, together with her angular features, gave an immediate impression of austerity; but as she offered me her hand, her face relaxed into a smile so warm and engaging that I felt as though I had been embraced.

'And this is William,' she said, standing aside. 'My son.'

Handsome and sturdily built, Merivale was almost as striking as his mother, but his face had about it the flush and fullness that come with high living and, though he couldn't have been above twenty-five years old, the hair had already begun to recede from his wide brow. He bowed formally from the waist as he gripped my hand.

I could see Miss Merivale out of the corner of my eye as I exchanged conventional courtesies with her brother, but I had no strong sense of her presence until she moved in on us, placing her hand on Merivale's sleeve but addressing herself to me. 'William,' she smiled, 'would be the perfect gentleman if he could only be persuaded to treat his sister with the consideration he extends to every other lady of his acquaintance. If I wait for him to introduce us, I may be obliged to stand here for another twenty minutes.'

I have never met anyone who could more aptly be described as exquisite. Her face resembled her mother's but was more delicately proportioned and of a milder cast – the high cheekbones less prominent, the fine jawline more unequivocally feminine. Her neck was long and slender, her fair skin almost translucent in its clarity. Although she had something of her mother's erect bearing, she stood a good six inches shorter, the top of her elegantly coiffed head barely above the level of my shoulder.

Merivale laughed quietly, a little easier, it struck me, for his sister's intervention. 'I am reproached,' he said with playful gravity. And then, with an odd, archaic flourish: 'My sister, Miss Esther Merivale.'

Miss Merivale proved to be as charming as she was beautiful, an accomplished conversationalist with a quick but unmalicious sense of humour and a flattering quality of attentiveness. Her questions about my life in England seemed neither intrusive nor superficial, and I responded with uncharacteristic warmth and openness, while she for her part spoke so engrossingly about her own circumstances that, by the time the dinner-gong sounded, I felt as if I had been granted privileged access to her family circle.

'This way, if you would,' called Vane, shepherding us towards the dining room. Merivale stepped up to Eleanor as though to escort her in. As he did so, Vane half turned and, evidently with the intention of blocking the manoeuvre, interposed himself between his daughter and the young man. I saw the blood rise to Merivale's face; saw Eleanor stiffen against the subtle pressure of her father's hand, placed momentarily against her slender waist as he guided her through the doorway ahead of him.

Vane occupied the seat at the head of the table, setting Mrs Merivale at his right hand and her daughter at his left. I had hoped that I might be seated next to Miss Merivale, but Vane motioned me to sit with the mother, while Bullen was accorded the honour I had coveted. With Eleanor at his other elbow, he sat directly across the table from me, stroking his beard and grinning broadly as if at some stupendous joke.

Eleanor, I thought, was trying to catch Merivale's eye, but as the soup was brought Bullen began to engage her in conversation, while Merivale leaned sideways and addressed himself to me. 'I understand,' he said, 'that you're here on a scientific mission.'

I smiled. 'You make it sound rather grand. I'm collecting specimens, but I'm an amateur in the field.'

'Nothing to be ashamed of in that. From the little I know of the subject, I'd say that a spirit of informed amateurism has always been the driving force behind the discoveries of natural science. The world is changing, Mr Redbourne, changing with dizzying speed, and the days of the amateur may well be numbered; but that doesn't invalidate either your own enterprise or the achievements of your predecessors.'

Merivale had been unduly modest: I realised as we continued to talk that he actually knew a good deal about the subject, and before long we were deeply immersed in a discussion that ranged from the theories of Darwin, through hybridism in plants and animals, to the shooting of hawks and owls. I had long been of the opinion that English gamekeepers were too vigorous and undiscriminating in their persecution of our native birds of prey, and I was delighted to find Merivale expressing comparable views in relation to his own country. 'Even if,' he said, leaning back to let the maidservant remove his plate, 'it were to turn out that these birds really were responsible for all the crimes laid at their door, imagine the loss to us when the whole tribe has finally been shot out of the skies. If I had my way, they'd be protected by law. When I look up and see a pair of wedge-tails soaring in the air above me, my heart soars with them – really, Mr Redbourne, that's the way it feels, as though I were up there alongside them, riding the updraughts. And though I'm not, properly speaking, a religious man, that's the way I'm able to imagine the experiences the mystics speak of – as uplift, the mind or spirit rising like an eagle into a clear sky.'

He paused, visibly excited and perhaps a little embarrassed at having expressed himself so unguardedly; and at that moment Bullen, who had evidently been eavesdropping on our conversation, leaned across the table, slapping the surface with his open palm.

'I don't imagine,' he said, 'that you spend much time giving your fellow farmers the benefit of your views. You'd get short shrift from anyone who's lost stock to the creatures.'

'I was speaking to Mr Redbourne,' answered Merivale, colouring.

I was doubtful whether Bullen had had time to drink more than two or three glasses of wine, but he'd certainly downed more than was good for his manners. As the rest of the party fell silent, he leaned back and addressed himself to the company at large, his face flushed and his voice appreciably louder and more emphatic than the circumstances seemed to require. 'It's the bane of our age,' he said. 'Sentimentalism. Looking for mysteries when the facts are staring us in the face. Turning aside from reality in order to indulge our finer feelings. Do you imagine the eagles share your finer feelings, Merivale? Not a bit of it. While you're busy examining the world through your tinted prism, they'll be dropping out of the sky to take one of your lambs.'

Vane was looking round the table with an expression of mild bewilderment, but Eleanor had clearly grasped the situation and, while Merivale blushed and stammered beside me, she cut in, quick and cold: 'What you call senti- mentalism,' she said, barely troubling to glance at Bullen, 'may be a refinement of the human spirit too subtle for your understanding.'

Vane gave her a withering stare. I would have intervened, but it was Bullen himself who restored a degree of order to the proceedings, breaking the silence with a high, barking laugh, as if to show that Eleanor's barb had failed to penetrate his thick skin. 'Your daughter's as sharp as a tin-tack,' he said, raising his wine-glass with mock ceremony and tilting it in Vane's direction. 'I'll wager she keeps you on your toes.' Eleanor glowered but said nothing, and the moment was past.

I should have liked to return to my discussion with Merivale but he had grown awkward and uncommunicative, as though Bullen's intervention had left him inwardly bruised. Bullen himself seemed oblivious to the young man's discomfiture, and as I listened to him holding forth loudly on a variety of topics about which he seemed to know next to nothing, I was struck by the sheer vulgarity of the fellow. By the time the coffee was brought, I was considering how best to ensure that our unfin- ished negotiations were not resumed.

'That was a grand dinner,' said Bullen, leaning back in his chair and wiping his beard with his napkin. 'I'll say this, Vane, you've done us proud.'

Vane smiled. 'At all events,' he said, 'it will be a dinner for you and Redbourne to remember when you're out in the bush snacking on frogs and lizards.'

'Nothing wrong with lizard,' said Bullen. 'But' – he gave me a conspiratorial wink – 'I doubt it will come to that. Trust me, Mr Redbourne, we'll eat well enough.'

'I'm sure we shall. And now, if you'll all excuse me, I'd like to take a turn in the garden.' I placed my napkin on the table and withdrew, leaning above Vane as I passed him. 'Perhaps you'd be good enough to join me,' I murmured, 'when circumstances permit.'

He looked up at me, his brow furrowed. 'I'll come right away,' he said.

The air of the terrace was barely cooler than that of the dining-room, but it was sweet with the mingled scents of the garden. As Vane caught up with me, I turned to make sure that Bullen had not followed us out, and caught a glimpse of him through the window, his head thrown back and his mouth wide. A yawp of laughter reached me on the fragrant air. Vane gave me a sidelong glance.

'I take it you've something on your mind, Redbourne.'

'Indeed. Listen, I'm grateful to you for introducing me to Mr Bullen, but you both seem to imagine that I've come to a decision on the matter of his employment. In fact, I'm not at all sure that he and I are likely to hit it off.'

Vane gave a throaty chuckle. 'So that's it,' he said. 'Well, I don't imagine that the pair of you are going to forge a lasting friendship, but the plain truth is that Bullen has precisely the experience needed for an expedition of this kind. He's not the most civilised of companions, I grant you; but then, you're not going to the most civilised of places. He's the right man for the job, depend upon it.'

Another outburst of laughter from the house, more prolonged this time. Vane tilted his head towards the sound. 'Look here,' he said, 'Bullen knows his way around the region. He knows many of the old trails – paths followed by the aboriginal tribes – and where he doesn't, he knows people who do. And he's a skilled hunter into the bargain. You might find a more congenial travelling companion, but you'd look a long time before you found a more useful one.'

I was silent for a moment, conscious of the force of his argument, but not entirely convinced. I should like to be able to claim that I had already recognised the brittleness beneath the rugged facade, but I believe that my unease owed more to a potent combination of resentment and snobbery than to any clear understanding of Bullen's character.

'You may be right,' I said at last. 'I'll sleep on it.'

'But not yet, I hope. Esther – Miss Merivale – has agreed to play for us. She's a talented pianist, Redbourne, genuinely talented – quite a favourite in the drawing-rooms of Sydney. I'm not a musical man myself but I know fine playing when I hear it. I can tell you, you're in for a treat.'

He turned and began to walk back towards the house. Bullen had put me severely out of humour and I should have preferred to plead fatigue and send my excuses to the company, but it was clearly impossible to absent myself without causing offence and, after a few seconds' hesitation, I followed.

I entered the drawing-room to find Miss Merivale already seated at the piano, while her brother busied himself with arranging the chairs in a shallow arc around one side of the instrument. As soon as he had finished, Eleanor made for the centre of the arc and sat down, motioning me to join her. 'You'll see her hands from here,' she said. 'Her nimble little fingers.'

Some quality of mischief in her tone and phrasing put me on my guard. 'I understand from your father that she has acquired quite a reputation round about,' I said, settling myself beside her.

'Oh, yes. She's clever girl, no doubt of it. And she knows it.'

I glanced at Miss Merivale to see whether she had overheard but if she had, she gave no sign of it. She was dusting the keyboard with a small lace handkerchief, her head slightly bowed. Someone had placed a lamp on the piano's polished lid, and her features shone in the soft light with something of the delicate translucency of a cameo portrait. She tucked the handkerchief into her sleeve and straightened her back, very calm and self-possessed. The room fell suddenly silent and she began to play.

François Couperin had been a favourite of my mother's, and I recognised the minuet at once. But whereas my mother's attempts had been stiff and hesitant, the work's intricacies always seeming a little beyond her grasp, Miss Merivale's rendition shimmered and flowed, its phrasing immaculate, its tone bright and confident. She played with gentle precision, perfectly evoking an age less frenetic than our own, an age still capable of celebrating, without irony or embarrassment, the ideals of harmony and just proportion. Each note was accorded its proper value; nothing was rushed, nothing snatched or fumbled. Even the trills – and her fingerwork was indeed extraordinary – gave an impresssion of spaciousness, as though she had all the time in the world to execute them. As she played, she half closed her eyes and tilted back her head so that you saw the long line of her throat; her slender body moved gracefully, swaying a little from the waist in time to the music.

She was playing from memory and as she reached the end of the piece, she moved seamlessly on to another. As she began the third, Eleanor leaned inward, her shoulder touching mine, her face so close I smelt the faint perfume of her skin. 'You do realise,' she whispered, 'that she's memorised dozens of these things? She might go on for hours.'

More mischief, I thought, edging away. I tried to return to the music but my concentration had been broken, and I was almost relieved when Miss Merivale, with an elegant flourish, brought the sequence to a close and turned to acknowledge our applause. I leaned behind Eleanor to address Mrs Merivale. 'You must be very proud of your daughter,' I said.

'Indeed, though I can take very little of the credit for her accomplishments. I have no musical talent of my own.'

'Then her achievement is all the more remarkable.'

Eleanor was shifting uncomfortably on her seat between us. Mrs Merivale reached out and placed her hand gently on the girl's shoulder. 'Of course,' she said, 'you know that Eleanor is musically gifted too.'

'Really? What instrument does she play?'

Eleanor whipped round to face me, her eyes flashing. 'Anyone would think you were discussing a clever five-year-old,' she said. 'I sing.'

'And very well too,' said Mrs Merivale soothingly. 'I'm sure Mr Redbourne would like to hear something from you.'

'I doubt it,' said Eleanor sullenly.

'Believe me,' I said, with as much conviction as I could muster, 'nothing would give me greater pleasure.'

'In that case,' said Mrs Merivale, 'Eleanor must sing. I know that Esther' – she beckoned imperiously to her daughter – 'will be more than happy to accompany her.'

Just a little less than happy, I thought, scrutinising Miss Merivale's delicately expressive features as her mother enlisted her services, but she made no objection. She returned to the piano, Eleanor following at her heels.

'I'm going to sing,' announced Eleanor bluntly, as though defying the company to stop her. She lifted the hinged lid of the piano stool and withdrew a slim clothbound folio.

'Schubert,' she said, letting the lid fall with a bang. 'We'll have a Schubert song.' She opened the songbook and bent it back on itself so sharply that I heard the glue crack in the spine; then she placed it firmly on the rack.

Miss Merivale seated herself on the stool and peered at the music. 'Not this one,' she said.

Eleanor stared down at her. 'Why not?' she asked coldly.

'I don't like it.'

'Don't like or can't play?' Scarcely above a whisper, but I don't imagine that any member of the company could have missed either the words themselves or the sting they carried.

Vane leaned forward. 'You'll mind your tongue, Eleanor,' he said quietly.

Miss Merivale turned to him with a thin smile, her slender hand raised. 'Please,' she said. 'If Eleanor particularly wants the song, I'm willing to accompany her.' She deftly flicked up the bottom corner of the page and half turned, lifting her eyes to meet Eleanor's. 'Are you ready?' she asked. Eleanor gave an almost imperceptible nod, and Miss Merivale began to play.

I had heard the song on a number of occasions, but the legend of the Erlking was in any case familiar to me from my childhood: indeed, I had at one stage become so morbidly obsessed by the little volume of folk-tales in which it appeared – and in particular by the sinister engravings that accompanied the text – that my father had eventually taken the unprecedented step of transferring the book to a shelf beyond my reach. Miss Merivale's performance compared favourably with others I had heard, but it was Eleanor's singing, thrusting me back into a shadowy world of half-remembered nightmare, that gripped my imagination that evening.

I don't want to give the wrong impression: Eleanor was, in strictly musical terms, comprehensively outclassed by her accompanist, and she certainly began very badly indeed. Miss Merivale, elegantly poised above the keyboard, held the rhythms – the right hand's percussive beat, the insistent growling of the bass – with exemplary precision, while Eleanor's rich but evidently untrained voice stumbled behind like an unseated rider. I saw a smile pass across Miss Merivale's face, a smile so signally devoid of warmth that it might have been construed as a smirk; and then everything changed.

I can locate it precisely, that moment of transition. As the frantic hoofbeats slacken, the Erlking moves in, creating a stillness at the heart of the storm, his mouth so close, it seems, to the ear of the panicky child that he barely needs to raise his voice. That was where Eleanor found what she was looking for, or where it found her. '*Du liebes Kind, komm, geb mit mir*' – that terrible, unrefusable invitation, the words welling from her throat as sweet as honey but laced with menace and, more subtly, with the sick yearning of the demonic for a world of human warmth and love.

Then off again, Eleanor utterly present now in the song, her voice – the child's voice – soaring in terror against the gathering pulse of the accompaniment, the quickening hoofs; and the father's words infused, in her interpretation, with the same terror, their sensible, humane reassurance so thrillingly subverted by that unspeakable otherness that I felt the hairs prickle at my nape. I was back there in the library, the book open in front of me in a pool of yellow lamplight, a small boy lost among the nightmare images: the father crouching low in the saddle, his hair flying in the wind, his cloak half concealing the wild-eyed child huddled in the crook of his left arm; and emerging from the tangle of briars and branches behind them, one long-fingered hand out-stretched, the Erlking himself. He is crowned as a king should be, but his clothes hang in tatters from his wasted body; his mouth is set in a famished grin. He doesn't seem to be moving with particular speed, but his narrowed eyes are lit with a terrifying certainty, as though he can already envisage the end of the story, the end of the hopeless, hectic ride. I heard the final words of the song ring out, stark and raw, in the space left by the suspended accompaniment; and then Miss Merivale, with studied understatement, struck the closing chords.

As the notes died away, Miss Merivale dropped her hands to her lap and drooped her head. She looked suddenly small and lost, her poise gone; in her face there was a kind of subdued panic, as though the song had told her something she would have preferred not to hear. Eleanor stood erect, staring out over our heads, her eyes brimming with tears. There was a long, uneasy silence, broken at last by Merivale.

'Bravo, ladies,' he called out, beating his thigh with the flat of his hand. 'That was splendid. Really splendid.' His sister looked up with a grateful smile, and the applause became general. I leaned back in my chair, feeling the tension begin to evaporate from my body, from the room. And then Eleanor's eyes met mine.

What did it signify, the gaze she turned on me then? Too intense for our surroundings, it might have reflected the frightful exhilaration of a night-ride whose hammering rhythms seemed still to echo in the air around us, yet it was focused on me, and on me alone, with a directness bordering on indelicacy. Recognition, was it? Accusation? Desire? For an instant that seemed an age I was transfixed, held like an insect on a pin; then she turned abruptly away and let me fall.

8

I had fallen asleep with Eleanor's singing still echoing in my mind but it was Daniel who visited my dreams, visible as a vague thickening of the darkness at my bedside, his voice sweeter and clearer than in life. *Come with me* he fluted, taking up the Erlking's theme, wheedling, coaxing. He moved in close and I felt his fingertips play lightly over my face, his lips brush my ear. *Come.* I started back from his touch and woke drenched in sweat, trembling with desire and dread. I lay in bed until the darkness began to draw off; then I rose and towelled my damp skin before dressing and making my way downstairs.

The eastern horizon was brightening as I left the house, and the air was ringing with bird-calls. Not the sweet tones of an English dawn chorus, but something altogether wilder and more disquieting – a babble of contending shrieks, whistles and warblings with an undercurrent of lighter piping sounds. More than anything I had yet experienced, those cries spoke to me of the distance I had travelled from my native soil, and as I walked out through the gates I was gripped by a spasm of something like vertigo and my heart lurched in my chest.

Once at a reasonable distance from the villa, I positioned myself among the shrubs at the edge of the track and waited, my gun at the ready. Vane had mentioned the passage, at dawn and dusk, of small groups of waterfowl, and I was eager to try my luck. I had barely settled back when a dozen or so duck winged over, low and fast. I jerked the rifle clumsily forward, fired both barrels and, as the second shot rang out, saw the hindmost bird stagger and drop.

I thought at first that I had lost it, but after a few minutes' searching I discovered the body half buried in a clump of low scrub, one wing twisted stiffly upward like a flag marking the spot. It was a beautiful thing, I saw, as I tugged it clear, its underparts a deep cinnamon-brown, flecked with darker mottling, and the gleam of its bottle-green head-feathers shifting with the loose swing of its neck. I placed it carefully in my satchel and returned to my makeshift hide.

I had no further success but I was pleased enough with my prize, and after a hasty breakfast I hurried down to the barn to skin the bird. Eleanor was there before me but her glance, as I entered, seemed less unfriendly than before, and I had no sooner placed the duck on the table than she set down her brushes and stepped over to my side.

'Teal,' she said. 'Chestnut teal.' She stretched out her hand and gently touched the bird's breast with the backs of her fingers. Something in the gesture – some quality of hesitant tenderness – stirred and confused me.

'So soft,' she said, with a little catch in her voice. 'Do you remember what Milton says about the waterbirds – bathing their downy breasts on silver lakes?'

'You've read Milton?'

She must have caught the note of surprise in my question. She bridled, glared. 'Why shouldn't I have done? You take me for a dunce, don't you? A little colonial flibbertigibbet.'

'Of course I don't. But I always think of Milton as a peculiarly masculine writer. I imagine that young ladies tend, as a rule, to prefer something a little less—'

'Perhaps,' she interrupted rudely, 'you need to widen the circle of your acquaintance.'

There was a moment of tense silence. Then she reached out and touched my arm, half propitiatory, half coercive.

'Come with me,' she said. 'I want to show you something.'

She marched over to the hayloft ladder, hitched up the front of her skirt and began to climb. I hung back, inhibited by a faint, unsourceable anxiety. As she reached the platform, she turned and held out her hand.

'Come on,' she said. 'It looks unsteady, but it's safe enough.'

'I'm not afraid of a fifteen-foot drop,' I said stiffly.

'What is it, then?'

I couldn't have explained it to myself, let alone to her. 'Nothing,' I answered, moving over to the ladder.

I'd imagined the loft very differently – hay bales, twine, dust and shadows; not that swept space, amply lit by the window and skylights and furnished like a nursery. Against one wall stood a low table, set as though for tea with a miniature porcelain service, sprigged with rosebuds; against the opposite wall, a small bench occupied by three exquisitely dressed china dolls. A blanket-chest, loosely draped with a fringed woollen shawl, had been positioned immediately beneath the skylight. Eleanor was looking at me, her head tilted a little to one side, evidently waiting for me to comment.

'I take it this used to be your playroom,' I said.

'In a manner of speaking. When I was sixteen my father told me I was to clear my bedroom of the trappings of childhood. That was the phrase he used. I said I wouldn't – told him I saw no reason to – but he wouldn't drop the matter. He quoted scripture at me – as if St Paul would have cared whether or not a young girl kept her dolls by her bedside – but I raged and cried, biting my wrists and knuckles until they bled, making him frightened I might do myself worse harm. In the end we agreed that I should be allowed a few keepsakes, so long as I removed them from the house. That was when I began to make a place for myself out here – a place where I can be as I am, not as he'd have me.'

Her voice, I noticed, had hardened as she was speaking; her expression was cold and distant. It seemed sensible to shift ground. 'You told me you had something to show me,' I said. 'Did you mean . . . ?'

'No, not these things. Something more important.' She stepped over to the blanket-chest, removed its covering and eased back the lid. Peering over her shoulder, I saw a neat bundle – a thick cylinder of tightly wrapped burlap about two feet long, tied at each end with a length of grubby cream ribbon – lying diagonally across the top of a disorderly heap of books. She removed the bundle, placing it carefully on the floor beside her, and rummaged through the books until she found the volume she was looking for.

'Do you know,' she said, quickly scanning the pages, 'I think no-one else has ever described things the way Milton does. Listen to this.' She settled back on her heels, angled the book towards the skylight and began to read.

And higher than that wall a circling row
Of goodliest trees loaden with fairest fruit,
Blossoms and fruits at once of golden hue
Appeared, with gay enamelled colours mixed:
On which the sun more glad impressed his beams
Than in fair evening cloud or humid bow,
When God hath showered the earth; so lovely seemed
That landscape: and of pure now purer air
Meets his approach, and to the heart inspires
Vernal delight and joy, able to drive
All sadness but despair: now gentle gales
Fanning their odoriferous wings dispense

Native perfumes and whisper whence they stole
Those balmy spoils.

She sighed and gently closed the book. 'Fanning their odoriferous wings,' she breathed, lifting her eyes to mine. 'Can you imagine?'

If, as I suspected, she had brought me to her hideaway in order to impress me with her little library and her modicum of learning, her rapture was no less genuine for that. I smiled, touched and faintly excited by her wide-eyed gaze. 'They're glorious lines,' I said.

'Yes, and frightening too.'

'Frightening? Why?'

'Because,' she said, and her mouth twitched uneasily, 'he's already there.'

'Who?'

'Satan. It's Satan approaching the garden. Prowling around, looking for a way in, plotting mischief. We've waited for our glimpse of paradise, and here it is at last, but he's there with us. And when we enter, we enter with him. Or he enters with us – I don't know exactly how it is. I want to see the garden pure and clear, and I can't. Milton won't let us. It's as if he's telling us the evil's deep in our own hearts and can't be rinsed out.'

'The gospels tell us otherwise. And Milton himself knew that the loss of paradise was only part of the story. It might be said that our fall can only be understood in relation to the act of redemption that follows it.'

'Are you a believer, Mr Redbourne? I mean, do you believe we can all be saved? Supposing someone sins – I mean a sin so terrible she can't speak of it, though it's not her fault – and goes on sinning because she has no choice. Might she still find her way back to paradise?'

'Everyone has a choice,' I said. 'That's the point. Sin is a choice, and so is repentance.'

There was a long silence before she spoke again. 'I don't believe that,' she said at last. 'It's too simple.' She turned away with an odd grimace and began to fumble nervously among the books in the chest. It struck me that I had not given her the answer she wanted.

'I'm no theologian,' I said gently. 'I may be wrong.'

She appeared not to have heard. 'Cowper,' she said, tugging a worn clothbound volume from the heap and handing it to me. 'All of Cowper's poems. And Crabbe's. Some of Byron's too. Bumped and battered, but that's all I can afford.'

'Don't you have access to your father's library?'

She gave an ugly, mirthless laugh. 'My father has no library,' she said. 'He thinks books are a waste of time and money. He'd be horrified if he knew of my own few shillingsworth.'

I opened the volume she'd handed me and made a show of examining the text, but found myself intrigued and vaguely distracted by the bundle on the floor. 'What's that?' I asked.

'I can show you,' she said, 'but you must promise not to say anything about it in my father's hearing.' Without waiting for a response, she lifted the bundle on to her lap, untied the fastening and began to unroll the cloth with quick, eager movements of her slender hands. I caught a glimpse of polished wood, a dusky gleam between the folds.

'Do you promise?' she asked, pausing suddenly in her task.

'I promise.'

She spread the cloth to reveal a carved figure lying on its back like a small brown baby, its stumpy legs slightly splayed and thrust a little forward from the hips. Neither the legs nor the skimpy arms suggested a great deal of care on the part of the carver, but the torso, though crudely modelled, was intricately decorated with tiny gouge-marks, and in the space where the thighs met under the rounded belly, the vulva was carefully delineated – a stylised leaf-shape bisected by a deep slit and fringed with finer incisions.

But it was, above all, the face that compelled attention: a polished oval, longitudinally ridged to form two distinct planes and dominated by the enormous, deeply sculpted eyes. I stared down at it, perplexed by its teasing inscrutability. It wasn't that the face was inexpressive, but that its expression was so deeply ambiguous as to engender a kind of confusion in my mind. Was the thing grieving, or were its features set, as the protruding tongue half suggested, in a mocking parody of grief? Was it angry? Lustful? Or had it perhaps withdrawn into some calm, contemplative space beyond the reach of passion? I stooped to examine it more closely and, as I did so, Eleanor smiled up at me.

'Don't you think she's beautiful?' she asked.

It wasn't the adjective I should have chosen. For as long as I can remember, I have been fascinated by sculptural form, and I regard the sculptors of classical antiquity as having attained a level of artistic expression unmatched, in any medium, either before or since; among their productions are works of such refined and exquisite beauty that I have, on occasion, been moved to tears in their presence. In what sense, I asked myself, could this crudely worked totem be said to share their qualities?

'The piece has a certain power,' I said. 'I wouldn't call it beautiful.'

'The power and the beauty are the same thing. I came across her in a curiosity shop down by the harbour and the minute I saw her I began to shake, my whole body trembling so that I had to lean against the counter to steady myself. There was something about the way she stood, so sure of herself among all that dust and clutter. And something in the set of her face too – look at it – as though she were saying, very simply and firmly: this is what I am. There's beauty in that, Mr Redbourne – in the thing she's saying and in the manner of her saying it – and though it's a kind of beauty I hadn't met with before, I recognised it at once.'

'I'm not persuaded,' I said, running my fingers across the roughly tooled surface, 'but perhaps I'm missing something.'

'I'm not trying to persuade you. Either you see it or you don't. But I want you to understand that, for me, the world changed when I found her.'

I was taken aback by the extravagance of the claim, and my face must have betrayed my feelings.

'I mean it,' she said, looking hard at me. 'Nothing was ever the same again. When I came home that evening I leafed through some of my watercolours, and it seemed to me I was looking at a kind of trickery – all soft tones in those days, washes so delicate they barely tinged the paper – and seeing clean through it. I couldn't stop thinking about what I'd found. And it wasn't just regret at having had to leave her in the shop—'

'So you didn't buy the piece there and then?'

'I couldn't. The asking price was two guineas.'

'Not a vast sum.'

'An impossible sum at the time. My father keeps a tight grip on my allowance – wants me to account for everything I spend. Every so often the odd shilling might stick to my palm, but two guineas called for extreme measures. I waited my chance and filched a couple of sovereigns from his purse one evening after dinner.'

It was her matter-of-fact tone as much as the disclosure itself that shocked me. 'Surely you knew that was wrong,' I said.

'He owes me more than that.' She was repacking the books, but her hands fell suddenly still and she lifted her eyes to mine. 'You've promised, remember. You're to tell him nothing.'

I nodded. She leaned over the little totem and placed her hand gently against the curve of the brow, the way a mother might touch her child in greeting or fond goodnight; then she swaddled it again and carefully returned it to the chest.

9

I had deliberately put Bullen from my mind, but when I returned to the house for lunch he was there on the veranda, lounging in the shade with a glass in his hand. He rose to his feet as I approached and strolled down to greet me. He was a little more relaxed in his manner than on the previous evening, and considerably more casual in his attire, his shirt collarless and partially unbuttoned beneath a loosefitting canvas jacket.

'I thought you might be game for an afternoon's shooting,' he said. 'If we set off directly after lunch we can ride down to the swamp, bag a few choice specimens and be back here in time for dinner.'

As I considered my reply, I saw Vane emerge through the french windows and step to the edge of the veranda. He raised his hand in salutation and rested his elbows on the rail, smiling in our direction. It seemed, in the circumstances, almost impossible to decline Bullen's invitation: the itinerary had clearly been arranged between the two of them, and a refusal might well be interpreted as doubly insulting, as much a gesture of disrespect towards my host as towards Bullen himself. I gave as warm a smile as I could summon up.

'Thank you,' I said. 'I should be glad to join you.'

I was not particularly hungry and Bullen, though apparently ravenous, showed no desire to linger over his lunch, so that by the time the groom appeared in the drive with our mounts we were ready to leave. Vane had provided me with a chestnut pony, rather short in the leg for a man of my height but sturdy and sure-footed, and we kept a steady pace for an hour or so, side by side at first and then, as the track narrowed, with Bullen leading the way. Eventually, as the track became too rocky for them to negotiate, we tethered the ponies and continued on foot.

It was hard going, and became even harder as we struck off at an oblique angle to the ridge and began to pick our way down the slope between the sandstone outcrops. The eucalypts here were stunted grotesques, their limbs twisted and their red boles pocked and rippled like diseased flesh.

'There,' said Bullen after a few moments. 'Do you see?' I caught the glint of sunlit water between the trees and eagerly quickened my pace, but Bullen reached out and grasped my sleeve, holding me back. 'Easy now,' he said. 'Easy and quiet.' I slowed obediently and we moved cautiously forwards until we stood on the edge of a worn lip of stone, gazing out over the swamp.

What was it, the sick tremor that afflicted me at that moment? In part, I suppose, it was a product of the heat, beating down remorselessly from the open sky but at the same time fanning upward from the hot rock like the blast from an opened furnace. There was the smell too, a soft odour of ooze and rot; and as I stood there, the shrilling of the cicadas seemed to swell around me and resonate through the bones of my skull with an insinuating force that made me think of madness. But above all, I think, I was disturbed by something in the look of the landscape – not pitilessness exactly, since the term implies the possibility of pity, but a blank imperviousness to our presence. In the gleaming foliage of the waterline mangroves, in the lazy flow of the inlet and the flat shine of its silted banks, I read nothing that seemed intended for my eyes, or for those of any intruder in that heartless, unblemished wilderness.

I heard the click of Bullen's safety-bolt and turned to see him braced against a eucalyptus bole, his rifle trained on the swamp below. I followed the slant of the barrel but could see nothing for the shine and dazzle of silt and water.

'What is it?' I whispered.

'You'll see.'

A pale form lifted from the water's edge, rising on broad wings in the instant before the shot sang out. I had a fleeting sense – seeing the wings at full stretch, the long legs just beginning to tread air – of explosive energy; then the bird crumpled and dropped back into the slime.

'Yes,' breathed Bullen, his face flushed, his eyes fixed on the spot. But the bird wasn't finished. It struggled to its feet and made for firmer ground, head and neck held low, its left wing trailing. Bullen slung his rifle back over his shoulder and began to scramble down the slope, his boots throwing up showers of dust and leaves. I followed at a slower pace.

I thought our quarry might have eluded us but its painful progress was clearly inscribed on the soft silt, and by the time I drew level with him Bullen was on his knees where scrub and swampland met, reaching into a thick clump of brushwood. He was breathless, agitated, his eyes glazed in an ecstasy of vicious excitement as he fumbled among the crackling stems.

'It's in here. Cover the other side in case it makes a break for it.'

I moved round obediently. He set down his rifle and kicked vigorously at the clump, breaking down the scrub and trampling it beneath his boot soles. Something stirred in the shadows. I caught sight of a glittering eye, a long, heavy bill; then Bullen lunged forward.

'Hah!' His cry of triumph was so wild and strident that I took it at first to have been uttered by the bird. There was a flapping and scrabbling, the snapping of dry brushwood.

'Over here, Redbourne. He'll not run now.'

Rejoining him, I found that he had one leg of the bird – which I now saw to be a squat, thickset heron – clamped in his right hand, and was groping with the other for a firmer hold on his prize. The heron was frantically resisting the manoeuvre, weaving its head from side to side and gripping the brushwood tightly with its free foot. I knelt to help, but as I did so, Bullen drew in his breath with a sharp hiss and jerked back his left arm.

'What's the matter?'

'Damn the brute,' he said. He extended his hand towards me, palm upward, and I saw the blood welling from a broad gash just below the ball of the thumb. 'Damn it to hell.' He yanked roughly at the bird's leg, bringing its breast hard against the enclosing lattice of twigs. It cried out, a single grating note.

'Careful, Bullen. The creature's in pain.'

He tugged again. The head lunged towards us, a string of mucus trailing from the corner of the bill. A stink of fish; the air electric with cruelty and terror. A spasm of revulsion went through me, and I rose to my feet and unslung my rifle.

'Stand aside, Bullen. I'll finish it off.'

He stared up at me, his eyes flashing. 'Damned if I will,' he said. 'This skin's almost unmarked. D'you think I'm going to indulge your finer feelings by standing back and letting you blast it to shreds?'

'It's the bird's feelings I have in mind.'

'It amounts to the same thing. Listen, Redbourne, these creatures don't suffer the way you or I would. Science tells us as much. A creature with a brain the size of a walnut – look, just cut this stem here, would you?

Here, below the foot. We'll have the brute out in half a minute.'

103

It was clearly not the moment for debate. I set down my rifle, took the clasp-knife from my pocket and began to saw at the woody stem, the dull blade squeaking as I worked.

Bullen gave a snort of impatience. 'Take mine.' He indicated with a glance the bone-handled hunting-knife hanging at his belt. I slipped it from its sheath and set to again. The steel was sharp and clean, and I worked with greater ease now, cutting away until something gave and Bullen hauled the bird clear of the tangled brush. He moved awkwardly, his bleeding hand held well away from the delicate plumage. The bird lunged again.

'The neck, man – get hold of its neck.'

I leaned forward and seized the extended throat, feeling with a subtle shock the hard, sinewy strength of the thing. Bullen breathed heavily at my ear. 'Flip it over,' he said.

Once the bird was on its back, it stopped struggling, though its eyes continued to move wildly in its angular head. Bullen edged forward, pinning the belly beneath his leg before setting the heel of his right hand firmly against the base of the throat and bearing down with the full weight of his shoulders. The bird quivered violently and beat the earth with its good wing in a pitiful travesty of flight; then it lay still.

Bullen rose stiffly to his feet, swinging the carcass up by the neck so that I saw the pinkish flush of the mudstained breast-feathers, the slack line of the throat. 'This one's mine,' he said, his voice harsh and a little aggressive, as though I had laid claim to the bird. He picked up his rifle and we retreated to the shade of the eucalyptus trees.

We had a good afternoon of it, all told, bagging between us several duck, a species of rail, an elegant blue and white kingfisher and a pair of small doves, modestly coloured but strikingly marked. I should have been delighted but my mood, as we rode back, was sombre. The stink of silt and fish hung heavily about us and my mind reverted continually to the same disquieting cluster of images: the sun hammering down mercilessly from the wide blue sky, light glinting off slime and water, the heron on its back in the dirt, and the two of us leaning above the bewildered creature like the fiends I once saw in a painting of the last judgement, meting out their dark, incomprehensible punishment to one of the damned.

10

Bullen returned to the villa several times during the following week, on each occasion taking me out for a day or half-day of shooting. I wouldn't go so far as to say that I was warming towards the man but I was learning to tolerate his company, and our excursions were proving so productive that I was increasingly inclined to overlook his intellectual shortcomings. Indeed, we were so successful that I was having difficulty in coping with the influx of specimens: by the end of the week such time as was not taken up with hunting the birds was almost entirely given over to preparing their skins.

'How many honey-eaters do you need?' asked Eleanor one morning, coming up behind me and surveying the heap of little corpses at the edge of my table.

I set down my scalpel, not entirely sorry to be interrupted. 'It's not a question of the number,' I explained. 'The thing is that slight variations between individuals — variations that might be overlooked in the field — could turn out to be important from a scientific viewpoint. At best, close examination might show one of these birds to be a new species. At the very least the group provides a valuable record, a basis for future research.'

'Give me one,' she said. 'That one, there.'

'What do you want with it?'

'I'm going to paint it.'

I handed her the bird. She held it in the cupped palm of her hand, scrutinising it intently before returning with it to her table. 'I want to paint it the way it is,' she said. 'Stiff and still.'

I caught the note of reproach in her voice and responded with a touch of irritation. 'Listen, Eleanor, you mustn't imagine—'

'Nell. I'd like you to call me Nell. Everyone does, except him.'

'Your father?'

'Yes. We argue about it. It isn't appropriate, he says.'

'He may have a point. It's not unreasonable for a father to want his daughter's name to reflect her station in life.'

'I have no station in life,' she said, spitting my own phrase back at me as though it disgusted her, 'but I have a right to be called by the name I choose.' She returned to her seat, laid the bird on the table in front of her and began to pin a fresh sheet of paper to her drawing-board. 'And you,

Mr Redbourne,' she continued: 'What name do you want me to call you by?'

There was a hint of insolence in the question, but a kind of bashfulness too: I saw the colour rise to her cheeks as she fumbled with the pin. 'If you wish,' I said, 'you may call me Charles.' And then, after a moment, regretting the stiffness of my initial response: 'I should like that, Nell.' She glanced up with a quick, brittle smile and reached for her paintbrush.

We worked for some considerable time without speaking, separately absorbed in our tasks. I had made a good job of the specimen in hand, and was just cutting the neck free at the base of the skull when I heard Eleanor sigh and set down her drawing-board. 'What do you think happens to them?' she asked.

'Wait a moment,' I said, working my scalpel-blade upward from beneath the vertebrae. 'There.' I lifted the body clear and dropped it to the floor beside my chair. 'Happens to what?'

'The birds. Once they're dead. Do you suppose they have any kind of after-life?'

I smiled at the fancy. 'A heaven for birds?' I asked.

'I don't know about heaven. Perhaps they just go on with their lives in some other form. Or in the same form but more shadowy, so we can't quite make them out.'

'Perhaps,' I said noncommittally. I turned back to my specimen and began to chip gently at the underside of the skull. When she spoke again, it was with an odd, compelling urgency that made me look up at once.

'Would you stop for a while?' she asked. 'Stop working, I mean. Just for a few minutes. I want to tell you about my brother.'

I laid down my scalpel and swung my chair round so that I faced her directly. 'Do you have brothers?' she asked.

'No,' I said. 'No brothers, no sisters.'

'Did you never feel the lack of company when you were growing up?'

'Not that I can remember. I'm not at all sure that I should have welcomed an addition to the family.'

'Well, when I was small I used to pray to be given a brother. And for a while I'd pester my mother about it, in a way that it shames me to think of now. Later, as I grew to understand such things a little more clearly, I began to realise that I was likely to be disappointed, and by the time she broke the news to me, I'd almost given up hoping. I can still remember my feelings – a kind of astonishment at first, and then joy, joy taking hold in me like a flame in dry tinder – when she told me she'd been blessed. That was how she phrased it, and I remember the look on her face too, a look of such sweetness that, even now, I find it hard to say that it was anything less than a blessing.

'We were both certain that the baby was a boy, and we talked of him so often that he became part of the family long before he was due to be born. I knew the places he'd want to go, and all my walks were taken with him in mind. And I'd talk to him as I went, as though he were really there, showing him the things I loved, and loving them all the more for being able to share them with him. I always imagined him slung on my hip, not heavy at all, moving so easily with my own movements that he might have been part of me.'

She stopped abruptly, half turning in her chair, twisting away from the light. Something in her face – some clouding or agitation of her features – made me uneasy. 'Maybe you should get on with your painting,' I said. 'Tell me about your brother some other time.'

'I've finished the picture. And maybe there won't be another time. Not for this. I want to tell you now.' She edged her chair clear of the table and leaned towards me, her forearms resting on her knees. 'He was to be called Edward,' she said. 'Like my father. I used to make believe I was looking into his eyes and seeing something of my father reflected there, and I'd tell him how like he was, the very image of his papa. And sometimes I'd call him by his name, very softly, and I'd teach him to say mine, pretending to myself . . . pretending—' She broke off again and began to rock gently back and forth, rubbing the palms of her hands against the rough fabric of her skirt.

'So your brother—'

'No,' she said sharply. 'I want to tell this the way it happened. The way it seemed to happen, anyway. One morning I woke early – I mean I was woken, woken by footsteps clattering through the hall downstairs, someone running helter-skelter, not at all the way the servants would normally have gone about their work. And it wasn't just that. All the other sounds were different too, as though I'd woken in someone else's house.

And my heart was beating very fast and hard, though at that point I couldn't really have known—'

'Don't do that, Nell'

'What?'

'That rocking. It disturbs me.'

She glowered at me, but sat back in her chair and composed herself a little before continuing.

'I ran out on to the landing, calling for my mother. But it was my father who appeared, banging back the dining-room door as he rushed out into the hallway. I can see him now, the way he looked that morning, staring up at me as I leaned over the stair-rail, his face grey like dirty pastry and his mouth twisted as though he were trying to smile and couldn't. "Get dressed," he said, "and stay in your room until I come up." Then he turned to go back into the dining-room, and at that moment I heard a cry – not a loud cry, but a kind of sobbing moan. I knew for sure then that something was amiss and I pelted down the stairs and caught up with him in the doorway. "I want to see Mama," I said, and made to squeeze past him into the room, but he moved to block my way, grabbing at my arm and knocking me sideways so that my head struck the door-frame. Not hard, but I fell to my knees; and as I tried to scramble out of his reach, I saw her lying there.'

'Your mother?'

'Yes, stretched out on the floor with the top of her dress unbuttoned and Mrs Denman kneeling over her, smoothing the hair back from her forehead. I must have stopped short at the sight of her – her face drawn with pain and the skin white and shining with sweat – because next thing I knew my father was bundling me back through the door and up the stairs. "Do as you're told," in he said. "Stay in your room and I'll come up when I can." He was trying to soften his voice, I could tell, but it came out wrong, and his fingers were gripping my shoulder so tight you could see the bruising for weeks after.' She put her hand up to the place, rubbing it gently as if it were still tender.

There was a long silence.

'And when your father came back?'

'He didn't. When I was dressed I sat on my bed for an age, and at last Sally – the maid we had then – came up and told me I was to go out and play, and wait for the baby to arrive. So I put on my shoes and my sun-hat and – have you been down to the creek?'

'Not yet.'

'Well, when you go, leave the main path at the fork and take the narrower track through the trees. After about half a mile you'll come to a small patch of rough grazing. Cross that and you'll find yourself at the edge of the most beautiful stretch of the creek. There's a bend where the water slows and deepens, and a stillness all around that frightens people who aren't used to it. That's where I go when I need to think. It's where I went that morning.

'I walked slowly along the bank, talking to my brother as I'd grown used to doing, pointing out the things he liked – dragonflies, spiders' webs, the swallows dipping over the water. But it seemed to me that he wasn't quite with me – drifting away as I tried to interest him in this thing or that, his attention wavering and fading like a dying candle-flame. Or perhaps it was me – my own attention somewhere else so I couldn't see him clearly or hear what he was thinking. After a while it became so difficult that I stopped trying and let him go. And that's when I saw Mama, standing at the edge of the grassland, her dress as pale as the silver stringybarks she stood against, so that I could hardly make her out at first. But as I looked, she seemed to come into focus – to sharpen somehow, I can't say how it was – and then I saw she was bareheaded, her hair unpinned and tumbling loose about her shoulders. And that was strange because I'd never seen her take a step beyond the garden gate without first putting her hat on; but it wasn't as strange as what happened after.'

She had begun to rock again, the chair creaking softly with her movements. 'I can't help it,' she said, catching my glance. 'When I think about these things—'

'There's no need to go on if it distresses you.'

'But it's important to tell you. I've never told anyone before – never met anyone I thought would understand.'

I was surprised to find myself blushing, flattered no doubt by her implied regard for my perspicacity, but stirred too, as I was later to acknowledge to myself, by the subtle suggestion of intimacy. I don't believe she noticed my discomfiture; at all events, she took up the thread again, moving smoothly on as though there had been no interruption.

'No, the really strange thing was this: one moment she was out there by the trees, and the next – I don't know how it happened because there's some gap, a blank space where something must have gone on that I didn't see or can't lay hold of – she was with me on the bank, almost as close as you are now. I remember thinking how young she looked, her features fine and her skin soft, but very pale, and her gaze so mournful I can still make myself cry by thinking about it.

'I'd thought when I first caught sight of her that she must have come to show me my brother, but now I saw that her arms were empty. "Where is he?" I asked. And then, because she appeared not to understand, I said his name, "Edward," very softly like that, the way I liked to whisper it to him on our walks together. That seemed to rouse her in some way, and she fixed her eyes on mine and held me with her gaze. Her lips didn't move, but I knew then, as surely as if she'd spoken, that she'd come to let me know that my brother was dead – that he wasn't coming to join me and I shouldn't wait any more.' She leaned forward again, cupping her chin in her hand, and I saw that her eyes were bright with unspilled tears.

'And your mother?'

'Not there, though I saw her clearly enough. She couldn't have been.'

'Couldn't have been? Is this a ghost story, Nell?'

'Not a story, but the plain truth. And my mother couldn't have been a ghost either, not in the way people usually think of ghosts. She didn't die until late that evening. But I suppose some part of her must have broken free before the end and wandered out to find me.'

I regarded myself at the time as a thoroughgoing sceptic in such matters, but there was something in her words – or perhaps simply in her guilelessly expressive features – that set my skin prickling.

'I think we should take a stroll outside in the sunlight,' I said.

'Let me finish.' She brushed angrily at her eyes with the back of her hand and stared hard at me as though daring me to move. 'I began crying then, whimpering like a hurt puppy, wanting it not to be true but knowing beyond all doubt that it was. But she reached out and took me up – I don't mean in her arms, and I can't say exactly what I do mean, but I felt myself gathered and raised, riding upward the way a boat lifts at its moorings as the tide turns in. And after she'd gone – and she seemed to slip away without my noticing – I was still held there, very quiet and still, sensing myself a little apart from the world but seeing it all so clearly – the ripples and creases on the surface of the water, the play of light on the eucalyptus leaves, the shadows sliding across the grass as the day wore on. And even that night, lying in bed, listening to my father sobbing and moaning in the next room, I could still feel myself supported, as if she were trying to . . .' She trailed off, lifting her eyes to the cavernous roof as though she might find among its shadows the words she was searching for.

'To console you?'

She seemed to consider this. 'Well,' she said at last, 'I suppose it was something of the kind. I felt she was offering me her protection, though I think in the end she wasn't strong enough to shield me from the worst. If she'd been able to give me everything she seemed to promise, the past ten years would have been very different. We'd have kept that gentleness about the household, the gentleness I remember touching us all – myself, my father, the servants – as she moved among us in life. And certainly my father would never have mistreated me as he does.'

'Come now, Nell. I can see that you and your father have your differences, but you're hardly—'

'You can see nothing,' she cut in angrily, starting to her feet. 'Nothing at all.' The colour was up in her cheeks again, her breathing fast and shallow. She leaned over her drawing-board and began to unpin the paper. 'I did this for you,' she said, 'but I might have saved myself the trouble.'

'Nell,' I said, moving towards her, 'you're not to talk like that. Do you hear me? Let me look.' She glared but made way for me, stepping back from the table so that I could see the painting more clearly.

What is it in art that opens our eyes and hearts to truths barely glimpsed in life? I had spent the best part of a morning staring at a succession of small corpses without registering what I was dealing with. Now, bending above Eleanor's painting – nothing, on the face of it, but streaks and clots of pigment on a cockled sheet of paper – I was jolted into awareness like a man roused suddenly from a profound sleep. The bird had been represented in profile and at such an angle in relation to the paper that, with bill slightly parted and neck extended, it seemed at first glance to be singing in blind ecstasy. Even the stiff left wing, held just wide of the body, might have been taken to indicate a taut vitality; but then the eye travelled to the dull badge of blood on the breast, to the legs, folded too close against the belly, and to the cramped grip of the feet on thin air. It was a remarkable achievement. By some expressive sleight of hand, Eleanor had contrived to suggest, more or less simultaneously, both the brute fact of death and the vibrant life from which the creature had been plucked; and it was in that poignant double focus that I discovered a truth which none of the morning's cutting and probing had succeeded in laying bare.

It was undoubtedly the image itself that moved me in the first instance, but it may be that what tipped the balance was Eleanor's giving of it – half sullen, half eager, her eyes lifted to mine as she handed me the sheet. At all events, my voice cracked as I thanked her, and I found myself, quite unexpectedly and with some embarrassment, on the verge of tears.

11

'You'll be pleased to know,' said Vane as we sat at lunch that afternoon, 'that Bullen has made arrangements for your expedition to the mountains.'

'He was here this morning?'

'He called by on his way to the store. You'll be starting out on Thursday, first thing. I suggested he join us for dinner this evening to discuss details with you.'

Bullen and I had, it was true, worked our way round, after a little unpleasantness and a certain amount of further haggling, to a broad agreement on the matter but I found myself vaguely disconcerted, not only by the fellow's high-handed assumption that he might plan our itinerary without further consultation with me, but also by the news that we were to leave so soon. I was debating the wisdom of saying anything on the subject when Eleanor spoke up.

'Mr Redbourne has scarcely been here a week,' she said. 'You're bundling him off into the bush before he's had a chance to settle.'

'Mr Redbourne is here with a purpose,' said Vane with a flicker of irritation, 'and Mr Bullen has kindly agreed to help him. It's not for you to interfere in their business.' And then, turning to me before Eleanor had time to reply: 'There'll be four of us tonight – I've invited Merivale.'

'Five,' said Eleanor. 'Five of us.'

'Male company,' said Vane brusquely. 'I think you might -prefer to take supper in the kitchen with Mrs Denham.'

'And then again,' she retorted, the colour rising to her cheeks, 'I might not.'

Vane gave her a long, hard stare. 'As you please,' he said, 'but I want no nonsense from you. You know what I mean. If you're addressed, you may speak. Otherwise, keep your thoughts to yourself.'

'Thank you, Father' – under her breath, the words themselves innocuous enough, but the insolence unmistakable. She laid her knife and fork carefully on the rim of her plate, rose to her feet and swept out of the room.

From the moment we sat down at the table that evening it was clear to me how profoundly Eleanor had subverted her father's plans: seating herself at Vane's side with Merivale to the left of her, she effectively isolated the young man from our company. I could see, glancing across as he bent smiling towards her, that he himself was by no means dissatisfied with the arrangement, but Eleanor's apparent determination to engage him in private conversation was plainly an irritant to her father. At intervals during the main course Vane would attempt to draw Merivale away, seeking his opinion on this or that matter of concern, but on each occasion Eleanor drew the young man back again, reeling him in as an angler plays a hooked fish, and Vane eventually abandoned him to her.

'The thing is,' said Bullen, glancing up as the maidservant reached over to set the fruit bowl on the table, 'that we'll have more equipment than we can carry. The train journey poses no problem, of course, but once we're out there we shall need assistance. I've made arrangements for one of the local guides to go out with us – fellow by the name of Billy Preece, highly recommended by one of my contacts in the area. More than willing to shoulder his share, I'm told, and knows the region like the back of his hand.'

I have a naturally romantic outlook, and Bullen's reference to the railway gave me a moment's pause. I had imagined us setting out from the villa on horseback, and plunging almost at once into the unknown: a train journey seemed altogether too mundane.

'Oh, you'll get your fill of the wilderness,' said Bullen, when I touched on the matter, 'once we're in the mountains. On ponyback first, and then on foot. By the time we return to civilisation you'll be more than ready to take advantage of its comforts.'

'No doubt,' I answered, 'but sometimes I think how the face of England has changed since my childhood – the railways reaching into all those quiet corners, the cities spreading outward like dirty stains – and I find myself wondering whether we may not be paying too high a price for the comforts of civilisation. Out here, with so much splendid scenery still unspoiled—'

'That's precisely the point,' interrupted Vane. 'There's so much of it that our own petty activities – railway construction, tree clearance, mining – make scarcely any impression. If I were to return to England now, I might well share some of your anxieties, but Australia's a different matter. You can't imagine it, Redbourne – the sheer immensity of the land, the resources we've scarcely begun to draw upon.'

'Besides,' said Bullen, 'there's nothing wrong with taking Nature in hand and letting her know we mean business. As a culture we possess certain skills, certain powers. They're the reason we're here – I mean, they're the reason we own the country and the blackfellow doesn't.'

'Well,' I said, 'we own it at the moment, but who's to say we won't be dislodged a century or two from now?'

Bullen shook his head. 'If we are,' he said, 'it won't be by a race of barefoot dreamers but by a civilisation even more forceful in its dealings with the world than we are.'

'True enough,' said Vane, selecting a ripe peach from the fruit bowl. 'I'm with Darwin there – it's the strong who inherit the earth. That's the way things work. And there's no doubt that the native tribes here have had their day.'

I sensed, rather than saw, that Eleanor had turned to look in our direction. 'Forgive me if I'm wrong, Father,' she said, cutting in with chilly precision, 'but isn't it the meek who are to inherit the earth? Or has that text had its day too?'

Vane ran his knife round the soft flesh of the peach, twisted the halves apart and set them carefully on his plate. 'I wasn't aware,' he said, 'that meekness was a quality you held in particularly high esteem, Eleanor.' He leaned forward and took up the decanter. 'More wine, gentlemen?'

As he reached across to fill Merivale's glass, Eleanor interposed her own. 'Thank you,' she said. I saw Vane hesitate.

Eleanor looked around the table. 'My father believes that good wine is wasted on young ladies,' she said.

'Your father believes,' said Vane, gruffly, 'that one glass is ample for any young lady worthy of the name.'

'But not,' Eleanor persisted, 'for a young gentleman.' She turned to Merivale. 'Do you think that's fair, William?'

The young man's confusion was almost comical. Undoubtedly flattered by her appeal, yet clearly conscious of his obligation to his host, he stuttered and goggled until Vane, perhaps out of pity for his predicament or perhaps simply in hope of restoring order to the proceedings, replenished Eleanor's glass.

'I don't think,' said Eleanor, picking up her thread as deftly as if the interruption had not taken place, 'that meekness means letting other people have their way at your expense, or being silent when you've a right or a duty to speak. I think it means being humble in the face of a universe we can hardly begin to understand. I think it means knowing when we should stop trying to set our stamp on everything we see – knowing when to stand back and admire the world instead of forcing ourselves on it.'

She took a gulp of wine and set her glass back on the table with clumsy emphasis. 'Mr Bullen seems to imagine,' she continued, 'that our culture will have fulfilled its destiny once it has taken everything else – the wilderness, other cultures, life itself – by the scruff of the neck and shaken it into submission.' Merivale shifted uneasily at her side and leaned forward as though to intervene, but if she saw the movement she chose to ignore it. 'We're cut out for better things, Mr Bullen – for higher things – but we live blindly, striking out at whatever displeases us, gathering up whatever takes our fancy. We don't see the damage we're doing or the suffering we cause. And until we do—'

'Whoa there, young lady,' cried Bullen, good-humouredly enough, I thought, given the circumstances. 'You can't hold me responsible for all the ills of the world.'

'I don't. Of course not. But when I hear you talk, I know where you stand – not in the clear light I want to stand in, but in some dark place, among all the other lost souls who've confused power with progress.'

Vane made a little lunge across the table, rapping lightly on the cloth with his knuckles. 'It seems to me,' he said with forced playfulness, 'that the ladies might reasonably retire now.'

Eleanor glanced at her father with an expression of such undisguised contempt that I felt myself wince on his behalf. 'I'll retire when I'm ready,' she said.

'In that case,' said Vane, reddening slightly but without faltering for a second, 'may I suggest that the gentlemen retire.' He drained his glass and rose unsteadily to his feet. 'If you'd care to join me on the terrace . . .'

Bullen and I fell in behind him but, looking round as I stepped out on to the veranda, I saw that Merivale was still in his seat. With one hand gripping his sleeve, Eleanor was literally holding him there, addressing him in low, urgent tones, her eyes fixed on his as though defying him to move. It crossed my mind that he might welcome my intervention but I couldn't be sure, and after a moment's hesitation I followed Vane and Bullen out into the darkness.

'. . . a mind of her own,' Vane was saying as I rejoined them, 'and I accepted that long ago. What I won't tolerate is being made a fool of at my own table, or having my guests insulted.' He turned as though to include me in the conversation, but seemed to think better of continuing. He felt in his breast pocket and withdrew his cigarette case.

'I believe Merivale will be with us directly,' I said after a moment, anxious to break the awkward silence. In the flare of his match I saw Vane's eyes lift towards the house. 'He's been detained by Eleanor,' I added.

'Detained at Her Majesty's pleasure,' said Vane sardonically. 'After an evening of my daughter's nonsense, I should think you'll be only too glad to get out into the bush for a couple of weeks.'

'It was an excellent evening,' I said.

Vane grunted and turned away, staring into the night. 'Fatherhood,' he said bitterly, 'is a mixed blessing.' And then, shifting his shoulders like a man easing away the afterweight of a slipped burden: 'You'll need the buggy early on Thursday, Bullen. What time shall we say?'

As they talked, I saw Merivale emerge on to the veranda, closely followed by Eleanor. The young man set his back against the rail and stood, starkly silhouetted against the french windows, his face turned towards his companion. As Eleanor closed in I lost sight of her behind his bulky form, but it was clear that she had not yet done with him: I heard her voice – not the words but the soft, insistent murmur of it – drifting out on the warm air. Merivale seemed to have little to say but his stance suggested that the girl had his undivided attention, and I was surprised when she broke abruptly away and stepped back into the house. He started after her, stumbling on the threshold so that he had to put out his hand to support himself.

What was it I saw then? I was tired and my mind was faintly clouded by the wine, but I thought Merivale reached out and grasped Eleanor by the shoulder, swinging her round – but her slight frame was scarcely visible at that point – to face him. I scarcely had time to register the movement before they were gone, passing swiftly across the windows and out of sight.

Bullen and Vane were discussing train times. 'If you'll excuse me,' I said, 'I think I'll turn in for the night.' My voice was thick in my throat and I was shaking with passion, as though the gripped shoulder or the grasping hand had been my own, but Vane, barely glancing my way as he bade me goodnight, appeared to notice nothing.

There was no sign of the couple in the dining-room, but as I stepped into the hallway I saw them there, in the half-light at the foot of the stairs. Merivale had been speaking but fell silent as I approached, shrinking further into the shadows, while Eleanor came towards me with a faint smile on her lips. I don't know quite what I had expected, but something in the assurance of her movements surprised and disconcerted me.

'I'm on my way to bed,' I said awkwardly, as though it were my own actions that required an explanation.

'Goodnight, Charles.'

Just that. I stood for a moment with one hand on the stair-rail, scanning her face for whatever clue might be visible in the dim lamplight. Not a flicker as she returned my gaze.

'Goodnight, Eleanor. Goodnight, Merivale.' I climbed slowly, my whole body suddenly slack with fatigue. As I reached the turn of the stair I almost looked back, but thought better of it.

12

I stretched out in extreme weariness but was unable to sleep for thinking of Eleanor down there with Merivale in the shadowed hallway. I told myself firmly that the girl's conduct was no business of mine but I couldn't settle, and after twenty minutes or so I rose from bed and seated myself at my desk with the idea that a little writing might steady my restless mind.

My journal, begun on shipboard as a simple aidememoire, had become increasingly important to me as the voyage progressed, and since my arrival in Australia I had begun to consider my writing in a new light. The field notes I had taken throughout the years of my youth and early manhood had been exemplary in their attention to detail but now, I realised,

I was looking for something more than scientific accuracy. I had been aware since childhood that the minutiae of the material world – the veining of a beech leaf, the whorl of a snail shell, a fox's pad-mark in the silt at the river's edge – were a kind of code, and I had sometimes had bewildering glimpses of the vast and infinitely complex truth they represented, but I had seldom attempted to find words to convey those insights. Now, as I wrote of the sheen on a beetle's carapace, for example, or the patterns scribbled on the pale bark of a eucalyptus tree, I found myself working with a new refinement, honing my phrases to an edge I hoped might be sharp enough to slip beneath the dazzling surfaces of things.

I was describing the clearing I had entered late that afternoon, and the subtle agitation set up by a pair of wrens as they foraged through the undergrowth in the softening light, when I was startled by a shrill cry. I set down my pen and listened. A brief pause and then a thud, followed by a second cry. I took up my lamp, opened the door and stepped out into the corridor.

It was Eleanor's voice, I knew, hearing it again as I approached her bedroom – a staccato phrase delivered in an intense undertone. I placed the lamp on the blanket-chest outside the room and rapped gently on the door.

'Eleanor?'

No answer. I called again and heard a voice rasp out, breathy and urgent: 'Tell him to go.'

I leaned against the door, my lips close to the keyhole. 'Merivale? Merivale, is that you?'

Dead silence, except for the slow ticking of the clock from the hallway below. And in that instant, driven not only by anxiety for Eleanor but also by an obscure sense of outrage, I turned the handle and threw back the door.

The scene presents itself to me now as a static tableau, its detail simultaneously vivid and equivocal. Vane stands beside the washstand, one hand resting on the marble surface, the other held to the side of his face. His jacket and waistcoat are draped over the back of the bedside chair; his pocket-watch, lapped in the gleaming coils of its chain, is on the seat. On the rug at his feet, in two almost equal pieces, lies a broken jug; water has soaked the fawn pile, forming a dark, irregular stain. Eleanor faces her father, backed up against the bed, but bolt upright. She is clutching the neck of her loose white night-dress, gathering the fabric at her throat. Her hair is unbound and dishevelled, her eyes fixed in a wild stare.

Is it just a trick of the memory, that impression of breathless stasis? Maybe so, but the impression is all I have: the two of them locked together in a world somewhere beyond the ordinary flow of things, utterly oblivious to my presence. The air seemed to have thickened around them, dense with undischarged energy and the coppery reek of sweat. And then, with a muffled grunt, like a man waking himself with effort from a disturbing dream, Vane swung round to confront me.

Never, before or since, have I experienced such acute embarrassment. Think of it: close on midnight, and a man of mature years and some social standing bursts into a young lady's bedroom in his nightshirt to find himself face to face with her father. It was the stuff of farce, without the leaven of humour. I gawped; I mumbled. 'I'm sorry. I thought I heard . . .'

'It's nothing.' Vane was breathing hard, his face and thick neck flushed, his brow gleaming with perspiration. 'Eleanor dropped the water-jug, that's all. There's no great harm done.' His face, I noticed as he lowered his hand, was marked, the cheekbone a darker, angrier red than the surrounding flesh. He squatted down on his heavy haunches and picked up the two pieces. Eleanor slumped on to the bed and sat there, shoulders hunched, hands thrust between her thighs, her face averted. She was trembling so violently that the bed-frame shook.

I leaned forward, trying to catch her eye. I was looking for a sign, for something that might tell me what kind of drama I had stumbled into, but her gaze was rigidly fixed on a point towards the far corner of the room and never so much as flickered in my direction. Awkward and uncertain, I turned back to her father.

Vane raised his arm and drew his shirt-sleeve across his forehead. 'I'm sorry you've been disturbed,' he said.

'Please don't concern yourself on my account. But Eleanor—'

'Eleanor has been a little over-excited by the events of the day. She needs to rest.' His breathing was returning to normal; his hand, cupping my elbow as he steered me round and guided me back to the door, conveyed nothing more than a host's natural solicitude for his guest's wellbeing.

But as we reached the doorway, Eleanor cried out – a stifled yelp of pain or fury – and I turned to see her rise from the bed and launch herself towards us. Vane hustled me quickly into the corridor, slipping out with me and slamming the door behind him. An instant later she was there, rattling at the handle, but Vane was gripping it firmly from our side, and the door remained closed. I heard her strike the wood with the flat of her hand, just once; and then she called my name.

An expression of something like panic crossed Vane's face, passing almost before I had time to register it. He jerked his head in the direction of my room. 'I'd advise you to get to bed,' he said. 'You can leave this to me.'

Close up against the door, Eleanor drew a long, sobbing breath. I hesitated. 'Perhaps I might have a word with her,' I said.

'Believe me, it's better you don't.'

I shifted uneasily from one foot to the other. 'Forgive me,' I said, 'but I feel there may be some advantage in letting me speak with her. In my experience—'

'I think,' he interrupted coldly, 'that I can be relied upon to know what's best for my own daughter.' And then, a little more civilly: 'Take it from me, Redbourne, there's nothing you can do for her.'

There seemed no point in persisting. 'In that case,' I said, 'I'll wish you goodnight.' I stooped to pick up the lamp and, as I did so, the rattling began again, followed by a heavy drumming against the panels. Vane flinched and tightened his grip on the door-handle. 'Go on,' he whispered hoarsely as I stood dithering. 'Get to your room.'

I was half-way back when she cried out again, the words ringing down the corridor with a terrible shrill clarity: 'He knows. He knows.' I turned to see Vane gesticulating wildly with his free hand, flapping me back as though I were a hen strayed from the coop. And then, even more stridently but no less distinctly, her voice cracking on my name: 'You hear me, Charles? You're my witness.'

Vane's features convulsed suddenly: a wincing grin, lips drawn back from the teeth, the eyes narrowed to slits. And still that panicky flutter, the hand wafting me back down the corridor. The air seemed charged with a kind of madness, a jittery, disruptive energy threatening my own stability, and it was with a measure of relief that I finally withdrew and returned to my room.

I reseated myself at my desk, still listening to the sounds from the corridor: the thick murmur of Vane's voice punctuated at intervals by his daughter's lighter tones, pleading, perhaps, or remonstrating. After a few moments I heard Vane's heavy tread on the boards as he drew closer. Then the door of his room creaking open; shut. The click as the catch snapped home.

I took up my pen again and wiped the clogged nib. There was something I had wanted to say about that moment in the clearing – something about the shifting, intricate patterns of sound and light set up around me as the birds flicked and piped among the leaves. I dipped the pen and wrote:

long-tailed and small-bodied, beautifully marked above. By good fortune, I was able to secure both with the same shot. The female died instantly but the male scurried across the dry litter and wedged itself tightly among the basal shoots of a small shrub. I thought I should be obliged to dispatch it, but by the time I had extricated it from its niche, it was already dead.

Even as I wrote, I knew that the moment was lost. I read back over my words with growing disappointment, then struck out the reference to my good fortune and paused for a moment over 'beautifully marked' before deciding to let the bland phrase stand. I left a two-inch space and then wrote again, more slowly now, and with some hesitancy:

I have just come from Eleanor's room, where

I sat back and looked at the words for several minutes; then I took my ruler and drew two lines through them, rendering them illegible. Beneath these and extending across the full width of the page I drew a third, indicating in my usual fashion the conclusion of the day's entry. I blotted the page carefully before closing the journal and retiring to bed.

13

I had anticipated a restless night but in fact I slept deeply, waking only at the sound of the breakfastgong. By the time I came down, Vane had already served himself and was seated at the table cutting vigorously at a thick wedge of gammon.

'Help yourself, Redbourne. This' – he held up a pink sliver on the end of his fork – 'is excellent. We rear and cure our own and, if I may say so, we do it rather better than most.'

I chose the eggs and joined him at the table. 'About last night—'

'Please,' he cut in briskly, his mouth full. 'Please don't apologise. You acted, I know, with the best of intentions and you've no reason to reproach yourself.' He swallowed hurriedly, dabbed at his mouth with his napkin and reached for the coffee-pot. 'May I?'

'Thank you.' I pushed my cup towards him. 'Where's Eleanor?'

'Still in bed, I imagine.' He gestured towards my plate. 'That's not much of a breakfast. Let me help you to a little more.'

I shook my head. 'It's not like her to lie in so late. I'm wondering whether last night's disturbance—'

'Don't concern yourself. Eleanor's an excitable girl – some taint on her mother's side – but she calms down quickly enough if left alone.'

'This has happened before, then?'

'Episodes of this kind, yes.' He sat back in his chair, slightly flushed, and took a deep breath. 'Listen, Redbourne, I must urge you not to involve yourself in any way. The worst thing we can do – I have this on sound medical advice – is to appear to sanction her follies or to give credence to her fantasies. Last night's display' – he gingerly fingered the bruise on his cheek – 'was an extreme form of the hysteria that has afflicted her periodically since her mother's death. No cause for alarm, you understand, but the situation requires careful handling. I hope I can rely on you.'

Something in his speech struck me as faintly artificial, as though he were delivering lines rehearsed in advance, and whether for this or some other reason, I was slow to respond to his implicit appeal.

He leaned forward again, jabbing at the air with his fork, his eyes fixed on mine. 'I said, I hope I can rely on you, Redbourne. The girl's health depends on it.'

'I can assure you,' I said, 'that I would do anything in my power to safeguard your daughter's well-being.'

He held me with his gaze a moment longer and then addressed himself once more to his breakfast, hacking at the gammon with renewed energy, chewing noisily on each mouthful. The conversation was clearly at an end, and as soon as I decently could I excused myself from the table and stepped out into the garden.

It was a morning of exquisite serenity, clear but not yet hot, the air rich with the scents of the warming earth. A small flock of finches moved erratically among the glossy leaves of the citrus trees, their white breasts gleaming as they caught the light. I watched the birds intently, hoping for that fleeting release I sometimes experience in such circumstances: the mind – or spirit if you like – vibrating for a moment in sympathy with the stir and shimmer of the natural world. But the events of the night were still with me, a dark, distracting undertone, and my concentration lapsed.

Although I considered returning to the house and knocking on the door of Eleanor's room, it seemed wiser, on reflection, to go down to the barn and await her arrival. But as I approached the building, I heard the clatter of something dropped or overset, and I knew she was already there. I hurried to the entrance and peered round the door.

Jem Poster

I thought at first that she was praying, down on her knees on the dirt floor, her head bent forward, her lips moving spasmodically, spitting out broken, unintelligible phrases. But both hands were at the back of her neck, and as my eyes grew accustomed to the gloom, I saw what she was up to – hacking with a pair of rusted sheepshears at her dishevelled hair. I stepped forward, crying out her name, but as she raised her head and looked towards me I saw that the tresses which should have mantled her right shoulder were already gone. She dropped her hands to her lap, sat back on her heels and stared up at me, her lips wet with spittle, her eyes lit with a terrible wildness. I thought of her father's injunction against involvement, but I could see that it would be a grave mistake to leave her, in such a state, to her own devices.

'What are you doing?' I asked, as calmly as I could.

'You can see what I'm doing.' She raised the shears to the back of her neck again. I knelt beside her and took up a loop of hair from the packed earth.

'Your father said—'

'What my father said' – I heard the blades clash and grind – 'won't have come within a country mile of the truth. Did he tell you about this?' She hauled sharply on the hair twisted in her left hand so that her head went back between her shoulders and her long pale throat lay exposed. Her teeth were bared in a fierce rictus, the breath hissing between them as she struggled, in grotesque pantomime, to free herself from her own unyielding grip. I leaned forward and took her gently by the shoulder.

137

'Don't,' I said. 'You'll harm yourself.'

'Not the way he's harmed me. But let him try it now.' She relinquished her hold and ran her hand with a vicious clawing or combing motion across the cropped side of her head. 'See? Try for yourself. Go on.' I could feel her trembling beneath my hand. 'I said, go on. Make to grab me by the hair as if—'

'Easy, Nell, easy,' I said, very softly but firmly, as though I were quietening a frightened animal. 'You're not to excite yourself.'

'Who says not?' She peered into my eyes, her face so close I could feel the warmth of her breath on my skin. 'I suppose my father's told you I'm brainsick, has he? A poor deluded child who doesn't know what day of the week it is?'

I lowered my eyes, unable to sustain the intensity of her stare. 'Not exactly. He told me that since your mother's death you've been prone to—'

'Damn him,' she cried, arching her body sideways and breaking my hold on her shoulder. 'Damn him and his lying tongue.' She set to once more with the shears, chopping and tearing frenziedly at the remaining hanks of hair. I snatched at her arm, a futile gesture in any event and, as it transpired, worse than futile. She gave a sharp cry and the shears clattered to the ground. I leaned behind her with the intention of retrieving them and saw the smooth skin of her neck broken, the blood seeping into the white collar of her blouse.

I remember the momentary silence, the acute and quite disproportionate spasm of anguish that went through me as

138

I gazed at the nick below the ragged line of her hair. I reached into my breast pocket for my handkerchief.

'Bend your head forward,' I said. I folded the handkerchief into a thick pad and dabbed gently at the cut. 'It's hardly more than a scratch. Certainly nothing to worry about.'

'Oh, I'm not troubled. Believe me, I'd take the blades to my face if I thought there was no other way of getting clear of it all.'

'This is wild talk, Nell. You're to stop it, do you hear?' I picked up the shears and slipped them quickly, blades first, into my side pocket.

'I'll talk as I please,' she said sullenly. She half turned, groping behind her with her left hand, then swung back violently to face me. 'Where are they?'

'The shears?' I fingered the protruding grip, feeling her touch still there in the warm steel. 'I have them.'

'Give them to me.'

'They're safer with me, Nell.' I rose cautiously to my feet and stepped back a couple of paces. 'You don't need them.'

'Of course I need them. I can't go back to the house with my hair like this.'

'You should have thought of that before you started.'

'I mean' – she tugged irritably at the last strands of uncut hair – 'with the job unfinished. Let me have them.' She held out her hand and stared up at me, her eyes daring me to refuse.

'I'll finish the job for you,' I said, 'but not with a pair of blunt sheep-shears. What were you thinking of, Nell?'

139

'I wasn't thinking. Just feeling. The shears came to hand, that's all – the way things do when they're needed.'

I went to my table, unfastened my satchel and drew out the case of instruments. I spread it flat and selected the larger of the two pairs of scissors.

'Come and sit here,' I said, pulling the chair away from the workbench and swivelling it round to face her.

'Just give me the scissors. I can do it myself.'

'You can have no idea,' I said, a little more brusquely than I'd intended, 'what kind of a mess you've made. Let me tidy it up for you.'

She stood still for a second or two, irresolute but visibly calmer now; then she stepped over and seated herself decorously in the chair. I pushed the door wide and the light came flooding in.

I trim my own hair as a matter of course and I had no scruples about dealing with Eleanor's, particularly since, as I was tactless enough to hint, her recent efforts had left so much scope for improvement. There's no great mystery to the craft: like the skinning of a bird, it requires a certain delicacy of touch but is otherwise largely a matter of patience and concentration. I worked with care, but with vigour and fluency too, running my hand smoothly upward from nape to crown through the thick curls, lifting and cutting, lifting and cutting, absorbed in the easy, repetitive movement. And it wasn't until the job was almost done that I was struck – feeling with a queasy tenderness the contours of her skull beneath my fingertips – by the strange intimacy of the whole business, and by some attendant notion of its impropriety. I withdrew my hand and straightened up.

'Have you finished?'

'Very nearly.'

'What does it look like?'

'A good deal better than it did ten minutes ago, but – hold still now.' I leaned over her again and snipped away a stray wisp of hair.

'But what?'

I snipped again. 'You'd better go in and see for yourself,' I said. 'I've done what I can.' I shook out the folded handkerchief and flapped the cut hair from the back of her neck.

'You're angry with me, aren't you?' She tilted back her head, staring up into my face.

'Angry at what you've done, yes. Angry at this wilful violation of your own beauty.'

'If my beauty's my own,' she said, colouring, 'I can do what I like with it.'

'That's not true, Nell. Your beauty is valued by others. This isn't simply an outrage against yourself, but against those who care for you.'

I saw her shoulders stiffen and go back. 'Outrage?' she said quietly. 'Violation?' Her voice was very clear and cold. 'You don't know the meaning of the words. I'll show you outrage. I'll show you violation. I'll show you how he cares for me.'

She rose to her feet and turned to face me, both hands at her throat. I had no sense at first of what she was up to; then the hands slipped an inch or two lower, and I saw that she was unbuttoning herself.

'What is this, Nell? What are you doing?'

She made no answer but continued, with deft, economical movements of her thin fingers, to unfasten her blouse. It wasn't the action alone that alarmed me but the terrible fixity of her gaze, her eyes trained on mine but seeming to look clean through me to the shadows at my back. I stepped forward to restrain her.

'No,' she said sharply. And then, as I hesitated, she put her right hand to the collar of her blouse and tugged it down over her shoulder so that her left breast lay exposed.

You have to bear in mind that, since the death of my mother, all my dealings with women had been of an essentially impersonal nature, and certainly nothing in my experience had prepared me for this – an act of unsettling complexity, simultaneously suggestive of licentiousness and trusting innocence, of vulnerability and barely suppressed fury. And if I was unsettled by the act itself, I was horrified by the damage it disclosed: what I was looking at was not the smooth pallor familiar to me from my days in the art galleries of France and Italy, but a blotched patchwork of scabs and bruises.

What should I have said? I felt the need of words, but for a long moment could only stare in appalled fascination at what I took to be a bite-mark, a ragged oval, visibly infected, an inch or so above the nipple; and when words came they were, as I knew at once, the wrong ones. 'That needs attention,' I said, gesturing awkwardly at the inflamed area.

'I am attending to it,' she said quietly. 'I always do.' She turned away as though belatedly registering the impropriety of the situation, and began to refasten her buttons.

'If there's anything I can do . . .'

She raised her head and glanced back at me over her shoulder. 'I told you,' she said. 'You're my witness.' Then she stepped out into the sunlight. I hurried after her as she strode purposefully up the path towards the house, her cropped head held high and her skirts swaying. It seemed to me that there was more to be said, but she never once slowed her pace or looked back.

Vane was leaning on the rail of the veranda, smoking. I saw his head jerk up as we approached; then he stubbed out his cheroot and struck diagonally across the lawn towards us, stumbling a little as he came, his eyes fixed on his daughter's face. As Eleanor drew level with him, he stretched out his arm, meaning, I supposed, to detain or embrace her; but she brushed past him as though he were an importunate street-beggar and swept into the house. As he gazed after her, I caught in his eye the most extraordinary expression of anguished entreaty, and I imagined that he would follow her; but he drew himself up sharply, rammed his hands into his jacket pockets and veered off towards the gates without so much as a glance in my direction.

I was seized by a longing for space and solitude. I left word with the servants that I should be away for the remainder of the day, then collected my net and killingbottle from the barn and set out for the creek.

Dinner that evening was a miserable occasion. Whether as a result of the turmoil of the preceding twenty-four hours or because I had spent too long in the full glare of the afternoon sun, I was oppressed throughout the meal by a sick headache that deprived me both of my spirits and my appetite. And Vane, too, seemed distinctly out of sorts: moodily preoccupied, he scarcely troubled to acknowledge my presence until we were half-way through the main course.

'I've come to realise,' he said at last, 'that I should have been more explicit about my daughter's condition. What I described this morning as hysteria might more appropriately be characterised as a form of mania. To put it bluntly, Eleanor suffers from delusions. I don't mean the fantasies natural to impressionable girls of her age, but ideas – usually of persecution or assault – that invade her mind and grow there until they become indistinguishable from the reality around her. It's a vile business, Redbourne, hard for her, and harder still on those who care for her. And of course' – he shot me a sharp glance – 'it makes her entirely unmarriageable. That's a heavy burden for a father to bear.'

I said nothing. Whatever I thought I had seen – up in Eleanor's room, out there in the shadowed barn – seemed to melt and blur, equivocal as the broken images of a midnight dream.

Vane picked up his napkin-ring and studied it carefully, as though it bore some arcane inscription. 'There's something else I have to say, Redbourne. I believe that your presence in the household may have contributed in some measure to these recent outbursts. Please don't misunderstand me — there's no personal criticism implied — but the coincidence is suggestive. I'm no expert in such matters myself, and I make no judgement, but the plain fact is that until last night she was showing every sign of having outgrown the more extreme manifestations of her illness.'

'If you're asking me to leave—'

'Please, Redbourne.' He reached out and gripped my sleeve with awkward familiarity. 'I wouldn't dream of it. You'll be gone by Thursday in any case, and that's all too soon for me. But I suggest that you avoid Eleanor's company in the interim — avoid it entirely. For your own good as well as hers.'

He placed the napkin-ring carefully beside the meatdish and glanced across at my plate. 'You're not eating,' he said.

I shook my head and felt a spasm of pain pass like fire from the back of my skull to my left temple. 'I seem to have lost my appetite,' I said. 'Do you mind if I retire?'

He leaned forward, scrutinising my face. 'You look flushed,' he said. 'Are you unwell?'

'A little. A touch of the sun, perhaps.' I rose unsteadily to my feet and made for the door.

'You'll bear in mind what I've told you, Redbourne?'

The words were clear as crystal but seemed to come to me from an enormous distance. I inclined my head vaguely in their direction, let myself out into the hallway and slowly climbed the stairs to my room.

I had made a vow to myself on leaving England that my opium-taking would in future be restricted to cases of medical necessity and, despite moments of temptation during the voyage, the bottle of tincture I had brought with me was still unbroached. I cracked the seal with my pocket-knife and eased out the cork. I took the tumbler from the washstand and poured into it a finger of brandy from my hip-flask. Then I added a few drops of the tincture, knocked back the mixture and eased myself, still half clothed, between the sheets.

It was a night of dreams, all forgotten now except the last. I was back in the swamplands where we had killed the heron, up to my calves in the silt at the water's edge. And she was there too, kneeling or squatting beside me, though in the half-dark – some dullness or misting of the air around us – I didn't recognise her until she spoke. Not in words, I think; but I knew clearly enough what she wanted and why she had joined me there, and I slipped the blouse back from her shoulders and began to wash the lacerated skin, scooping up the water in cupped hands and letting it fall from above so that it ran in rivulets down her throat and breasts. Swamp water, yes, but shining as it fell; and her skin taking on the shine, the scars and bruises fading as I worked. And then, because I knew that this, too, was what she wanted, I knelt and placed the tips of my fingers lightly against the healed flesh.

I can't get back to it now – not to the charged heart of the dream. But I remember that, lying there in its thrilling afterglow, I conceived the notion that the waking world and the world of the dream were one and the same; and in my confused or exalted state I imagined myself padding down the corridor to Eleanor's room and gently rousing her from sleep to ask whether she knew in what miraculous fashion we had both been blessed.

14

Eleanor wasn't at breakfast the next morning, and Vane seemed scarcely able to acknowledge my presence, let alone to maintain a civilised conversation. He ate with nervous, preoccupied haste, and only when he had cleared his plate and poured himself a second cup of coffee did he raise his eyes to mine.

'I've sent for Bullen,' he said. 'I thought you'd want another day out before you leave.'

'Thank you, Vane, but I'd prefer to stay here. I've two skins to prepare, and I shall need time to pack for tomorrow's journey.'

'Bullen won't be here until eleven. I imagine that will give you time enough.'

His anxiety to have me off the premises was so painfully evident that I decided not to argue the point. 'I'll set to work now,' I said. 'No doubt I can arrange my affairs around the excursion.'

'Thank you, Redbourne.' His features softened into a weak smile. 'I know you appreciate the delicacy of the situation.'

'Is Eleanor any better this morning?'

'It's hard to say. She's quieter, as she generally is after one of these episodes, but she's still far from well.'

'Has the doctor examined her?'

'There's no need.' Vane drained his coffee-cup and set it carefully back in its saucer. 'He'd prescribe complete rest as usual. If she keeps to her room for the next few days, she'll gradually return to a more orderly state of mind.'

'I hope I shall be able to see her before I leave.'

'I'm afraid that won't be possible,' he said, rising abruptly to his feet. 'But I should be glad to pass on any message you may have for her.'

I was quite unprepared for the wave of desolation that swept over me at that moment, and it took me a second or two to recover my equilibrium. 'Thank you,' I said. 'You might just tell her that I look forward to seeing her fully restored to health on my return.'

It was barely a flicker, but the expression that crossed Vane's face told me as clearly as words could have done that I shouldn't presume on boundless hospitality on any future visit to the villa. 'I mean,' I added hastily, 'when I call by to collect my trunk.'

'Of course,' he murmured, but even as he spoke I could see from his expression that something – perhaps some small sound from beyond the door – had distracted him. He stood alert for a moment, head lifted like that of an animal scenting danger, and then, scarcely troubling to excuse himself, strode swiftly past me and out of the room.

I was glad at first to get out to the barn but I found it difficult to concentrate and I made a poor job of the first specimen, tearing the delicate skin in several places. The second bird fared even worse, its pale breast-feathers stained with bile as a result of my carelessness and, on a sudden nauseous impulse, I disposed of the entire mess in the scrub outside the door. It was Eleanor, I realised, as I wiped my instruments and returned them to their case, who had distracted me, her presence so deeply engrained in the place – or perhaps simply in my receptive mind – that it was impossible to be there without thinking of her.

I made my way back to the house in a state of subdued agitation, and as I rounded the shrubbery and looked up I saw her at the window of her room, her face close against the glass. I was unable to interpret either the words she mouthed at me or the fluttering action of her raised right hand but I judged it best, in the first instance at least, to remain where I was. I ducked back out of sight of the house and waited.

I heard the rustle of her skirts as she approached, and knew from the sound that she was moving fast, half running towards me across the open lawn. As she drew level with the end of the shrubbery she caught sight of me and veered round with a movement so impetuous as to bring her within an ace of falling into my arms. And seeing her standing there, her face lifted to mine and her hand flat against the base of her throat as though to steady her own quick breathing, I was struck by the thought that a man differently reared or constituted – a man, in short, of less ambiguous temperament than myself – would hardly have let such an opportunity slip for want of a welcoming gesture.

She was flustered and dishevelled, her eyes hollow in her pale face and her hair standing out from her head in absurd tufts and spikes, yet her beauty remained somehow inviolate, too deeply seated, it seemed to me, to be dislodged by the accidents of life.

'I wanted to see you before you left,' she said. 'To say goodbye. I couldn't bear not to.'

I should have liked to tell her of my own desolation, earlier that morning, at the thought of leaving without sight of her, but the words wouldn't come. 'Your father told me you were keeping to your room,' I said. 'I'm glad to see you up and about.'

'Keeping to or kept to?' she snapped, her eyes flashing anger. 'There's a difference.' And then, more mildly: 'I'm sorry you've been witness to so much disturbance over the past few days, Charles. It must have been distressing for you.'

'I suppose it has been. Listen, Nell, I need to understand this clearly. Your father—'

'Not now.' She drew back with a little shake of her head. 'One day, perhaps. In any case, it's all done with.'

'And Merivale? What was I witnessing there the other night, at the foot of the stairs?'

'Oh, that.' She shrugged. 'William has been stealing kisses from me since we were children. He knows it's not appropriate any longer, but that doesn't stop him trying. I was telling him it's high time he went out and found himself a wife.'

'And he, I imagine, was telling you – maybe not for the first time – that he's already found what he wants, here on his doorstep.'

I saw from her expression that I had hit the mark, but there was no embarrassment in her reply. 'He needs to look further afield,' she said. 'It would be better for him.'

'And you?'

'I've never entertained the idea of marrying William. Even if my heart had been in it, it wouldn't have done. He sees his future here, in the valley. I can't tell him why that's impossible for me.'

I felt a faint exhilaration, a lightening of my breath as though some weight, far down, had eased or shifted, and at that moment I heard Bullen calling out to me from the terrace.

'You may have to go down and fetch him' – Vane's voice, curt and clear on the still air.

Eleanor pressed herself back against the dense mass of the shrubbery and gripped my sleeve. 'Go,' she said, tugging feverishly at the fabric. 'Quickly.' I brushed her fingers gently with my own, just once, and then stepped out to meet Bullen.

15

I had told Bullen that, short of coming across a significant rarity, I wasn't anxious to add to my collection that afternoon, and we set off on foot without any particular destination in view. I had in mind a few hours' gentle rambling in the immediate vicinity, allowing us to arrive back in good form for our departure on the following morning, but Bullen seemed to find the idea unappealing, and we were soon striding along with our customary briskness, though rather more convivially than usual.

Bullen deflected my questions about Eleanor's illness but offered instead, with uncharacteristic frankness, a series of glimpses into his own life. I learned for the first time of the disciplinarian father who had bought himself out of his

Lancashire regiment in order to begin a new life in Queensland, only to succumb to fever within a year of his arrival; the haphazard upbringing by a mother whose beauty was once a local legend but whose fondness for drink had drawn her progressively deeper into an underworld that had eventually destroyed her; the unfinished education provided at the expense of one of his mother's admirers and the hunger for success in a world that seemed repeatedly to balk his best efforts. It was a tendentious and sometimes disjointed account but I felt, by the time we turned and began to head back towards the villa, that I had gained a considerably fuller picture of the man fate had chosen for me as my travelling companion.

We had walked considerably further than I had intended, threading the narrow paths into the heart of the valley, and the afternoon was well advanced by the time we reemerged on to the main track. As we crested the rise the breeze hit us, not cool exactly, but a welcome relief after the heavy stillness among the trees below. Bullen set his hat to the back of his head and wiped his sleeve across his brow.

'Best foot forward,' he said, 'and we'll be back in time for dinner.'

I think I was the first to see them, just off the track a couple of hundred yards ahead of us, three figures squatting in the shadow of a sandstone outcrop, their heads turned in our direction. As we drew near they rose to their feet, and the tallest of the three stepped out on to the track and hailed us.

'It's all right,' said Bullen, perhaps misreading my excitement at finding myself, for the first time, face to face with one of the indigenous inhabitants of the country. 'I know this fellow.'

The man appeared old, his beard and hair almost completely grey, but his body was spare and upright and his movements easy. He was barefoot and bareheaded but dressed in European clothes: a pair of flannel trousers, rolled up at the ankles and tied at the waist with a length of cord; and a threadbare black jacket, patched at the elbows with a lighter cloth. He wore no shirt; the jacket flapped open to reveal an almost fleshless torso, the collarbones prominent and the ribs individually visible.

'You keeping well, Mr Bullen?'

'Well enough, Amos.' Bullen gave a curt nod in the man's direction but didn't slacken his pace; barely looked at him. The encounter might have passed without incident if I hadn't lagged a little, curious to see the man's companions, who hovered a few paces behind him. They stood shoulder to shoulder, brother and sister, I thought, or perhaps a young couple. Their features were strong and handsome, but their eyes were uneasy, reluctant to meet mine. The youth wore a cotton shirt, loosely tucked into the waistband of his grey breeches; the girl was dressed in a cream blouse, far too large for her slender frame, and a print skirt, evidently home-made, which barely reached her calves. Her hands were clasped in front of her and I saw, around her thin wrist, a bracelet of reddish spines punctuated at intervals by small bunches of bright yellow feathers.

As Bullen slowed, half turning as though to urge me on, the old man thrust his hand into his jacket pocket and tugged out a short-stemmed briar. 'You'll take a smoke with me?' he asked.

Bullen's face darkened. 'You mean you want me to fill your pipe for you?'

The old man shrugged his shoulders and held out the briar.

'If that's what you want,' said Bullen aggressively, 'then why not say so?'

The man took a pace backward, his eyes wary. 'You have tobacco?' he asked.

'I can sell you some.' Bullen extended his hand, rubbing together his thumb and forefinger. 'Do you have money?'

A shake of the head. Bullen turned away. 'No money,' he said, 'no tobacco.'

I saw the old man's face fall. 'Give him a pipeful,' I said.

'I give nothing for nothing,' said Bullen grimly. 'It's a simple policy and a sound one.'

'The girl's bracelet,' I said. 'Will they let us have that?'

Bullen leaned close, sly, conspiratorial. 'If we lay out enough tobacco,' he murmured, 'you can probably have the girl as well.'

I ignored the remark. 'Ask him,' I said. 'Will they trade the bracelet?'

Bullen peered at the object. 'It's made of thorns,' he said. 'Thorns and feathers. Completely worthless.'

I could see that the materials were of no intrinsic value, but I liked the brilliance of the little yellow tufts and the way the thorns fanned out against the girl's dark skin. 'Items like this have a certain cultural significance,' I said defensively.

'Some do. This looks to me like something she's made herself. These people here' – he lowered his voice – 'aren't the certified goods, if you take my meaning. Neither one thing nor the other.'

'Even so,' I said, 'I should like the bracelet.' Bullen shrugged and turned back to the old man.

'You hear? My friend wants the bracelet.' He leaned forward and grabbed at the girl's wrist, but she flinched and stepped back out of reach. Bullen tapped his own wrist. 'Bracelet,' he said. 'She gives us the bracelet, you get tobacco. Understand?'

The old man stared up at him from beneath his matted fringe. 'How much tobacco?' he asked.

Bullen held up his left hand, fingers extended. 'Five,' he said. He reached into an inner pocket and drew out a large wash-leather pouch. 'Look.' He loosened the drawstring and removed five small plugs of tobacco, placing them in a neat row on the gritty surface of the rock. The old man considered them for a moment, then shook his head vigorously. He held up both hands.

'Ten,' he said.

Bullen glanced sideways at me. 'Are you sure you want the thing?' he asked.

The question irked me and, at the same time, hardened my resolve. 'Of course I'm sure,' I said. 'Give him the tobacco. You can trust me to pay you back in full.'

'No doubt, but there's an issue of principle involved. It doesn't do to let these people think they can get the best of a deal.' He took two more plugs from his pouch and laid them on the rock with the others. 'Seven,' he said. 'No more.'

The old man reached out and gathered up the dark oblongs. He slipped them into the pocket of his tattered jacket and turned to address the girl, speaking in his own tongue.

I could see at once that the transaction wasn't going to be straightforward. The girl muttered under her breath and backed away, covering the bracelet with her right hand. As the old man stepped towards her, one arm raised, she dodged behind the youth, who half turned to address her. It wasn't necessary to understand the language: it was clear enough what was going on. I glanced at Bullen.

'Let's leave it,' I said. 'She doesn't want to part with it.'

'Leave it be damned. They've got my tobacco.'

'Ask him to return it.'

Bullen grimaced. 'The deal's been done,' he said, 'and no one's going back on it.' He unslung his rifle and let it hang, lightly balanced, in the crook of his arm. The action seemed casual enough, but something in his expression alarmed me. And then I heard the dull click of the safety-bolt.

The others heard it too. They fell silent and turned towards us again. They might have been waiting for Bullen to speak, but he said nothing. He just stared, gazing into each of the three faces in turn. As he fixed his eyes on the girl, she lowered her head and removed the bracelet; then she placed it on her palm, stepped over and held it out to me.

I am embarrassed to recall the scene. The girl – hardly more than a child, I thought, looking closely at her downturned face – stood before me, hand outstretched, like a schoolboy malefactor awaiting the sting of the master's cane. I remember the smallest details – the spring and twist of her thick hair, the quick pulse at the side of her neck, her bare foot scuffing the dust. Her expression was unreadable but her arm, I noticed, was trembling.

'For God's sake, Redbourne, take the thing.'

I reached out and picked the bracelet gently from her palm. 'Thank you,' I said, as though it had been a gift offered in love or friendship. 'Thank you very much.'

I wanted to catch her eye, wanted to tell her with a glance or a smile that I had meant no harm, but she didn't look up. Bullen slung his rifle back over his shoulder and turned away.

'Let's go,' he said. 'It's getting late.'

After dinner that evening I laid the bracelet on my writing-desk and examined it closely. Out there in the light of the afternoon sun, vivid and changeable against the skin of the girl's wrist, it had seemed a prize worth having; now, staring at the object stretched out in the lamplight against the polished wood of the desk, I wondered what I could have been thinking of. I opened my journal, dipped my pen and wrote, beneath the date:

First encounter with indigenous people. Purchased a bracelet, an unsophisticated affair of red-brown thorns strung on a stout thread and interspersed with tightly bound tufts of yellow feathers. The girl who sold it to me

I set my pen back on the inkstand and took up the bracelet again, letting it swing from my fingers for a moment; then I opened the top drawer of the desk and dropped it in. No point in brooding on the matter, I told myself, ramming the drawer home again, but I was unable to obliterate the after-image of my last view of the group: the two men retreating together to the shade of the outcrop, leaving the girl gazing after us from the middle of the track, her legs a little apart and her arms folded across her chest, her print skirt lifted and ruf-fled by the stiffening breeze.

III

16

My first sight of the mountains was something of a disappointment. The modest ridge that rose up ahead of us as we crossed the plain bore no relation to the towering crags and pinnacles created by my imagination on the basis of an earlier conversation with Vane, and I couldn't help remarking on the fact.

Bullen turned from the window with a thin smile. 'Just wait,' he said. 'I've no doubt we shall be able to impress you soon enough.'

He was right, of course. As the train climbed steadily higher, the grandeur of our surroundings became apparent. Where the land fell away from the track I was able to look out across the treetops and see how the forest stretched to the horizon under a soft bluish haze, while sporadic outcrops of grey and ochre sandstone hinted at sterner beauties to come. The occasional farmsteads and trackside settlements served only to emphasise the scale of the surrounding wilderness: watching a flock of cockatoos lift and wheel against that astonishing backdrop, I remembered Vane's assertion that the country's vastness made it almost impervious to human activity, and I wondered fleetingly whether I might have been too quick to dismiss the idea.

On alighting at the station we arranged temporary storage of our luggage before setting off on foot. Bullen had been given to understand that Billy Preece lived in a hut just beyond the edge of town, but we had been walking for upward of half an hour, and had left most signs of civilisation some distance behind us, by the time we reached our destination. We heard the cluck and cackle of barnyard fowl and then, rounding a bend in the track, found what we were looking for.

Built almost entirely of overlapping boards, roughsawn and untrimmed, the hut was of a design too primitive to be entirely prepossessing, but I could see at once that it had been soundly constructed and well maintained. The threshold was a good two feet above ground level, and the low doorway was served by a little run of three wooden steps. To left and right of the building, an untidy fence of stakes, branches and brushwood marked what I took to be the front boundary of the property.

'Holloa!' shouted Bullen. 'Is anyone at home?' The sound of slow, uneven footsteps across bare boards, and then the door swung open.

The man was not above middling height and his body, as he stood there in the doorway, was twisted noticeably out of true, but something in his demeanour suggested power and presence. His hair and beard were grey, but vigorous in their growth, his face thin but strong-featured. He seemed in no hurry to come forward, addressing us from the threshold with an easy familiarity. 'You'll be the gentlemen from Sydney.'

Bullen advanced towards him. 'Billy Preece?'

'I'm Owen Preece. My son's round the back.' He stepped down and approached us with a stiff, lopsided gait, his right hand extended. 'I'm pleased to meet you, gentlemen.' His handshake was firm and his gaze, as he looked into my eyes, was clear and direct. He indicated a gateway in the fence and bowed us through with an odd, old-fashioned courtesy. 'This,' he said, touching the barrier as he followed us in, 'is meant to keep out the wallabies. I can't claim that it's entirely successful, but at least' – he turned to me, his tanned face creasing into a smile – 'it makes them stop and think.'

'There's only one way to stop a wallaby,' said Bullen. He slapped his ammunition-belt twice with the flat of his hand. 'Ask any grazier.'

There was a moment of strained silence before Preece brought us to a halt. We were looking down a long, gently sloping strip of land, so completely unlike the surrounding bush that we might have stepped into a different country. Close at hand, vines ran riot over a rough trellis, their arching stems festooned with clusters of small purplish grapes, while further down I could see staked rows of beans, the brighter greens of assorted leaf-crops and the gleam of melons and pumpkins lying in the shadow of their own broad leaves. Half-way down, a boy, barefoot and stripped to the waist, his brown skin glistening, was bending over a patch of freshly dug earth.

It was an extraordinary sight, that rectangle of lush colour laid down among the subtler shades of the bush. I brushed my hand across the vine-leaves, as though I might apprehend their soft lustre through the skin of my palm. Preece glanced sideways at us, waiting, I thought, for our response.

'It's a veritable paradise,' I said. 'I can't imagine how you maintain such a fertile garden out here.'

'Oh, it's simple enough, but not easy. Half a dozen cartloads of dung each winter and bucket after bucket of water raised from the gully throughout the summer. In this weather you might be at it from dawn till dusk. I'd be down there now, only my leg's been giving me trouble all day.'

'At least you have assistance,' I said, glancing down the slope just as the boy turned to look at us.

'Yes, in that respect I count myself fortunate. I've only been blessed with one son, but I couldn't wish for a better helpmate than he's turned out to be.' He threw back his head and called out, 'Billy! Come up and meet the gentlemen.'

I had assumed, seeing the half-naked brown body stooping above the turned soil, that the boy was a hired hand, one of the aboriginals of the neighbourhood, and I was glad to have recognised my error without having revealed it. Billy straightened up and wiped his palms on the seat of his ragged breeches before starting up the slope towards us.

He moved lightly and with a dancer's grace, his slender arms held out a little from his body, his feet sure and nimble. As he drew level with us, he swept the tangle of black curls back from his forehead and flashed me a smile of such unguarded warmth that my own more formal greeting died on my lips. Bullen gave the boy a curt nod and turned aside.

'You're Mr Redbourne, aren't you?' said Billy, looking into my face with undisguised curiosity. 'Da says you've come from England.' His voice was deeper than his childlike manner and physical slightness had led me to expect, and I saw, examining his features more closely, that his cheeks and chin were lightly downed with dark hair.

'Yes,' I said, 'that's where I live. Very far away, Billy, on the other side of the world.'

Even before he replied, I could see from the change in his expression that I had struck the wrong note. 'I know where England is,' he said stiffly. 'I've not had much schooling but I'm no dunce, and we're not short of books and maps. You'll see when you step inside.'

'If you gentlemen are agreeable,' said Preece, cutting in quickly, 'we'll have a bite to eat now. Billy will take the ponies down to the station and collect your luggage.'

Bullen gave a grunt, which I took to signify assent. Preece indicated a low bench in the shade of the vines. 'If you'd like to sit there for a moment,' he said, 'I'll call you in when it's ready.' And then, turning to Billy, who was showing signs of wanting to resume his discussion with me: 'Go on now – the sooner you're off, the sooner you'll be back.' The boy flitted away towards the gate with Preece following on at his own slow pace.

I sank gratefully on to the bench. Bullen made no move to join me there but stood looking down the garden, tugging irritably at his beard.

'What is it?' I asked. 'Is anything wrong?'

He swung round savagely. 'For God's sake, Redbourne, you can see what's wrong. We've been palmed off with shoddy goods. As scrawny a runt as I've ever clapped eyes on, and a bloody half-and-half into the bargain. If I'd known—'

'Quietly, Bullen. Preece will hear you. And in any case, I don't see any great difficulty. Assuming Billy's up to the job—'

'How could he be up to the job? I'm prepared to believe that he knows the territory – these people always do – but how's he going to cope with his share of the baggage? We need a man with the strength of a mule, and we're lumbered with a skinny boy.'

'Appearances can be deceptive. And no one in his senses would set himself up with a job he knew to be beyond his capabilities.'

'These are poor people, Redbourne, scratching a living from the dirt. You can see how it is. I send word that we're willing to pay good money for certain services, and of course they'll come forward claiming to be able to provide those services. Whether they can be relied upon to do so is another matter.'

What little I had seen of our hosts inclined me to give them the benefit of the doubt, but all my attempts to reason Bullen into a more charitable frame of mind proved futile. I was relieved when Preece appeared at the window and called us in to eat.

It took me some moments to adjust to the gloom of the interior but there wasn't, in truth, a great deal to see. Bare walls and floor, the sleeping area curtained off from the living room with a length of plain burlap; four shelves supported on iron brackets, three lined with books and one piled untidily with cooking utensils; a small blackleaded stove, a sturdy pine table set for our meal and four wicker-seated chairs that had evidently seen better days. There was only one item of any distinction: against the side wall stood a dresser of dark oak, beautifully crafted and speaking with mute eloquence of another time and place.

'It's not what you're used to, perhaps,' said Preece, catching my glance, 'but you'll get used to worse once you're out in the bush. And I'll guarantee,' he added, motioning us to our seats, 'you'll not taste food as good as this again before your return.' He leaned over the stove and began to ladle thick orange-brown stew into an earthenware bowl.

At certain junctures in my privileged but not entirely happy life, I had found solace in contemplating the pleasures of a simpler existence. Imaginary pleasures, I would tell myself, returning obediently on each occasion to the cares and duties I was born to; but sitting at my meal with Preece that afternoon, listening as he discoursed with quiet passion on his own experience of simple living, I was seized again by the old longings, and forcefully struck by the notion that a man might take more pleasure in a single well-managed acre than in a neglected estate.

Bullen was clearly less favourably impressed than I was. I could see him out of the corner of my eye, shifting and fidgeting as Preece veered from agricultural matters to philosophical speculation, and at last he set down his spoon, scraped back his chair and rose to his feet. 'I'm going for a stroll,' he said. 'Do you want to join me, Redbourne?'

'No,' I answered, irritated by the interruption and scarcely troubling to glance up. 'I'll stay here.'

'As you please.' Bullen picked up his rifle and strode to the door. 'Call me when the boy arrives with the luggage.' I heard the rap of his boot heels on the steps, and then he was gone.

17

I was, to tell the truth, glad to be rid of Bullen for a while, and I sensed that Preece felt much the same. His manner became more confiding, his matter more directly personal, and I, for my part, was sufficiently intrigued to encourage his disclosures. I don't mean to imply that there was anything culpably indiscreet about his conversation, but it seemed to me that I was being offered privileged access to his life, and I was flattered by the thought. His childhood, I gathered, had been a happy one, and he had been considered something of a scholar in the small-town school he had attended, but he had chosen to follow his father into the mines, moving westward in his early twenties as the industry expanded.

'It wasn't what my parents had wanted for me, but I was doing well for myself, earning good wages. My lodgings were cheap and I'd no family to support, nor any vices to speak of, so I was able to put something by. I'd had it in mind from the time I started at the mine that I should work there until I was thirty and then get out and buy myself some property – a few acres, a small herd of cattle. I'd even chosen the spot. There's a stretch of land along the Hawkesbury river, a little beyond Wise-man's Ferry, that I used to visit with my parents when I was a child – meadows so fresh and green they seemed to glow with their own light. That was where I thought I'd fetch up, though as you see . . .' He leaned back in his chair and spread his calloused hands palm upward.

'It seems to me, Preece, that you're very well placed here.'

'Oh, don't mistake me. I'm where I belong, and glad of it. But in those days I thought a man – any strong-willed man – could choose his path through life, and I had to learn through suffering that that's not so. I had a notion that by bending my body to my will I could bend the world, and the closer I drew to my thirtieth birthday, the harder I drove myself. In the end I was working all the hours I could keep myself upright, sometimes two shifts back to back. I won't say no one questioned it, but no one stopped me. There was an under-standing: they needed the labour – and when I was whole there wasn't a man in the company could match me load for load – and I wanted the money. And though I'd begun by imagining a small-holding, I came to think – well, it was a kind of madness, Mr Redbourne, dreaming of myself as a big

172

landowner in a fancy house. Thoroughbred, servants, society wife, the lot. I'd got it all mapped out in my head, that other life, so different from the one I was leading. And though I knew it for a dream, I couldn't rid myself of it.'

'Young men are bound to dream,' I said. 'It's natural. And there's no telling how their visions may inform the pattern of their future lives.' I was thinking, in fact, of my own case, of the strange, late flowering of my youthful ambitions in a land as extraordinary as any I had ever dared to imagine.

'True enough. But I think this was a dream gone wrong, like clear spring water souring where it pools. And what I was about to tell you is that it came near to destroying me. It was a sweltering evening in early January, and I rolled up for the night shift half dead on my feet with weariness. My mates could see at once that I wasn't fit for work. "You go home," they said, "go home and get some sleep." It was good advice, but I wouldn't heed it. And that was the night the dream came to an end.'

There was a crash from outside, the echoing report of a rifle-shot. Preece eased himself to his feet and stepped over to the doorway, squinting into the sunlight. 'It sounds as though your friend is starting as he means to go on,' he said drily. There was, I thought, a hint of reproof in the observation, but I didn't respond. After a moment, he returned to his chair and picked up the thread of his tale.

'I was working, I remember, in a kind of daze, keeping at it by sheer force of will. I was hunkered down when it happened, reaching for my pick, my cheek up close against the coalface so I couldn't see clearly. I heard it all right, though – a hard, tearing sound as the lump split from the seam – and if I'd had my wits about me I might have got clear in time, but I was slow on the uptake and slow on my feet. I remember one of my mates crying out, but I think I was already under it by then, pinned by the legs and twisting from side to side like a crushed snake.

'I was lucky to be alive, I see that now, but that's not the way it seemed then. I was screaming fit to wake the dead as they lifted the fallen coal, moaning and crying out as they stretchered me down to my lodgings. When Dr Milner told me the left leg would be fine, I knew at once what he was going to tell me about the other, and I began to blubber like a baby. He'd have had it off there and then, but I wouldn't let him. "You think it over," he said at last, "and I'll call by again first thing." I let him dress it as best he could, but I wouldn't take the morphine he gave me, for fear of weakening my resolve.

'When he arrived next morning, I told him I wanted more time. "More time for what?" he said angrily, and then, a little more gently: "You must believe me, Owen, the leg's too badly smashed to mend." There were moments I thought so myself, but there was a kind of stubbornness in me kept me going, though the pain gave me no rest. "You're putting your life in danger", Dr Milner told me when he called again that evening. "If you won't let me amputate, I'll take no further responsibility for you." Even then I wouldn't let him. I was waiting. I can see that now.'

'Waiting? For what?'

'For her. The third morning after the accident she turned up at the door. Let herself in as though she'd been summoned, though I know for a fact that no one had sent for her. I'd had a terrible night, I remember, the pain a little dulled by that time but lodged close, if you take my meaning, as if it had moved deeper into my body and meant to stay. And I can see it now, how she steps in – yes, with the shine from outside making a path from the doorway to the foot of my bed so that she seems to be walking on light – and unslings a small basket from her shoulder. And though she comes towards me so softly—'

'Who is this, Preece? Who are you talking about?'

'My wife. I mean the woman who was to bear my child, though at the time I'm speaking of, I'd no more idea of that than – but that's not quite right. Because what I was going to say was that as she approached the bed, I began to tremble, and my heart banged away at my ribcage like a steam-hammer.'

'Love at first sight,' I suggested, smiling.

There was no answering smile. He was staring out through the open door, his eyes glittering in his thin face.

'Love didn't come into it,' he said. 'Not then. Just the certainty that she was there by way of answer to some cry or prayer I'd been too proud to utter. And it was fear I felt – no doubt of it – but something else too: a sense of being visited by a power that wasn't my own. Not hers either – not exactly – but streaming from her like sunlight off a looking-glass. I'd been a chapel-goer all my life and I'd often thought about those early Methodists, the way they'd known the call when it came. Well, this was my call, Mr Redbourne, only it came from a quarter I'd no knowledge of – had barely thought about. And perhaps that's the nub of the matter: we know it's the real thing because it's like nothing we could ever have invented for ourselves.'

'So this was some kind of religious conversion?'

He seemed to consider the phrase. 'I don't know what you'd call it,' he said at last. 'What I do know is that from the moment she walked through the door I understood that my life was set to change, bottom to top.'

'And your leg?'

'I was coming to that. She set her basket on the floor and pulled the coverings down to the bed-end. And it might have been because of the pain and fever, but I felt no shame at that, nor when she lifted my nightshirt and pushed it back. And she, for her part, didn't flinch, though knee to ankle looked like something you'd find on a butcher's slab. Everything was strange, yet nothing seemed out of place, if you see what I mean. I remember her holding the leg, just above the damage – her hands very cool against my skin. And with that, the pain drew off, and the fear with it, and I found myself watching her with a kind of curiosity, as though her actions had nothing to do with me. She reached down and took a little knife from the basket – not a steel knife, but one of the chipped stone blades they make. And even though I thought at first she was going to cut me, I wasn't remotely troubled by the idea.'

'But she didn't?'

'Cut me? No. She stretched out her arm and rolled up the sleeve of her blouse. Then she nicked the flesh' – he tapped the spot on his own arm – 'just here, on the inside of her elbow, and began sucking at it.'

I said nothing, but my expression must have given me away. 'Maybe we're the unnatural ones,' he said, looking hard at me. 'Anyhow, you can't judge this until you've heard the upshot. After a while she spat the blood into her palms and rubbed it over the upper part of my leg, very gently at first and then with firmer movements. And as she worked – I can't explain this, Mr Redbourne, I can only tell you what happened – as she ran her hands back and forth, my leg began to throb and twitch, and the life flooded back into it like water through a lifted sluicegate. I don't want to call it a miracle – it was weeks before I was able to walk again and, as you see, I'm still slow on my feet – but the point is, the leg was saved. And that's not the whole of it, either, because whatever happened on that morning set my mind off in new directions. I had plenty of time for reflection in the days that followed, of course, and little by little I came to see what a fool I'd been, reaching out for a dream while the life I'd been given slipped by without my noticing. She showed me what I'd almost lost, and made it all real to me again. Just ordinary things, you might say – the sound of rain beating on the panes or the doorsill, the smell of hot bread, her footfall as she crossed the floor to tend to me – but coming at me so sharp and sweet they brought the tears to my eyes . . . Does this make sense to you, Mr Redbourne?'

I nodded. It crossed my mind that I might tell him something about Eleanor, but before I could speak, he rose stiffly to his feet and pulled open one of the drawers of the dresser. 'I'd like you to see this,' he said, handing me a photograph mounted on a dog-eared rectangle of green card. 'It doesn't do her justice, but it catches something of the look of her.'

The photograph itself was scarcely larger than a postcard and I had some difficulty in making out the detail, but it seemed at first sight to be a rather conventional studio portrait. Preece's tale had led me to expect a figure altogether more dramatic than this full-featured housewife, a little beyond the first flush of youth, her hair pulled back from her face in the European fashion and her dark skin set off by a plain white blouse. But peering more closely, I was struck by something in her gaze, some quality of abstraction or inward concentration, as though she'd taken the measure of it all – the photographer and his paraphernalia, the absurd painted backdrop she'd been posed against – and decided that it didn't concern her. It wasn't haughtiness exactly, and certainly not contempt, but she had the look of a woman whose mind was on higher or deeper things. I handed back the photograph. 'Mrs Preece was evidently a woman of character,' I said.

'She never took my name. To tell you the truth, we didn't marry, though that wasn't for want of asking on my part. "We have what we have," she used to say. Sometimes I wondered whether she'd already given herself – to one of her own people, I mean – before she came to me, but she never said, and it didn't seem right to question her. I didn't even know where she came from – she certainly wasn't from the mountains – but after a while there seemed no need for questions. She was right: we had what we had, and though I wish she'd been with us for longer, you'll not hear me complain.'

I sat very still, waiting, watching his face. He seemed to have withdrawn into a state of quiet meditation, and after a while it occurred to me that he had said all he wished to say, and that I should leave him to his thoughts. But as I made to rise, he looked up sharply, as though at some unwarranted interruption, and I realised that there was more to come.

'They were the best years of my life, no doubt of it, the years I spent with her. Once she had me back on my feet again I found work in the company office, but I knew that wasn't for me. I was biding my time, Mr Redbourne, waiting for the next thing. Not fretting, just waiting. And one day she looked across at me as we sat at breakfast – and I remember her having to raise her voice a little against the rattle and clank of the freight-wagons going by on the track beyond the back yard – and she said, very simply and firmly, "I don't want the child to grow up here." That was how she broke the news to me, and it was the sign I'd been waiting for. Within a fortnight I'd found this plot, and by the time Billy was born the hut was built and furnished, and I'd started to clear the scrub out back. And as I worked, the strength returned to my arms and shoulders, and the hope to my heart – not the mad hope of wealth and power that had led me astray, but a sweet and steady sense of the worth of what I was doing.

'We weren't well off – I'd left my job as soon as I was sure that the plot was mine – but I was never worried on that score. And Billy – well, the child was a revelation to me. I mean, I hadn't known I could feel such tenderness, such patient tenderness. He was just a scrap of a thing at first, so small the midwife doubted he'd survive, but when I cradled him for the first time in the crook of my arm and felt the softness of his skin against mine – do you have children, Mr Redbourne?'

I shook my head. 'I'm not married,' I said. 'I've only recently begun to consider what I might have missed.'

'Well,' he said, manoeuvring with a tact and delicacy that took me by surprise, 'a child's no guarantee of happiness, nor a wife neither. But speaking for myself, I felt truly blessed. It was a kind of heaven we lived in then – she and I grown so close for all our differences, and the child drawing us closer still. I remember sitting with them one day in the shade of the back wall, looking down over the ripening crops. And I thought, I want nothing more than this. If that wasn't heaven, Mr Redbourne, I don't know what is. And heavenly too because, strange as it sounds, I had no thought of it coming to an end, no thought at all.'

He faltered and broke off, evidently caught off guard by his emotions. I should have liked to be able to respond with greater compassion, but I knew too little about the man and his sorrows, and I simply sat back in respectful silence until he resumed.

'It was like a bolt of thunder from a cloudless sky. I'd been out until dusk, splitting wood for the stove, and I came in to find her in her chair, exactly where you're sitting now, with her head in her hands. And that was strange because there was no food on the table and she wasn't one for sitting around when there was work to be done. She raised her head as I came close, but slowly, as though it were weighed down in some way, and

I could sense then that something was amiss. I dropped the firewood I was carrying and knelt beside her there, reaching for her hand. And as soon as I touched her skin, I felt the chill of it, a chill from somewhere far down in her body. "What is it?" I asked her, and my heart was banging already as though it knew something my head didn't. "What is it?"

'It was a gift she had, to be able to tell me what was in her mind without putting it into words – with a look, it might be, or with something less than a look. She just lowered her eyes, and something in the manner of her doing it frightened me horribly – as if she were saying, *Enough* or *It's over.* "I'll fetch the doctor," I said, knowing full well she'd no more want to see one of our doctors than plunge her arm in scalding water, but I was in a panic, d'you see, not knowing what to do, and that was all I could think of. Anyway, she shook her head, very slow and sad, and placed her hand over mine, and we just sat there watching as night came on and the stars brightened in the sky. After some time she told me I should go to bed – insisted on it, with a kind of anger I'd not seen in her before, though I sorely wanted to stay – and I left her there, her arms folded across her breast, her body hunched and twisted a little to one side, leaning out into the darkness.

'It was just getting light when I woke to see her over by the window, kneeling beside the dilly-bag she'd brought with her when she first moved in with me. When I saw that – saw her packing a spare skirt and blouse, her ebony hairbrush, a velvet ribbon – I thought perhaps I'd misunderstood, and that she'd simply decided to go away for a while. But there was something in the set of her face that told me otherwise, and at last she straightened up and said very quietly, "I'm going home." "This is your home," I said, and with that I hauled myself out of bed and stepped towards her. But she backed away as though she didn't know me, as though I might harm her. "To my people's lands," she said, and then, very softly: "It's time."

'Of course I was in a terrible state – you can imagine – but not wanting to let on, not wanting to hinder her. "What shall I tell Billy?" I asked. "I've spoken to Billy," she said. Then she picked up her bag and walked out, quite slowly and carefully, the way people do when they're in pain, but not hesitating at all. I wanted to hurry after her and catch her in my arms, but I could see that wouldn't be the right thing. She stepped away down the track, very clear at first in the early sunlight, then half lost against the shine and shadow of the trees. I watched her out of sight, but she didn't once look back.'

He leaned forward in his chair and stared out through the doorway, his mouth clamped tight and his eyes glistening.

'And you had no word from her?'

'Never. Nor expected it. But for weeks after she'd gone I dreamed of her, night in, night out. Always in the same flat landscape – very harsh and dry, scattered with boulders. No shadow, the sun beating down on her. I can't tell you what it was like to see her out there time after time, very small and lost, with the desert stretching as far as you could see on every side. And she was searching, it seemed to me, always searching, so that I found myself desperate to help, but because I wasn't allowed to be with her – I can't say exactly how it was, but that

much was plain – there was nothing I could do. There was a
time I thought it would go on like that for the rest of my life
and maybe beyond, the same vision over and over; but one
night, a couple of months after she'd left, I saw her walking
along very fast, her head up and all her movements firm and
certain. No searching now, and her step so light that her feet
barely touched the sand. There was no change in the landscape – none that I could see – but I knew she'd found what
she was after. And as I looked, her form thinned and dwindled
like a scarf of mist when the sun breaks through, and I woke
with a cry of joy on my lips or in my ears – her cry or mine,
it wasn't clear, and it didn't matter – and hurried to the doorway. It was still dark, but with that faint stirring or softening
that you sometimes feel in the few moments before dawn. And
as I looked out, I knew there was no call to fret about her any
more, and my heart – well, I was weeping like a child, but there
was no bitterness in the tears. After that—'

He stopped and raised his head. I had heard it too, an inarticulate shout ending on a rising note, half roar, half yelp. A second
or two of blank silence followed, and then a string of sharply
delivered expletives. 'Something's got Mr Bullen's dander up,'
said Preece grimly, levering himself to his feet. He limped over
to the doorway and peered about, one hand lifted to shade his
eyes, then stumped down the steps and out on to the track.

It was Billy, I saw, as I followed Preece out, who had aroused
Bullen's wrath. The boy stood between the two ponies, his
head thrown back in sulky defiance, while Bullen berated him
in a vicious undertone. '*Damned fool of a boy*', I heard as we

approached. '*Cack-handed incompetent*'. The reaction might have
been excessive and the language uncalled-for, but the reason
for Bullen's rage was immediately apparent: the ground was
strewn with cartridges, evidently spilled from the open ammunition box that Billy was clutching in his left hand.

'What's going on?' asked Preece.

'You can see what's going on. The lad's been scattering our
ammunition about like seed-corn.'

'I've done nothing wrong,' said Billy. 'The box fell open as
I was unloading it. Look.' He held up the object and shook
it, making the hinged lid clack and swing. 'If it had been
properly fastened—'

'That's enough, Billy,' said Preece, leaning forward and laying a hand on the boy's arm. 'There's stew for you in the pot.
You go on in and leave us to attend to the baggage.' He eased
the box from the boy's hand, dropped awkwardly to one knee
and began to gather up the spilled ammunition.

'It's as well I arrived back when I did,' said Bullen, turning
to me as Billy stalked off. 'There's no knowing what damage he
might have done.'

Preece looked up over his shoulder. 'It was an accident,
Mr Bullen,' he said. 'Just an accident.' Bullen opened his mouth
as though to reply, but seemed to think better of it. He stepped
over to the nearer of the two ponies and began to unfasten the
luggage-straps.

By the time we had the luggage indoors the sun had sunk
behind the trees, and the sky outside was fading to a softer
blue. I should have liked to sit and rest, but with Preece

wordlessly tidying the room around us and Billy huddled over a book in the corner, pointedly refusing to acknowledge our presence, it seemed sensible to get out of the hut and to take Bullen with me.

A light breeze was springing up as we left, stirring the eucalyptus leaves into whispering life. Bullen strode off at an unnecessarily brisk pace, still visibly angry and showing no sign of wanting either my company or my conversation. We had travelled a good half-mile along the track before he slowed and turned to address me. 'What a pair of fools we've been landed with,' he said. 'I've been badly let down over this business, Redbourne, I don't mind telling you.'

'It's too early to make a judgement. Give the boy a chance to prove his mettle.'

'And each as bad as the other,' he went on, ignoring my intervention. 'The son incapable of carrying out the simplest task and the father a fount of nonsense. And you should know better, Redbourne – it's no kindness to encourage a man of his sort by listening to his ramblings.'

'It seemed to me,' I said cautiously, 'that some of his views were worthy of serious consideration.'

'Preece is a fool and his views are balderdash. What kind of progress do you think we'd have made in a country like this if we'd been guided by such views?

Make no mistake about it, Redbourne, the wilderness doesn't want us here. We're engaged in a war, an unending battle with a heartless enemy, and men like Preece, with their crackbrain dreams of harmony, are a menace to us all.'

'Yet there's something persuasive in his arguments. Listening to him, I had some notion of a better future – for myself certainly, maybe for all of us.'

'But look at the man, Redbourne, look at the way he's living. He's a throwback, barely one rung up from the savages he evidently consorts with. If I believed that the future of humankind rested in the hands of men like that, I'd cut my throat.'

I wasn't inclined to let him have the last word on the subject, but as I meditated my reply I became aware of a clamour in the air overhead. I looked up. 'Ravens,' said Bullen, lifting an imaginary rifle and drawing a bead on the flock. They were calling as they flew, not in the guttural tones of our own ravens, but high and clear, a disconsolate wailing sound. I watched them cross the pale strip of sky above us, drifting over like flakes of soot, and as I stood gazing, something in their sombre progress and the melancholy music of their cries stirred me so deeply that, just for the barest instant, I imagined myself in uncorrupted communion with the wilderness and the luminous skies above it.

Perhaps Bullen felt something too. As the cries died away, I saw him shiver and clutch his jacket more tightly about his body. Then we turned, moving in unison as though at some inaudible word of command, and made our way slowly back to the hut.

18

It was still dark when we rose the next morning, but by the time the ponies had been watered and loaded up the light was beginning to filter through the mist. Billy appeared to have dressed up for the occasion, in a pair of fawn-coloured breeches, frayed but neatly pressed, and a startlingly white shirt or blouse of unconventional cut, loose-fitting and wide open at the neck. Flitting ahead of us as we set off down the track, he seemed to shimmer and dance on the air, more spirit than substance.

The mist drew off with remarkable suddenness, exposing a serene sky, clear blue overhead but stained towards the west by a long, flattened band of mauve cloud. The sun was still low but it touched the tops of the eucalyptus trees, making the red tips of the leaves glow like fire. Preece and Bullen appeared to be in sombre mood, but I was in a state of strange excitement, my mind alert and all my senses heightened. Everything delighted me – the beaded threads of gossamer strung among the shrubs, the drone of a passing insect, the wet shine of the fern-leaves, the fragrance exhaled from the freshened earth. Every so often I would stop to examine the plants growing beside the track, not with a botanist's interest but with the curiosity of a child. Running my hand lightly across a cluster of vivid blue florets, I was struck by the thought that I had no name for the plant that bore them, nor for any of the other small plants whose flowers glowed in the muted light beneath the trees. In normal circumstances my ignorance would have irked me, but that morning I took a deep pleasure in the very namelessness of the things around me and I remember wondering, not entirely playfully, whether Adam's fall might have begun not with the eating of a fruit but earlier, with the arising of the desire to catalogue the animals and plants in his teeming paradise.

The air quickly grew hot but we pressed on without stopping, and a little before midday we emerged on to a tract of more open land, a long slope of grass and low brush punctuated at intervals by small sandstone outcrops. From somewhere higher up, I heard the mellow warbling of an unseen bird and, closer at hand, the faint trickle of water. Preece led the ponies a little uphill, hugging the shade, before bringing them to a halt and beginning to disburden them.

'Is this it?' asked Bullen.

Preece gestured obliquely across the slope below us. 'A couple of hundred yards on, where the scrub thickens again, you'll start to take a line along the cliff face. It's not as dangerous as it sounds, but it's no route for a pony, laden or unladen. Nor,' he added with a wry smile, 'for a man with a gammy leg.' He tugged a bundle clear of its fastenings and handed it to Billy. 'We'll just get this done, and then we'll see about lunch.'

Looking back, I invest that meal with a significance it could hardly have held for me at the time. The sweetfleshed fowl we shared, the bread we broke, the clear water lifted in cupped hands from the trickling rill, all appear now as emblems of untainted wholeness, and our eating and drinking as a valedictory ritual. But then? I was, quite simply, impatient to get on. I remember moving away from my companions as the meal drew to a close and gazing down at the faint line of the track ahead, eagerly tracing its meandering course, its sudden drop and disappearance into the scrub.

'A word with you, Redbourne,' said Bullen, stepping up alongside me.

'What is it?'

'The boy's fee. Preece is asking for payment now.'

'Of course.' I fumbled in my pocket for my purse but Bullen drew close and gripped me by the arm. 'Offer him half now and half on our return,' he whispered into my ear. 'That way we'll be sure of the pair of them.'

Something in his words, in his absurd conspiratorial posture, filled me with disgust. 'For God's sake,' I said, shaking myself impatiently free of him. 'If we can't trust people like Preece and Billy, who can we trust?'

'For my part,' he said coldly, 'I trust no one. You may do as you like.' He turned on his heel and stalked off.

I called Preece over and paid him the modest fee he requested. He resisted my attempt to give him an additional sum for our food and lodging, observing, with a turn of phrase that would have done credit to a man of a far higher station in life, that he had been amply rewarded by the pleasure of my company and required no other recompense for his hospitality. 'And this,' he said, shifting ground before I had time to pursue the matter, 'is where it begins in earnest. You've a testing time ahead, no doubt of it.'

'You seemed earlier to be making light of the dangers.'

'I said that the route's not as dangerous as you might imagine, but it's no Sunday stroll either, and you've more baggage than I'd recommend for the journey. Go carefully. And please', he added, glancing up anxiously, 'look after Billy.'

I smiled. 'I thought Billy was here to look after us.'

'Oh, he knows the land well enough – I'm not troubled about him on that score. But he's had very little experience of dealing with people, and Mr Bullen' – he hesitated, lowered his voice – 'Mr Bullen is a difficult man.'

'I give you my word,' I said. 'Billy will come to no harm.'

'Thank you, Mr Redbourne. I'll be waiting here with the ponies five days from now, Wednesday midday. Billy can time it right, just so long as he's not hindered. Would you see to it that Mr Bullen doesn't interfere with his planning?'

I looked up to where Bullen and Billy were stooping together over our kit, their heads almost touching. 'You've no cause for concern,' I said. 'Mr Bullen will be as keen as any of us to ensure that everything runs according to plan.' Preece was silent. I had the distinct impression that he was waiting for me to continue, but there seemed nothing more to say, and after a moment we moved slowly back up the slope to rejoin the others.

Preece was not, it struck me as he took his leave of us, a man given to dissembling his feelings: the perfunctoriness of his farewell to Bullen was in marked contrast to the warmth with which he shook me by the hand. 'I'll wish you a safe journey, gentlemen,' he said. And then, without any of the awkwardness or embarrassment I remember my own father displaying on similar occasions, he took his son in his arms and held him close. 'And you, too, Billy,' he whispered, releasing the boy at last and turning quickly away. He mounted the taller of the two ponies and, with the other falling into step behind, rode off the way we had come.

I have to confess to being gripped, as I watched him disappear from view among the trees, by a spasm of some-thing close to panic. With Preece at our side, I had barely given a thought all morning to the wide and increasing distance between us and the civilised world, but in that instant I saw with disquieting clarity just where I stood. I mean, literally so: out on that open slope, surrounded by the bush and its wild denizens, under the blank glare of a cloud-less sky. I felt my legs trembling beneath me, and it was a moment or two before I felt able to join Bullen and Billy at their work.

They had divided our baggage into three units, two of which had been bound with leather strapping and thick twine to form bulky packs. Bullen was working on the third, while Billy was attaching an array of smaller items to the other two – a kerosene lamp, a cooking-pan, an iron ladle, a length of coiled rope. What had seemed a modest enough load when conveyed by other means now appeared intimidatingly large and cumbersome.

'Do we really need all this?' I asked.

Bullen raised his head and fixed me with a cold stare. 'If we didn't,' he said, 'we wouldn't have brought it. Give me a hand with this strap.'

Once the packs were ready, Bullen sent Billy to fill the water-canteen. 'Your pack,' he murmured, leaning in close as the boy moved away, 'isn't as heavy as it looks. I've taken care to distribute the items appropriately.'

'Appropriately?'

'You'll be carrying less weight. There's no point in wearing you out.'

'Then your own pack—'

'Billy's pack, Redbourne. Billy will take up the slack.'

'You mean he'll carry the heaviest load?'

'Exactly. It's what we're paying him for.'

'He's here as our guide, not as a beast of burden.'

'Guide and porter, Redbourne. That's what he signed on for.'

'Even so, he's a young lad, and not strongly built.'

'The very point I was making yesterday. "Give him a chance to prove his mettle," you said. Well, he has his chance, and we'll see what he makes of it.' He glanced up as Billy began to walk back towards us. 'Best to say no more about this,' he whispered. 'With any luck, he won't even realise.'

Billy lashed the canteen to one of the packs and tugged tentatively at the straps. 'Not that one, Billy,' said Bullen. 'This is yours.'

It crossed my mind that I might, by a sleight Bullen would be obliged to ignore, exchange my pack for Billy's, but the boy was already squatting down, wrestling his burden on to his narrow shoulders. I saw him stagger as he rose, his thin frame taut with strain, and I stepped forward to steady him.

'It's all right, Mr Redbourne. I'm stronger than I look.' He straightened his back a little and took a few careful steps. 'I've carried heavier loads.'

'You're to tell me if it becomes too much for you. Do you hear me, Billy?'

He glared up at me from beneath his dark fringe. 'I'm not a child,' he said. 'There's no call to fuss over me.' It seemed best to drop the matter. Bullen and I shouldered our own packs, and the three of us set off, moving cautiously down the slope towards the shadowy edge of the scrub below.

19

Bullen seemed particularly ill-humoured that afternoon, and I quickly tired of his company. Wherever the track narrowed I would drop back and slow down, hoping that he would press ahead, but on each occasion he simply matched his pace to mine while Billy, trailing some twenty or thirty yards behind us, did the same. From time to time, guiltily conscious of the weight the boy was carrying, I would turn to make sure that he was bearing up. He would nod or raise his hand in casual acknowledgement, but he made no attempt to close the gap.

Late in the afternoon we reached an open space, a small clearing where the wall of rock above us curved away from the path in a wide, irregular arc to create a flat arena of rough grassland. Bullen stopped and looked around. 'Perfect,' he said. 'We'll set up our base here.'

I stepped off the path and immediately found myself ankle-deep in soft ooze. 'We can't camp here,' I said. 'Look at this.' I stood on one leg, extending my muddied boot towards him.

Bullen gave me a patronising smile. 'Not in the swamp,' he said carefully, as though speaking to an obtuse child. 'I meant over there.' He indicated a point a little further on, where the curve of the cliff wall brought it back to the edge of the track.

As we advanced, I realised what had attracted his attention. The section of the cliff he had pointed out to me was extensively eroded, undercut from a height of about ten feet to form a shallow recess. I could see at once that the protection afforded by the overhang, though limited, would be useful. Moreover, I noticed as we reached the spot that the sandstone floor of the recess projected forward from the line of the cliff, a platform of firm, dry ground raised a little above the level of the swampland. There was no sign of running water in the vicinity but, that apart, the site seemed ideal.

Bullen slipped the straps from his shoulders and eased his pack to the ground. 'We'll set up a lean-to against the rock,' he said. 'Just there, where the undercut's deepest.' He turned to Billy who was labouring up the path towards us. 'You hear that, Billy?'

The boy dropped his burden and squinted up at the rock face; then, without a word, he was off, picking his way along the margin of the swamp until he reached the platform of solid rock that fronted the recess. Bullen shot me an irritable glance.

'It's not intentional,' I said. 'He's tired. You can see it in his face.'

'What I see in his face,' said Bullen sharply, 'is insolence. Sheer insolence. What's he up to now?'

Billy was standing beneath the overhang, peering from side to side, his face close up against the sandstone wall. I saw him reach up and place his palm against the hollowed surface, then step away and stumble wearily back to rejoin us.

'Good enough for you?' asked Bullen sardonically. 'Do you think you'll be comfortable?'

'Not here,' said Billy. 'I'll find us a better place.'

'Better than this? Where?'

'A little further down the track.'

'How much further?'

The boy shrugged. 'About an hour,' he said vaguely. 'Maybe two.'

'It's getting late,' said Bullen, glancing up at the sky. 'We're staying.'

'Not here,' insisted Billy, stubbornly. 'We mustn't stay here.'

'Mustn't? What the devil do you mean by that?' Bullen swung round to face him, flushing with anger.

Billy shifted uncomfortably from foot to foot, his head averted. 'This place belongs to my mother's people,' he said quietly. 'It's a gathering place.'

Bullen looked up and down the track in exaggerated dumb-show. 'I don't see any sign of a gathering,' he said. 'Do you?'

'They're here whether we see them or not. The ancestors, I mean. People from the faraway time. Except they're not people, not exactly. They're . . .' He faltered and turned towards me, holding out his arms in silent appeal, as if he thought I might be able to explain or amplify his halting phrases for Bullen's benefit.

'Listen, Billy,' I said gently. 'Mr Bullen thinks this is a suitable place, and I have to say that I agree with him. The stories your mother told you when you were a child shouldn't be allowed to govern your life now that you're growing to manhood. When we're young we're entitled to indulge our fancies, but maturity entails a more stringent vision of the world.'

'But the stories are true stories. My mother said so.'

Bullen gave a snort of exasperation. 'We're stopping here,' he said, 'and that's the end of it. We need poles, Billy, a dozen strong poles. Ten of them about my height, and a couple of longer ones. Take this' – he tugged his hand-axe from his belt and held it out – 'and see what you can find.' Billy hesitated for a moment, standing stock still, his eyes fixed ferociously on the ground in front of him; then he reached out, snatched the axe and strode back down the track the way we had come.

'It seems to me,' I said, as soon as I judged the boy to be out of earshot, 'that the matter will require careful handling. Billy clearly believes—'

'I don't care what he believes, Redbourne. He's in our employ and he'll do as I tell him. It's as simple as that. You can see he's been indulged by his father – all these sulks and silences when he feels he's been thwarted or put upon – and it's about time someone took him in hand.' He drew out his knife and began hacking savagely at the scrub, cutting from the base of each plant and piling the stems and branches alongside the track. 'We'll need plenty of this,' he said. 'Perhaps you'd be good enough to help me?'

It was his tone, rather than the request itself, that irked me. 'In a moment,' I answered coolly, moving away. I was reminding him, of course, that whatever authority he had assumed in his dealings with Billy he exercised none over me; but I was also genuinely curious to see what had aroused the boy's interest. I made my way to the rock face and scanned the shadowed wall beneath the overhang.

It took me a little time, but once I realised what I was looking for, I saw them everywhere: delicate handshapes outlined with a haze of reddish pigment, the fingers spread wide. They were concentrated in a ragged band around chest height, but some could be seen as high as the curve of the overhang, and several within a couple of feet of the platform. Where, at one point, the rock had been differentially eroded in such a way as to form a narrow shelf just above ground level, I found two hands aligned as though stretching towards one another on its horizontal surface.

'Bullen,' I called. 'Come and look at this.'

He clearly shared none of my excitement. 'I've seen such things before,' he said brusquely, turning away without a second glance. 'It's their idea of art.'

I should have liked to know more, but it was apparent that Bullen wasn't the man to ask. 'You wanted my help with the brushwood,' I said.

'If you can spare the time.'

The insult was delivered almost casually, and it seemed best to let it pass without comment. I took out my pocket knife and set to, working with a vicious energy that doubtless owed something to my resentment, and by the time Billy returned, trailing two slender saplings, topped and trimmed, I was drenched in perspiration and breathing hard. He dropped the saplings at the edge of the platform, and was moving off again, without a word, when Bullen called out to him: 'Billy, those aren't straight.'

Billy stopped in his tracks and turned back. 'The shorter ones are better than these,' he said, 'but nothing grows straight in this part of the forest. These are as good as you'll get if you want the length.'

'Those are the long ones? They'll need to be longer than that. The shelter has to be wide enough for the three of us.'

Billy shook his head. 'Just for you and Mr Redbourne,' he said. 'I'll not sleep here.'

Bullen shrugged and stooped to his task again but Billy, who had evidently been brooding on the matter, broke out in sudden fury: 'You think you know best, don't you? You think you can do what you like out here, trampling and cutting and breaking things down without thought of the spirits you're disturbing, without please or thank you or sorry. And you won't listen. You hire me as your guide but you won't be guided by me.'

I saw Bullen stiffen. He straightened up slowly and wiped his knife-blade twice across the rough fabric of his breeches. His voice, when he eventually spoke, was thick with suppressed anger. 'I hired you to show us the way and carry our kit, not to instruct us in the superstitions of a dying race. If you know what's good for you, you'll do the job you're being paid to do and keep your opinions to yourself. Do you hear me?'

'You'll see I'm right, Mr Bullen. You'll find out.'

Bullen lurched towards him but I was there first, seizing the boy by the elbow and steering him back towards the track. 'I'll help you carry up the other poles,' I said quickly. And then, under my breath, feeling the resistance in his trembling arm: 'Don't argue, Billy.' Only when I felt him fall into step with me did I consider it safe to relax my grip. We walked on for a minute or two in uncomfortable silence.

'If my father had known Mr Bullen was going to treat me like this,' he said at last, 'he'd never have let me come.'

'I think,' I said judiciously, 'that Mr Bullen might have behaved better. But the same applies to you, Billy. You must to learn to curb your anger.'

'If I'm angry, it's his fault. And anyway, it's not just anger. I'm frightened too.'

'What are you afraid of?'

'The ancestors.' He came to a sudden halt and glanced nervously around as though expecting ambush. 'I'm afraid for you and Mr Bullen if you build the shelter where you shouldn't. I'm afraid for myself if they think I'm to blame for bringing you here.'

Now that we had stopped walking, the trembling of his body was more noticeable and his face, as he turned towards me in the shade of the trees, looked drawn and grey. I reached out and gently touched his shoulder. 'There's nothing to worry about,' I said. 'The dead won't harm us.'

'Not if we treat them as we should, no. If you respect them, they'll look after you – keep you from danger, guide you home when you're lost. But if you anger them . . .' He paused, staring beyond me into the shadows, and I took advantage of the moment to shift ground.

'Those decorations on the rock face,' I said. 'The hands. When were they made?'

He shrugged his shoulders. 'A hundred years ago. A thousand. What does it matter?'

'I'm interested, that's all. It's natural to be curious about things we don't understand.'

'Maybe. But you might have to learn to understand them in a new way.' And then, his tone softening: 'You know how it's done?' He opened his mouth and mimed the placing of some object or substance on his extended tongue; then he held his left hand in front of his face, palm outward and fingers splayed, and blew softly against it. And just for a moment he seemed to draw away from me, his entire being concentrated in that mimic act, and I glimpsed fleetingly – a filigree of roots extending endlessly through subterranean channels – his dark, inexplicable connection with his mother's land.

I had imagined that I should have to spend the evening keeping Billy out of Bullen's reach, but the boy took matters into his own hands, slipping silently away as soon as he had brought up the last of the poles. Bullen, for his part, seemed barely to notice his absence, preoccupied as he was with the building of the shelter. He worked steadily and with uncharacteristic concentration, lashing the poles firmly together to form an irregular box and filling the sides and the sloping top with a taut lattice of twine before weaving in the strands and clumps of cut brushwood. He gave particular attention to the roof, selecting the densest vegetation and packing it as thickly as the slender framework allowed. At intervals he would rap out a curt instruction – 'Hold this', he'd say, or 'Tie that' – but he showed no sign of wanting to involve me more fully in the operation.

The finished structure, sited beneath the overhang but projecting a good three feet beyond it, looked neither neat nor entirely stable, but Bullen assured me that it would meet our needs for the next few days. 'Of course,' he added, stepping back to survey his handiwork, 'it may be more than we need, but up here the rain can sweep in so fast you hardly see it coming. It's as well to be prepared for the worst.'

'And Billy?' I asked. 'What protection will Billy have from the rain?'

'Billy has made his choice. If it proves to have been a foolish choice, that's not our fault. I want to make this clear, Redbourne: we've not brought the lad along for his benefit, but to make the journey easier for ourselves. And let me warn you now against taking his side against me. I've noticed it on more than one occasion, and you can bet your life he's noticed it too.'

I was stung by the accusation. 'I'm not taking sides,' I said heatedly. 'It's natural to have some concern for the boy's welfare.'

'He's a sly one, Redbourne. If it serves his turn, he won't hesitate to set us at loggerheads. Just bear that in mind next time you're tempted to stand up for him.' He broke away and strode over to the edge of the platform. 'Bedding,' he said tersely, squatting down above the ooze and hacking savagely at the marsh-grass with his knife. 'Give me a hand with this.'

By the time we had finished our task the light was fading. I was more tired than hungry, and I stretched out on my grass couch while Bullen lit a fire and boiled water for tea. I must have dozed off for a minute or two: I remember sitting up with a start, momentarily disorientated, then scrambling to the doorway and looking out.

I wonder now what it is about that scene that keeps it so vividly present in my mind: Bullen stooping redfaced over the flames while the eucalyptus twigs spit and crackle, his right arm extended as he tips tealeaves carefully from a screw of white paper into the steaming pan; behind him, the looming mass of the bush and, above that, the deepening colours of the evening sky. It has something to do, I suppose, with the incongruity of that little ceremony out there in all that unimaginable vastness; but I think, too, that the scene offers me a way of rehabilitating Bullen – of visualising him not simply as an invasive presence in a world too subtle and delicate for his clouded understanding, but also as the improbable heir of those aboriginal rock-painters, a keeper of the human flame in a dark, inhuman wilderness.

He glanced up as I emerged. 'Tea, bread and jerked beef,' he said. 'Not on a par with Vane's dinners, but good enough for now. Given a reasonable day's hunting, we'll no doubt eat better tomorrow evening.'

'Any sign of Billy?'

He bent to lift the pan from the fire. 'I imagine he's still sulking. He'll be back when he gets hungry.'

I ate a few mouthfuls and sipped at the scalding tea, but absently, my thoughts running on the boy. 'We might have expected him to show up by now,' I said. I rose to my feet and called his name, but there was no response. 'I'd better go and look for him.'

Bullen paused in his chewing and stared up at me. 'I'd not advise it,' he said. 'The lad's not far away, depend upon it. And he'd be only too pleased to think he's got you running around after him. I say we leave him to his own devices.'

'I can't do that. I'll not sleep easily until I know he's safe.'

Bullen shrugged. 'I tell you,' he said, 'you're fretting for nothing. But you must do as you please. I'm turning in for the night.'

He was right, of course. I wasn't twenty yards down the track before I saw Billy moving towards me, the white cloth of his shirt glimmering in the dusk. As he drew close I could see or sense a kind of wariness in him, as though he were uncertain what kind of reception he might expect.

'Did you call me, Mr Redbourne?'

'I was concerned about you, Billy. I'd expected you to join us for supper. Will you come up now?'

He shook his head. 'It's not a place for everyday doings. Anyway, Mr Bullen doesn't want me there. I can tell.'

'But you must eat. Shall I bring you some food?'

'I'm not hungry tonight. You've no need to worry about me, Mr Redbourne. I can look after myself.'

'You've no shelter. If it rains—'

'If it rains, I shall build my own shelter. But it won't rain. Not over the next few days. I could have told Mr Bullen that if he'd asked me.'

'Even so, I don't like to think of you out there alone.'

'I'll be safer out there than you'll be in your bushhut. At least I'm showing the ancestors the respect they deserve.' And then, more gently, as though to soften the implied reproach: 'Thank you for thinking about me, Mr Redbourne. And listen: if you see anything unusual, don't go near it. Leave the place as quickly as you can.'

'What kind of thing?'

'Maybe something like a human figure, or maybe some wild creature. But not an ordinary creature – you'll notice its strangeness as soon as you set eyes on it.'

I smiled. 'Billy,' I said, 'you have to remember that all the creatures here look strange to me.'

There was no answering smile. 'When people see them,' he continued, 'they know. Sometimes they can't even describe the thing they've seen, but they always know.' He gave a little shiver and drew the loose cloth of his shirt more closely around his shoulders.

'You'd better stop this talk, Billy. You're only frightening yourself.'

'I'm telling you things you need to understand. But I don't think you'll listen.' He turned and began to move off, slipping away from me into the darkness as Daniel had done that night at the Hall, and I cried out in sudden anguish: 'Billy!'

He stopped and looked back over his shoulder, his features invisible now. 'What is it, Mr Redbourne?'

'Nothing, Billy. Sleep well.' He turned again, and I stood and watched until the pale gleam of his shirt was lost among the shadows.

20

I was roused at first light by the echoing crash of riflefire, two shots in quick succession. I turned stiffly on my grass couch to find Bullen gone, his blanket thrown untidily back against the side wall. I pulled on my boots, rinsed my mouth with water from the canteen and went out to investigate.

I found him a couple of hundred yards up the track, squatting beside the path in a haze of tobacco-smoke, his back against the cliff wall and his rifle propped against a projecting branch. As I approached, he took the pipe from his mouth and hailed me.

'You're up early,' I said.

'I had a restless night. Dreams, noises, night-sweats, heaven knows what.' He ran his hand wearily across his face and I saw that he was trembling.

'What noises? I heard nothing.'

'Murmurings. Breathings and groans. I might have imagined them but they seemed real enough at the time.' He thumbed out his pipe and rose heavily to his feet. 'I'm glad you're here, Redbourne. You can give me a hand with these.'

Until that moment I hadn't noticed the bodies. Two wallabies, huddled on their sides against the cliff wall, the brown fur of their flanks streaked with blood.

'Right and left.' Bullen mimed the two shots. 'One after the other, dropped as they broke cover. I tell you, Redbourne, I'm as sharp now as I was twenty years ago.' He stepped over to the bodies, motioning me to follow, and then, leaning above the nearer of the two, gripped it by the wrist and dragged it on to the track. The head lolled back as the upper part of the body twisted round and I saw, with a shock of grief and astonishment, the rich orange fur of the creature's chest and throat. I stooped to examine it more closely and, as I did so, the muscular hindlegs twitched and kicked. I started back.

'It's still alive.'

'Barely.' He flashed me a grim smile. 'I'm not expecting it to recover.'

'But you can't—'

'I'll handle it. You take the other.'

He grasped the base of the tail and swung the wallaby over his shoulder, staggering a little under the weight. I found myself faintly unsettled by the rolling movement of the animal's slack mass against his back as he steadied himself and began to walk back down the track towards the camp, but I was relieved to see that there were no further signs of life. I bent down and tugged the second carcass clear of the cliff wall.

It was the weight, I suppose, of a young child – nothing unmanageable, but I had to brace my mind as well as my body before heaving it up, and I was glad to shrug myself free of it on reaching the platform. I had rather hoped that I might leave the skinning of both specimens to Bullen, but he ducked quickly into the shelter and re-emerged with a pair of skinning knives. 'You'll need this,' he said, handing me the smaller of the two.

'I prefer my own instruments.'

'They're too delicate for this job. Use the knife.' He straddled the larger carcass and heaved it on to its back. I remember the arms spread wide from the bright chest, the still eloquence of the small black hands; and then the knife moving slowly down from the throat to the genitals, fur and skin parting beneath the blade. I looked quickly away.

'I've not skinned anything like this before,' I said, turning over the second carcass.

'You've skinned a rabbit?'

I nodded.

'Think of it as a rabbit.' He gave a sharp bark of laughter. 'A bloody big rabbit. It's no different.'

It was, in fact, very different. In part, it was a question of the creature's size – the sheer bulk and density of the dead flesh – but I was struck too, leaning above the body, by the refinement of the long features and by some quality of gentle resignation in their expression. I hesitated for a long moment before beginning the incision.

'You'll need to bear down more firmly,' said Bullen, glancing across at me. 'You're not skinning a fairywren.'

I was sweating in the strengthening sunlight. A thick, musky odour came off the dead animal, and I felt the bile rise in my throat. I straightened up and threw down my knife, surprised by my own distress.

'I can't do this,' I said.

Bullen stepped over and shouldered me aside. 'Firm and smooth,' he said, drawing his blade down the creature's vivid bib. 'It's not difficult.'

I saw it, I think, a little before he did, the quick movement of pink flesh squirming back from the light as the flap of the cut pouch fell aside. I had read, of course, of the remarkable breeding habits of the continent's marsupial fauna, but for a second or two I was unable to interpret what I had seen. Then Bullen fumbled in the soft belly-fur and drew out the naked, writhing scrap, and I realised, with a renewed pang of grief, that he had shot a nursing mother.

He made light of my concern. 'Kill a female wallaby,' he said, turning the tiny oddity about in the palm of his hand, 'and it's ten to one you'll find her nursing. And at this stage' – he prodded at the translucent skin with a bloodstained forefinger – 'it's barely an animal at all. It doesn't do to get dewy-eyed about such things.' And as if to reinforce his point, he dropped the hapless creature to the ground and crushed it beneath his heel.

If I were asked to provide a rational explanation for my apparently irrational behaviour, I should say that I was responding to the casual cruelty of Bullen's action, but there was more to it than that. As the nailed heel came down, I experienced its weight as though the crushed spark of life were my own, and I felt myself, for the briefest instant, lost in a smothering darkness. I struggled like a man in the grip of a nightmare; then, as the darkness cleared, I rounded on Bullen with vituperative passion, my voice harsh and my whole body trembling.

'The creature couldn't have survived,' he said, cutting in quickly as I paused for breath. 'Surely you can see that? What kindness do you think there'd be in leaving nature to take its course?'

I breathed deeply, steadied myself. 'In themselves,' I said carefully, 'actions are neither cruel nor kind. Kindness and cruelty are qualities of the human heart. I saw no sign that your action was informed by kindness.'

'And what's in your own heart when you lift your rifle and draw a bead on a choice specimen? Where's the kindness then?'

I was searching for an answer when I became aware of Billy standing motionless on the track below, looking towards us, one hand pushing his thick hair back from his forehead and the other shading his eyes. 'Let's drop the matter,' I said brusquely. And then, in a more conciliatory tone: 'I'm afraid I wasn't thinking very clearly.' Bullen grunted and turned back to his task while I, with an obscure feeling of failure, busied myself with preparations for the day's expedition.

Bullen was by no means happy about having to deal with both wallabies himself. He had wanted to make an early start but the morning was well advanced by the time we set out from the camp, and for the first mile or so he seemed to find it impossible to open his mouth without venting his displeasure. I was careful not to respond, while Billy, now burdened with nothing weightier than the day's provisions, strode purposefully ahead, just out of conversational range. As we pressed on, however, the mood lightened a little, and our spirits were further lifted by the discovery of fresh water running in a thin cascade down the rock face above the track. Bullen held the canteen to the warm trickle until it was full, and we drank by turns until our thirst was quenched.

It has often struck me that my approach to the natural world is imaginative rather than analytical, and it was borne home to me with increasing force, as we plunged deeper into the wilderness, that my expectations concerning this part of our journey had been tinged with fantasy. In particular, I had vaguely supposed that our travels would bring us progressively closer to some teeming source or centre of life, and it was only when I traced this notion back to its origin – a painting remembered from boyhood and depicting a patently implausible gathering of exotic mammals and birds massed rank on rank in a dark-tinted forest or jungle setting – that I saw clearly the childish extravagance of my imaginings.

Even so, there was birdlife in fair quantity, as well as evidence – odd scufflings in the undergrowth, a sloughed snakeskin by the side of the track – of other less visible lives, and we took a good number of specimens, including three brilliantly coloured parrots and several small passerines of quite remarkable beauty. 'Nothing of great rarity,' observed Bullen, taking them from his satchel and examining their vivid plumage as we rested at the side of the track in the noontide heat; but to me, encountering them for the first time, the birds were extraordinary, each bright body a minor revelation.

I had found myself unable to eat earlier in the day, but now I was hungry. I unpacked the remaining bread and a few strips of jerked beef from Billy's knapsack, and began to eat. Billy followed suit but Bullen rose impatiently to his feet and picked up his rifle. 'I may as well scout ahead,' he said, moving away down the track. 'Come and find me when you're ready.'

Conversation with Billy was appreciably easier in Bullen's absence and we were talking with some animation when the first shot rang out. A heartbeat's space, and then a second report. 'A couple more for the bag,' I said, looking casually over my shoulder as the echoes died away; but Billy rose to his feet and stood stiff as a ramrod, listening, his head cocked to one side.

'He's left the track,' he said. 'He's somewhere lower down.' He gathered up the debris of our lunch and crammed it into his knapsack before throwing back his head and calling out, his voice unnaturally high and clear: 'Mr Bull-en! Mr Bull-en!' There was no reply.

Billy slung the knapsack over his shoulder and stepped briskly forward, motioning me to follow.

The ground below the track fell away more gently here, a rocky slope patchily covered with tall scrub. 'He's down there,' said Billy, stopping suddenly. As he spoke, I saw the vegetation tremble and part some twenty feet below, and Bullen emerged and scrambled towards us, breathless and visibly excited.

'Did you see it?' he called.

I waited for him to rejoin us on the track. 'We've seen nothing out of the ordinary,' I said.

'Believe me, Redbourne, this was very much out of the ordinary.' His eyes, I noticed, were abnormally bright, his cheeks suffused with a hectic flush.

'A bird?'

'A dream of a bloody bird. I didn't get a clear sighting, let alone a good shot at it, but I know it's nothing I've ever come across before. The colours on it, Redbourne, the way it lifted as it flew off. And not a small bird either – hard to judge from the glimpse I had, but maybe a foot or more in length.'

'What kind of bird?'

He shrugged. 'Long-tailed, I think. Could have been a parrot. All I can tell you for certain is that I'm not budging from this place until I've had another crack at it.'

'You may be in for a long wait,' I said, scanning the expanse of scrub. 'It could be anywhere among that lot. And in any event it's not likely to return with the sound of rifle-fire fresh in its memory. I suggest we press on now and look for it again on our way back.'

'I'm not interested in your suggestions,' he said. 'I'm staying here. You do as you like.'

I was stung by the sharpness of his tone. 'In that case,' I said, with equal asperity, 'expect us back in three hours' time.' I made to move off but Billy edged forward, blocking my way, speaking urgently under his breath.

'Tell Mr Bullen he should come with us,' he said.

Bullen leaned towards him. 'What's that, boy?'

'I said you should come with us, Mr Bullen. You'll be safer.'

'I can't see any particular danger. Can you?'

'Nothing particular. Only—'

'I can do without your protection, thank you. You look after Mr Redbourne. I'll look after myself.' He turned abruptly and began to pick his way back down the slope. Billy hesitated, but I could see that any further intervention on his part would be a mistake.

'Three hours,' I called out, moving quickly away and signalling to Billy to follow. I remember Bullen raising his hand in acknowledgement before edging into the scrub and disappearing from view.

'Don't worry about Mr Bullen,' I said, as Billy fell into step beside me. 'There's no need.'

'More need than you'd think, Mr Redbourne.'

I stopped in my tracks. 'What do you mean by that, Billy?'

He stood in silence for a moment, fingering the strap of his knapsack, his eyes avoiding mine. When he spoke, his voice was hushed, so soft I had to strain to catch his words. 'I dreamed about Mr Bullen last night,' he said. 'I can't say exactly what was happening in the dream, but I know he was in danger.'

'We dream all sorts of things, Billy, but few of our dreams have much bearing on the events of our waking lives.'

'That's not what my mother told me. She said I was to pay attention to my dreams and to let them guide my life.'

'I think we should move on,' I said firmly. Billy glanced once over his shoulder but raised no objection, and we set off again at a gentle but reasonably steady pace. I was soon thoroughly absorbed in my quest for specimens, and it was only much later, when we sat down to rest, that Billy voiced his anxieties again.

'But you must realise, Billy, that Mr Bullen knows what he's doing.'

'Mr Bullen knows less than he thinks he does,' said Billy bluntly. 'And he sets himself at odds with the world. He damages the things he touches, and doesn't understand there's a price to be paid for the damage. If he'd heeded me when I told him about the ancestors, he wouldn't be sick now.'

'Whatever makes you think Mr Bullen's sick, Billy?'

He looked up sharply as though surprised by my question. 'You can see it,' he said. 'You can see it in his face.'

'He's a little out of sorts, perhaps. But he's a man of moods – up one minute and down the next. I can guarantee that if he's bagged the bird he's after we'll find him in excellent spirits on our return.'

Billy glanced away. 'I think,' he said slowly, 'that it would be better for him if he didn't kill it. He doesn't know what it is.'

'That's exactly the point, Billy – that's why he's so excited about it. He believes he may have stumbled upon a rarity, or even an unrecorded species.'

He was silent for a moment, gazing out across the valley. 'I mean,' he said at last, 'that it mightn't be a bird at all.'

I laughed at that, but he turned to me with a look of such ferocious intensity that the laughter died in my throat. 'Mr Bullen knows it was a bird he saw,' I said. 'It's just that he doesn't know what kind.' The boy continued to stare at me, his expression gradually softening into what I took to be a kind of bewilderment. I remember thinking that he had failed to grasp some essential detail of my discourse; only later did it occur to me that the failure was my own, and that I had missed his meaning entirely.

21

Bullen was waiting for us. He was sitting beside the track with his elbows resting on his knees and his head bowed, the very picture of despondency.

'It's in there somewhere,' he said, rising to his feet as we drew level with him, 'but God knows where.' His voice was dull and his movements, I noticed, as he slung his rifle across his shoulder and stepped forward, were heavy and listless. 'I shall have to come back tomorrow.'

'I understood,' I said, 'that we had other plans for tomorrow.'

'I want that bird, Redbourne, and I'm damn well going to get it. The valley can wait.'

Our agreement had been vague, admittedly, but his words implied a thoroughly unacceptable interpretation of the arrangement between us. I was about to respond, and sharply too, when I caught the look in his eye. I don't want to overstate the case, but I had the fleeting impression of something crazed there; not much more than a glimmer, but sufficient to give me pause. I held my tongue and we moved off in strained silence, a silence not broken until we reached the cascade.

Billy was there first. He put his face to the rock and sucked up the water in long, noisy draughts while Bullen unstrapped the canteen and pulled out the cork.

'Let me in,' he said, elbowing Billy aside.

The boy gave ground, but with evident reluctance. 'There's enough for everyone,' he said. Bullen made no reply, but held the canteen in the wavering flow until it was full. I saw him lift it to his lips, then lower it suddenly, thrusting it at Billy, his eyes fixed fiercely on a point further along the track and a little above head height. 'Take it,' he muttered. And then, more urgently, still without looking at the boy: 'Take the bloody thing.'

Billy could have had no clearer understanding of the situation than I had, but he reached out and snatched the canteen from Bullen's outstretched hand. Bullen slipped his rifle from his shoulder and took aim, and it was only then, following the line of the barrel, that I became aware of the bird.

I could only just make it out, a wedge of fragmented colour half concealed among the leaves of an overhanging banksia, but I knew at once that this was Bullen's dream-bird, and that he had been given a second chance. I caught a glimpse of the long tail-feathers and, as the creature turned on its perch, a startling flash of red.

It could hardly have been an accident – Billy, usually so sure-footed and circumspect, stepping forward at that precise moment with a townsman's clumsiness, stirring the dry litter with his feet. The shot was snatched and an instant too late: the bird was already winging away low and fast under cover of the scrub. Bullen dropped his rifle, swung round and caught the boy by the shoulder, ramming him back against the blotched bole of a paperbark. I stepped in quickly, dragging at his outstretched arm. 'Let the lad alone, Bullen. You'll hurt him.'

He drew back his hand and whipped round to face me. 'That was deliberate,' he said hoarsely. 'Malicious sabotage.' And then, rounding once more on Billy: 'What in the devil's name do you think you're playing at?'

Billy looked up at him, his eyes sullen under his dark brows. 'You've ripped my shirt,' he said flatly. 'You shouldn't have done that.'

'Damn your shirt, boy – you can get yourself another.'

'There isn't another. Not like this.' He was probing the torn cloth, running his fingers over the exposed skin below his collarbone. 'My mother gave it to me,' he said, and with the words his face crumpled and he began to cry, quietly at first and then more wildly, his thin body racked by long, shuddering sobs. Bullen stared down at him for a moment, then turned on his heel and stalked off down the track.

I pulled a handkerchief from my jacket pocket and held it out. 'Here,' I said. 'Stop that and dry your eyes.'

He snatched the cloth and passed it quickly over his face, but the sobbing continued almost unabated. He struggled to speak, the words catching in his throat. 'She didn't want to leave' – he swallowed hard, dabbed at his eyes – 'but it was time. She folded it up . . .'

There was a long pause.

'The shirt? She folded the shirt?

He nodded, dumb with misery; the tears poured down his cheeks. He began to mime the act, moving with such poignant delicacy that I seemed to see the woman's dark hands passing across the white cotton, tucking, folding, smoothing. 'And then,' he said, 'she put one hand up like this' – he reached towards me, the gesture bringing her so close that I felt the brush of her fingertips on my own skin – 'and she told me . . .' He pressed his knuckles to his mouth and closed his eyes.

'Told you what?'

He turned away, shaking his head helplessly from side to side; and as I looked at his quaking shoulders, something of my old longing quickened and flared. It even occurred to me that I might take him in my arms and comfort him but Daniel was mixed up in it all too, that troubled soul whose unassuageable grief had shown me the inefficacy of my own confused love, and the impulse faltered and died. I glanced down the track to where Bullen brooded, still as a statue, above the valley rim.

'We need to get on,' I said, moving away. 'Dry your eyes now and join us when you're ready.'

Bullen turned as I approached, his face still dark with anger. 'We should have known better,' he said savagely. 'I'd sooner have no guide at all than that misbegotten half-and-half.'

'Go easy on him, Bullen. He's not much more than a child.'

'Exactly. And we're not nursemaids. I tell you, we'd be a good deal better off without him.'

'Sssh. He'll hear you.' I glanced over my shoulder. Billy had evidently managed to stem his tears and was moving slowly down the track towards us.

'I don't give a damn whether he hears me or not. He's lost me a prize, Redbourne, a real prize, and I see no reason to spare his feelings.'

Billy had undoubtedly heard him. As he drew close to us he lifted his head, addressing himself pointedly to me. 'I can leave now if Mr Bullen wants me to,' he said.

'Mr Bullen is angry, Billy. He doesn't mean what he says. We're both grateful to you for accompanying us.'

The colour deepened in Bullen's hollow cheeks. 'I'll thank you to let me express my own opinions,' he said. 'I've a tongue of my own, and what I've said, I'll stand by.'

'This is absurd, Bullen. We need the boy's help. Besides, we have some responsibility for his welfare.'

'You've no call to worry on my account, Mr Redbourne. I'm as safe in these mountains as I am in my da's back yard.'

Bullen flung out his hand in a brusque gesture of dismissal. 'Let him go,' he said. 'I can find the way back.'

Was it some premonitory tremor that passed through me as he spoke? I was suddenly swept by an anxiety so intense that, just for a second or two, I felt myself on the brink of falling. I remember reaching out and grasping convulsively at Billy's arm. 'You're not to leave,' I said. 'Do you hear me? Don't listen to him.'

I can hardly blame the lad. He would have seen in my momentary panic an opportunity to hit back at his tormentor, and the temptation must have been irresistible. I saw his eyes narrow.

'I'll stay,' he said, 'if Mr Bullen tells me he's sorry.'

Bullen shot the boy a look of such undisguised malevolence that I wondered whether he might drop him on the spot. Then he turned abruptly and moved off down the track. I hoped that might be the end of the matter, but Billy sprang forward, tucking in behind him like a terrier at his master's heels.

'Come on,' he shouted excitably at Bullen's broad back, his brown feet dancing on the dry leaves. 'Say it. Sorry. Sorry. Like that. It's not so much to ask for, is it?'

Bullen spun round, his face contorted. 'What you're asking for,' he shouted, 'is a prime thrashing, and I've a good mind to give it to you.' I could see again the terrible wildness in his eyes, and it struck me with disquieting clarity that Billy was making a serious misjudgement. I stepped forward quickly. 'Billy,' I said, 'calm yourself. Let Mr Bullen alone. He'll apologise in his own good time.'

Bullen raised his head slowly, as though with difficulty, transferring his unsettling gaze to me. 'Apologise?' he spat. 'To this jumped-up by-blow? I'd as soon beat myself senseless with an iron bar.'

The boy muttered something under his breath, inaudible to me, I confess, but Bullen started forward and let fly at him. More a cuff than a punch, but delivered with vindictive force. Billy dodged back and the blow fell short. I thought at first that it was Bullen, teetering with his left hand extended at the edge of the drop, who was in danger; but in fact it was Billy who, stumbling sideways, lost his footing and was gone.

If he made any sound – any utterance, I mean, any cry of despair or alarm – I don't recall it. Only the rush of loosened debris slipping away down the cliff face and pattering through the canopy below; and, in the appalling hush that followed, the quick rasp of my own breath. I stepped to the edge and peered down into the gloom.

'Holloa!' I called, scanning the shadows for any sign of movement. 'Can you hear me, Billy?' My voice echoed briefly from the rocks around, but there was no answering shout.

'You heard him,' said Bullen, lurching towards me and laying hold of my arm. 'You heard what the pup said to me.'

'Never mind about that. Did we bring the rope with us?'

He was staring at me as though I had addressed him in a foreign language.

'The rope, Bullen. Where is it?'

'Back at the camp. Look, you saw how it was. I'd never knowingly—'

'We can discuss it later.' I broke his hold on my sleeve and hurried down the track as fast as the failing light and the dangerous terrain allowed.

The rope was coiled on the platform just outside the lean-to. Unnecessary weight, I had thought, watching Bullen lash it to Billy's pack the previous day, but now the coil struck me as regrettably insubstantial, a bare thirty feet, at a rough reckoning, of flimsy hemp. I seized it and stumbled back up the track.

Bullen was exactly where I had left him, but squatting on his haunches now, his shoulders bent forward and his head between his arms, as though he were trying to lose himself among the rocks and scrub. I was almost upon him before he looked up.

'What use do you imagine that will be?' he asked, eyeing the rope.

Darkness falling, the rock face dropping away below us to indeterminate depth, the rope itself not much above a tether's length. The question was, in its way, a good one, but I was finding in action some antidote to the panic at my heart. I hitched one end of the rope to the base of a sturdy sapling and tugged the knot tight.

'The lad's dead,' Bullen continued. 'Dead or dying. If he weren't we'd have heard him call out by now.'

I passed the free end of the rope once round the base of a second tree, looped it beneath my arms and tied it securely. 'Let it run as I need it,' I said. 'No slack. I'll give a shout when I'm ready to come up again.'

'It's a pointless risk. Leave it until daylight, at least.'

I positioned myself above the drop. 'I'm going down,' I said. 'With or without your assistance.'

'You're a fool, Redbourne. Take it from me, there's nothing to be gained by a display of schoolboy heroics.'

225

I was stung by the remark, but not deflected. 'Are you going to help?' I asked.

'You've no experience in these matters,' he said. 'You'd do well to defer to mine.'

It was, given the circumstances of the accident, an astonishing remark, and I think Bullen himself recognised as much. At all events, he stepped abruptly forward and took up the rope, bracing his left hip and shoulder against the sapling it was tied to. I leaned back gently, gauging resistance; then I dropped to my knees and eased myself over the edge.

The face was steep but not quite vertical, and though I could see very little, I found no great difficulty in feeling my way down. I went cautiously at first, testing each hold offered by the sandstone or the stunted scrub, acutely aware of the slenderness of the rope that half supported me; but as I continued my descent I began to move more freely, with a confidence – no, more than that, with an exhilaration generated, I think, by the very precariousness of my situation. I had a fleeting recollection of my childhood dreams of power – the delirious fluency of the body's progress across landscapes strewn with irrelevant obstacles – and then my right foot, feeling for the next toehold, found nothing but air. Hopelessly unbalanced, I slid sideways, scrabbling at the rock, and fell into space.

The shock of my fall and the jolt as the rope arrested it were almost simultaneous. For a long moment I hung inert, turning and swaying with the movement of my fragile lifeline, staring down into the shadows under my feet; then I raised my head and looked around.

I could see at once how matters stood. I was suspended immediately beneath an outcrop of rock, an irregular protrusion heavily undercut from below. It was on the overhang, I realised, that I had lost my balance, feeling for a foothold that simply wasn't there. I knew that, provided the rope held, I was in no immediate danger; my task now was to bring my feet back into contact with the cliff-face.

'Bullen! I shouted. 'Haul me up. Easy as you go.'

His answer came back, but very faintly, the words lost on the breeze. I hung there, listening, waiting, alert to every tremor of the rope. I had my eye on a tuft of scrub a few feet above my head. When I draw level with that, I said to myself, I shall be back in control. I watched intently for a minute or more, and with each lapsing second I felt my terror mounting, blind and ungovernable as a rising tide.

'Bullen!' I yelled again, my voice shrill now, and horribly raw. 'Bullen! Pull me up!'

There are, I imagine, few circumstances so terrible that the imagination cannot make them more so. As I hung there, revolving slowly in my flimsy harness above that inscrutable vacancy, it came to me that Bullen must have decided to do away with me. Later, reflecting on the moment, I would discover or invent reason enough for having entertained such an idea, but what flashed through my mind at the time had nothing to do with reason. It was an image, shadowy but compelling: Bullen's tall figure stooping beside the sapling at the far end of the rope, his long fingers fumbling at the knot.

I kicked out in panicky spasm and strained upward, gripping the rope as high above my head as I could reach. The lack of any purchase for my feet made the action peculiarly difficult and, as I jerked and twisted in the void like a hooked fish, it occurred to me that my struggles might be futile. But fear lent me strength: little by little, hand over hand, I drew myself upward until I felt my boot soles strike rock.

'Praise,' I remember my mother saying, 'must be heartfelt or it is nothing.' As I established my footing more securely, wedging my boots firmly against cleft stone and knotted scrub, it seemed to me that I knew for the first time what heartfelt praise might be. In other circumstances, I might have dropped to my knees and raised my voice to the heavens; as it was, I set my lips against the dry sandstone, feeling with a giddy exultation the day's heat still contained in it, and breathed thanks for my deliverance.

The line went taut: Bullen taking up the slack, hauling me in. It was easy now, my body held and steadied, my feet and hands clever in the deepening gloom. As I drew level with the top, Bullen knelt and took hold of my collar, but I had no need of his assistance. I remember crying out, with a mixture of relief and triumph, as I breasted the lip and threw myself face down on the track; and I recall, too, the pungent scent of some herb or shrub coming off the stained sleeves of my shirt, sharp as smelling salts. I lay still, breathing deeply, feeling my heart hammering against the packed earth.

When I raised my head I found Bullen still kneeling close at my side, watching me intently. 'Well?' he asked. 'Did you find him?'

I have to confess that Billy's plight had been thrust to the back of my mind by my own trials. I must have hesitated, because Bullen found it necessary to prompt me. 'The boy,' he said. 'Is there any sign of him?'

'I've found nothing, but that doesn't mean there's nothing to find.'

He opened his mouth as though to reply, but swayed suddenly from the waist and lurched sideways. He put one hand to the ground to steady himself and I saw, in the violent trembling of his extended arm, how deeply the fever had taken hold. I recognised then the preposterousness of my earlier expectation: in health Bullen might conceivably have hauled my dead weight up from beneath the overhang, but his sickness had made him as weak as a baby. I scrambled to my feet, slipping free of the rope.

'Come on,' I said firmly. 'I'll help you back.'

He rose with difficulty, moving as though dazed. 'I don't say there's nothing to find,' he said slowly, 'but I can tell you there'll be nothing worth the finding.' He shuffled over to the sapling and bent stiffly to unfasten the rope.

'Leave it,' I said, more sharply than I had intended. 'We'll come back at first light and try again.'

He shook his head wearily but said nothing. I gathered the rope in loose coils and dropped it at the side of the track. 'We must do everything we can,' I said. 'We certainly can't leave the area without making a more thorough search.' I took up his satchel, feeling the meaty weight of the birds' bodies as it swung from my hand, and we moved on.

I must have appeared rather brutal, urging him on over that rough terrain when it was clear that each step drew heavily on his diminishing reserves of strength. Every so often I would grip him by the elbow, trying to support and steer him where the track seemed most uneven, but each time he shook me off. After a while he stopped and lowered himself unsteadily to the ground.

'I'm dead-beat,' he said. 'You go on. I'll rest here for a moment.' He leaned back against a spur of sandstone and closed his eyes.

'We can't be more than a couple of hundred yards from the shelter now. You'll rest more easily there.' I stretched out my hand, but he ignored it.

'Water,' he said dully. 'Where's the canteen?'

'I thought you were carrying it.'

His hand went up to his shoulder and fumbled the crumpled fabric of his shirt where the canteen–strap should have been; dropped to his lap again. 'Billy,' he whispered. 'Billy had it.'

'I believe we may have a little water in the shelter,' I said. I knew for certain that we had none, but I wanted Bullen on his feet and walking.

'Bring it here.'

I stood silent, embarrassed by the exposure of my childish stratagem. He leaned forward, suddenly animated, prodding the air with his forefinger in a febrile show of anger.

'Don't play games with me, Redbourne. Do you hear? I'll get down to the camp in my own good time.'

'Please yourself.' I turned and walked away, but I hadn't gone twenty paces when I heard the clump and shuffle of his boots on the track behind me. He called out once, his voice thin and tremulous, but I judged it expedient to ignore him and I didn't slacken my step until I reached the shelter.

I had already lit the lamp by the time he joined me. His face, as he ducked under the flimsy lintel, was blank with fatigue, and he barely glanced my way before lowering himself to his couch. I removed his boots and drew the blanket over his shivering body, and after a few moments his eyelids flickered and closed.

Once I was sure he was asleep I unfastened the satchel and laid our specimens on the ground beside the lamp, the three parrots a little apart from the smaller birds. In the cold yellow shine their colours seemed oddly lusterless, and such small pleasure as I was able to derive from close examination of their plumage was quickly stifled by darker emotions. He's out there, I thought, imagining Billy's slender form spreadeagled on the valley floor, the white cloth of his shirt stained and tattered, his thick hair matted with blood and dust; out in the dark alone. I bowed my head, meaning to pray for him, but no words came.

I gathered up the stiffening bodies and dumped them in the corner, beside the wallaby skins. Then I eased off my own boots, doused the lamp and curled up on my spartan bed, tugging the blanket tightly around me.

22

It was still dark when I woke, roused by a soft scrabbling, the rustle of shaken vegetation. Some small marsupial, perhaps, moving through the brush outside? But the sounds continued, and as I listened, I was able to locate them more precisely: not outside, I realised, but within the walls of our flimsy shelter.

Lying in bed as a small child, I would shiver as the owls called from the beechwood or feel the hairs on my neck prickle at the vixen's scream as she quartered the dark fields in search of a mate. 'There's nothing to be afraid of out there,' my mother would say, leaning over me with a candle in her hand, her fine features irradiated like those of the angel in the east window of the church; and when I was a

232

little older, no less fearful but ashamed to call out, I would repeat her words like a charm as I lay listening to the stir of nocturnal life in the darkness outside. Now, in a wilderness shared with blacksnakes and death-adders, I was learning a fear scarcely less intense than my childhood terrors, and altogether more rational. I felt my arm trembling beneath me as I eased myself forward and fumbled for the lamp and matches.

But it was Bullen, I saw, as the flame steadied on the wick, who had disturbed me. He was lying on his back, arms raised, groping blindly to and fro across the ferny ledge behind his head. I threw back my blanket and scrambled towards him.

'What's the matter?'

'My pillow.' His voice was hoarse and plaintive, like a troubled child's. 'I can't find my pillow.'

'You have no pillow,' I said. 'Lie still now and rest.'

He screwed up his eyes as though he were about to cry. In the dull lamplight his brow and neck glistened with perspiration; his shirt was drenched.

'My mother's gone for water,' he said, 'but she'll be back soon. She knows where my pillow is.'

I pulled a shirt from my pack, folded it neatly and slipped it beneath his head. He lay quiet for a moment, then rose awkwardly on one elbow, leaning towards me but with his gaze fixed fiercely on the shadows at my back. His tongue moved restlessly between his cracked lips.

'What is it?' I seized him by the shoulder, leaning close, trying to intercept his crazed stare.

'I thought she'd be back by now,' he said. And then, with sudden, startling vehemence: 'Damn the bitch. Out dancing while her own son dies of thirst.' His head drooped and he began to rock back and forth, whimpering softly to himself.

'Sssh,' I said, as soothingly as my own unease allowed, 'lie back now.' I patted the folded shirt with the flat of my hand. 'There's your pillow.'

'But no water.' He seemed to reflect for a moment. 'Are we in hell?'

'No. Not in hell.'

'Then there must be water.'

The logic was wild but the fact was indisputable. 'Yes,' I said, 'there's water.' I picked up the lamp and took the pan and ladle from the rock-shelf. I could feel his eyes on me, anxiously following my movements.

'Don't worry,' I said. 'I shall be back in a few minutes.' I ducked outside and made my way to the far edge of the platform.

I knew, of course, that it would have been safer to walk back up the track at first light to collect fresh water from the cascade. But think about it: a three-mile trek with no better container than a couple of chipped mugs and a lidless cooking-pan, Bullen helpless with fever and racked by thirst, Billy perhaps waiting for rescue . . . My reasoning, I would maintain even now, was essentially sound; but if my experience out there taught me anything at all, it was that we live in a world that cares nothing for reason.

234

The wallabies' carcasses, I noticed, had been disturbed by scavengers, the soft flesh of their bellies torn open. I raised the lamp. A slick shine off the spilled entrails, off the pooled water around them; a whiff of staling blood. I skirted the remains and picked my way across the plashy ground until I judged myself well clear of their taint; then I squatted down and began to fill the pan, dipping the ladle where the water lay deepest, careful to avoid stirring the sediment below.

As I worked, I became aware of Bullen's voice drifting out to me on the quiet air, the words incomprehensible but edged with anger or desperation. I finished my task as quickly as I could and hurried back to the shelter.

He was staring up at the roof but turned his face to the light as I entered, scarcely pausing in his monologue, his eyes wide and vacant. I spoke his name softly, but he gave no sign of having heard. 'Bullen,' I said again. 'It's Redbourne.'

His gaze flickered. 'I know who you are,' he said aggressively. 'What do you want?'

'Nothing. You were talking to yourself.'

'Not to myself. To my mother. She's come back without. Says I can get my own damned water. Her very words. That's not natural, now, is it?'

'Your mother's not here, Bullen. Only me.' I set the lamp and the pan of water on the ground beside him.

'And Billy?'

'Sit up now.'

He eased himself laboriously on to his left side and propped himself on his elbow again. 'I dreamed I'd killed him,' he whispered.

'Drink this.' I dipped the ladle and held it to his lips.

He drew back, averting his face. 'Poisoned,' he said. 'I can smell it.'

'Come on, now. You'll feel better for it.'

'Poisoned,' he insisted. 'Smell for yourself.' He pushed the ladle away and slumped sideways to the ground.

I bent forward and sniffed at the water. The faintest tang of iron and rot; nothing to speak of. 'It's not as fresh as it might be,' I admitted, 'but we've no choice at present.'

'There's running water somewhere. Listen.'

I could hear nothing but the dry whisper of the breeze in the eucalyptus leaves and the monotonous croaking of the frogs. 'I'll get you fresh water when I can,' I said, 'but you'll have to make do with this in the meantime.' I slid my right hand beneath his head and tried to raise him, but he twisted away.

'I can't drink that filth,' he said.

'Then you must go without.' I banged the ladle angrily back into the pan, but he reached out and gripped me by the wrist. 'Give me the water,' he said, bearing down on my arm as he raised himself again. 'I shall have to drink something.'

He grimaced as he swallowed, like a child taking medicine; then he snatched the ladle from my hand, refilled it and drank more greedily, the water spilling in a small clear runnel from the corner of his mouth. He wiped his forearm across his chin and lay back, letting the ladle drop.

His breathing was quick and his colour high, but the agitation was gone from his face and his movements seemed calmer. After a moment his eyes closed and, judging that he had no further need of me, I extinguished the lamp again and returned to my couch.

23

On the edge, legs braced against the gritty sandstone, my back and shoulders quivering as I pull on the rope. The body bumps slowly up the rock face, the white shirt snagging and tearing on scrub. The head lolls sideways, the arms hang limp. I haul my burden level with the cliff-top, hitch the rope around a broken branch and lean over. The rope twists as I draw it towards me; the face turns, staring into mine. *Daniel?* My mouth is dry, my whole body shaking. The loop is tight around his neck and I realise, with a spasm of guilty terror, that I have made a terrible misjudgement. *Daniel?*

What's happening? The boy's lips move in response, but silently. In the instant before I wake, it occurs to me that

I know what he has to tell me, but as I open my eyes the unvoiced message fades from my mind.

'Billy!' I sat up, kicking myself free of my rucked blanket, and hurriedly pulled on my boots. Bullen was stirring, moaning softly and stretching one hand towards me. As I made for the doorway, I heard him whisper my name.

'I'll be back shortly,' I said.

'I need a drink.'

I took the pan from the shelf and helped him to a ladleful of water. He drank slowly, with evident distaste or discomfort. I dipped the ladle again. 'Do you want more?' He grimaced and shook his head. I lifted the ladle to my own lips and drained it. A little like blood, I thought, running my tongue over the roof of my mouth; the same metallic aftertaste. 'It's not so bad,' I said.

He had begun to moan again, burrowing back down among the tangled folds of his blanket, but my mind was on Billy. I scrambled out of the shelter and ran up the track in the early light. The air was cool and moist, but by the time I reached the spot I was sweating profusely, my shirt cleaving to my back.

Apart from a slight roughening of the surface a few feet above the loop, the rope showed no sign of damage. The sun was still far too low in the sky to illuminate the cliff face directly but, peering down, I was able to make out the bulge of the outcrop I'd hung beneath on the previous evening; and then, a few yards below that – I craned downward, suddenly alert, staring into the shadows – the outside edge of a second projection, a flat ledge fringed with scrub.

I had no doubt that I should have to go down again, and less fear than you might imagine about making the descent alone. I retied the knot around the sapling, shortening the rope by a good six feet; then I slipped the loop under my arms and let myself over. This time I could see what I was about, and within a couple of minutes I was braced just above the overhang, the rope at full stretch and my body canted backward from the rock face. I turned my head and looked down over my right shoulder.

The floor of the valley was carpeted with mist but the air around me was brightening by the second, and I was able to see clearly the line of the ledge below. Not an isolated projection, I realised, but a trackway as broad as the one we had been travelling on, running as far in both directions as the crowding undergrowth allowed me to see.

'Billy!' I shouted. 'Billy! Can you hear me?'

My voice reverberated among the rocks and died away. I listened, straining into space, but there was no answering cry.

I twisted round in my harness, leaning out sideways above the ledge now, desperate for a sign. Was that faint localised darkening of the track's surface a disturbance of the leaf-litter? Even if it were, my reason told me, I could hardly read it as evidence of Billy's survival. It might denote almost anything: a wallaby startled into sudden activity, a lyrebird scratching for food, the boy's body – and I felt my own body tighten in sympathetic spasm – striking the shelf before continuing its headlong descent to the valley floor.

It was difficult to see what more I could do. I climbed back
to the top, untied the rope and coiled it loosely about my arm
before making my way back to camp.

I thought at first that Bullen must be on the mend. He had
left the shelter and was kneeling at the edge of the platform,
staring out across the swamp. Then his body convulsed and
he pitched forward on to his hands, retching violently.
His breeches, I noticed as I approached, were unbuttoned and
gaping wide, his shirt-front stained. He wiped his mouth and
glanced up at me. 'The water,' he said. 'You wouldn't listen,
would you?' His face was white, his whole frame quaking.
I could tell that the fever had abated, but his extraordinary
pallor made him appear sicker than ever.

'That's nonsense, Bullen. You were already ill when you
drank the water.'

He screwed up his face as though he were struggling with a
complex idea. 'The fever's one thing,' he said slowly. 'This is
another.' He eased his body wearily to the ground and lay with
his knees drawn up, his hands clutching at belly and groin.
He glanced briefly up at me; then his eyes closed.

'You can't sleep here,' I said. 'Not in full sunlight.'

He let me help him back to the rock face and huddled in
the shade of the overhang, a few yards from the shelter. I was
about to turn away when he stretched his arm weakly towards
me, palm upward, like a beggar asking for alms. 'I need water,'
he whispered. 'Fresh water. And' – I leaned down to catch his
words – 'opium for this damned flux.'

'I'll try to find water,' I said, moving away.

'And opium? Do you have any?'

I hesitated, not turning back but feeling or imagining his gaze fixed on the space between my shoulderblades. 'Yes,' I said at last. 'I have a little tincture in my pack.'

I ducked into the shelter and fumbled among my belongings for the bottle. I removed the cork and sniffed it, the smell taking me back, as it invariably did, to my childhood: my mother stooping above my bed, administering comfort from a tiny silver beaker.

Bullen appeared to be drifting off again, but he roused himself at my approach and leaned forward on one elbow.

'Open your mouth,' I said, kneeling at his side.

'I can dose myself without your help. Give me the bottle.'

He reached out and, as he did so, I caught the stink coming off his body, and felt my gorge rise. I struggled for control. 'You're very ill, Bullen. You'd do better to let me attend to your medication.'

He was clearly in no state to prolong the debate. He opened his mouth wide and I sprinkled a few drops of the paregoric on to his discoloured tongue. He swallowed hard. 'Is that all?' he asked, eyeing me as I recorked the bottle.

'For the moment, yes. I'll give you more later.'

He sighed, letting his head sink back to the ground. 'And you'll fetch fresh water?' he asked.

I nodded. 'I shall be gone for an hour or two. Try to rest while I'm away.'

I returned the tincture to my pack, collected the pan from the shelf and set out in the direction of the cascade. The smell of Bullen's sickness seemed to hang about me like a poisonous fog as I walked, and by the time I reached the site of Billy's accident, I knew beyond doubt that the sickness was also my own. I squatted at the side of the track and voided myself in long, racking spasms.

To continue would have been out of the question: it was as much as I could do to drag myself back down the track to the camp. I made straight for the shelter, dropped to my knees and rummaged frantically through my pack for the tincture, persisting until it became apparent that the bottle simply wasn't there.

'Bullen,' I shouted, giddy with rage and nausea. 'Where's the paregoric?'

No reply. I stumbled back into the sunlight. Bullen was lying, sound asleep, more or less where I had left him, but he had clearly found sufficient strength to make the short journey to the shelter and back in my absence: the bottle stood on a low ridge of stone a couple of feet in front of him. I snatched it up and held it to the light.

He had evidently dosed himself generously, but the situation might, I reflected, have been worse: he had, at least, left more than enough for my immediate needs. I put the bottle to my lips and sipped, feeling the familiar restorative warmth like a golden wafer on my tongue; and then, for good measure, I sipped again.

I should like it to be understood that I tended Bullen throughout the course of that long, bewildering day as conscientiously as my own condition allowed. I assisted him to the edge of the platform as his needs dictated, even, on one occasion, helping him to clean himself – though the fact is that my own needs were almost equally pressing. At intervals I administered small quantities of paregoric. I took no more myself: I was rationing the supply, intending to take a powerful dose immediately before turning in for the night.

Despite the medication, Bullen grew increasingly restless as the day wore on, shifting and turning irritably on the platform's uneven surface. Some time late in the afternoon, as the sun began to sink behind the trees, he lifted himself on one elbow and called out: 'I need more medicine.'

I fingered the fluted surface of the bottle in my pocket. 'There's none left,' I said. 'We've finished it.'

If he recognised the falsehood, he gave no sign of it. He raised his head for a moment and stared out across the swamp at the encroaching shadows; then he slumped back with his arm angled across his face, like a man who has seen more than he can bear.

By nightfall he was delirious again, moaning and gabbling, his fever rising as the air around us cooled. I roused myself and helped him back to the shelter, coaxing and tugging as he crawled painfully over the unforgiving sandstone. I guided him to his makeshift bed and pulled the blanket over his trembling body.

I had some compunction about taking the opium in his presence, but no serious fear of discovery. Kneeling in the darkness beside my bedding like a man at prayer, I silently eased out the cork; then I raised the bottle to my parched lips and took what I thought I needed to see me through the night.

I dreamed vividly and confusedly, and the shout that woke me may well have belonged to that strange interior world of luminous streetscapes and predatory figures, though at the time I assumed that Bullen had cried out. I lit the lamp and held it up.

Bullen had thrown off his blanket and was lying on his back, his eyes wide open and rolled slightly upward. He was whispering to himself, but the words made no sense. I remember thinking, carefully isolating the ideas from the haze that surrounded them, that he must be talking in code to avoid detection, and that unless I could persuade him to speak in English, his secret would be lost for ever.

'Bullen,' I said, 'what is it?'

His lips stopped moving but there was no change in his expression.

'Bullen?'

He turned towards me; his gaze wavered and came to rest on the lamp. 'Thank heaven,' he said. 'I thought the night would never end.'

I set the lamp on the ground and moved to his side. I had some sense of his delusional state and a fainter if more unsettling awareness of my own, but I was unable to dispel the notion that he had something of the most immense importance to tell me. I leaned over him and placed one hand on his shoulder, and at that moment the flame guttered on the wick, burned suddenly low and went out.

Bullen whimpered in the darkness. 'I can't see,' he said. 'I'm dying, aren't I?'

My tongue moved clumsily in my mouth, searching its dry recesses for the words I needed. 'The lamp's gone out,' I said.

A long pause, and then: 'Can't you light it?'

'We've no oil.'

'They'll have plenty next door,' he murmured. 'I'd go myself, only . . .'

I sat back on my heels and felt his misery flood the little space between us, unignorable as a child's cry. I fumbled for his blanket and tried to draw it over him, but he reached out convulsively and grasped my forearm. 'Please,' he breathed. 'I must have light.'

I gently loosened his hold. 'Sssh,' I said, and the sound shivered and broke far down in my body like a spent wave lapsing on the shore. 'We need to rest.' I crawled back to my own side of the shelter and took a quick pull at the paregoric. Then I sank down and lay on my back listening to the deep, unhurried breathing of the wilderness.

24

The sky was just beginning to lighten when I opened my eyes to see her crouching at the entrance, her back towards me and her head bowed.

'Nell?'

She swivelled round to face me and I saw the baby cradled in her skirts. It was swathed in a filthy shawl, its head hidden deep in the folds, but its smooth brown legs stuck out beyond the hem, kicking stiffly to the jittery rhythms of my pulse.

'Where did you find it?' I asked.

She looked at me with a strange, sly smile. 'I thought you knew,' she said. 'The child's ours.' She loosened the shawl around the baby's head and tilted the face towards me. 'Can't you tell?'

I strained forward, trying to make out the features, but could see only the sheen of the brown skin. Then Eleanor slid her hand beneath the folds and slipped the shawl right back to the shoulders so that the wicked little face came clear, its glittering eyes staring back at me from beneath the high, domed brow. I knew then that it wasn't a baby at all, and wanted to tell Eleanor so, but she was gazing down at it with such rapt adoration that I hadn't the heart to say anything.

After a while she raised her head again. 'Would you like to hold her?' she asked.

I drew back, feeling the bile rise in my throat, but she thrust the bundle towards me. 'Go on,' she said. 'Take her.' It was impossible to refuse. I held out my arms and, as I did so, the thing lunged at me. I felt its wet mouth clamp on the flesh at the base of my thumb, and its tongue, rough as a cat's, begin to rasp the skin. 'Little mischief,' said Eleanor softly, 'she's hungry.' She tugged the creature away and returned it, kicking and squirming, to her lap; then she undid the buttons of her blouse and laid bare her left breast.

'Look at her face,' she said. 'She knows what she wants.' She lifted the creature and settled its head in the crook of her arm. I saw its mouth widen to receive the nipple, and I cried out a warning, starting forward and scrambling across the sandy floor; but Eleanor twisted quickly round and, without a word or a backward glance, rose lightly to her feet and walked away.

'Bullen,' I whispered. 'Bullen, did you see her?' I knelt at his side and shook him gently by the shoulder.

It was the first time I had touched a corpse, but I could tell at once what I was dealing with. Bullen was lying on his side with his face turned away from me and half buried in the folds of his blanket. Sleeping peacefully, I might have said from the look of him, but my fingertips knew better, and my heart contracted in terror. I remember staggering from the lean-to and stumbling barefoot down the path, as though I might find help out there; then my guts clenched in spasm and before I could get my fingers to my belt, I had fouled myself.

We deceive ourselves constantly, in ways at once so subtle and so fundamental that only the sharpest of blows can bring us to our senses. Until that moment I had been a hero or, to put it more accurately, I had been playing the role of one of the heroes of my childhood reading, battling gamely against a dangerous but ultimately tameable universe. I don't mean that I hadn't been frightened, but my fear had been tempered by the unspoken assumption of my own invincibility. Now, weak and giddy, lost in that vast wilderness like a glass bead dropped in a cornfield, I felt myself jarred into some new and terrible understanding. Nothing clear, nothing readily explicable; not strictly an illumination, but a tremulous recognition of the darkness that lies concealed beneath our intricately woven fictions. I stood shivering in my soiled breeches and howled at the sky.

I must have cut an abject figure, yet I would have given anything just then, out there in that inhuman solitude, to have been gazed upon by human eyes. I don't know how long

I stood there, but after a while it came to me that I should wash myself down. I made my way slowly to the edge of the swampland and stripped off my clothes; then I squatted above the stagnant seepage and cleaned the filth from my legs as best I could.

Each small action seemed to require an inordinate effort, and by the time I had ferreted out my spare clothes and put them on, the chill had gone from the morning. The still air in the lean-to was growing heavy: a sweetish smell of excrement, a darker undertone of decay. I dosed myself with the last of the paregoric, draining the bottle dry, and then turned my attention to Bullen.

Certain ideas are so firmly established in our minds that it is almost impossible to eradicate them. I realised at once that I possessed neither the tools nor the physical resources to bury the body, yet I found myself unable to dislodge the conviction that it was my duty to do so. After a moment or two of confused deliberation, I knelt at Bullen's side, gripping his shoulder with one hand and laying the other on his bony hip; and it was only when I felt the body's stiff resistance to my tentative coaxing that the sheer absurdity of the enterprise was borne home to me. I sat back on my heels and felt the heat rising through my own body, licking upward like an unguarded flame.

'Burn it,' she said.

I started and swung round, expecting to see her there at the entrance again, but there was no sign of her. Yet the voice had been as clear as if she had been standing at my shoulder. I stumbled outside and looked up and down the track.

'Nell,' I called, and my voice came ringing back to me from the cliffs, mingled with hers. 'Now,' she said. 'Do it now.'

I ducked back into the lean-to and gathered up my belongings, stuffing them haphazard into my pack; then I spread my blanket and piled on to it the wallaby skins and bird carcasses, a foul jumble of sticky fur and dulled feathers. I folded the blanket over them and roped it up to form a loose bale. The effort left me trembling and breathless, and while I was resting she drew close again, so close that I could feel her voice resonating in the aching hollow of my own throat.

'You can't carry these things,' she said, and I felt her hand pass across my face, light as breath and moving with such expressive delicacy that the tears sprang to my eyes. 'You don't have the strength.'

'I'm only taking what needs to be taken.'

Some faint stir in the air around me signalled disapproval. 'Let it burn,' she said. 'Everything.'

I remember the anger rising in me then, anger at her persistence, at her unwanted interference in my affairs. 'It's not your business,' I shouted, tugging at the bale, manoeuvring it clumsily towards the entrance. But as I cried out, something flared and roared – whether within me or around I couldn't tell – and I staggered and fell heavily against the wall of the shelter. Then I knew that I should have to do as she said.

There was no shortage of tinder – the ground inside and around the shelter was littered with eucalyptus leaves – but in my weakened state I took some time to gather all I needed. Little by little I raised a small mound of the brittle debris at the entrance before transferring it, in rustling handfuls, to the space between Bullen's body and the brushwood wall.

I struck a match and leaned over and, as I did so, I was seized by anxiety. Was some ritual required? Some form of words? If you had asked me six months earlier, posing the question in theoretical form, I should doubtless have said that the freed soul has no need of ceremony and that – supposing such a place or state to exist – it will find its way to heaven unaided. Now, stooped above Bullen's earthly remains, I was tormented by the fancy that some omission on my part might doom his spirit to an eternity of aimless wandering among the trees and lowering crags. I blew out the match and began to pray, cobbling together such phrases as I could remember from the prayer book with others of my own invention. When I ran out of words, I took a handful of leaves and scattered them over the body.

Whether because of the trembling of my hands or the faint dampness still in the leaves at that early hour, I found it more difficult than I had anticipated to ignite the heap. The oils would flare and sputter at the touch of the match and then, almost as suddenly, the flame would die back along the blackened edges of the leaves. After the third attempt, I sat back on my heels and drew out my pocket-book. I tore half a dozen pages from the back and twisted them loosely, one by one, inserting them at intervals along the base of the heap. And as I did so, Daniel's mournful face slipped from between the pages and fluttered to the ground.

Nothing could have prepared me for the violence of her intervention, the terrible jolt of anger she sent through me as I stared down at the photograph. She said nothing, nothing at all, but her intention was as plain as if she had screamed the words in my ear. I picked up the little scrap and placed it on the pyre. Then I struck another match and set it to the twists of paper, coaxing each in turn into flickering life.

That did the trick. The flames licked up the heap and began to eat at the base of the wall so that the brushwood crackled and spat. I piled on more debris, but there was no need. I felt the heat strike upwards as the fire took hold, and I withdrew from the shelter and moved upwind of the blaze, my eyes smarting.

I might attribute my languor to sickness, or to the effects of the opium; or it may have been that the flames offered a spectacular and welcome diversion from darker thoughts. Whatever the reason, I stood gazing in a kind of trance as the blaze intensified, and it was only when the breeze stiffened and veered, scattering sparks and burning leaves in my direction, that I saw with any degree of clarity the implications of my action. 'Nell,' I whispered, thinking she might have further instructions for me, but I could hear nothing through the roar of the burning brushwood.

It was the smell of scorched flesh and feathers, reaching me as the wall lurched inward and the roof subsided, that spurred me into action. I stumbled to the track and set off in the direction of a civilisation whose very existence in this wild and remote corner of the earth seemed suddenly questionable.

25

I had no strategy; I was in no condition to formulate one. Weak and confused, I had only the vaguest notion of the distance I should have to travel or of the time it might take me to cover the ground. The nausea and cramps were less troublesome now, but I was afflicted by a raging thirst and so preoccupied by my immediate need for water that nothing else seemed important. Every so often I would stop and listen, and occasionally I would hear, or perhaps merely sense, what might have been a thin trickle through overgrown or subterranean channels; but each time, my investigations proved fruitless.

I'm not sure how long I had been walking when I came upon the gully, but the sun was high in the sky, filtering through the branches almost directly overhead. The terrain below the track was less precipitous here, a rocky slope falling away into densely wooded shadow. The gully cut through it at right angles to the track, its course marked by a lush growth of fern and sedge.

I leaned out cautiously and sniffed the air. Moist earth and leaves; a cleaner undertone I could only interpret as fresh water. I stepped gingerly on to the slope and began to follow the line of the gully down, hugging its edge. The shadows deepened around me and the air grew cooler.

I don't know whether it was the change of atmosphere, operating on a system sensitised by illness, that affected me at that moment, but I found myself suddenly struggling for breath and balance. My legs trembled violently and my vision dimmed. I sat down heavily among the tumbled rocks and, as I reached out to steady myself, the singing began.

I call it singing, but there was nothing melodic about the sound. A chant perhaps, a rhythmic, humming monotone swelling and diminishing among the trees, vocal rather than percussive, yet unlike any human voice I had ever heard. I listened for a minute or two, maybe longer, and little by little it dawned on me that the sound came from the gully. I scrambled to my feet and looked over.

The creature was only a few feet below the lip, crouching among the ferns, but I couldn't make it out at first. I mean, I could see the curve and pale sheen of the bowed back, a white heel braced against a fissure in the sandstone, but I couldn't make any sense of what I was looking at. I squatted down, angling for a better view, and as I did so, the thing raised its head and I saw that it was Daniel huddled there, stripped to his glistening skin and quivering like a trapped rabbit. His mouth was open but the singing, I realised in that instant of astonished recognition, had stopped.

He stared up at me, his eyes gleaming; his voice was as light as the breeze in the eucalyptus leaves. I leaned forward, straining to catch his words.

'I could have stayed,' he whispered, 'only you wouldn't have it. Sent me out into the dark alone.'

I said nothing, watching his eyes the way you'd watch the eyes of a wild animal. He ran his tongue along his upper lip. 'You could let me in now,' he said.

He raised his arms above his head like a small child asking to be picked up, but the opium had made me as cunning as he was, and I could see at once what he was after. I backed away from the edge and turned to run, but he hauled himself up the slope and lunged at me, clutching at my ankles so that I stumbled and went sprawling among the ferns. I felt his hands fumbling at my back – a soft fluttering, at once tender and malign. Then he began to test the space between my shoulderblades, pressing insistently on the spine, and I braced myself and clenched my heart like a fist, knowing that if he were to find a way through to its warm chambers, I should be lost.

'Let me in,' he pleaded. I looked over my shoulder and saw his face hanging above me, but crumpled now and streaked with tears. I shook my head and his features seemed to shift and blur like the contours of a stone seen through running water. 'Daniel,' I said very gently, my fear subsiding as the pressure on my back diminished, 'you died. Last winter, in Jack Waller's barn.'

He bent close to my ear and spoke again, but there were no words any more, just the faint whisper of breath passing between his fading lips and out into the damp air. He brushed my face with his fingertips and I raised my arm to push him away, but he was already drawing off, dissolving among the trees like a scarf of mist.

I lay there for a moment, my cheek pressed to the ground, trying to bring my trembling limbs under control; then I rose clumsily to my feet and dusted the debris from my jacket. I was anxious to leave the shadows and rejoin the track, but it was obvious that I couldn't expect to travel much further without water. I listened again, holding my breath, staring into the gloom until something came clear: a curved ridge of stone overhung by ferns, black water brimming at the lip. Thinking about it later, I wondered how I could have seen the pool from where I stood, but I'm tolerably certain that, as I scrambled down the slope to the gully floor, I knew already what I should find and where I should find it. I pushed my hands in among the fronds until my palms touched water; then I crouched down, beastlike, and drank greedily, sucking cold mouthfuls from just beneath the oily surface.

The climb back to the track left me breathless, but I was eager to press on immediately. The water was seething and churning in my gut, but I had been refreshed by it, and for some time I tramped steadily without any particular thought of my situation. 'One foot in front of the other', my father would say, urging me on when, as a child, I trailed behind, complaining that I could go no further; one foot in front of the other.

It was a fallen branch, lying at an angle across the track, that checked me in my stride. Literally, yes, but I mean more than that. As I raised my right leg to step over it, the loose cloth of my breeches snagged on a projecting twig and I heard the dry wood snap, sharp as a pistolshot. I staggered backward, physically unbalanced but startled, too, by a bewildering flash of recognition: I had stepped over the same branch earlier in the day.

My first thought was that I had turned the wrong way on rejoining the track and was now retracing my steps. But that explanation, I sensed darkly through a rising wave of panic, was at odds with the evidence. The memory triggered by the crack of the breaking twig was not a recollection of having approached the branch from the opposite direction, but one that conformed in every detail to the more recent event. Even the twig itself, hanging now by a thread of bark and swaying erratically to and fro, seemed obscurely familiar. I stared down at it, my mind reeling.

I stood for a long time, rigid in the middle of the track, not so much attempting to make sense of the aberration as waiting for some clue or signal that might make sense of it for me. The silence deepened around me; the twig stopped dancing on its thread and hung still.

I moved, in the end, simply because the alternative was unthinkable. I stepped over the branch and continued on my way, but more slowly now, dogged by uncertainty. I remember stopping at intervals and scanning the undergrowth at the edge of the track, the way a traveller might search an English road-side for a milestone smothered by meadowsweet or dog-roses; but if I had been asked what I was looking for, I should have had no answer.

I had grown used to the dappled shade of the trees, and the full sunlight, when I emerged into it, hit me like a fist. Here the cliff plunged sheer below the track on one side; on the other a stand of stringybarks, monumental columns of solid white light, dazzled and perplexed me. My eyes watered and the sweat poured from my skin.

Surely I remembered this from our outward journey? Looking backward as we stepped into the shade, Bullen and I together, to see Billy toiling up the slope behind us in the pun-ishing glare, bent under his burden. The sweep of the cliff-top behind him as he rounded the track's long curve. Or had that been somewhere else entirely? I struggled to hold and clarify the vision, but the equivocal fragments fused with the scene in front of me, and I gave up the attempt.

I edged back into the shade and sat down. My head throbbed, not painfully but heavily, and the landscape pulsed and shuddered. Like a living thing, I remember thinking queasily, squinting upward to where the stringybarks stood in loose formation, their pale limbs lifted to the sky; and it was at that moment that I saw the lories.

A small flock of the elegant creatures perching among the twigs, the whole tableau seeming, at the precise instant of my glancing up, so unnaturally still that I might have been looking at an extravagant example of the taxidermist's art. Just for that instant; then a breeze lifted the loose strips of hanging bark, rattling them softly against the tree's white bole, and everything was in intricate motion – the twigs and leaves dancing and shimmering while the birds wove their elaborate patterns of sound and colour among them. And as I followed their movements, something stirred in the cramped recesses of my heart, forcing a cry from my lips, a cry of exultation that rose through the branches above me and was absorbed in the luminous air. Praise at its purest – wordless, impassioned praise, flying straight as an arrow to heaven. Yes, and the birds rising too, flashing crimson and azure against the softer blue of the sky, and some part of myself caught up in the winnowed air so that I had to place the flat of my hand against the hot earth to remind myself where I belonged.

It was love that had lifted me, I realised, whirling me up among the beating wings; and love, I thought, looking down the track and seeing him standing there in a blaze of light, his white shirt fluttering in the breeze, that had brought Billy back from the world of the dead to guide me home. He was looking in my direction, one hand sweeping the dark curls clear of his face in a gesture at once familiar and disquieting. I called out and scrambled to my feet, but he started like a frightened deer and began to run back the way he had come.

'Billy!' I staggered into the sunlight and picked my way clumsily down the slope, calling and waving, but he neither slackened his pace nor looked back and, as I gazed after him, he rounded the bend in the track and was lost to view. Dazed by the glare and trembling with weakness, I should have been glad to return to my seat in the shade; but it was in my mind that he intended me to follow, and I drew myself together and stumbled after him.

By the time I reached the bend myself, I knew that such strength as I had been able to summon was failing. I remember thinking, carefully if not quite lucidly: I'm coming to the end. Perhaps I articulated the thought; at all events, I have a vivid but confused recollection of the words echoing through or around me as I raised my head and looked up the track to see Billy walking back towards me, no longer alone but accompanied by a taller figure. I stood staring into the light in a perplexity of hope and doubt.

If I was slow to recognise Preece, that was doubtless due in part to my own confused state, but also to the fact that the man himself appeared transfigured. He was bearing down on me with a force that seemed to disguise his halting gait, his mouth set in a thin, hard line and his eyes burning. Like an Old Testament prophet, I thought, as he drew up in front of me with his staff held menacingly before him, a prophet fired with rage against sinful humanity. And it struck me as a little absurd to be extending my hand to such a figure in such a place, but the formal greeting was, at that moment, all I was capable of imagining. He seemed barely to notice me.

'Preece,' I murmured, and my voice rang in my skull like a cracked bell. 'I can't tell you—'

'It's not you I want,' he said curtly, glancing over my shoulder. 'Where's Bullen?'

I must have stood gawping like a fool. Preece leaned in close. 'Bullen,' he repeated. 'Where is he? I tell you, Redbourne, I'll have the hide off his back for what he did to Billy.'

'Bullen's dead,' I said. I sank down at the side of the track, put my face between my hands and began to cry.

Water, I remember, fresh water from a tilted flask. And I remember them raising me to my feet, Preece on one side and Billy on the other, and helping me forward. I tried to keep step with them but my legs were weak and clumsy, and after a few paces my determination lapsed. We moved slowly. Sometimes the track narrowed, and one of my companions would drop behind; at one point I was obliged to negotiate a particularly difficult stretch unaided, and did so on my hands and knees. Billy spoke only to urge me on; Preece, as far as I can recollect, said nothing at all until we reached the upland clearing where the ponies were tethered. Then he turned to me, his gaze milder now and his voice soft. 'You'll take the lad's mount, Mr Redbourne. Billy's legs are good for a few miles yet.'

I wanted to thank them both, but the words wouldn't come. Billy helped me up and I sat slumped in the saddle like the proverbial sack of meal while Preece adjusted the stirrups. 'You're a lucky man,' he said. 'Lucky we found you.

And lucky' – he straightened up and gestured back the way we had come – 'the wind's in the right quarter. If that bush-fire had been moving in this direction it's ten to one you'd have been burned to a cinder.'

I twisted round and looked over my shoulder. The late sunlight was still bright on the nearer treetops, making them shine like polished copper, but out in the middle distance a long smudge of grey smoke hung above the forest, dulling the air for what must have been mile upon smothering mile. My head swam and I swayed forward, clutching at the pony's mane. Preece swung himself, stifflegged, into his saddle. Then Billy clicked his tongue twice against his palate and we moved on.

26

I can't fault Preece's treatment of me. He took me back
under his roof and surrendered his bed to me; he
cooked the little portions of bland food my weakened
body needed, and served them up at appropriate intervals;
and when I woke crying and trembling in the dark, my skin
slick with perspiration, he would rise from his mattress at
the far end of the room, draw up a chair and sit at my side
until I was able to sleep again. But there was a subtle
constraint in his dealings with me now, a reticence that I
interpreted as a form of reproach. I had the impression that
he was waiting, courteously but with something less than
complete equanimity, for the day I should be well enough
to leave.

I can hardly blame him. Heaven knows, I've reproached myself often enough for what I've come to think of as culpable inertia. In the course of our brief, abortive journey Billy had been routinely mistreated, and finally assaulted, by a man ostensibly in my employ. Although I had spoken up once or twice in the boy's defence, I had done far too little for him: he owed his survival not to my half-hearted interventions but to a combination of good fortune and his own youthful agility. I was mortified to learn that he had been huddled on the ledge when I began my first descent of the rock face but had chosen to scurry away and conceal himself, judging me incapable – he said as much, and the accusation smarts even now – of protecting him from Bullen's vindictive anger. That he should have considered it safer to return home alone under cover of darkness than to make the journey in our company reflects almost as poorly on me as it does on Bullen.

There was no refuge. Catching Preece's eye for an instant as he stooped to tuck in my blanket, or hearing through the hot boards the lilt of a whistled tune as Billy went about his business in the garden, I would remember again, with undiminished shame, how I had failed the boy. And to make matters worse, the hatchet-faced constable who came to question me on the evening after my return seemed to be exercised at least as much by the attack on Billy as by Bullen's death. 'I've two of my own,' he said grimly, 'and heaven help anyone who laid a finger on either of them.' He leaned forward in his chair, bringing his face uncomfortably close to mine.

'Bullen was ill,' I said. 'I don't believe he knew exactly what he was doing.'

'Not so ill that he couldn't throw a punch at the lad.' I could see the sweat beading the man's brow and upper lip; his short hair stuck out from his scalp in damp spikes. I leaned back wearily against the iron bars of the bed-head.

'Mr Redbourne has been very sick himself,' said Preece, stepping forward protectively.

The constable nodded. 'I've almost done,' he said, rising to his feet. 'If we should need to find you once you've left the mountains, Mr Redbourne . . . ?'

I gave him Vane's address, spelling it out slowly for him as he bent over his pocket-book. 'And the dead man's family?' he asked.

'I'm fairly certain there were no close relatives. I shall make . . .' My head swam as I groped helplessly for the word. 'Enquiries,' I said at last. 'I'll let you know.'

'Thank you, Mr Redbourne.' The air around us seemed to flicker and dim; I could barely make him out as he stepped over the threshold and into the gathering dusk.

Just once, on the third morning of my enforced stay, the atmosphere lightened briefly. I was up and about for the first time since my return or, to put it more accurately, I was seated at the table with my pencil in my hand and my journal open in front of me, my mind as blank as the page I was staring at. Billy was sitting just inside the doorway with his shirt on his lap, carefully stitching the torn fabric, his eyes narrowed against the sunlight and his bare feet braced against the door-frame, while Preece busied himself with his broom, sweeping the dust into a small heap just in front of the boy's chair.

'It's a strange thing,' said Preece, straightening up with a smile, 'how some people have a knack of putting themselves in other people's way.' He was looking in my direction, but I saw from his expression that his words were intended for Billy's ears. Billy continued with his stitching, giving no sign of having heard.

'I said,' Preece persisted with humorous emphasis, leaning over the boy and ruffling his hair, 'it's a pity I can't get to the doorway for the great lummock skewed across it.' Billy let his needle fall and grasped his father's wrist with his left hand, at the same time aiming a gentle punch at his ribs with his right. The broom clattered to the floor as Preece moved in close and held him in a lock or embrace, the two of them laughing as they struggled together. Watching their good-natured scuffling from across the room, I should have liked to laugh with them, but found myself instead on the point of tears.

I can't say exactly what it was, the grief that welled up in me at that moment, but I know that I seemed to be standing at the boundary of some charmed enclosure, like a soul exiled from its true habitation, looking for a way in. And as Preece released Billy and turned back to his task, his face still creased with laughter and his eyes shining, I heard myself say, in a voice not quite my own, 'Give him his due, Preece, he's a fine young man,' and then, following through with feigned nonchalance: 'Clever, too. He might go far with a good education. If you wanted to send him to Sydney to continue his schooling, I've no doubt we could come to some arrangement.'

It was as though a cloud had passed across the sun. Preece's features stiffened, the laughter fading from his eyes. 'Thank you, Mr Redbourne,' he said coldly. 'Billy's getting a good education here – better than any schoollearning could give him – and he'll go as far as he needs to go.'

'Even so,' I said, taken aback by the severity of his tone, 'there would be certain advantages. With the right kind of schooling—'

'How do you think the boy would fare, cooped up in a city classroom, learning by rote things that'll draw him from the soil he's rooted in and give him nothing worth having in exchange? Who knows what damage he might suffer?'

'I shouldn't have made the offer if I hadn't believed it to be in Billy's best interests.'

Preece's gaze relaxed slightly, though his voice was still hard. 'I believe you mean well, Mr Redbourne,' he said, 'but you've no call to concern yourself with such matters. It's not your place.'

Billy rose silently, draped his shirt across the back of his chair and slipped away into the sunlight. I stared at the floor, rigid with misery. 'You're right,' I said at last. 'I shall leave tomorrow.'

We set off early, Preece and I on ponyback, Billy loping easily beside me, one hand on the bridle. I had been touched by the boy's insistence on accompanying us and felt under some obligation to make conversation, but neither he nor I seemed able to strike the right note, and we soon lapsed into silence.

I was still far from well – frail and feverish, my eyes confused by the riddling interplay of glare and shadow on the dusty track in front of me and my mind troubled by elusive fragments of the night's dreaming. By the time we reached the station, I was already exhausted. I remember Preece helping me down from the pony as though I had been a child, and holding me lightly by the arm as we made our way to the platform.

He had allowed ample time, and we had a good halfhour to wait. We sat in the shade, Preece on one side of me and Billy on the other, our talk sporadic and constrained, while the heat intensified around us. I stared down the track into a distance creased and distorted by the quivering air, and imagined the long, hot miles ahead.

It seemed to me that I had never known time pass so sluggishly, but at last I heard the wail of the whistle, and the train steamed in with a racket that set my raw nerves jangling. Preece helped me to my feet and across the platform to the nearest carriage. He threw open the door and held it back, hovering solicitously behind me as I hauled myself in.

I pulled the door to, lowered the window and rested my elbows on the frame, queasy with the stink of grease and sulphur. Preece lifted his eyes to mine. 'I should think you'll be glad to get back to your own world,' he said.

It came to me that I should be hard put to it to locate my own world again but the notion, glimpsed through a dull haze of fatigue, refused to come into focus, and I let it pass. 'I can't thank you enough,' I said – and the words fell dead from my lips, though I meant them sincerely – 'for all you've done for me.'

Preece took a step backward and glanced away down the track. 'I've done by you as I'd have done by any man,' he said.

There was an awkward pause. I tugged my purse from my pocket and withdrew two sovereigns. 'I must have been a drain on your resources,' I said, proffering the coins. 'I hope this will square accounts.'

He shook his head. 'There's no need.' The train jerked into motion with a squeal and clash of couplings, and began to glide slowly forward.

'For Billy,' I said. 'Take it for Billy.'

Preece made no move. Billy's face was turned in my direction, but I couldn't read his expression. Puzzlement, was it? Embarrassment? I leaned out in desperation as they began to slip away from me. 'Billy,' I cried, holding out the coins on my open palm; and then, almost beside myself with anguish, I lunged forward and tossed them on to the platform at his feet.

He didn't stoop. His father reached out and placed one hand on his shoulder. I watched the two conjoined figures dwindling away down the shimmering platform as the train gathered speed. They might have been made of stone.

IV

27

I had imagined that I should quickly recover my health once I was back at Tresillian Villa, but I was wrong: my return precipitated a nervous collapse of paralysing severity. Even as I stepped down from the buggy into the punishing sunlight I could feel some deeper dissolution setting in. True, I was able to respond to Vane's handshake with a firmness that might have passed for warmth, and as he ushered me into the house I answered or deflected his enquiries with what I imagine to have been a reasonable show of civility; but I felt that my body – my feet, my tongue, my prickling eyes – didn't entirely belong to me, and I grew sick and giddy with the effort of controlling it. As soon as I decently could, I slipped away to my room and locked the door.

I sat on the edge of my bed, hearing the sounds of other lives beyond my window – the piping of small finches in the shrubbery, the clang of a pail set down on a stone surface, a faraway lowing of cattle – and watching the lozenges of sunlight lapse slowly across the floor and walls. In a moment, I kept telling myself, I shall rise to my feet, wash, change my clothing and go downstairs; but the moments passed and I barely moved. Just once, hearing Eleanor's voice drift up from the garden, I was stirred into action: I leaped up, crossed to the window and looked out. She was out of sight beyond the corner of the house, and too distant for me to be able to distinguish more than the occasional phrase of what was evidently a slightly irritable conversation with her father. 'You should have called me,' I heard her say at one point, her voice sharp with accusation; and then Vane's light bass cut in, cool and placatory, and the two of them moved away.

A little before sundown I heard footsteps approaching along the corridor, and then a gentle rapping at my door. I sat tight, said nothing.

'Charles?' Eleanor's voice again, very soft and close now. I imagined her out there listening for my reply, her cheek resting against the varnished wood. I held my breath. My heart lurched in my chest.

'Charles, shall you be dining with us? Mrs Denham needs to know.'

The mundane detail – that casual reminder of a world in which meals are served at set hours by capable domestics – steadied me a little. 'I'm afraid not,' I called. 'I'm rather indisposed.'

There was a long silence before she spoke again, urgently now, dropping her voice to a low whisper. 'Come to the door, Charles. I want to see you.'

I eased myself back and laid my head on the pillows. 'I'm in bed,' I said. 'I'll see you tomorrow.'

Another pause and then, so quietly I could barely hear her: 'I'm glad you're back.' She turned, the fabric of her dress brushing the door, and I raised my head and strained forward to listen as her footsteps died away down the corridor.

As darkness began to fall, the rapping and whispering began again: *Open the door* – the words repeated two or three times as I rolled over on to my side, burying my face in the pillows. *Yes*, she breathed, and an instant later, her voice so close behind me that there could be no doubt of it, *I'm with you now.* A little sigh, and then the pressure of her body against my back, the warmth of her mouth at my ear. *There's nothing to be afraid of*, she said, and because it was my mother's voice I heard then, my mother's reassurance echoing back to me across the years, I turned, whimpering, and let her draw my head to her breast. *Hush*, she whispered, rocking me gently in her arms, and the sound stirred me and set my hands working at the soft fabric of her garments, peeling back layer after layer. Easily at first, and with a subdued excitement; but as I worked on, I felt the stuff disintegrating beneath my probing fingers, clumps of feathers breaking away and drifting across the bed in smothering clouds so dense that I struggled for breath and, crying out, startled myself from sleep.

Is it possible, I wonder, to convey any sense of what followed? Not a night punctuated by terrifying dreams, such as I had experienced under Preece's roof, but a night of unalleviated terror in which I slipped confusedly between sleep and waking without finding even momentary respite from the images and sensations that stormed round or through me. It's the landscapes I remember best, and this most clearly and terribly of all: a vast tract viewed at first as though from a great height or through the wrong end of a telescope – rock and forest, swamp and river, the sunlight thickening in a brooding sky. As I stare – and I know already that something frightful is about to happen – I see below me, dead centre of my field of vision, a lick of orange flame springing up like a flower. I raise my head and another starts up towards the horizon and, further still, a third. I clap my hands over my eyes to protect the land from my own incendiary gaze but I can see clean through my palms, and the fires continue to break out wherever I look. And then – it's the same landscape, but in some sombre aftermath, and I'm down there now, stumbling across the hot earth – the drifts of ash, the blackened, skeletal trees, the light draining remorselessly away; and in the choking air, little tatters of soot or darkness swirling around me as I wake, sweating, and reach for my pocket watch.

If, indeed, I did wake. I looked at the dial and saw that it was a few minutes past midnight; but how, I asked myself later, could I possibly have seen what I thought I'd seen? Not just the watch, but the entire room in daylight detail – washstand and writing table, ewer, basin and oil-lamp, all in essence as I knew them to be, but twitching and quivering with a horrible, restless energy. And something twitching, too, at the corner of my left eye, a sooty flake from the smoking waste I'd just passed through. I reached for my handkerchief and dabbed frantically at the shadow, but it slid sideways across my vision like a shutter and I was back among the blackened tree-trunks again, staring helplessly into the deepening gloom.

Beneath the confusion ran an inarticulate longing for daybreak but, in the event, I missed the moment and the sun was well up when I woke to Vane's voice, low and insistent, calling my name. I sat bolt upright in a kind of panic, clutching at the damp cloth of my shirt.

'What is it?' My pulse was racing, my mouth dry. I heard him try the handle.

'Are you all right, Redbourne?'

A simple enough question, but the answer seemed beyond me. I made my way unsteadily to the door, unlocked it and let him in. It struck me, as his eyes met mine, that he was reading the answer to his question in my face; and at the same moment I lost my balance and lurched sideways against the door-edge.

'I shall have to sit down,' I said.

He helped me back to the bed and sat beside me, eyeing my crumpled clothes. 'You're in no condition to be on your feet,' he said. 'I'll have your breakfast sent up to you.'

'I've little appetite at the moment.'

'Would you like me to send for Dr Barton?'

'It's not necessary. I shall feel better when I'm properly rested.'

He rose to his feet. 'Whatever you need,' he said with a formal inclination of his head, 'is at your disposal. You've only to ask.'

'Thank you, Vane.' I swung my legs on to the bed and sank back against the pillows as the door clicked shut.

Towards midday, as I lay staring listlessly at the ceiling, Eleanor entered bearing a bowl of broth on a lacquer tray. 'You're to drink this,' she said, without preamble, as I struggled upright. 'I've had it made specially for you.' She was brisk and businesslike, studiously avoiding my eyes, but I saw, as she handed me the tray, that her arms were trembling. She drew up a chair and perched on the edge of the seat, emphatically present but poised as if ready for retreat, her hands braced on her thighs.

'How are you, Nell?'

She glanced away, flushing faintly. 'I've missed you,' she said simply. 'Since you went I've been . . .' She raised both hands palm upward in a delicate, hesitant gesture and let them drop again. I felt a tremor pass through me, head to heel, a swift shock of pleasure and apprehension.

'I was afraid,' she continued, 'that you wouldn't come back. Just a vague worry at first, the kind of feeling you might have about anyone you care for when they're away from you. But then the dreams began, and it came to me that you were in danger. I thought you were going to die out there.'

'Dreams about me?'

'Dreams of disaster. I thought they concerned you, but I could never get close enough to see the faces. I don't want to talk about it.'

'Has your father told you about Bullen?'

She nodded. 'Drink up your broth,' she said, 'while it's still hot.'

I dipped my spoon obediently and took a mouthful. 'You're terribly thin,' she said. 'Your face is different. Sharper and harder. If I didn't know you, you'd frighten me.'

'I've not had sight of my own reflection for days.'

She stepped over to the washstand and picked up the looking-glass. I reached out to take it from her.

'Finish that first,' she said.

I supped the broth quickly but without relish. She stood over me until the bowl was empty, then handed me the mirror.

I could see at once what she meant. In part it was the beard, still at the stage at which it accentuated rather than concealed my jawline and the hollow contours of my cheeks, that gave my face its forbidding appearance; but there was something in the eyes, too, a look I didn't recognise as my own. It was as though the wilderness I'd walked through, or some essential element of it, had lodged in me, giving my gaze an unfamiliar depth and darkness. I wiped the glass nervously against the counterpane and handed it back. 'I need a shave,' I said.

'You need a bath.' She wrinkled her nose. 'Have you been sleeping in those clothes?'

'Is it so obvious?'

'I'll ask Mrs Denham to arrange it.' She returned the mirror to the washstand and picked up the tray. I could feel her drawing off, slipping away from me into a world I wasn't yet fit to face, and I leaned anxiously after her as she moved towards the door. 'Will you come back?' I asked.

'Later. I'm working on something out in the barn. I want to keep at it while the idea's still clear in my mind.'

'A painting?'

She shook her head. 'You'll see,' she said. 'When you're ready.'

I had expected to feel better for my bath and change of clothes, but in fact I returned to my room in a deeper state of exhaustion. Not only that, but the fluttering tag of darkness was back, dancing away at the margin of my vision. I strained to take it in, swivelling my eyes or turning my head to find it always just out of range, a faint shadow flickering in sunlight like an inverse will-o'-the-wisp, simultaneously elusive and insistent. I spent the afternoon in a state of morbid anxiety, and though I heard Eleanor's knock I didn't respond immediately.

'Charles, it's Nell.'

I rose to my feet and let her in. Another bowl of broth; a slice of buttered bread on a white porcelain plate. 'I'm not hungry,' I said, scanning the tray.

'You must keep your strength up. How can you get better if you don't eat?' She stepped past me into the room and motioned me towards the bedside chair. It seemed pointless to resist.

'Does your father know you're looking after me like this?' I asked.

She handed me the tray and drew up the other chair, setting it directly in front of my own, a little closer than seemed necessary. 'Of course,' she said.

'Has he no objection?'

She glanced towards the door, silent for a moment, her lips compressed. 'I don't need my father's permission to visit a sick friend,' she said at last. Something in her words, or perhaps in her defiant tone, caught me off guard: the room blurred suddenly, and I set the heels of both hands to my eyes in a vain attempt to stem the tears.

'Do you have many friends?' she asked. 'In England, I mean.' She was watching me closely, I sensed, but her voice gave no hint of distaste or embarrassment. I shook my head, still fighting for self-control.

'Suppose you were ill at home,' she continued. 'Who would visit you there?'

I shrugged, fumbled for my handkerchief. 'I have a manservant,' I said.

'That's not what I meant.' She leaned forward in her chair, her head tilted to one side. 'What's the matter with your eye?' she asked.

'The darkness?'

An absurd question. She frowned, visibly puzzled. 'The twitching,' she said. 'At the corner.' She reached tentatively towards my face, her hand raised in the air before me as though in blessing.

'I don't know.' It crossed my mind that I might tell her about my dreams – about the burning and the desolation – but I couldn't think how to begin. 'It's been troubling me since last night.'

It was the simplest thing – just a continuation of that interrupted forward momentum, the fingertips coming to rest lightly against the outer edge of my eyelid, the side of the palm against my cheek – but I think I knew even then that there was power enough in that touch to alter the course of a life. I stiffened, froze.

'Does it hurt?'

I felt the tears well up again and, as I struggled to speak, the tray tilted on my lap and slid forward and the whole lot crashed to the floor. I sat in a kind of stupor, staring at the debris – the plate broken into half a dozen angular shards, the bowl spinning on its side, the thin broth spreading out across the polished boards; and then, as though the accident had given me permission, I began to cry without restraint.

She made no move to rise. Instead, she leaned closer and pressed my head to her shoulder, slipping her other arm around my own shoulders. She held me to her as my sobbing intensified; continued to hold me as it subsided. I felt myself drift on the rise and fall of her breathing, light as a leaf on a tidal swell. 'No,' I murmured, drawing away a little, breaking her hold.

'What is it?' she asked.

I gestured weakly towards the debris. 'All this,' I whispered. 'This mess. This damage.'

'But not only this?' She was gazing into my eyes with an expression of such searching intensity that I began to tremble. 'Tell me,' she said.

I have never talked to anyone as I talked to Eleanor that afternoon. I spoke with desperate eloquence, hearing the words spill out as though from someone else's lips, mapping out a world of irreparable hurt and loss. I recognised the element of confusion in my breakneck narrative, but I could see at the same time how everything was linked: the heron flapping helplessly in the dust, Billy stumbling sideways before dropping from sight over the cliff edge, the slender arms of the dead wallabies spread wide in mute entreaty, Daniel walking out into the pelting night, the black girl's averted gaze as I pocketed her bracelet, the flames spreading outward from beneath my hands to consume a fragile, extravagant wilderness. Each thread seemed to lead ineluctably to another, and I was still talking when the gong sounded for dinner.

'I must go,' she said, rising from her chair.

'Nell, I'm sorry. Your clothing . . .' She followed my gaze, holding the skirt wide to inspect the damage: a long, greasy stain running diagonally from knee-level to hemline.

'It's nothing,' she said. 'Nothing that soap and water won't remedy.' I bent forward awkwardly, making to gather up the fragments of porcelain at her feet, but she prevented me.

'Leave it,' she said. 'I'll send one of the girls up to attend to it.'

'I've taken up so much of your time. It was good of you to listen to me.'

'I listened because I wanted to listen.' She crossed to the window and raised the sash a couple of inches. 'A little air,' she said, putting her palm to the aperture, 'now that it's growing cooler.'

A faint breeze rustling the leaves, the hum of insect life from the flowerbeds below. She turned to face me, framed against the softening light. 'You're not to worry,' she said quietly. 'There's no cause.'

I remember her words precisely, but the words were only part of it. Standing there in front of the window, her cropped hair forming a jagged aureole about her head, she seemed at once abstracted and concentrated, as though she were communing with a world beyond our own; and fanciful as it might appear, I saw her at that moment as something more than herself – a priestess, perhaps, called upon to interpret some profound insight for the benefit of suffering humanity – and heard her simple words as a form of absolution. I felt my breathing ease, my spirits lighten and lift.

I should have been glad to prolong the moment, but she turned abruptly and made for the door. 'Shall I get the girl to bring you some fresh broth?' she asked. I was silent, caught off balance, trembling between worlds.

'Charles?'

'That would be nice. Will you come back later?'

'Tomorrow.'

The tremor was starting up again at the corner of my eye, the flickering wisp of darkness re-insinuating itself. 'Nell,' I called.

'What is it?'

'Did you understand what I was trying to tell you about Daniel?'

She paused, one hand on the door-knob. 'You loved him,' she said, 'in your own way. The harm wasn't in the loving.' She threw the door wide and the curtains billowed inward from the windowsill, lifted on a draught so sweet it might have come fresh from Eden's fields.

28

Vane came to my room several times over the next few days, but on each occasion his demeanour suggested that the visit was little more than a courtesy, while I, for my own part, must have made it plain enough that I had no interest in prolonging our stilted exchanges. I was vague and easily distracted – by the creak of a floorboard in the corridor, the murmur of voices from the hallway – and Vane, who was, after all, no fool, could hardly have failed to realise that it was Eleanor I wanted to speak to.

I don't think I was capable of such insights at the time, but I see clearly now how strangely our roles had changed. Excitable, irreticent and prone to fits of weeping, I clamoured incessantly for Eleanor's attention during her visits while she, listening intently or speaking with gentle gravity, drew me patiently back to a world I had ceased to care for. I sensed a fine judgement at work there: she seemed to know what I needed before I knew it myself, and showed considerable skill in countering my irrational resistance to her suggestions. I remember in particular how adroitly she brought me round, on the evening of my fourth day back at the villa, to her view that it was time for me to leave my sick-room and get out of the house. I was not, I told her peevishly, well enough to do so, but she was insistent.

'I'm not asking you to go far. Take breakfast with us tomorrow, and then come down to the barn with me. You'll feel better for the change of scene.'

'And worse for the journey. I've only to stand and my legs start shaking.'

'The more reason to set them moving. I'll wake you at seven tomorrow.'

'Eight o'clock would suit me better.'

'I shall be taking breakfast at half past seven.'

'I shall come down,' I said grudgingly, 'and perhaps take a turn round the garden. I very much doubt that I shall be able to accompany you to the barn.'

I saw her smile very faintly, as though with satisfaction at something accomplished, before rising from her chair. 'We can discuss that over breakfast,' she said.

The clock had barely struck the half-hour when I came down the next morning, but Vane and Eleanor were already at breakfast, eating in silence at opposite ends of the table. Vane rose as I entered, extending his hand in greeting.

'Welcome back to the land of the living,' he said with a brittle smile. 'It's good to have you with us again.' He seated me in the chair beside his own and poured me a cup of coffee. 'What will you have?'

I settled for a slice of toast. 'We'll soon build you up,' said Vane, sliding the butter-dish towards me. 'Soon put the flesh back on your bones.'

I looked down at my wrist, so thin and frail against the dense weave of the linen tablecloth, and wondered with a flash of panic whether I should ever find my place again in the solid world of everyday things. I took up my knife and began to spread the butter, trying to disguise the trembling of my hands.

There was a light tapping at the door, and a maidservant entered. 'Post for Mr Redbourne,' she said, holding out a letter.

'Leave it there,' said Vane brusquely. The girl placed the letter on the sideboard and withdrew, but she had no sooner gone than Eleanor rose deliberately to her feet, crossed the room and retrieved it.

'Charles might want to read it now,' she said, addressing her father over my head as she set the letter beside my plate.

The air seemed to thicken around us. Eleanor stood at my side, leaning a little inward, her body so close to mine that I felt, or imagined I felt, the warmth of it on my own skin. Vane's face, I saw, glancing up, was rigid with suppressed fury. I picked up the letter and slipped it into my inside pocket.

'It's from my uncle,' I said. 'I'll read it later.'

Eleanor stepped away and returned to her place. She sat down, rolled up her napkin and slipped it into its silver ring; then she leaned back, folding her hands demurely in her lap. Vane ate slowly, chewing each mouthful with a thoroughness that seemed in some obscure way to be directed at, or against, his daughter, but at last he pushed back his chair and we all rose together.

As we reached the french windows, I stood aside to let Eleanor pass, and was about to follow her out when Vane plucked at my sleeve. 'Might I have a word with you, Redbourne?'

Eleanor stopped in her tracks and turned to face us. 'Charles has promised to come down to the barn with me,' she said. 'I have something to show him.'

'And I,' said Vane coldly, 'have something I wish to say to him. Perhaps you'd be good enough to leave us alone for a few minutes.'

I sensed that Eleanor expected me to respond. What should I have said, though, caught there between father and daughter on the sunlit threshold? I said nothing, and after a moment Eleanor stepped back. 'I'll wait for you on the path,' she said. She flung away and strode off down the slope, her skirt swaying with the vigour of her move-ments.

Vane watched her until she disappeared from view behind the long curve of the shrubbery. 'Let me advise you,' he said, 'not to let my daughter monopolise your time. I shouldn't like your convalescence to be hindered by any demands she might make on your resources.'

'I believe,' I said carefully, 'that she has my best interests at heart. It's difficult to judge such matters but I suspect that her attentions have, if anything, hastened my recovery.'

'Indeed?' He drew out his cigarette case but paused on the point of opening it, and returned it to his pocket. 'There's something else,' he said. 'Your correspondence with your uncle . . . The fact is, I'd be grateful if you'd avoid any mention of my domestic difficulties when you write. I mean, I hope you won't touch on the matter of Eleanor's illness.'

'I wouldn't dream of it.'

He gave me a crooked smile. 'You're a good man, Redbourne. I shall be sorry to see you go.'

I could hear the struts and slats of the veranda ticking softly as the sun heated them. Vane placed his hands on the rail and stared out across the garden, his shoulders hunched.

'As soon as I'm strong enough—'

'Please,' he interrupted. 'You mustn't imagine that I'm hurrying you on your way. You must take your time. I won't hear of you leaving a moment before you're ready.'

There was a long, awkward pause. 'If you don't mind,' I said at last, 'I shall go and find out what Eleanor wants to show me.'

Vane turned slowly towards me. I imagined from his expression that he had something more to say, but he drew himself up stiffly and strode past me into the house.

I was weak, certainly, and the path to the barn was more heavily overgrown than I remembered, but the walk was not the ordeal I had imagined. At breakfast I had managed to swallow a few mouthfuls of Vane's strong coffee, and now my spirits lifted as I followed Eleanor down, a little hesitantly but without great difficulty. My senses had been refined by my illness, the sense of smell above all, and I remember snuffing the air in a state of febrile excitement, almost over-whelmed by the heady mix – the subtle perfume of Eleanor's hair and clothing, flowerscents wafted from the garden, the heavier undertones of vegetation bruised by my boot soles, the rich smell of cattle-dung rising from the meadows below.

And then, as she pushed back the barn door, the tang of freshly cut eucalyptus wood. I could see at once what she had been up to in my absence: just inside the doorway, in the middle of a scatter of chippings, stood a pale upright form some three feet in height, vigorously rather than cleanly sculpted, its contours unmistakably feminine.

'Is this what you wanted to show me?' I asked, stooping to examine the piece. It was evidently unfinished, its surfaces still rough, but it was apparent to me that Eleanor had discov-ered, whether in the medium or elsewhere, a new and exhilarating source of inspiration. The figure was incomplete, like a piece of damaged Greek statuary – headless and all but limbless – yet charged with vitality. Above the truncated thighs and the broad curve of the buttocks the waist narrowed and twisted sideways and backwards, the torso drawn taut against the sustaining fullness at its base; the armpits were exposed and hollowed and the breasts and shoulders raised, as though the missing arms were reaching for heaven. Not strictly naturalistic yet suggestive of a deep understanding of natural forms, it was a remarkable achievement, and all the more so in that Eleanor appeared to have had only the most basic implements at her disposal: ranged on the floor behind the sculpture were a rusted saw, a broad-bladed gouge, a large iron file and a primitive mallet crudely fashioned from a length of reddish timber.

She squatted down among the chippings and lifted her face to mine. 'There's no one else I can show it to,' she said. 'And even you . . . I couldn't be sure you'd like it. You do like it, don't you?'

'Very much indeed.' I wanted to reach out and touch the figure but some sense of the gesture's subtler implications held me back. 'It's a wonderful piece.'

'There's more to be done, but only surface work. The lines of the carving are all there, almost exactly as I envisaged them when I began. And you know, Charles, all the time I was working on her I knew she was going to come out right. I can't explain it very well, but it seemed to me that she was lodged in the wood like a tree-spirit, and that if I just let the grain guide my blade I should find her. Does that make sense?'

'Of a sort, yes.' I straightened up and stepped back for a longer view, conscious that she was scrutinising me as carefully as I was scrutinising her handiwork; and it was at that moment that I recognised the connection between what I was looking at and the stumpy totem she had shown me in the hayloft. It was far from obvious, because the relationship wasn't traceable in the form itself but in what lay beneath the form – some dark, illicit knowledge of appetite and power.

'Yes, of course,' she said, when I delicately touched on the matter. 'From the moment I walked into the shop and saw her there, I knew I wanted to make something as strong and beautiful as she was. But you can't just copy someone else's work. I had to come at it my own way, and I could only do that when the time was right. This is the right time. And this,' she added, unbuttoning the cuffs of her blouse, 'is only the beginning.'

I dragged a chair to the doorway and, as she worked, sat staring out into the light, lulled into a state of reflective ease by the rhythmical rasp of her file. At long intervals she would break off and we would exchange a word or two but, perhaps divining my mood or perhaps simply absorbed in her task, she left me largely to my reveries. My thoughts ranged widely but I found them returning repeatedly to the walled garden at the Hall, an admired ornament to the estate in my father's time but pitifully neglected in my own. With its cold-frames smashed, its peach trees blighted and its espaliers unpruned it had become, over the years, an emblem of my own despair.

Yet Preece had fashioned his garden out of raw wilderness; all I needed to do was to restore order to a plot of fertile land cultivated by my ancestors for more than a century. Yes, I should take the garden in hand, and the orchard too; and then, why not set new fruit trees in the meadow beyond? And beyond that again? I imagined the slope as it might appear in some future spring, clouded with blossoms, or glowing red and gold in late summer as the fruit sweetened on the boughs.

I lost track of the time, but it must have been close to midday when I eventually roused myself and rose unsteadily to my feet. Eleanor was on her knees in front of the figure, her back turned towards me so that I saw, with a hot, tender shock, the small bones of her neck above the collar of her blouse. Her sleeves were rolled back to her elbows and she held the file loosely in her left hand. As I watched, she ran the flat of her other hand with a long caressing movement down the figure's skewed flank and across the belly, dislodging a shower of pale dust; and with the action I experienced a surge of giddy exultation so intense that I reeled sideways against the warped boards of the door.

Eleanor looked round sharply. 'What's the matter?' she asked.

'Nothing,' I answered, steadying myself as best I could. 'Nothing to speak of.'

Back in my room that evening, I opened the top drawer of my writing-desk and took out the aboriginal girl's bracelet.

For Eleanor, I thought, shifting its small weight in the palm of my hand. I slipped it into the pocket of my outdoor breeches but I had no sooner done so than I began to wonder how she might construe such a gift, and I spent the night in a foolish agony of indecision, sleepless through hours of darkness so miserably protracted that it seemed the dawn would never come.

29

As my strength increased over the following days, Vane's temper seemed to worsen. I stayed out of his way as far as circumstances allowed, taking short walks around the estate or reading in the shade of the trees at the end of the lawn while he, for his part, made no attempt to bridge the widening gulf between us. It was clear that he would have liked me to maintain a similar distance from his daughter for the remainder of my stay, but that proved impossible. Although I made a point of avoiding the barn, I was unable to prevent Eleanor from seeking out my company elsewhere.

'You can't send me away just because he doesn't like seeing us together,' she objected one morning, as I tried to reason with her. We were standing on the lawn in full view of the house, and I glanced up anxiously at the veranda as she spoke. 'He's not there,' she said, registering the movement, 'and even if he were, our friendship's no concern of his.'

'You're his daughter and I'm his guest. We each have certain obligations to him.'

'I've no such obligation.'

'All daughters have a duty to their fathers.'

'Only when their fathers have honoured their own obligations. I owe him nothing. And sometimes,' she added after a thoughtful pause, 'we have to think of our duty to ourselves.'

I considered the phrase. 'Surely,' I said, 'you don't mean that we should all be allowed to do exactly as we want?'

'Not quite. I mean that there are times in our lives when what we want is so important that we can't allow ourselves to be knocked off course by other people's wishes, especially when those people may not have our best interests at heart.' And then, turning to look me full in the face: 'I know what I want, Charles. What do you want?'

The directness of her challenge caught me entirely off guard. What I experienced then was a faint, sweet aftertaste of the exhilaration I had known in the barn as her hand moved smoothly over the swelling contours of her own creation, but I could find no way of translating the sensation into an appropriate answer to her question. 'I don't know,' I answered lamely.

'Maybe you should find out.' She gave a little laugh. 'That's your homework,' she said. 'I'll ask you again next week.'

'I may not be here next week, Nell. As soon as I'm strong enough I shall travel to Sydney and book my passage home.'

I saw the smile fade from her face. 'But you can't go yet,' she said. 'You've hardly seen anything of the country.'

I wanted to tell her that I had seen more deeply into the country than I had either expected or wished, but I thought the claim might sound presumptuous. 'I've learned a lot,' I said simply.

'There's always more to learn.' She turned and looked out across the valley before swing back to face me again. 'There's something in particular,' she said. 'Something you should see before you go. I'll take you there this afternoon.'

'Listen, Nell, your father—'

'I'll deal with my father. We'll leave after lunch.' She broke away with a little shake of her shoulders and marched up the slope towards the house.

Despite Vane's absence from the table, or perhaps in part because of it, our conversation over lunch was horribly constrained. Eleanor was visibly unsettled, her features taut and her movements nervy and graceless, though the impression of imbalance was offset by something in her eyes and in the set of her jaw.

'He's taking lunch in his study,' she said tersely, in response to my query. And then, as I debated whether to question her further: 'John will have the ponies saddled up by the time we've finished.'

The remainder of the meal passed in near-silence, but as we rose from the table Eleanor's spirits seemed to lift, and by the

time we had ridden through the gates and out on to the track
she appeared to have recovered not only her equilibrium but
something of the girlish insouciance that had struck me so
forcibly at the beginning of our acquaintance. I remember her
urging her pony forward with little whispered endearments,
her mouth at the creature's ear, and then turning to me with a
smile of such childlike simplicity and openness that I scarcely
knew how to respond.

We had been travelling for perhaps half an hour when the
slope above the track abruptly changed character – the trees
stark and black, the ground beneath them strewn with
charred branches. A faint bitterness rose from the ashy dust
stirred by the ponies' hoofs. I know this landscape, I thought,
feeling the hairs rise on the back of my neck. 'Where are we
going, Nell?'

'We've arrived.' She reined her pony to a halt and slipped
nimbly from the saddle. I dismounted more gingerly.

'You wanted to show me this?'

'I want you to see how the bush grows back.' She led me off
the track and across the soft scatter of charcoal to a small group
of eucalyptus saplings. 'Look at these.'

What I had registered initially was a scene of devastation, the
ravaged landscape of my fevered nightmares. Now, looking
more carefully, I saw that the damage was only part of the picture. From the base of each sapling sprouted a ring of fresh
shoots, while the blackened trunks had erupted at irregular
intervals with similar outgrowths, vigorous tufts of translucent
green foliage flushing to red where the leaves were newest.

Eleanor reached out and brushed one of the tufts gently with the palm of her hand. 'You see?' she said. 'Hardly more than two months ago, the whole of this hillside was ablaze. From the house you could see the glow of it two nights running, and the sky grey with smoke by day. Now the land's healing itself. It always does.'

I was struggling to control my emotions, staring at the luminous foliage, half blind with tears. 'What I'm saying,' she continued after a tactful pause, 'is that you've done nothing to the land that the land itself can't mend.' Her head lifted suddenly and her eyes narrowed. I turned, following her gaze, to see what had distracted her.

Two figures were moving slowly towards us down the track, a man and a woman, both walking with a terrible languor under the weight of the tattered bundles they carried on their backs. Watching their approach, I sensed that the woman was gravely ill: her head hung low and her bare feet dragged in the dust. She was quite young, I realised as she drew close, but her features were stiff and hollow, the bones prominent beneath her dark skin. Her arms swung loosely a little forward from her sides, the wrists as thin as a child's below the frayed cuffs of her blouse.

Her companion was almost as thin, but evidently not as frail. He held his head as high as his burden allowed, walking with grim concentration, his eyes fixed fiercely on the track ahead of him. As the two of them drew level with us I called out a greeting, but they pressed on without so much as a glance in our direction.

Our actions are not always entirely explicable, even in retrospect, but I can see clearly enough how one unsatisfactory encounter with the indigenous people of the region might have stirred memories of another. I cried out, I remember, then started forward and stumbled after the couple, tugging the bracelet from my breeches pocket as I went. I can't imagine what they must have thought of me as I fell in alongside them, jabbering excitably, thrusting the thing towards them. Had they seen it before? Did they know the girl it belonged to? Could they get it back to her? Would they take it anyway? As I stopped to draw breath I saw the man shake his head from side to side, slowly but emphatically, his tangled locks sweeping the sides of his gaunt face. He might have been answering any or all of my questions but his eyes steadfastly avoided mine, and I interpreted the gesture more generally as a refusal to have anything at all to do with me. Disconcerted, I stepped back and rejoined Eleanor.

'I had an idea they might know her,' I said. 'The girl who owned the bracelet.'

'It's not impossible. But look at them, Charles. They've cares enough of their own.' She stared down the track, following the couple's painful progress for a moment before turning back to me. 'Let me see it,' she said.

I held out the bracelet in the palm of my hand. 'It's beautiful,' she murmured, taking it up between her finger and thumb and examining it closely. 'So delicately made.'

'She didn't want to part with it. We forced her.'

'You told me. Bullen threatened her. Threatened them all.'

I was watching the movements of a thickset grey lizard as it hunted among the stones at the far side of the track. 'Yes,' I said, 'but the fault was mine. If I hadn't wanted it—'

'You saw the beauty in it.' She draped the bracelet across the back of her hand so that the spines fanned out as they had against the dark skin of the girl's wrist. Something in that subtle collocation startled and moved me, bringing the words to my lips before I had time to consider them. 'Will you have it?' I asked.

The stillness was so profound that I could hear the tiny snap of the lizard's jaws as it took its prey. 'No,' she said after a moment. 'No, I can't.' My expression must have betrayed me for she reached out and touched my forearm like a mother comforting a disappointed child. 'I mean,' she said gently, 'that it doesn't belong to you, and can't belong to me.' She held up the bracelet so that the yellow feathers trembled and glowed in the sunlight. 'We'll leave it here.'

'Do you think she'll find it?'

She shrugged. 'What's important,' she said, 'is that we don't keep it.' She bent one of the fresh eucalyptus shoots towards her and slipped the bracelet over the tip, easing it down until it hung close against the blackened bark of the trunk. 'You'll travel more lightly without it.'

'I shall be going back almost empty-handed. My uncle's letter asks how the collection is progressing. I'm steeling myself to report the truth – that the sum of my endeavours is a few dozen insignificant specimens, most of them taken within shouting distance of my host's front door. I set out with grander designs.'

'If you stayed on, you could organise another expedition.'

'I've no stomach for it. The fact is, Nell, that I'm coming round to your position on the matter – the grasping, the killing. It seems to me that I've done enough damage.'

'But I don't want you to leave. Not just yet.'

The ponies were jostling one another, tetchy and restless, eager to be moving. 'I must,' I said. 'I want to get back to England. I have plans for my estate.'

'Then take me with you,' she said, the colour rising to her cheeks.

I felt my own face grow hot and my heart quicken. 'You know I can't do that, Nell. You must see how such a course of action would compromise us, you as well as me.'

'Not if we travelled as man and wife.'

Her phrasing was sufficiently ambiguous to leave open in my mind the possibility that she was suggesting some kind of subterfuge. She must have read the uncertainty in my eyes, because she stepped forward and took me by the wrist, looking intently into my face. 'I mean,' she said, with careful emphasis, 'that we might be married.'

I stood speechless, listening to the wind whispering among the black branches overhead. She leaned close, so close that I felt the touch of her breath against my throat as she spoke. 'Mightn't we?'

Sheer madness, I thought, beginning to tremble the way I'd trembled out there on the cliff face that evening as I jigged and spun at the rope's end above unfathomable space; but her gaze was so clear and sane and the pressure of her hand on my wrist so tenderly compelling that it was not, in the end, unduly difficult to give her the answer I hardly dared believe she wanted.

30

Eleanor was in favour of broaching the subject with her father on our return to the villa that evening, but I held out for a more cautious approach. Nothing of our intention, I insisted, was to be revealed to Vane, either directly or indirectly, while I remained in the house as his guest. It was apparent to me that Eleanor was unconvinced by my arguments, but she complied with my wishes.

Early next morning I rode into the city and paid a month's rental on a set of rooms in a small but reasonably well-appointed boarding-house within easy walking distance of the harbour. I had intended to be back at the villa in good time for lunch, but my mount was slow and fractious, and by the time I entered the dining-room Vane and Eleanor were half-way through their meal.

'There's soup in the tureen,' said Vane, scarcely troubling to glance up. I helped myself and sat down beside Eleanor. As I picked up my napkin she reached out and placed her hand on my wrist – just for the barest instant, but I could see from her father's expression that neither the gesture nor its significance had been lost on him. I should have preferred to leave my announcement until the end of the meal, but it was clear that I now had no choice in the matter.

'I've been to arrange my accommodation,' I said. 'I shall be living in lodgings in the city for the next few weeks.'

'You'll get a berth easily enough,' said Vane. 'I doubt whether you'll need to stay as long as that.'

'The fact is that I may need to stay a little longer. Longer, that is to say, than I would if it were simply a matter of booking myself on the first available passage. There's something else – I mean, I don't intend to leave at once because—'

It was absurd. A man of middle years and some sophistication, and I was blushing like a schoolboy, mumbling my words, searching hopelessly for the elegant phrases I'd prepared during the morning's ride. 'Because what?' snapped Vane. 'Because you want to wed my daughter?'

I nodded, simultaneously relieved and humiliated by his intervention. 'Yes,' I said. 'I should like to ask for Eleanor's hand in marriage.'

'I'm not a fool,' he said. 'Do you think I couldn't see what was going on under my own nose?'

I leaned back in my chair and drew a deep breath, steadying myself. 'There was no intention of deceiving you,' I said quietly.

Vane grunted. 'Eat your soup,' he said, 'before it gets cold.'

'And your answer?'

In the stillness that followed I could hear the servants' voices rising from the scullery; slopped water, the clank of an iron vessel. 'You have my permission,' he said at last. He pushed away his plate, flung down his napkin and, without another word, stalked out of the room.

Once away from the villa, I quickly established a healthy regimen: a brisk walk to the harbour each morning upon rising and then, after breakfast, a longer excursion, sometimes through the bustling thoroughfares of the city but more often to a quiet spot on the shoreline where I would sit and gaze at the ocean, lulled by the sound of the breaking waves. In the afternoons I would retreat to my rooms to read or write.

Eleanor was almost constantly in my thoughts, but in a distant, rarefied way, as though she were a figure from a half-remembered dream. My future wife, I would think, repeating the phrase to myself like a charm in the hope of calling her before me in slightly more substantial form, but the girl herself – the moving, breathing creature – seemed always out of reach. The letters I sent her reflected something of my perplexity: detailed but reticent, solicitous but without warmth.

I had been in the city for more than a week before I heard from her. Her letter, which I took to have been supervised or even dictated, informed me simply that she and her father would call on me at eleven o'clock the following morning to discuss the wedding. I tore the envelope apart in the hope that she might have slipped some small note into its recesses, but there was nothing to be found.

They arrived punctually, Vane rapping on the front door with his cane as the clock in the hallway chimed the hour. It had struck me that our discussion might be more agreeably conducted in the open air than in the confined space of my dingy sitting room and Vane fell in at once with my suggestion that we should stroll down to Farm Cove, though he showed no sign of wanting to initiate conversation. Eleanor walked between us, talking nervously and almost incessantly about nothing in particular, and it wasn't until we were within sight of the shore that her father turned to the matter in hand.

'I'm not planning a grand celebration,' he said bluntly. 'Aside from the Merivales, you know none of our neighbours, and it's a little late in the day to be making introductions. In any case, Eleanor has expressed her own preference for a modest affair.'

'I shall be grateful for whatever you see fit to arrange.'

He raised his hand in a brusque, dismissive gesture. 'A dozen or so families from the neighbourhood will be invited back to the villa for luncheon after the ceremony. I'll have trestles and an awning set up on the terrace, and there'll be no shortage of food or drink, but that's as far as it goes. I've no doubt you'll be marking the occasion in your own fashion on your return to England.'

'I'm sure,' I said, more truthfully than he might have supposed, 'that I shall be unable to better your own arrangements.'

There were other matters, all of an essentially practical nature and requiring little more than my acquiescence. Eleanor seemed subdued, staring at the ground in silence until her father brought up the question of best man. 'I've sounded young Merivale on the subject,' he said. 'I know he'd be glad to do it.'

I sensed Eleanor's agitation even before she spoke. 'You had no right,' she said. 'That was Charles's business, not yours.'

'I'd thought of it myself,' I said quickly. 'I'm delighted to have the matter so neatly resolved. I shall write to him this evening.'

'Then I'll take that as settled,' said Vane.

Eleanor stepped up close, taking me by the elbow. 'I should like a word with Charles,' she said, leaning across me to address her father. 'A word in private.'

Vane glared at her but she was already walking me away from him, towards the shoreline. 'It's out of the question,' she said, barely waiting to get beyond her father's hearing. 'What are you thinking of?'

'I don't know what you mean.'

'You can't ask William to be your best man,' she said. 'Don't you see? You'd be rubbing salt into an open wound.'

'He's entitled to refuse.'

'William's too much of a gentleman for that. If you ask him, he'll feel honour-bound to accept.'

She continued to press her case but I held out, citing both the wisdom of humouring her father and the absence of any other candidate. 'Besides,' I said, 'if your father has put the idea into his head, I might well give offence to both parties by failing to follow up.'

There was a long pause. 'You may be right,' she said at last.

'Thank you, Nell.' I drew away, anxious to rejoin Vane, but she called me back.

'Not yet,' she said, and then, so softly I could hardly make out the words: 'I've something more to say.' She gazed out over the foreshore to where a flock of small waders dipped and scuttled at the water's edge. 'That business with my father,' she murmured. 'It went on for years.'

I knew that she was giving me the opportunity to release myself from our hastily framed compact and felt obscurely touched by the gesture. I should have liked to take her hand but refrained, inhibited by Vane's presence at our backs.

'You must forget the past,' I said. 'You're about to begin a new life. A new life in a new world.'

She shook her head. 'We carry our past with us,' she said. 'I have my hopes for the future, but I don't expect to forget.'

I glanced over my shoulder. 'Your father's waiting,' I said.

'Do you hear what I'm saying, Charles?' She reached out and gripped my sleeve, shaking my arm vigorously as though to rouse me. 'Do you understand?'

The birds rose and wheeled as one, their wings flickering against the rippled shine of the water. 'We can talk about it later,' I said. I turned, breaking her hold, and began to make my way back to where Vane stood stiff as a statue in the midday glare.

In the event, Merivale carried out his duties throughout the ceremony and the succeeding festivities in such exemplary fashion that I found myself wondering, as the luncheon drew to a close, whether Eleanor might not have exaggerated the extent of his interest in her; but as we rose from the table I saw him look towards her with an expression so unguard-edly tender and desperate that it seemed impossible she should not be pierced to the heart by it. I glanced sideways, half fearful of surprising her in some small act of betrayal, but she was listening with rapt attention to her neighbour, her slender neck and shoulders twisted away from us, and it was my own heart that smarted for the young man and his wrecked hopes. I took him by the arm and walked him down the slope of the lawn towards the citrus grove.

'Eleanor has told me,' I said gently, 'that your own feelings for her—'

'My feelings are of no account. But I should like you to know, in case you have any doubts on the matter, that the indiscretions were all mine. Nell gave me no reason to suppose that my clumsy pursuit of her would ever be rewarded. On the contrary, she made it plain that I was wasting my time. But she was never cold, Redbourne, never unkind – though perhaps it would have been better for me if she had been.'

'You must feel free to write to her – to write to us. And should you ever find yourself in England . . .'

He shook his head, as though the possibility were too remote to be entertained. 'I like you, Redbourne,' he said. 'I like you very much indeed, and I don't mind telling you that I had some notion when we first met that we should come to know one another a good deal better in due course. I believed, to be frank, that you were the man my sister had been waiting for, and nothing' – he came to a halt and looked back up the slope to where Esther and Mrs Merivale stood talking together in the shade of the awning – 'would have given me greater pleasure than to have welcomed you into our own family.'

Was there mischief in that little speech? Nothing deliberate, I thought, scanning Merivale's open features, but I found myself profoundly unsettled by his words. I had voyaged to the far side of the world, ostensibly in the service of science but actually, as recent reflection on the matter had made increasingly clear to me, in quest of a wife. Not an unworthy venture in itself, of course; but what gave me pause at that moment was the thought that I had travelled all that distance only to snatch at the first opportunity that presented itself. What other vistas might have opened up before me if I had waited longer or explored more widely? And what had determined my choice? A wild song, the meeting of eyes across a shadowed drawing-room, a few small kindnesses offered at a time when my spirits had been at their lowest ebb and my judgement clouded – were these adequate foundations for a marriage?

'Thank you, Merivale,' I said. 'And thank you, too, for standing alongside me today. A lesser man would have refused.'

'I considered it an honour. But you mustn't imagine that my duties have been entirely easy for me.'

'All the more credit to you for discharging them so ably.'

'Ably enough, no doubt, but not as gladly as I could have wished.'

'You're a young man,' I said consolingly, 'and, if I may say so, an extremely eligible one. My mother used to say that weddings are like troubles – they never come singly. Allow me to hope that the next will be your own.'

He gave me a wan smile. 'I've never wanted anyone but Nell,' he said simply. And then, turning abruptly away: 'Perhaps we should rejoin the others.'

As we walked back up the slope Eleanor came hurrying towards us, half stumbling on the cumbersome folds of her gown. 'You can have no idea,' she laughed as she joined us, 'how much I'm looking forward to wearing my everyday clothes again.' She wriggled her shoulders, playfully suggesting the irksomeness of the gown's heavy fabric, and threw back her head, exposing the long line of her throat.

It wasn't a wanton gesture – indeed, there was a kind of innocence about it – but neither was it a ladylike one. And though I was stirred by it, my pulse quickening as I gazed, I felt it, and her words too, as a subtle affront. 'Mrs Redbourne,' I murmured, half jocular, half chiding, as I grasped her arm and drew her to my side. I felt her lithe body stiffen against me.

Merivale shifted uneasily, tugging at his cuffs. 'We're in for a storm,' he said, nodding towards the darkening horizon. 'It's a blessing it didn't blow up an hour earlier.'

There was a huddle of guests in front of the veranda, all waiting, I surmised, to bid us farewell, but as we approached the terrace Esther and her mother stepped briskly forward to intercept us. 'I'm sorry,' said Mrs Merivale, reaching for Eleanor's hand, 'that we've made so little of our last opportunity to speak with you before you leave. The truth is, my dear, that the right words seem so hard to find. It's the happiest of occasions, of course, but you'll forgive me – and I hope Mr Redbourne will forgive me too – for telling you that I've shed tears at the thought of your going, and that I've no doubt I'll shed more when you're gone.' Even as she spoke, her eyes brimmed, and Eleanor, with a quick, impulsive movement drew her close and held her.

I turned away, faintly embarrassed, and addressed myself to Esther. 'I'm glad to have met you, Miss Merivale, and to have heard you play. I shall treasure the memory of your impromptu recital.'

She took the compliment as a lady should, modestly but without embarrassment, her fine features irradiated by a smile of unmistakable warmth. 'I wish,' she said softly, 'that we'd had time to get to know one another better.' She clasped my hand briefly in her own, then leaned over to Eleanor as

Mrs Merivale drew away. 'Goodbye, Nell,' she said. 'I hope you'll send us news of your life in England.'

'She has promised,' said Merivale. 'Hold her to it, Redbourne. And' – he turned quickly on his heel before the words were out – 'look after her.' He hurried towards the waiting carriage, his mother and sister following at a gentler pace. I stood staring after them, listening to the hollow sound of the awning as it flapped and billowed in the rising wind.

31

Vane had insisted that we remain at the villa until the morning of our sailing, but there were no concessions to our new status. My old room had been made up as before and I spent my wedding night alone, listening, between spells of troubled sleep, to the noise of the rain and the buffeting wind.

Those last two days in the house were lived in a strange state of suspension. Eleanor seemed gloomily abstracted, moving like a ghost from room to room or staring out from the veranda across the sodden lawn; and though Vane spent much of the time shut away in his study, leaving us largely to ourselves, our conversations were awkward and inconsequential. I drank more tea and coffee than was good for me and passed the hours between meals listlessly scanning the pages of Vane's farming magazines.

On the second afternoon Eleanor and I walked down to the barn to oversee the packing of her sculpture and her little cache of treasures. The rain had eased off over the preceding hour or so, but as we picked our way between the dripping shrubs it began again with renewed force, and by the time we ducked into the doorway we were wet through.

The two servants were manoeuvring the blanket-chest down the loft ladder as we entered, and neither acknowledged our presence until they had set it safely on the ground.

'That's everything from up above, Miss Eleanor,' said the older man as he straightened up. 'It's all in here, and well padded.'

'Thank you, Norwood. And there's that too.' She indicated the sculpture, scarcely advanced, I noticed with surprise, since I had last seen it.

'We've brought down a couple of old blankets,' said Norwood. 'We'll wrap it in those before we crate it up.' He crossed over to the figure and ran his hand over the smooth surface of the shoulders. 'It's a nice piece of work,' he said.

I saw the younger man smirk. Eleanor brushed past him and began to climb the ladder. 'I'm going to have one last look,' she said, glancing back at me as she hauled herself on to the platform. 'I shall be down in a minute.'

My specimens were still where I had left them, ranged on the shelves of the battered dresser over against the far wall. While the men roped the blankets around Eleanor's sculpture,

I picked out a few of the more beautiful skins, laying them on the dresser's dusty surface for closer inspection – lory and lorikeets, a spinebill, the kingfisher, the chestnut teal. I took up the teal and turned it in my hands, twisting its eyeless head this way and that to catch the muted light, but the iridescence was gone and the dense breast-feathers, which I had once fancifully thought of as bearing the impress of Eleanor's fingers, were stiff and damp.

By the time Eleanor rejoined me, I was more than ready to leave and she, for her part, seemed close to tears, her face rigid with strain. 'It's all in hand,' I said. 'There's no need to stay.'

As we reached the doorway, Norwood looked up. 'What about the birds, Miss Eleanor? Are those to be packed too?'

Eleanor glanced sideways at me. I hesitated.

'Charles?'

'No,' I said. 'Get rid of them.' I turned up my collar and stepped out into the rain.

We rose in darkness next morning, and were on the road by daybreak. Vane had seated himself beside Eleanor, obliging me to sit on the opposite side of the carriage, and I spent much of the journey staring out of the streaming window, trying to avoid his gaze. He had assured me that we should be in good time, but the road had been damaged by the heavy rains, and our progress was frustratingly slow. At several points on our journey we came to a place where the rainwater, pouring in a torrent from the slopes above, had scoured a broad groove through the sandy surface, and on each occasion I held my breath, listening to the rush and swirl beneath us as we eased forward into the flood.

We reached the quayside with barely twenty minutes to spare. Vane took matters in hand at once, leaping out to collar a passing porter before I had so much as risen from my seat. While he supervised the unloading of our luggage, I paced restlessly up and down, anxious to be on board but inhibited by a sense of occasion: this was no ordinary parting, and a casual farewell, I thought, was out of the question.

Vane evidently held no such view. Turning back to us as the last of our bags was handed down, he simply gripped me by the hand and wished me well, then took Eleanor briefly in his arms. 'Write to me when time allows,' he said, as he stepped back to let us go. His voice was flat, his handsome face as blank as the grey sky above us. Eleanor gazed into his eyes for a long moment; then she lowered her head and turned away.

Once aboard, we made our way to the stern. Despite the driving rain, the deck was crowded, and though my own height gave me a good view of the well-wishers gathered on the quayside, Eleanor was unable to see beyond the massed bodies of our fellow passengers.

'I have to see him,' she said breathlessly, bobbing and weaving, searching for a gap, a vantage-point. 'I have to wave him goodbye.'

'We've said our goodbyes, Nell.'

'Don't you understand? It's for ever.' She ducked down and began to force her way through the crowd, moving erratically but with savage determination. I lost sight of her for a moment and then she reappeared, close to the rail, just as the ship's engines shuddered into life. I saw her scanning the quayside, her head thrust forward; and then her hand went up.

Vane had placed himself so close to the edge of the wharf that I was unable to see him from my own position until the ship drew away. The quayside crowd had begun, almost as one, to wave and shout, but Vane was standing starkly upright, a little apart from all that noise and agitation. He stared after us for a long minute and then, raising one hand in brusque salute, turned and was lost to view among the waving arms, the flourished hats and handkerchiefs.

It was clear that we were in for a rough spell. As we approached the mouth of the cove, the wind stiffened, sending the rain slantwise across the running deck, and I felt the steamer lift and lurch on the swell. The passengers began to make their way below, bracing themselves against the unfamiliar movement. I assumed that Eleanor would rejoin me but she remained at the rail as the deck cleared, gazing out over the white foam of our wake, apparently oblivious to the pelting rain. Something in her huddled posture and air of dark absorption troubled me, and I made my way towards her, moving as quickly as conditions allowed and calling her name as I went. She gave no sign of having heard.

'You'll be drenched to the bone,' I said, drawing up behind her.

She was silent, straining forward as the wharf blurred and dwindled behind the shifting veils of rain. I reached out and touched her shoulder. 'Come now, Nell,' I said. 'We should go below.'

She twisted towards me, her hands still gripping the rail, her gaze hard and angry. 'I'll come when I'm ready,' she said.

'When you're ready? What do you mean by that?'

'I mean exactly what I say.'

Ill-tempered little minx, I thought, with a dull flush of anger; a pert, cross-grained piece, and spoiled goods into the bargain. 'Do as you please,' I said, 'but I've no intention of catching my death on your account.'

As I turned my back on her the foghorn vented a long, mournful blast, a sustained note that seemed to pass through the planking and up into my shivering body; and as the sound died away, a cry went up from behind me as if in answer – a human cry, but so wild and raw that I felt my skin crawl. I stopped in my tracks and whipped round.

Eleanor had started after me and stood with her feet splayed on the tilting deck, her head thrown back, howling at the sky. Her mouth was wide, drawn down at the corners so that the sinews of her neck stood out; the skin around her eyes was creased and puckered like that of an old woman. I stepped forward and took her in my arms in a helpless confusion of pity and embarrassment, trying simultaneously to assuage her unfathomable grief and to shield her from the curious stares of the few passengers still up on deck. I remember thinking, holding her stiffly to my breast and rocking her distractedly to and fro, that I had fooled myself into marriage: the visions I had seen in the soft light of my sick-room – the loving companion, the ministering priestess – had been nothing more than the projections of my own longing.

Little by little her weeping subsided and her breathing grew more regular, and after a while she eased herself back against my cradling arms, lifting her face to mine. Her ruined face, I thought, coldly appraising the blotched skin and swollen eyelids; but as my mind framed the words she reached up and touched my own face, pressing her hand gently against the line of my jaw as though to communicate, through the flesh, matters too vast or too complex to be entrusted to language. And then, as her gaze steadied and locked with mine, I saw it all suddenly clear for an instant, knowing that what I held was the irreducible sum of things – squalor and splendour, vision and nightmare; the pathos, the pettiness and the doomed, undeniable beauty; the wise adept and the broken child. I drew her close again, feeling the delicate trembling of her body through the folds of my coat.

She took a deep, shuddering breath; then she pulled away and swung herself lightly round to stand at my side.

'I'm ready now,' she said.

ACKNOWLEDGEMENTS

A number of individuals have helped, in a variety of ways, during the writing of this novel. Particular thanks are due to Luigi Bonomi, Richard Griffiths, Stephanie Hale, Beth Hanley, Kathryn Heyman, Richard Johnstone, Keiren Phelan, Martin Thomas, Mark Tredinnick, Carole Welch, Gilly Withey and Tim Woods.

I'm also grateful to the President and Fellows of Kellogg College, Oxford, for a period of sabbatical leave in 2002; to Southern Arts and the Senate Research Fund of the University of Wales, Aberystwyth, for financial assistance with visits to Australia in 2002 and 2004 respectively; and to Arts Council England for one of their Writers' Awards in 2003.